THE MODERN THEOLOGIANS

The Modern Theologians

An Introduction to Christian Theology in the Twentieth Century
Volume I

Edited by David F. Ford

BLACKWELL
Oxford UK & Cambridge USA

Copyright © Basil Blackwell Ltd. 1989

First published 1989
Reprinted 1990, 1992, 1993, 1994

Blackwell Publishers
108 Cowley Road, Oxford, OX4 1JF, UK

238 Main Street
Cambridge, Massachusetts 02142, USA

British Library Cataloguing in Publication Data
A CIP catalogue record for this book is available from the British Library.

Library of Congress Cataloging in Publication Data
The Modern theologians: an introduction to Christian theology
in the twentieth century / edited by David Ford.
    p.   cm.
Includes bibliographies and index.
    ISBN 0–631–15371–3 (v. 1)—ISBN 0–631–15372–1 (pbk.: v. 1)
    1. Theology, Doctrinal — History — 20th century.   I. Ford, David,
1948–
BT28.M593   1989
230'.09'04—dc19

Typeset in Palatino
by Hope Services, Abingdon
Printed and bound in Great Britain by
Biddles Ltd, Guildford and King's Lynn

This book is printed on acid-free paper.

Contents

Preface

The main aim of these volumes is to introduce the thought of most leading twentieth-century Christian theologians and movements in theology. The period for our purposes begins with the First World War, 1914–1918. Two criteria for selection were that the theologians should have written constructively on a broad range of theological issues, and that they should be widely studied at present, especially in universities, seminaries and by others at third level. There were also the more controversial criteria of quality and significance.

The contributors are all based in Europe or North America and come from a wide range of institutions, denominational backgrounds and countries. Most are themselves constructively engaged in modern theology, and their purpose has been both to produce a scholarly account of their subject and also to carry further the theological dialogue in each case. So the aim has been partly 'historical theology' but also the sort of engaged discussion that comes from those who are practitioners in the field.

The chapters try to help readers to think in a way appropriate to a theologian while also encouraging dialogue and argument. The only way this can happen adequately is by close study of a theologian's writings, and it is to this above all that we aim to introduce readers. The main intended use of these volumes is, therefore, to prepare for, accompany and aid reflection on the study of texts. Yet few will be able to read all these theologies, so the complementary intention is to give some grasp of the rest of the field.

There is a common pattern followed by most of the contributors: introduction, survey, content (concentrating on the main issues), the debate about the theology, an assessment of its achievement, the agenda it sets for the future, and a short bibliography. In addition each part has a brief introduction and each volume includes a list of important dates and a glossary of the key words and phrases which a student entering the field might not have met already.

This first volume is mainly about major figures of continental European theology. Among them are the most likely candidates for 'classic' status in this type of theology so far this century: Barth, Bonhoeffer, Bultmann, Tillich, Rahner, and Balthasar. Barth, Bultmann, and Tillich were key participants in the upheaval in Protestant theology after the First World War and its further testing in the face of Hitler's National Socialism, and they were still dominant figures until at least the end of the 1950s. Bonhoeffer's reputation as a prophet and martyr under Hitler is now being complemented by an expanding discussion of his theology, and in some ways his achievement (his works often in fragments, his life intensely involved with contemporary events and ethically ambiguous to many critics) is 'classical' in a more typically modern sense than the others. Rahner and Balthasar represent two very different approaches to the renewal of Roman Catholic theology, although, for a fuller picture of it, Lonergan, Congar, Schillebeeckx, and Küng, as well as David Tracy and Latin American liberation theology in volume II, need to be considered. Protestant theology after Barth and Bonhoeffer is represented on the one hand by Torrance and Jüngel, who develop very different theologies which yet have the common factor of a close and largely sympathetic dialogue with Barth, and, on the other hand, Pannenberg and Moltmann, whose contrasting theologies tried to move continental theology beyond the debate between Barth and Bultmann by rethinking Christian concepts of history and eschatology.

The coherence of this volume therefore revolves around Protestant and Roman Catholic theologies which were largely centered in German-speaking areas of continental Europe – Torrance, Lonergan, and Schillebeeckx are only partial exceptions to this in terms of the main influences on their thought. An important further dimension has been the ways in which the Protestants and Catholics have influenced each other in this period, as seen in Bonhoeffer's conception of the church and spirituality or Balthasar's and Küng's outstanding studies of Barth. Indeed it has become commonplace to remark that the main distinctions between academic theologians have generally ceased to run along denominational lines, although influence, mutual respect and common themes should not be exaggerated into a marginalizing of church tradition, especially for those theologians in parts I, III and IV.

The grouping of theologians into the five parts of this volume should not have too much read into it. The arrangement has not been arrived at easily, because other schemes had almost equal advantages. The introductions to each part try to explain the selection, but the overriding concern has been for the particularity of each theologian as understood by another theologian. As for the order of the parts, it is largely historical. Barth and those closest to him are first because of his initiating role in dialectical theology. Bultmann and Tillich were also associated with that, so they and their group come next. Rahner, Lonergan, Congar, and Balthasar were all born within a year of each other, and there is no significance in their order of appearance. Finally, Pannenberg and Moltmann emerged latest, in the 1960s.

The coverage of the volume is by no means comprehensive, and there are major contributions to theology which are not included, such as Scandinavian theology, Friedrich Gogarten, Emil Brunner, Gerhard Ebeling, Walter Kasper, the political theology of Johann Baptist Metz, other French theologians besides Congar, and other theologians working in Holland besides Schillebeeckx (though Berkouwer is included in volume II, chapter 7).

There are also many ways in which theology has been done other than by those who treat directly the key issues in the tradition of dogmatic or systematic theology. There are in particular those scholars who have done biblical theology – for example, Oscar Cullmann and Ernst Käsemann in New Testament, and Gerhard von Rad in Old Testament – and have profoundly affected many of the theologians discussed. Indeed, for many in the 1950s and 1960s biblical and hermeneutical theology was a substitute for systematic or dogmatic theology. In this volume these theologians are only represented directly by Bultmann, but there are many others.

There are also theologians in church history, spirituality, practical theology, philosophical theology, and philosophy of religion, as well as a multiplying range of "theology and . . ." approaches (sociology, psychology, the natural sciences, literature and the arts are the most prominent). Volume II does more justice to some of these forms of theology, but still the main formal criterion is that a theologian deals with a broad range of the classic Christian issues and offers a constructive response to them and to modernity, while the secondary guideline is that these volumes are intended to be an introduction to those theologians who are most widely studied at third level.

David F. Ford

Acknowledgments

During the three years of editing these two volumes I have incurred large debts of gratitude. Julia Mosse of Blackwells began the project and Stephan Chambers and others have sustained it in many ways. The stage of selection and arrangement was greatly assisted by friends in the Society for the Study of Theology and the American Academy of Religion, and also by several participants in the 1986 conference in Cambridge on the thought of Donald MacKinnon. Shirley Hanson has, with insight and precision, done most of the work on the Glossary, a major undertaking, and she has been ably assisted by Ann Ind and Steve Wigley.

I am deeply grateful to each of the contributors, above all for the quality of what they have produced, but also for a general amenability to guidelines and to requests for changes. Several classes and seminars responded to successive versions of the Introduction to volume I, and Werner Jeanrond and Míchaél Ó Siadhail contributed many suggestions to the final draft. Dan Hardy has accompanied these volumes at every stage, and I am deeply grateful for his support, advice and conceptual creativity. Even before this project was conceived, he created the course in modern theology in the Department of Theology in the University of Birmingham which I shared with him in teaching for many years, and which has been the context for engaging with many of the theologians treated in these volumes. My mother-in-law, Perrin Hardy, has been wonderfully encouraging, patient and simply full of life as she has coped with two families engaged in the same project. My mother, Phyllis Ford, gave a week's intensive secretarial and all-round support to bring the volumes together at the end. My wife, Deborah, has been important beyond words.

But in so far as it is proper at all for an editor to dedicate a work, this one is offered in memory of Hans Frei, who died on September

12, 1988. He was a teacher and friend to me and many others. His generosity, his wisdom and the rigor and fruitfulness of his thinking have been a great gift to the fields of theology and religious studies, and far beyond. In relation to this work, in conversation and through his 1987 Edward Cadbury Lectures in the University of Birmingham he helped in planning the project and in thinking through the Introduction to volume I at an early stage. So, with great gratitude to him and in deep sympathy with his wife Gerry and all his family, these volumes are dedicated to his memory.

Notes on Contributors

Richard Bauckham is Professor of New Testament Studies in the University of St Andrews, Scotland. He was born and educated in England. His publications include *Tudor Apocalypse* (Appleford, 1978); *Jude 2 Peter* (Word Biblical Commentary vol. 50; Waco, Texas, 1983); *Moltmann: Messianic Theology in the Making* (Basingstoke, 1987); *The Bible in Politics: How to Read the Bible Politically* (London, 1989/Philadelphia, 1990); *Jude and the Relatives of Jesus in the Early Church* (Edinburgh, 1990); *The Theology of the Book of Revelation* (Cambridge, 1992); *The Climax of Prophecy: Studies on the Book of Revelation* (Edinburgh, 1992).

J. A. DiNoia OP is Professor of Systematic Theology in the Dominican House of Studies, Washington, DC, and Editor-in-Chief of *The Thomist*. He was born in the United States and studied in Washington and in Yale. His publications include *The Diversity of Religions: A Christian Perspective* (Washington, 1992).

David F. Ford is Regius Professor of Divinity in the University of Cambridge, England. He was born in Dublin, studied there and in the Universities of Cambridge, Yale and Tübingen. His publications include *Barth and God's Story: Biblical Narrative and the Theological Method of Karl Barth in the Church Dogmatics* (Frankfurt, Berne, New York, 1981; 2nd edn. 1985); *Jubilate: Theology in Praise*, with Daniel W. Hardy (London, 1984), US title *Praising and Knowing God* (Philadelphia, 1985); *Meaning and Truth in 2 Corinthians*, with Frances M. Young (London, 1987, Grand Rapids, 1988).

John D. Godsey is Emeritus Professor of Systematic Theology in Wesley Theological Seminary, Washington, DC. He was born in the United States and educated there and in the University of

Basel. His publications include *The Theology of Dietrich Bonhoeffer* (Philadelphia and London, 1960); *Preface to Bonhoeffer: The Man and Two of his Shorter Writings* (Philadelphia, 1965); and *The Promise of H. Richard Niebuhr* (Philadelphia, 1970). He is the editor of *Karl Barth's Table Talk* (Richmond, 1963) and co-editor of *Ethical Responsibility: Bonhoeffer's Legacy to the Churches* (Lewiston, N.Y., 1981).

Daniel W. Hardy is Director of the Center of Theological Inquiry, Princeton, New Jersey, and formerly Van Mildert Professor of Theology in the University of Durham. He was born in the United States and educated there and in the University of Oxford. His publications include *Jubilate, Theology in Praise* with David F. Ford (London, 1984), US title *Praising and Knowing God* (Philadelphia, 1985), and articles on creation, rationality, theology and science, and church and society.

Werner G. Jeanrond is Senior Lecturer in Theology and Fellow of Trinity College, University of Dublin. A native of the Saarland, Germany, he studied at the Universities of Saarbrücken, Regensburg and Chicago. His publications include *Text und Interpretation als Kategorien theologischen Denkens* (Tübingen, 1986), translated as *Text and Interpretation as Categories of Theological Thinking* (Dublin and New York, 1988); *Theological Hermeneutics: Development and Significance* (London and New York, 1991); and, together with Jennifer L. Rike, eds., *Radical Pluralism and Truth: David Tracy and the Hermeneutics of Religion* (New York, 1991).

Robert W. Jenson is Professor of Systematic Theology in St Olaf College, Northfield, Minnesota. He was born in the United States, educated there and in the Universities of Heidelberg and Basel. His publications include *Alpha and Omega: A Study in the Theology of Karl Barth* (New York, 1963); *The Knowledge of Things Hoped For: the Sense of Theological Discourse* (New York, 1969); *God after God: The God of the Past and the God of the Future, seen in the Work of Karl Barth* (New York, 1969); *The Triune Identity: the Christian Interpretation of God* (Philadelphia, 1982); and *America's Theologian: A Recommendation of Jonathan Edwards* (New York, 1988). With C. Braaten he edited and contributed to *Christian Dogmatics*, 2 vols (Philadelphia, 1984).

David H. Kelsey is Professor of Theology in Yale Divinity School, New Haven, Connecticut. He was born and educated in the

United States. His publications include *The Fabric of Paul Tillich's Theology* (New Haven, Conn., 1967); *The Uses of Scripture in Recent Theology* (Philadelphia, 1975); *To Understand God Truly* (Louisville, 1992).

Hugo Meynell is Professor of Religious Studies in the University of Calgary, Canada. He was born and educated in England. His publications include *God and the World* (London, 1971); *An Introduction to the Philosophy of Bernard Lonergan* (London, 1976); *Freud, Marx and Morals* (London, 1981); *The Intelligible Universe* (London, 1982) and *The Theology of Bernard Lonergan* (Atlanta, Ga, 1986).

Robert Morgan is Lecturer in Theology and Fellow of Linacre College, University of Oxford. He was born in Wales and educated in the Universities of Cambridge, Durham and Tübingen. His publications include *The Nature of New Testament Theology* (London, 1973); with M. Pye, *Ernst Troeltsch: Writings on Theology and Religion* (London, 1977); and, with John Barton, *Biblical Interpretation* (Oxford, 1988).

Aidan Nichols OP is Professor of Dogmatic and Ecumenical Theology in the Pontifical University of St Thomas, Rome. He was born in England. His publications include *The Art of God Incarnate. Theology and Image in Christian Tradition* (London, 1980); *Yves Congar* (London, 1989); and *The Theology of Joseph Ratzinger* (Edinburgh, 1988).

John Riches is Professor of Divinity & Biblical Criticism, University of Glasgow. He was born in England and studied there and in Germany. His publications include *Jesus and the Transformation of Judaism* (London, 1980); (ed.) *The Analogy of Beauty* (Edinburgh, 1986); and *The World of Jesus* (Cambridge, 1990). He edits *Studies of the New Testament and its World* (Edinburgh, 1981–) and the English translation of H.U. von Balthasar, *The Glory of the Lord* (Edinburgh, 1982–1991).

Robert Schreiter CPPS is Professor of Theology at the Catholic Theological Union in Chicago. He was born in the United States and studied there and under Edward Schillebeeckx in the University of Nijmegen, Holland. His publications include *Constructing Local Theologies* (New York, London, 1985); *In Water and in Blood: A Spirituality of Solidarity and Hope* (New York, 1988); with M. C. Hilkert, *The Praxis of Christian Experience: An Orientation to Schil-*

lebeeckx (San Francisco, 1989); and (ed.) *The Schillebeeckx Reader* (New York, 1984; Edinburgh, 1988); and *Reconciliation* (New York, 1992).

Christoph Schwöbel is Lecturer in Systematic Theology in King's College, London. He was born and educated in West Germany. He has written *Martin Rade* (Gütersloh, 1980); and he has edited *Karl Barth-Martin Rade. Ein Briefwechsel* (Gütersloh, 1981) and *Martin Rade. Ausgewählte Schriften* vols I–III (Gütersloh, 1983, 1986, 1988).

J. B. Webster is Associate Professor of Systematic Theology, Wycliffe College, University of Toronto. He was born and educated in England. His publications include *God is Here* (London, 1983); and *Eberhard Jüngel: An Introduction to His Theology* (Cambridge, 1986); and a translation of Jüngel's *Theological Essays* (Edinburgh, 1989).

Editorial Note

Where a book is referred to in the notes to a chapter and appears also in the bibliography, place and date of publication are given in the bibliography only.

A date of first publication refers to the first edition in the original language.

Introduction to Modern Christian Theology

David F. Ford

Christian theology in this century has been immensely varied. This has not just been a matter of diverse approaches and conclusions, but also of fundamental differences about what theology is, what modernity is and what Christianity is, and which questions within these areas are to be given priority. This makes an overview difficult, all the more so because many of the theologians are still alive and producing new works and some of the movements are still young. This introduction attempts to give, not an integrating picture, but sufficient background and general understanding of the field to help readers approaching it for the first time to find their bearings, and to assist more experienced readers to explore it further.

WHAT SORT OF SUBJECT IS MODERN CHRISTIAN THEOLOGY?

Between the European Middle Ages and the end of the nineteenth century there were many major events and transformations of life and thought, often originating in Europe but with global conse-quences. Chief among these have been the Renaissance and Reformation, the Enlightenment, the American and French Revol-utions, the rise of nationalism, the Industrial Revolution and the development of the natural sciences, technologies, medical science, and the human sciences. There has also been the combined impact of bureaucracies, constitutional democracy, new means of warfare and of communication, mass education and public health programs, and new movements in the arts and in philosophy and religion.

Theologians have been members of societies, churches, and academic institutions through this innovative, traumatic period, and their theology has inevitably been influenced by it. That is how, in a minimal sense, their theology is modern: by taking account of these and more recent developments, even if sometimes in order to dismiss, criticize or try to reverse them. In addition, today they face the issue of 'postmodernity', which will be treated in the Epilogue which concludes volume II.

Some may wish to repeat a past theology, but this is not possible. The context has changed, and what is actually communicated and understood today can be very far from the original meaning. Yet Christian theology always requires some continuity with the past, so the question is how there can be appropriate continuity without simple repetition.

What is the significance of modernity for the content and method of theology? What is the importance of Christianity for a proper appreciation and response to modernity? And might it be that a religion with the discontinuity of the crucifixion at its heart enables a creative way of coping with the novelty and disruption of modernity? Such questions, which are broadly in the area of interpretation or hermeneutics, are inextricable from others about the nature of Christianity and of theology. All the theologians treated in these volumes have to handle them, and it can be helpful to note some of the main strategies they use.[1]

Imagine a line punctuated by five types of theology. At one end, the first type is simply the attempt to repeat a traditional theology or version of Christianity and see all reality in its own terms, with no recognition of the significance for it of other perspectives or of all that has happened in recent centuries. At the other extreme, the fifth type gives complete priority to some modern secular philosophy or worldview, and Christianity in its own terms is only valid in so far as it fits in with that. So parts of Christian faith and practice may be found true or acceptable, but the assessment is always made according to criteria which are external to faith and which claim superiority to it. Neither of these extremes is represented among the theologians studied in this book, the first because it is hardly modern in the sense intended, the fifth because it is hardly Christian.

That leaves three types in between. Type two gives priority to the self-description of the Christian community (which is, of course, by no means uncontroversial) and might be characterized by Anselm of Canterbury's motto, 'faith seeking understanding'. It insists that Christian identity is primary and that all other reality needs to be construed in relation to it, but also that Christianity itself needs continually to be rethought and that theology must engage seriously with the modern world in its quest for understanding. Karl Barth is a leading representative of this approach, though this type-casting by no means exhausts his theology – and the same is true of attempts to pigeonhole most of the other theologians. Robert Jenson's essay (chapter 1) takes as its leading theme how Barth responded to Enlightenment and later thinkers by refusing their terms and developing his own framework through Jesus Christ and the Trinity. Further examples of this type are Bonhoeffer (though some would dispute this, especially as regards his latest letters and papers), Torrance, Jüngel, Congar, Balthasar and, to be discussed in the second volume, postliberals and some Evangelicals and Eastern Orthodox theologians.

Type three comes exactly at the middle of the line. It is a theology of correlation. It brings traditional Christian faith and understanding into dialogue with modernity, and tries to correlate the two in a wide variety of ways. It does not claim any overarching integration of Christianity and modernity – neither one that would subsume modernity within Christian terms nor one that would exhaustively present Christianity in specifically modern terms. In its classic modern representative, Paul Tillich, it takes the form of the basic questions raised in contemporary life and thought being correlated with answers developed through interpretation of key Christian symbols. In a period of fragmentation and pluralism the method of correlation is especially attractive as a way of keeping going a range of open dialogues. It is a component in most theologies and is particularly important in Schillebeeckx, Küng, and many of those in both Britain and North America who could be called revisionist. James Buckley in volume II, chapter 4, defines revisionists as those 'devoted to shaping Christian practices and teachings in dialogue with . . . modern philosophies, cultures and social practices'.

The fourth type uses a particular (or sometimes more than one) modern philosophy, conceptuality or problem as a way of integrating Christianity with an understanding of modernity. It wants to do justice to both and sees the best way of doing this to be the consistent reinterpretation of Christianity in terms of some contemporary idiom or concern. Robert Morgan's essay (chapter 5) sees Rudolf Bultmann in these terms, using existentialism as the key to interpreting the New Testament. Morgan's critical comments suggest that Bultmann's position would benefit by being opened up to the approach of the third type. Other examples of this fourth type might be Pannenberg, Lonergan, process theology, those Buckley describes as liberals, and many representatives of volume II's new challenges in theology who see the need for liberation and justice in specific areas of modern life as the decisive integrator.

Such a scheme is too neat to fit the whole of any major theology, but it helps in mapping some of the main possibilities in relation to a central and unavoidable matter, the interaction of Christianity with modernity. It also enables us to notice some theologians in whom apparently no one type is dominant. Karl Rahner, as freshly interpreted by Joseph DiNoia (chapter 9), is irreducibly pluralist, even though many standard readings of him make him seem, in his use of a particular philosophical anthropology, to fit the fourth type. It can be immensely significant for a theologian's reputation and reception to liberate him or her from inadequate typing, and when a particular theology seems to fit well into one type there must be special effort to discern the ways in which the type is also transcended.

A final caution is the observation that many of the deepest differences about important matters, and even whole ways of doing theology, cut across the above types. This applies, for example, to the role of practice or of decision in Christianity, and to some conceptions of human freedom, divine action, the shape of the church and much else. There is no substitute for engaging with issues of content, and often in the intensive grappling with key questions the rather formal and abstract concern about mapping the types is swallowed up in the adventure of a particular intellectual, spiritual, and practical journey.

KEY MODERN ISSUES

What have been the main issues in twentieth-century theology? The following five sections explore what has been characteristic: the continuing importance of the inherited agenda of doctrines, the problem of how to integrate a theology, the recovery and criticism of the past, the special significance of the nineteenth century, and the conditioning of theologies by their contexts and interests.

The Systematic Agenda

The traditional topics of what is variously called systematic theology, dogmatic theology or constructive theology are: God and revelation, predestination (or election), creation and providence, human being, sin and evil, Jesus Christ, atonement (or redemption or salvation), the Holy Spirit (or grace) and Christian living (including justification, sanctification, vocation, and ethics), the church, ministry and sacraments, and eschatology. These doctrines (or dogmas or *loci*) can be seen as a concentration of the main events and issues in the Christian overarching story from before creation until after the consummation of history. They continue to be important for modern theology, and even when a theologian has a very different framework the questions raised by these doctrines will have to be answered.

Among those topics, there have been some characteristic modern emphases. At least until the 1960s the distinctive contributions of twentieth-century thinkers have been in the areas of God (especially the reconception of the Trinity and the relationship of suffering to God), revelation (very different approaches, represented for example by Barth, Bultmann, Tillich, Rahner, and Pannenberg), Jesus Christ and salvation in history (closely tied to the previous two issues), human being, and eschatology. Eschatology deserves special mention. The century opened with the rediscovery by academic theology of its importance in the New Testament. Secular eschatologies (of progress, socialist revolution, empire or race) have had immense influence in modern times, but mainstream Christianity had largely ignored the eschatological dimension of its own origins. When it was widely recognized, partly under the pressure of secular alternatives and the crisis of European culture and society manifest in the First World War, then it gave a new standpoint for thinking through Christianity. There was a great variety of eschatologies, and the unavoidability of the question has been one of the distinctive marks of twentieth-century in contrast with nineteenth-century theology.

It becomes increasingly difficult to generalize or have any adequate perspective on more recent years. Certainly any neglect of sin and evil (especially in the aftermath of the Holocaust, the Gulag and Hiroshima) is being corrected in recent theology. As the Pentecostal movement spread, not only in new independent churches but also through millions in the traditional denominations, the Holy Spirit has also been a major topic, though some would see this as just a variation on the typically modern preoccupation with subjectivity and immediate experience. Christian ethics and the church have also had increasing attention, in line with emphases on praxis and community.

Integrations

How is a theologian to relate these various topics to each other? One tendency (corresponding to the second type described above) is to see Christianity having a certain coherence in itself. The doctrines together are the intellectual description of this. So Lindbeck, (volume II, chapter 13) compares doctrines to the statement of the basic grammar or rules showing how a language or culture hangs together. This makes the Christian community the main home of Christian theology (cf. Barth's *Church Dogmatics*) and asserts the priority of a distinctive Christian identity, as expressed above all in the Bible. The way theology is integrated in such an approach is through something internal to the tradition, usually the Bible or one or more key doctrines. Other worldviews and disciplines are discussed and may contribute, but not as equals or superiors.

Other theologians (in the third and fourth types) see integration with modernity as more important and even as essential to a modern theology. Typical concerns are to work out a theological method comparable with other disciplines, often trying to show that theology can justify its claims to rationality and knowledge (Lonergan, Pannenberg), or to affirm the relevance of Christian faith by reinterpreting it in relation to a modern philosophy (existentialism, process thought) or urgent issues (oppression, gender, race, nuclear war, ecology, relations between religions).

Overall, these theologies display a tension between the identity, of Christianity and its relevance to modernity. At the international and institutional levels this has in the twentieth century been dramatized most publicly in ecumenical theology. Lindbeck's contribution offers a provocative interpretation of this, symbolizing it in the two aims of Vatican II, *ressourcement* (renewal through return to sources) and *aggiornamento* (renewal through relevance).

Recovering and Criticizing the Past

A major feature of modernity has been its concern with history. Underlying this is a heightened awareness of change and innovation. The tools that have served this are new.methods of research and new criteria for historical reliability. These, together with the greatly increased scale of historical work, have had the most obvious effects on theology. The Bible and the rest of the Christian heritage have been examined afresh and traditional opinions often challenged. But that has been just one manifestation of a more comprehensive problem.

Modern historical consciousness recognizes that meaning is closely bound up with changing contexts and that we today are also conditioned by many factors as we try to understand the past. Is the whole enterprise of 'true' interpretation possible? For Christian theologians it has seemed unavoidable to attempt it, and the most fundamental reason for this is that Christianity (and it is not alone in this) cannot do without the authority of the past in some form. So a great deal of attention has been paid to what is often called hermeneutics, the art and theory of interpretation. How do we cope with the 'hermeneutical circle', the problem that in understanding the past we tend to draw conclusions based on our own pre-suppositions, interests and involvements? Is the meaning or truth of a text such as a gospel necessarily bound up with its being historically factual? There are very broad questions about language and self in relation to reality (there has been a great deal of reflection on metaphor, narrative, objectivity, and subjectivity), and other questions about genre, the intention of the author, or the relative roles of disciplines such as philology, literary criticism, sociology, psychology, comparative religion, philosophy, and history. And often there is a divergence between those who see much of the Christian past as on the whole worth recovering, and others who see it more as something from which liberation is needed and who use a 'hermeneutic of suspicion' to do so.

The themes of suspicion, doubt, and radical critique are constantly present in modern thought, raising most sharply the issues of authority and reliability. For many the very discipline of theology has disintegrated and lost its intellectual integrity in the face of all this. So most theologians discussed in these volumes are engaged in a recovery of Christianity in the face of unprecedently devastating, sophisticated and widely disseminated dismissals of both Christianity and theology. That, at least, is the situation in the West and in those influenced by it. But some of the developing theologies of volume II, part IV try to redefine the concerns and context of theology so that the confrontation with doubt, agnosticism, atheism, and the intellectual world of the modern West takes second place to serving a praxis of liberation.

In addition (and sometimes, as with Marx, accompanying a fundamental strategy of suspicion) there has been the challenge from modern overviews of history as alternatives to the much-criticised traditional Christian story stretching from creation to consummation. Does Christian theology need a renewed over-arching conception of history? Pannenberg and Rahner would say so, but Bultmann would see such an idea as dangerously mytho-logical, and many others too have serious reservations.

That and all the issues mentioned thus far can be seen as aspects of a pivotal modern theological concern: the relationship of faith and

history. In continental European Protestant theology this was a
fundamental matter dividing Barth and Bultmann. When they were
found wanting by successors such as Pannenberg and Moltmann it
was again this issue that was central. It has likewise been a
dominant concern in much British, North American and Evangelical
theology, and many of the new challenges in theology also focus on
it in their own ways. It is perhaps in Roman Catholic theology that
the implications of modern thinking about faith and history are
most sharply underlined. This is partly because it was only in the
third quarter of the twentieth century that Roman Catholic theologians
could use modern historical methods without official disapproval.
So since the Second World War there has been a hectic period of
assimilation, reinterpretation, and controversy. It is symbolized in
Schillebeeckx's journey from a tradition in which philosophy, not
history, was the main partner of doctrine, through *ressourcement* and
hermeneutics to a massive and controversial treatment of the main
topic in the nineteenth and twentieth century debate about faith
and history: Jesus Christ.

The Nineteenth Century: Creativity and Crisis

In the recovery and criticism of the past a theologian frequently
gives a special place to particular periods or contributions. It is often
more true to say that a theologian seems gripped in this way, and is
immersed in texts and debates which have an authority that
permeates his or her theology. The Bible is most widely treated in
this way, and the patristic period is likewise usually privileged. The
other two main reference points before the modern period are
medieval theology and the Reformation. Periods, traditions and
theologies interanimate each other in subtle ways, and it is often
crude to draw clear lines of influence. Yet it remains important to
understand with whom a theologian finds dialogue most worthwhile.

One period, however, stands out as the most helpful in understanding what it means for twentieth-century theology to be
specifically modern: the nineteenth century. That was the century in
which the issues of modernity were tackled comprehensively for the
first time, and most of the main Christian responses to them
explored. So it is not surprising that the main dialogue partners for
twentieth-century theologians outside their own period tend to be
either nineteenth-century figures or movements of thought which
were shaped then. Even though most theologies are, of course, deeply

indebted to other periods as well, in their understanding of them the philosophical and historical habits of nineteenth-century thought are usually very influential. Barth, for example, who wanted to break with much of what he saw as characteristic of nineteenth-century theology, was steeped in it and has to be understood in relationship to it. The cost of ignoring the nineteenth century is often paid in energetically repeating the exploration of options which were developed and thoroughly discussed then, and most twentieth-century theologians know this.

It is therefore worth surveying the nineteenth century in its importance for these volumes. The brevity of this can best be expanded through two capable treatments of this field, one by Claude Welch[2] and the other edited by Ninian Smart and others.[3]

There were three thrusts in nineteenth-century thought which especially need to be appreciated in relation to twentieth-century theologians. The first was the rethinking of knowledge and rationality, and the accompanying need to reconceive theology. This will be treated below through Kant, Schleiermacher, and Hegel. The second was the development of a new historical consciousness joined with the application of critical historical methods to religion. This will be traced through Hegel and Strauss. The third was the challenge of alternative explanations of religion, as seen in Feuerbach, Marx, Durkheim and others. In the middle comes the awkward figure of Kierkegaard, and at the end the summing up of all the issues in Troeltsch.

Immanuel Kant (1724–1804) died just inside the nineteenth century and is the crucial figure linking it to the eighteenth century and especially its rationalist tradition. He offered an account of knowledge, and especially of the human knower in interaction with the object of knowledge, according to which claims to knowledge by both 'natural theology' and 'revelation' were disallowed. In place of his denial of knowledge he affirmed a faith which was practical and moral rather than theoretical, and which was not especially religious. The central notion is that of freedom. Its reality cannot be either proved or disproved by 'pure reason', but it is reasonable to postulate it in order to make sense of human action and morality. This is the realm of 'practical reason', through which Kant argues for the rationality not only of freedom but also of God and immortality. His own main theological work, *Religion within the Limits of Reason Alone*,[4] is a thorough 'moralization' of religion, and in its pruning of Christianity to fit his philosophy is a good example of the fifth type of theology described above. Yet he is decisively theistic, with an austere conception of God as the 'unconditioned' or 'absolute', whose reality is beyond all knowledge or experience but is mediated through our sense of moral obligation.

We see in Kant the most influential statement of the modern tendency to distinguish fact (pure reason) from value (practical reason) and to categorize religion and morality together under the latter. We see also the emphasis typical of so many modern theologies on the practical or ethical content of Christianity, and especially the centrality of freedom. Sometimes this is developed focusing on personal freedom and intersubjectivity, as in existentialism's concern for encounter and decision. In others, such as Moltmann and liberation theologies, the practicality takes a social and political form and is more affected by postKantian ideas of history and society.

It is worth reflecting why Kant's stress on the ethical, practical, and intersubjective in religion continued to be attractive. Partly it is because Kant shared common roots with many theologians in a Lutheran faith constituted by a dynamic interactive relationship between the believer and God. For those who came later it also represented an appealing response to the most dangerous threat which modernity posed not only to theology but also to the whole realm of value, ethics, and the personal. There were the challenges of naturalistic and other 'reductionist' explanations of religion which by the end of the century had been built up to massive proportions by such figures as Strauss (critical history), Feuerbach (philosophy), Marx (politics and economics), Durkheim and Weber (sociology), Frazer (comparative religion), William James (psychology), Darwin (evolutionary biology) and Nietzsche (philosophy). These have decisively shaped the 'common sense' of many twentieth-century educated Western people about religion, and in the face of them the claim of Kant that the realm of freedom and practicality could not be reduced to any 'objective' explanation offered theologians something which was both widely appealing beyond Christianity and a medium through which to express Christianity.

Kant's ethical interpretation was challenged by two major alternative ways of conceiving Christianity and theology in the early nineteenth century, those of Hegel and Schleiermacher. Friedrich Schleiermacher (1768–1834) is usually regarded as the outstanding theologian of the century. At the root of his achievement was a reconception of religion. For him it is primarily neither morality nor belief (knowledge) but is an immediate self-consciousness or feeling of absolute dependence on God. So the roots of faith are pre-moral and pre-cognitive, and this religious consciousness is common to all people, though very variously recognized and expressed. While in Kant God (the absolute or unconditioned) is present in our sense of moral obligation, in Schleiermacher God is present in an immediate dynamic relationship that grasps our whole being. Christianity is the specific form of this God-consciousness shaped through Jesus Christ and the community of faith in him. This was a view of religion which had an integrity of its own in the subjective realm of feeling or consciousness, but which yet could be reflected upon and discussed intellectually in theology and could inform the whole of practical living. It offered an idiom through which all of Christian doctrine could be expressed afresh. *The Christian Faith*[5] is his culminating work, offering a method of theology which relates it to other disciplines and working out the content of faith with central reference to Jesus Christ and the experience of those with faith in him.

Schleiermacher's influence has been immense (see Jenson's essay on Barth, chapter 1). Besides his powerful account of religion's validity rooted in the dynamics of awareness of God, he pioneered modern hermeneutics, offered a 'noninterventionist' account of God's relation to the world which included a critique of religious language, suggested a restructuring of the whole theological enterprise which was, due to his advocacy, partly embodied in the new University of Berlin, and in his public ecclesiastical, cultural, and political life represented a lively and effective integration of modernity and Christian faith. All this was seen by him as in continuity with the Protestant Reformation and its evangelical tradition.

The twentieth century began with a reaction against him led by Barth, who yet always acknowledged his greatness. Schleiermacher is the grandfather of those who attempt to correlate or integrate faith with modernity, and particularly of those who see the point of contact in human interiority – Tillich's 'ultimate concern' or Hick's religious consciousness. He is the principal creative sponsor of the whole revisionist and liberal enterprise, but he himself constantly eludes simple categories: in those used above he seems, according to interpretation, to oscillate between the third and fourth.

The second major early nineteenth-century challenge to Kant came from G. W. F. Hegel (1770–1831). He criticized both Kant and Schleiermacher for having an inadequate notion of rationality. Both of them had left the concept of God (the absolute, or unconditioned) relatively untouched. Hegel developed a system in which the absolute was conceived as rational and dynamic, realizing itself through a dialectical process in history. He saw the Trinity as the supreme reality, in which God differentiates himself and becomes

actual in Jesus Christ and enters into suffering and death on the way
to the ultimate reconciliation of all in the Spirit. The system thus had
a dialectical logic embracing history with its developments and
conflicts, and Hegel surveyed all of history, including the religions,
in order to show the basic forms of life, society, and religion in their
evolution. He also saw himself as a Christian, Lutheran philosopher
recovering the truth of the basic doctrines of Trinity, creation, fall,
incarnation, reconciliation and the Holy Spirit. For him Christianity
was religion in its absolute expression, but, while its content could
not be surpassed, philosophy could give a more adequate conceptual
expression of it as truth, uniting it with all other truth.

The nineteenth-century shift towards more historical, process-
oriented ways of understanding reality was profoundly affected by
Hegel. Kant had separated the self from other reality: Hegel offered a
comprehensive, historical integration of subjectivity and objectivity
in which reason and even logic took on dynamic form, and Kant's
restriction of theoretical reason in knowing God was overcome.
Hegel daringly reconceived the idea of God and his involvement
with the world (sometimes described as a type of 'panentheism'); he
placed the issue of truth, not religion, at the top of the agenda; and
he encouraged rational and historical reconsideration of key doctrines.

The twentieth-century theologians who have wrestled most
thoroughly with Hegel have often emerged deeply ambiguous about
him as a Christian thinker – this is true in various ways of Barth,
Jüngel, Rahner, Lonergan, Pannenberg, Balthasar, and Küng. One
reason may be that in so far as he can be related to our types he, like
Schleiermacher, oscillates according to the interpretation. But with
him it is between the fourth and fifth types: some see him offering
an appropriate modern conception of Christianity, others as absorbing
it into his system on his own alien terms. But both by setting an
agenda and in his contribution on specific issues (a way of
conceiving the integration of history in the Trinity in Barth, Rahner,
Pannenberg and Moltmann; the death of God in Jüngel and
Moltmann; Rahner's and Lonergan's ways of affirming reality as
rational; Pannenberg's concepts of rationality and universal history,
Küng's approach to incarnation) he is still shaping theological
debate.

In addition, the reactions provoked by Hegel resonate through the
rest of the nineteenth century and into our own. One of the most
passionate, that of the Dane Søren Kierkegaard (1813–58), went
virtually unnoticed in his own time, but exploded in early
twentieth-century existentialism and especially influenced Barth,
Bultmann and Tillich. Kierkegaard rejected Hegel's rational inte-

gration, accusing him especially of failing to take account of the existing, deciding individual, and he put forward a radical concept of Christian subjectivity which was not dependent on rational or historical justification. We live life forwards, with no neutral or overarching standpoints. We are faced with decisions and have to choose without any guarantees that we are right. We are constituted by such decisions and through them become different in ourselves. All ethical and religious existence is participated in in such self-involved and self-transforming ways. The gospel faces us with the most radical decision of all, which probes us to the depths and challenges us to go the paradoxical way of the cross. In this Kierkegaard is expanding the practical side of Kant and giving it more full-blooded Christian content. He denies both Kant's and Hegel's versions of how reason relates to faith and sees instead the paradoxical reality of incarnation and cross eliciting the leap of radical faith.

More typical of the nineteenth century was the development of Hegel's stress on history, but rejecting his tendency to give ideas and concepts primacy over empirical research. David Friedrich Strauss (1808–74) was the most controversial figure in this. He applied historical critical methods to the accounts of the life of Jesus, found a great deal that he called 'mythical' (that is, religious ideas given in the form of historical accounts) and decided that there was little reliable factual information about Jesus.

The issue of the historical Jesus in relation to the Christ of faith was now firmly on the theological agenda.The rest of the nineteenth century saw many other developments in historical study which are part of the essential background to the twentieth century, especially in the fields of history of dogma and (more widely) historical theology (outstanding figures being Ferdinand Christian Baur and Adolf von Harnack), but the controversial center of the field remained the figure of Jesus, a focus which has been a legacy to many theologians treated in these volumes. British scholarship (especially after the volume *Essays and Reviews* in 1860) also increasingly joined in the research and discussion, beginning the tradition described by Stephen Sykes in chapter 1 of volume II.

The middle third of the nineteenth century saw many attempts to rethink and restore orthodox Christianity in Germany, Britain, the United States and elsewhere and many of these have continued to be influential, generally within particular churches or traditions (for example, biblical fundamentalism, Anglo-Catholicism, various types of confessionalism). It was also the time when new critiques of religion, such as proposed by Ludwig Feuerbach (1804–72), began to be developed. They multiplied as the century went on, as religion was scrutinized through the disciplines of history, literature, philosophy, geology, biology, psychology, sociology, politics and economics, and comparative religion. These, as mentioned above, were to help cause a major intellectual and cultural crisis in Western Christianity in the twentieth century. but they have also been engaged with in a variety of ways by theologians, and the critical dialogues with them are a major theme running through theologies in the late nineteenth and the twentieth centuries -- for example, Bonhoeffer with sociology; Tillich with socialism, depth psychology and much else; Lonergan, Pannenberg, Moltmann, Küng, and Tracy with almost every area; Teilhard de Chardin and process thought with evolutionary biology; and Moltmann and liberation theologies with Marxism.

Finally, overlapping the two centuries is Ernst Troeltsch (1865–1923), who in many ways summed up the nineteenth century and is the indispensable background for the twentieth. He saw the Enlightenment, not the Reformation, as the genesis of modernity, and the main nineteenth-century development as that of a comprehensive historical consciousness. So, while constantly in dialogue with the theology of Schleiermacher and the philosophies of Kant and Hegel, he saw them all as needing to be criticized through a more thoroughly historical method. He was immersed in late nineteenth-century history of religions and sociology, and wrestled with the enduring problems raised by them, such as the absoluteness of Christianity, the role of the historical Jesus in Christian faith, and the inseparability of all religion from its social and historical context. He arrived at a complex critical and constructive position: resisting naturalistic, reductionist explanations of religion; emphasizing Christianity's distinctive values worked out through the centuries in interaction with different situations, and calling for a fresh, creative social embodiment of those values in twentieth-century Europe; and stressing the ambiguities of both Christianity and modernity.

After the First World War, the dialectical theologians, especially Barth, tended to see his main achievement as negative, showing the *cul de sac* arrived at when theology tries to move from human experience, history, and religion to God. But Troeltsch has also been continually influential, as in Bultmann's historical critical approach to the Bible, the later Tillich's method in dealing with historical patterns and the world religions, Pannenberg's conception of a theology that is consistently and critically historical, North American attempts to work out a practical and sociologically aware theology in a pluralist society, the widespread demand to take local contexts more fully into account in doing theology, and the discussion in theologies of religions about the uniqueness of Christianity.

The above account of the nineteenth century as it has affected the theologians discussed in these volumes has been largely centered on Germany and oriented towards the theologians in this first volume, and towards others in so far as they are in dialogue with them and their forebears. This is because that German tradition, while by no means all-inclusive,[6] is the most sustained and intensive example of engagement in the enterprise of modern theology, as already defined, and is the most direct way of introducing historically the typical problems of modernity, such as knowledge and rationality, historical consciousness, and alternative explanations of religion. There are of course other important traditions, which will be indicated where most relevant, mainly in volume II.

Contexts and Interests

The nineteenth- and twentieth-century historical and sociological insights urge theologians to take fuller account of the situation in which theology is done and for whom and by whom it is done. The history of ideas is not enough. Theology needs to be seen in relation to the many forces and events helping to shape it through the centuries. The twentieth century has added its own conditioning, such as the Holocaust and concentration camps; the unprecedented scale of mass killing of fellow human beings in wars; the Russian, Chinese, and Iranian revolutions; the emergence of new, post-colonial societies; the spread of mass communications, business corporations and technology of many sorts; struggles against racism and sexism; the ecological crisis; and the vast expansion of professions and academic disciplines and institutions. More specific to religion have been the Pentecostal movement, Christian and inter-religious ecumenism, the World Council of Churches, the Second Vatican Council, the spread of Islam and Christianity (especially in Africa), new religious movements outside the main world religions, the multiplication of 'basic communities', liturgical reforms and new translations of the Bible. Most of these feature in the theologies of these volumes, though many are only implicit, or are ignored by theologians in ways that call for more explicit recognition.

More narrowly, there is the significance of the social and institutional context in which theology is produced. All of the nineteenth-century theologies mentioned above and most of the theologies in these volumes, as well as the essays on them, were written in universities or, to a lesser extent, seminaries. They are therefore at home in an academic, largely middle-class 'high culture', which, in its main centers in continental Europe, Britain, and the United States has been remarkably stable through a century of traumas. One of the main tensions in Christian theology has been between its participation in this wider academic culture and its relationship to the Christian community. That has been sharpened by the growing professionalization of the clergy. In German-speaking countries academic theology and clergy education has been integrated in state-financed universities, so that theology has been drawn both towards being an academic discipline on a par with others and towards serving the needs of a profession. These two easily conflict, and the results for theology are symbolized in the debate about the Jesus of history (academic emphasis) and the Christ of faith (clerical requirement).[7]

In Britain similar tensions developed, and, as Sykes describes in volume II, there was an attempt to separate institutionally the more 'academic' from the more contentiously 'ecclesiastical' subjects. In the United States the separation of church and state tied theology more exclusively to seminaries and divinity schools and therefore to the clerical profession. This has tended to polarize theology and religious studies, often in different institutions. It has also contributed to the present situation in which religion is widely practiced and influential but theology tends to be seen as a specialized *professional* discipline and is marginal within both academic and wider culture.

The marginalizing of theology has also happened in varying degrees in Britain, Germany, and elsewhere. It poses a problem for most of the traditions of theology dealt with in this volume: given the largely academic setting together with the academic marginalization of theology, what sort of academic discipline is it? The main temptation within academic life is clearly to become increasingly specialized and allied with other specialized disciplines. That is just the temptation to which the sort of theology covered in these volumes cannot completely succumb, because it is about major issues and their interrelation and inevitably crosses disciplines. But if theology does not fragment into specialties or become absorbed into other disciplines, how does it understand itself? Other related hard questions follow. What is theology's relation to religious communities and their need not only for professional training but also for critical and constructive thinking? How should it handle its own 'ideological' tendency to serve the interests of a particular group, culture, class, religion or profession? Does theology abandon or compromise or fulfill its academic commitments by fuller involvement in practical social and political matters, whether radical or conservative?

Another way of looking at such questions is to ask how theology relates to its three main 'publics': the academy, the churches, and society.[8] Most of the theologians who are the subjects of these volumes are members of all three but concentrate mainly on addressing two of them, usually academy and church. Many of the new challenges in volume II question this in favor of more attention to addressing and changing society. But such an overview needs to be made more complex by noting major contemporary features of each public.

The academy has become more pluralist and self-critical and, at the same time (especially in the West), more subject to pressures to serve the economy in short-term and direct ways. The pluralism of methods appropriate to different disciplines and the increasing awareness by other disciplines of their own often ideological character have somewhat undermined the self-confident positivism and secularism that contributed to theology being marginalized; while the economic and political pressures have put many other disciplines in both humanities and sciences in a marginal position, especially in Britain.

As for the public in the mainstream churches, there has been more corporate social and political controversy and involvement this century, especially in liberal and radical causes – two major instances are the World Council of Churches and post-Vatican II Roman Catholicism. In this context it has become harder for a 'church' theologian to cover the major areas of Christian thought without grappling with social and political issues.

For the 'public', that is society around the world, matters of religion or quasi-religion have been (often tragically) prominent this century, so that it has become less easy with integrity to privatize or cordon off religion and reduce its public significance. It has likewise become in some ways easier to make the case for the need for high quality public discourse within religion as well as about it.

The theologians treated in *The Modern Theologians* try to provide such discourse. They have worked at the leading edge of this century's Christianity and contributed to the making of its history. They are of interest both as a 'religious study' of twentieth-century Christian thought and also as examples and partners for those who follow them in their discipline. The coverage is not complete; but even including the omissions mentioned in the Preface it is worth remembering that the field of such theology is even wider. A great deal of theology is done by those who write little or who may not write it down at all. A lifetime's wisdom may be channelled into teaching or other activity, or may issue in one powerful book. That sort of theology cannot be treated directly here, but it helps to keep the whole enterprise in perspective to remember that at the origins of the two traditions most influential on the theologies of these volumes are Socrates and Jesus, neither of whom left us any writings.

NOTES

1 This typology was suggested by Hans W. Frei in his Cadbury Lectures in the University of Birmingham, 1987, which are unpublished at the time of writing.
2 C. Welch, *Protestant Thought in the Nineteenth Century*, 2 vols.
3 N. Smart et al., *Nineteenth Century Religious Thought in the West*, 3 vols.
4 New York, 1960. First published 1793.
5 Edinburgh, 1928; New York, 1948.
6 See Welch, *Protestant Thought*, for a much fuller picture of Protestant theology, especially in Britain and the United States; and Smart et al., *Nineteenth Century Religious Thought*, for a still broader account.
7 Hans Frei in his Edward Cadbury Lectures (see note 1 above) developed this idea.
8 See David Tracy, *The Analogical Imagination*, ch. 1.

BIBLIOGRAPHY

Primary

Cunliffe-Jones, H. (ed.), *A History of Christian Doctrine* (Edinburgh, 1978).
Gruchy, J. de (general ed.), *The Making of Modern Theology. Nineteenth and Twentieth Century Theological Texts*, 8 vols on Schleiermacher, Bultmann, Tillich, Bonhoeffer, Barth, Harnack, Reinhold Niebuhr, Rahner (London, 1988–89).
Heron, A. I. C., *A Century of Protestant Theology* (Cambridge, 1980).
Hodgson, P. and King, R. H., *Christian Theology. An Introduction to its Traditions and Tasks* (London, 1983).
Macquarrie, J., *Twentieth Century Religious Thought*, 4th edn (London, 1988).
Marty, M. E. and Peerman, D. G., *A Handbook of Christian Theologians* (Nashville, Tenn., 1984).
Nicholls, W., *Pelican Guide to Modern Theology*, vol. 3, *Systematic and Philosophical Theology* (London, 1971).

Schoof, T. M., *A Survey of Catholic Theology 1800–1970* (New York, 1970).

Smart, N., Clayton, J., Katz, S. and Sherry P. (eds), *Nineteenth Century Religious Thought in the West*, 3 vols (Cambridge, 1985).

Welch, C., *Protestant Thought in the Nineteenth Century*, 2 vols (New Haven, Conn., and London, 1972, 1985).

Secondary

Ebeling, G., *The Study of Theology* (London, 1979).

Farley, E., *Theologia* (Philadelphia, 1983).

Feuerbach, L., *The Essence of Christianity* (New York, 1957).

Kant, I., *Religion within the Limits of Reason Alone* (New York, 1960).

Lindbeck, G., *The Nature of Doctrine. Religion and Theology in a Postliberal Age* (Philadelphia, London, 1984).

Lonergan, B., *Method in Theology* (New York, London, 1972).

Moltmann, J., *Theology Today* (London, 1988).

Schleiermacher, F., *Brief Outline on the Study of Theology* (Richmond 1966, first published 1810, 2nd edn., 1830).

Sykes, S. W., *The Identity of Christianity* (London, 1984).

Tracy, D., *Blessed Rage for Order. The New Pluralism in Theology* (New York, 1975).

Tracy, D., *The Analogical Imagination* (New York, 1981, London, 1982).

Troeltsch, E., *Protestantism and Progress. The Significance of Protestantism for the Rise of the Modern World* (Philadelphia, 1986; first published 1912).

Part I

Corresponding to Revelation

The First World War brought about a major crisis in European culture and society. This was the context for Karl Barth's *The Epistle to the Romans* and the explosion of dialectical theology, followed by Barth's attempt to rethink the whole enterprise of modern theology.

Robert Jenson argues that, far from being a conservative revival of premodern theology, Barth's theology takes full account of modernity and could even be seen as going beyond it into 'postmodernity'. Barth transforms the human autonomy of the Enlightenment by identifying Jesus Christ as the one with true autonomy; he intensifies the modern critique of religion; and he offers a God-centered account of reality in place of a mechanistic, atheist universe. Jenson follows Barth through *The Epistle to the Romans* to his pivotal discovery through Anselm of the form of rationality appropriate to Christian theology. He then gives a survey of the *Church Dogmatics*, including an explanation of its structure and approach, before concentrating on two main aspects: its christological description of reality, which puts the life history of Jesus in the place often occupied by an abstract concept of God; and the Trinity as the way of conceiving God in his self-revelation. The conclusion suggests lessons to be learned, especially in Britain and North America.

John Godsey shows Bonhoeffer's theology to be in close but not uncritical relation to Barth's. His life and theology are described in their remarkable coherence of belief, action and reflection, culminating in martyrdom. His main works are summarized (with considerable attention given to the fundamental but less well known early dissertations), and the key integrating themes are seen to be Jesus Christ and sociality. Bonhoeffer's later theology was only published after his death, and Godsey traces its reception and the debates it has stimulated.

Thomas Torrance and Eberhard Jüngel represent post-Second

World War theologies strongly influenced by Barth. Torrance is in a Scottish tradition of theology (Stephen Sykes situates this in the context of British theology in volume II), which has close links with continental Europe. Daniel Hardy describes and assesses his work: its combination of a positive, scientific position with an approach to history that challenges most modern hermeneutics; its appreciation of the stimulus to intellectual vision given by Christian faith; and its overall standing as the 'most highly developed version of realism'. He engages especially with Torrance's relating of theology and natural science, a subject that is something of a blind spot for most of the other theologians in this volume, Lonergan and Pannenberg being partial exceptions.

Jüngel, the youngest of this group, has, in line with Barth, what John Webster describes as 'a resolute theological realism'. Perhaps his main contributions to this realism are his reflections on language (especially metaphor, parable, and analogy), his concept of possibility as part of reality and his wrestling with the theme of the death of God. He has also tried more than anyone else in this period to explore how the theologies of Barth and Bultmann can contribute to each other.

All four share a concern that above all theology should rationally and faithfully 'correspond' to revelation, whose givenness, graciousness, and objectivity are emphasized in various ways. In Bonhoeffer the correspondence is worked out especially in its ethical dimension as 'conformity to Christ'. Torrance offers the most thorough theoretical account of such correspondence. Jüngel, besides his exploration of language and possibility, has most fully responded to the common criticism (made, for example, in chapter 11 below) that Barth's approach to corresponding to revelation fails to do justice to human freedom and responsibility.

1

Karl Barth

Robert W. Jenson

INTRODUCTION: LIFE

In the summer of 1911 the 25-year-old Karl Barth became pastor at Safenwil, a small town in his native Switzerland. Parish experience in this community, most of whose breadwinners worked in industry, was expected to season him for a scholarly career; instead it threw him into theological convulsion.

Barth had studied under Adolf von Harnack at Berlin and Wilhelm Herrmann at Marburg, great masters of the 'liberal' theology in its last effloresence. Thus he went to Safenwil as a professional of the Christian *religion*, as one trained to cultivate a particular tradition of humankind's quest for unity with the divine. Pastoral work broke this conception of his calling.

The young pastor had now to preach, from appointed texts; therefore he now read the Bible differently than he had read it in classrooms. He found that the Bible is not about our religion, but about something called the Kingdom of God. What that might be, he did not know, but he saw that it could not be what liberal exegesis had taught him it was: the final success of our religious quest. Indeed, Barth discovered in the Bible an entire 'strange new world': a reality which one might *inhabit* and in which everything goes differently than in our apparent world, a world unified not by our religious relation to God but by God's sovereign relation to us, the world, he said in amazement, 'of God'.[1]

As Barth observed his working-class parishioners, in the unmistakable oppression that shaped their lives, he was driven to acknowledge that cultivation of their religious experience was, under the actual circumstances, a gratuitous enterprise. Hope for a Kingdom of God, whatever that might turn out to be, seemed more to the point – and precisely to the social-democratic point.

And as the years went by in Safenwil, Barth watched the suicide of the Western bourgeois culture for which liberal Christianity had provided the ideology. It was exactly the outsider-position of a Swiss, *viewing* the national representatives of that civilization devour themselves, which made the first 'World War' a conceptual torment for him. How could the European nations, liberated by Enlightenment and exquisitely cultivated through two centuries, suddenly fall barbarously upon one another, and for no reasonable or even ascertainable *casus belli*? How could his old German teachers suddenly call for loyalty above all to *Kaiser* and *Vaterland*?

Barth's radicalization thus came from all sides, but it made only one experience. Born in Basle, on May 10, 1886, into a churchly and academic family, he had hardly been expected to be a rebel and an overthrower. After initial study done somewhat unwillingly at Berne, he had his years in the splendid theological-academic world of Berlin, Tübingen and Marburg. After a year's service to the German-speaking congregation of Geneva, he went to Safenwil, to meet his undoing.

As a proper young academic, he did his struggling in print, producing lectures and papers[2] and the book which theologically divides the twentieth century from the nineteenth, the second attempt (1922) at a commentary on Paul's letter to Rome, *The Epistle to the Romans*.[3] This book became the banner of a generation of the German-speaking church's young pastors and teachers. A childhood memory of groping in a dark church and accidentally yanking the bellrope, to bring the whole village running, became Barth's metaphor for its publication.

In 1921 Barth was called to a teaching post at Göttingen, then to Münster and in 1930 to Bonn. There events again overtook him and he became a theological leader of the 'confessing' opposition to National Socialism's attempt to rule the German church, and chief drafter of the opposition's 'Barmen Declaration'. In consequence he was in 1935 forbidden to teach in Germany. He returned to Basle and remained there the rest of his life, teaching, writing the *Church Dogmatics* and a stream of papers and smaller books, and with relish playing the role of famous theologian, for students and visitors alike. On the morning of December 10, 1968, his wife of 55 years failed to awaken him with the music of his beloved Mozart.

MODERNITY

Our volume is dedicated to major theologians of the twentieth century. The position of Karl Barth in such a volume would seem assured, and yet a certain paradox appears. For while Barth is commonly supposed to be among the century's giants, if not to be its single greatest theologian, he is in English-speaking parts of the church also commonly supposed to be a sort of throwback, perhaps to the seventeenth century. Thus in the last years of the 1950s, when Barth was still at the height of his powers, when his fame was greatest, and when it would seem that the general tenor of his views should have been widely known, the university of Basle attracted American students from the 'evangelical' wing, who had pilgrimaged there on the impression that his thought was a 'conservative' reaction to modernism. English and North American theologians from the opposite pole have had the same impression with different evaluation; Barth has been routinely denounced as a theological reactionary, who tried to save the faith from the acids of modernity by locating it in a sealed compartment of biblicistically revealed truth.

In fact, Barth's thought is drastically 'modern'. That is to say: his thought is determined both in its structure and in its warrants by the Western church's mandatory and continuing effort to come to terms with the Enlightenment. Indeed, if there is such a thing as 'postmodernism', Barth may be its only major theological representative so far, for his work is a vast attempt to transcend not merely the Enlightenment but also 'modern' Protestantism's defining way of making that attempt.

Modernity had a beginning: the eighteenth century's creation of a new intellectuality to replace that inherited from 'the ancients'. We call it 'the Enlightenment'. Arising first in Holland and England, nearly simultaneously vital in Scotland and America, and exported first to France and then to Germany and the rest of Europe, the current had by the turn of the century nearly undone Christianity among the élites of Europe and North America. It is the effort to recover this loss, *without* denying the truth which the Enlightenment brought forward, which has determined the goals and boundaries of modern theology.

Attempting to characterize the Enlightenment within the confines of an essay on another subject, I am necessarily condemned to superficiality. That said, I may then suggest that for present purposes three slogans will sufficiently evoke the Enlightenment's spirit.

The first is one provided by Karl Barth himself in *Protestant Theology in the Nineteenth Century*: the Enlightenment, he said, was the emergence of a specific sort of '*Mensch*', of human person, the 'absolutist' human person. This is the person who understands him/

herself in that he/she 'discovers his own power, his own ability, the potential that slumbers in his . . . humanity simply as such, and who understands this as something . . . in itself justified and mighty, and who therefore sets this potential in . . . motion in every direction'.[4] The Enlightenment was a declaration of independence by the human subject, from every limitation but faithfulness to him/herself. Necessarily, a specifically religious declaration of independence was central to this project, and had to amount to renunciation of Christian tradition and canon. For how are we to follow no guide but our own free judgment, and worship the God spoken of by Isaiah or Aquinas?

A second slogan for Enlightenment aspiration can be 'critique', a label much beloved of Enlighteners and made definitive for the movement by its perfecter, Immanuel Kant. 'Critique' is an intellectual policy, of suspicion over against all 'appearances' of truth. It is our initial experience that reality *presents* itself to us, but if we are to be autonomous subjects, we cannot accept such impositions as veridical. We will instead ask the question of the proverbial American 'man from Missouri': I know that is what the thing *looks* like, but now what is it *really*?

The seventeenth-century triumph of 'modern science' had many elements. But culturally decisive was the policy of persistence in the critique of appearances. Copernicus and Galileo provided the paradigm. It certainly looks as if the sun goes round the earth; the great triumph consisted in asking and continuing to ask, But does it really? Through the seventeenth century, such questioning produced an unprecedented outpouring of fascinating and useful knowledge. As soon as this record of success could be seen and reflected upon, the hope had to arise of applying the same policy to the intractable questions of humanity's own life. Therewith arose the great assignment of the eighteenth century, and the hope that constituted Enlightenment.

The first and obsessing target of the eighteenth century's critical enterprise was the established religion of Europe and America. Moreover, it was precisely those elements of the Christian religion which make it specifically *Christian* – the worship of God as Trinity, confession of 'original' sin, and confidence in God's sovereign grace – which both most offended the passion for autonomy and seemed most vulnerable to critique. For traditional Western theology had divided the West's religious substance between 'natural' doctrines and practices – i.e., in fact, those derived from classical antiquity – and doctrines and practices based on 'revelation' – i.e., on the Scriptures and the theological experience of the church. The

Enlightenment adopted this very division as its critical principle, trimming 'revealed' religion to the standards of 'natural' religion. The outcome was a sort of repristination of classical antiquity's religion, minus the cultic relation to society that had made it vital.

A third slogan can be 'mechanism'. The *results* of seventeenth- and eighteenth-century science became culturally and intellectually pervasive in the form of a metaphysical expansion, by inspiration of a specific root metaphor. There is nothing in Newtonian physics themselves to require interpretation of the universe as mechanism; it was the technology *enabled* by the new science that suggested the metaphor. With or without adequate warrant or methodological care, what one may call the vulgar Enlightenment believed the new science had provided an encompassing and superior worldview: of the universe as a vast machine.

It is plain that such a worldview is flatly incompatible with trust in anything like the Christian gospel. For the very deity of the gospel's God is invested in what within a machine-universe can only appear as 'interventions': Israel's rescue from Egypt, Jesus' resurrection, and the final new creation. As 'free-thinkers' of every stripe rightly argued: if the great Engineer made a perfect machine in the first place, he does not need to interfere in its running; whereas if the machine needs constant fixing, how was its Engineer God?

I am already in position for a first characterization of Barth's theology. For it has a clear and by no means undialectically antagonistic relation to each motif of Enlightenment.

Inescapably, what the Enlightenment thought of as freedom is what the classical Christian tradition means by 'sin' – and Barth's revival of classical teaching about sin is most of what English-speaking 'neo-orthodoxy' took from him. The would-be autonomous subject, self-contained over against every instance by which his/her intention or judgment might be relativized, is precisely the person 'curved in on him/herself' of Reformation teaching, the person 'who wants to be Lord himself, the judge of good and evil, who wants to be his own helper' – the *Church Dogmatics'* primary description of sin.[5] And yet – central among Barth's examples of typical eighteenth-century figures is Mozart himself.[6]

With some plausibility, it might be said that Barth's objection to the Enlightenment's passion for autonomous humanity is not so much to the ideal of the autonomous human as to the eighteenth century's identification of who this human person is. The *Church Dogmatics* is a single massive description of that specific human person in whom being the human he is and being the Lord and judge of good and evil indeed coincide, who truly is in himself both helped and Helper; and it is a statement of our ontological identity with and in precisely this person.

The critique of religion was interrupted by Friedrich Schleiermacher – to whom I am coming – but then taken up with intensified acuity by the great outsiders of the nineteenth century. And the line from Feuerbach through Nietzsche and Overbeck has perhaps had no more enthusiastic theological student than Barth in the days of his radicalization. The whole of Barth's work could be summarized by saying that he carried the Enlightenment's critique of religion to its final possibility, attacking the West's established religion not by the standard of one of its own religious components but by the standard of an instance external to all of them, that strange and contingent message called the gospel.

Finally, there is of course no common ground between the mechanistic worldview and Barth's vision – or any other Christian vision. Yet precisely as a unitary description of Christ, the *Church Dogmatics* is one long ontological treatise, one great vision of unified reality. The casting of such specifically Christian metaphysical visions had been a central work of Patristic Christianity, but the usual theology of the medieval and modern West had thought such enterprises no longer needed. Barth stands directly in the line of those thinkers of the nineteenth century, most notably G. F. W. Hegel, who were challenged by the vulgar Enlightenment's mechanistic metaphysics again to build specifically Christian alternatives.

SCHLEIERMACHER AND THE LIBERAL THEOLOGY

Barth did not, of course, directly confront the Enlightenment. Between him and it lay his primary resource, inspiration and *bête noire*: the German theology of the nineteenth century. By around 1800 the great Enlighteners had done their work. Christianity's nineteenth-century theological recovery, an integral part of the general explosion of energy with which Christianity astonished its gravediggers, was very largely the work of one man. That he was a German made Germany the center of the theological world for a century and a half.

Indeed, the recovery was very much the work of one *book*: *On Religion: Speeches to its Cultured Despisers*.[7] Friedrich Schleiermacher was first and foremost a figure of the flowering of German arts and letters between, let us say, 1780 and 1850. That this renaissance occurred resulted in part from the particular way in which the Enlightenment had been received into Germany (tracing that, however, would be beyond the scope of this essay). Central to the great German time was a new vision of humanity, nurtured through the last decades of the eighteenth century by such thinkers and *litterati* as Lessing, Herder, and Goethe. This was the vision of the human person as his/her own work of art: of the person as formed through his/her history into something like a classical sonata-movement, in which the greatest possible diversity is held together in a transcendent temporal unity. Schleiermacher's apologetic, lamentably summarized, was: if you indeed want to fulfill the Goethean vision in your own personhood, if you seek both great and various experience and the unity of your experience in itself and with the universal, then you must cultivate your religious life, for it is only therein that historical multiplicity finds unity.

The *Speeches* made Schleiermacher 'the church father of the nineteenth century'. They did not do so in virtue of Schleiermacher's specific positions – for example, the famous definition of religion as 'feeling' – but in virtue of their general pattern of analysis and argument. The *Speeches* begin with an analysis of human existence, to show that 'religion' is a necessary component of complete personal life and is, moreover, the component by which all others are brought together into unity. There follows an analysis of religion's possible modes and manifestations. Then comes stipulation of Christianity's specific identity among the religions, done by reference to the figure of Christ. And finally there is argument that of all possible religions, Christianity best fills religion's place in life. Along the way, a conceptual creation occurs: of the concept 'religion' as we now use it.

Without Schleiermacher, Barth's theology would have been as impossible as would any other German theology of the nineteenth or early twentieth centuries. For Barth fully adopts Schleiermacher's concept of religion. For both, the attempt to unify and make overall sense of our lives is the inescapable and necessary center of human existence. Indeed, Barth's theology too circles around this phenomenon. Barth's break with the nineteenth century may – with only a little pushing – be described by saying that he just turned the Schleiermachean pattern around. Instead of interpreting Christianity by the general characteristics and functions of religion, he interprets religion, including and especially Christian religion, by Christianity's differentiating specifity. Instead of analyzing human existence, in order then to inquire after Christ's contribution to it, he analyzes Christ's existence, in order then to inquire after our place therein.

There was a century between Barth and Schleiermacher. Schleiermacher's pattern of theological procedure could be and was filled in most variously. The initial analysis of human existence was derived in different ways. Material specification of religion and its relation to other aspects of life varied. And argument for the superiority or appropriateness of the Christian religious option was conducted by different sorts of warrants. The names of Barth's teachers show what line of nineteenth-century theology, among the several possibilities, was his immediate context and target: the 'liberal' theology.

Liberal theology properly so called was the dominant movement of the last part of the nineteenth century and its hangover into the twentieth. Typically, liberal theologians derived their analysis of human existence and the location therein of religion from Immanuel Kant: religion was understood as the interior presupposition of moral action, and religious doctrines as 'value judgments', which only in their naive form may appear as statements of metaphysical fact. Definitive for the movement, however, was the particular way in which Christ was thought to fit into and influence religious existence – as 'the historical Jesus'.

Christianity is the deepening of religious life by Christ; this, to repeat, was the shared supposition of the century. But Christ, said the liberals, is an historical phenomenon or he is nothing. Here enters a motif of the German vision which was present in Schleiermacher but was not central for all subsequent schools: its historicism, its understanding of human life as essentially worked out through time. Moreover, since the liberals had interpreted confession of Jesus' resurrection as a confession of values rather than of facts, they had at least initially to think of Christ as a phenomenon of *past* history. So the liberals asked: how do we have to do with the past Jesus? Their answer defined their theological movement: we can have to do with the past Jesus only in the same way we have to do with any other figure of history, by study of the evidence. One could almost say that for liberalism historical method was the great sacrament: we have to do with Jesus by historical study of Scripture, and in converse with him the possibilities of moral life are transformed.

Karl Barth came to see liberal theology as nothing less than a betrayal of the faith. Yet here again his relation to his past was no mere contradiction. Liberal theology was a radically christocentric theology. If all assertions about God and the soul – metaphysical propositions in their apparent form – are in fact meaningful only as value judgments, and if Christians make their value judgments in converse with Jesus, then it is only in converse with Jesus that Christians can speak meaningfully about God and their own souls. Barth learned this argument from Wilhelm Herrmann, and retained its conclusion as a great maxim, even when he replaced its premises. Perhaps the one aspect of Barth's early theology that is generally known to English-speaking theology is his polemic against 'natural theology'. Although Barth came to see the liberal theology as specially addicted to this vice, his polemic was initially a straight-forward *continuation* of liberalism's polemic against 'metaphysics', against claims for religious assertions' meaningfulness outside reference to Christ.

Moreover, that to speak of persons, whether God or creatures, is to speak of history, was as foundational for Barth as ever for the liberals from whom he initially heard it. He came to reject the liberal axiom that the only historical events are those of which historical-critical research is the appropriate cognition, but that in talking of Christ and ourselves in God we are talking of events arrayed in time's before and after, was a principle in which he wavered only for a moment.

THE COMMENTARY ON ROMANS

The Epistle to the Romans was the break, between the two unequal parts of Barth's career and between the nineteenth and twentieth theological centuries. This book is the conceptual version of his pastoral and political convulsion.

The theology of *The Epistle to the Romans* was rightly labelled 'dialectical', by foe and friend. The work is a sustained conscious repristination of the Socratic dialectic, of Socrates' assault on Athenian certainties, learned from passionate study of Plato and Socrates' Danish disciple, Søren Kierkegaard. As Socrates invented ever new contradictions, to break down Athens' claim to *possession* of righteousness, of any direct line from what justice meant in Athens to what justice means in itself, so Barth generated contra-dictions to break down Christendom's claim to possession of righteousness, of any direct line from what virtue or faith could mean religiously to what they mean in the gospel.

The Epistle to the Romans was written as a direct assault on the reader. It is not so much intended to inform as to transform. When we read it, the chief thing is to *experience* the dialectic, to be *rendered* critical of our own religiosity – and so to be freed to hear from Paul about *God's* righteousness. Religion, Barth agrees with

Schleiermacher, is the highest possibility of humanity, our quest for that beyond ourselves in which alone we can be fulfilled; but just so it is our attempt to use eternity for our own purposes, and so the denial of it as eternity.[8] Christ is the savior in whom religion is perfected – by being abandoned, 'who bridges over the distance between God and man – in that he tears it open'.[9] 'The No which meets us is *God's* No. What we lack is just what helps us. What shuts us in is new country. What cancels all the truth of the world is also its foundation. Exactly because God's No is complete, it is also his Yes'.[10] God 'acknowledges us as his in that he takes and keeps his distance from us'.[11] He is 'known as the unknown . . ., not man and just *therefore* the first and last truth . . . of man'.[12]

It is treacherous to attempt a statement of 'what *The Epistle to the Romans* teaches'. But Barth did himself say in his Foreword, 'If I have a system, it consists in what Kierkegaard named "the infinite qualitative difference" between time and eternity . . .'.[13] And of the many images with which Barth evokes the relation of time and eternity, there is one which can perhaps compendiously show how time and eternity, in their qualitative difference, touch by not touching. Time is touched by eternity, Barth said, as a circle is touched by a tangent line – perhaps he might better have spoken of a cylinder and a plane. The plane does touch the cylinder, and beings inhabiting the surface of the cylinder would find themselves stopped when they came to the line of tangency. Yet the plane occupies no space on the cylinder; there is no stretch of the cylinder-world which is also a stretch of the plane; the cylinder-worldlings would see nothing stopping them, could get no purchase on their impediment. The line of eternity's tangency to time, said Barth, is death. Christ is savior in that he occupies that line perfectly.

'DIALECTICAL THEOLOGY' AND AFTER

The group which rallied around *The Epistle to the Romans* lasted only a decade; we may date it by the survival of its journal, *Zwischen den Zeiten*. Other leaders of the 'dialectical theologians' went on to become great names in their own rights: Rudolf Bultmann, Emil Brunner, Friedrich Gogarten, and – a bit on the fringes – Paul Tillich. In 1933 they suspended joint publication, having discovered they were no longer a group.

Manifestly, the theology of *The Epistle to the Romans* could be no more than a polemic moment – though for Bultmann it came close to providing a permanent system. One need only ask: how would you *preach* by its lights? Having once said, 'All your religion is but a grasping after God, who refuses to be grasped,' what would you say the next time? The dialectical theology was a christocentric theology, yet it was crippled in its ability to speak about Christ. Christ is said to be savior as the supreme occupant of the line of death; in consequence, dialectical theology remarkably copied its liberal antagonists in being unable to speak materially about the risen Christ. Yet it did not have liberalism's alternative; it could not proclaim the historical Jesus, since this would make the gospel dependent on historical research and so on prior culture.

The dialectical theology was above all polemic: it was the perfecting of the Enlightenment's critique of religion, and marked exactly the *break* with previous theology. When the dialectical theologians were compelled to say what they *affirmed*, they found they had been united mostly in their negations. None recanted the negations, except perhaps Tillich if he ever held them; each found his own way to constructive thought. The ways they found account for most of the options of twentieth-century theology.

Barth's own renewed search is documented in papers and lectures and two books: the strange book about Anselm[14] and the first volume of a *Christliche Dogmatik* (*Christian Dogmatics*) of which the second never appeared. The way he found may be characterized in two complementary ways.

A short formula for traditional theology's problem in modernity can be that the Enlightenment's critique undid the faith's claim to rationality, undid the warrants by which theology had vindicated the coherence and plausibility of faith's statements. Schleiermacher had provided a new set of warrants, derived by analysis of human existence. But *The Epistle to the Romans'* intensified renewal of religious critique, now in the name of faith, undid these also – thereby, since no new warrants were evoked, sawing off faith's own limb. The rationality of *The Epistle to the Romans'* discourse is at every moment precarious.

Barth found his way by seeing that also in this matter modernity's proceedings could be simply reversed. Why should faith find the warrants of its rationality in analyses conducted 'prior' to faith? Why should discourse about the Kingdom seek cognitive plausibility by attachment to discourse about the world? *Why not the other way around?*

The assertions of faith, he said in the book about Anselm, have their own internal coherence, and demonstration of faith's rationality consists in tracing the spiderweb of their connections. Nor is this the coherence of a freely-invented conceptual system, since the whole which thus obtains is a single witness to an event outside itself, an event which demands exactly this witness as its cognition.[15] Moreover, such knowledge, if it is knowledge, must itself be the decisive knowledge also of the world, for if the faith is true then all things exist as mirrors of the Christ to whom faith and its reflection witness.[16]

Thus we are led to the alternative, christological way of describing Barth's move. The positions of the dialectical theology were not to be abandoned: the dialectical dissolution of religion and the reference of all churchly discourse to Christ are right. But how to do both? Barth never states it in so many words, but those who read must see how he made his move. In effect, Barth transposed the dialectic of time and eternity into christology. Time and eternity join without joining, draw the line of death along their tangency, *not* as a general border between God and creatures but as the determinants of *one* creature's existence, as the life, death, and resurrection of Jesus the Christ of Israel; only *so* does the 'infinite qualitative difference' encompass our lives also. The *Church Dogmatics* is all christology; and as it traces the connections and movements of Christ's reality, the lineaments of *The Epistle to the Romans* are followed.

As Barth made his epistemological-christological move, two closely related ambiguities of his previous thought resolved themselves. A hasty reader might earlier have thought that Barth's polemic against 'natural theology' was against one *kind* of theology, for which he wanted to substitute another, the 'revealed', kind. In the later writings, it is unambiguous: *all* theology is natural theology, in that our theological thoughts are necessarily 'natural' to us, necessarily emerge from our religious attempt to benefit from God. The question is whether any of our theology is also *true*; and that issue is in God's hand, not ours.

Moreover, *The Epistle to the Romans* is genuinely ambiguous at a central point. Is Barth against religion's attempt to bridge the difference between God and us because he thinks God and we are so far apart that the effort is hopeless? Or is Barth against the religious quest because he thinks that God is not missing in the first place, and so does not need to be pursued? In the *Church Dogmatics* and elsewhere, it becomes plain that the latter is the case. The 'infinite qualitative *difference*' between God and us is not a *distance*. On the contrary, as this difference constitutes the reality of Christ, it constitutes precisely God's nearness. The religious effort to get closer to God is wrong because it is unbelief, because it supposes that God is away from us and must be quested after.

THE *CHURCH DOGMATICS*

It is time to turn directly to the *Church Dogmatics*. In this section I will briefly survey the overall structure of the massive and daunting publication. Then in the next two sections I will seek more material access to it. The choice of topics for the latter exercise must be somewhat arbitrary; there is, in my judgment, no intrinsically favored access to the work. Perhaps I may first probe where my own study of Barth began: with his christological doctrine of reality.[17] Then I will describe his trinitarianism. And that can – or anyway must – suffice.

The *Church Dogmatics* is structured as a series of 'volumes', each of which is in fact a multi-volumed material part of the work; I will in the following speak of 'Part I', etc. for these large units and reserve 'volume' for its normal use. Part I, in two volumes, deals with the possibility of theology, with what in modern theologies has come to be called 'Prolegomena'; this is, in Barth's understanding, the doctrine of the Word of God. Part II, in two volumes, contains that part of the doctrine of God not already treated in Part I. Part III, in no less than four volumes, treats of creation – Barth's wind is increasing even from its previous majestic status. And Part IV occupies three completed volumes, of which the third had again to be subdivided, and breaks off with a fragment of an intended fourth volume; it holds the doctrine of 'reconciliation' – that is, of christology and atonement. Part V was to have brought the eschatology, under the title of 'redemption'; Barth did not live to create it.

The work is intensely, even ferociously systematic, in that very particular sense which Barth saw as appropriate for Christian theology. It is just such a web of mutually demanded insights as Barth postulated in the book on Anselm. But a single deductive 'system' it is not at all. Rather, the total work marches to the pattern of the old method of '*loci*', in which each topic develops a complete theology, organized around a specific theme. With each 'volume' Barth initiates his reflection anew. It is therefore possible to begin reading the work at the beginning of any part; none absolutely requires its predecessors for its comprehension. This may also be the place to note the role of the long sections in small type: these include everything from what would in another book be footnotes to chapter-length excurses. They are some of the most interesting parts of the work, but on a first reading may well be skipped.

I may begin description of Part I with a final hint to new readers:

always pay the most careful attention to the theme-propositions which Barth sets at the beginning of each numbered 'paragraph' – that is, by usual standards, chapter. Thus paragraph 1, on the 'task' of dogmatics, has: 'The theological discipline of dogmatics is the Christian church's scientific [*wissenschaftlich*] self-examination, with respect to the contents of its distinctive speech about God.'[18] That the church *does* speak about God, and in its own specific way, is a fact. That it *can* speak about God, is a claim which is either believed or rejected. The question of prolegomena, as must follow from everything we have so far said of Barth, can for him only be: *how does it happen* that the church does and so can speak of God? And to that question, his founding answer is: the church can speak of God because God is the particular God that he is.

Therefore, following a relatively brief development of theology's formal characteristics, Barth proceeds immediately to that locus by which the specific God of faith is *identified*: the doctrine of Trinity. This occupies the first segment of a chapter on 'The Revelation of God', a second segment of which is then a complete christology – the first of several in the total work – and the third a consideration of the anthropological reality and possibility of revelation, as a doctrine of the Spirit. Only after all this can Barth return to a more complete formal treatment of dogmatics' role in the church, to what is usually thought of as prolegomena.

The beginning of Part II, on God, to the likely surprise and distress of the beginning reader, traces all this ground anew, now under the rubric of our *knowledge* of God. How can we know God? Because he is the God who makes himself known, and for no other reason. Because he in fact makes himself the object of our in itself all-too-'natural' theology.

Then three mighty chapters speak of God himself. The first invokes the 'reality' of God; this comprises his *being* and his 'perfections' – in the older language, his 'attributes'. The first theme-proposition of this chapter states the whole: 'God is, who he is in the act of his revelation. God seeks and creates communion between himself and us, and so he loves us. But he is this Loving One, as Father, Son and Holy Spirit, also without us, in the freedom of the Lord who lives from himself.'[19] God is the one who loves in freedom.

The next chapter brings the doctrine of election or predestination, which will be further described in the next section. Here I must note but two points. First, the doctrine comes at *this* point because it is, according to Barth, the description of the *actuality* of God's being, of his love-that-is-freedom and freedom-that-is-love. Second, Barth's treatment has made a revolution of the doctrine, making of it explicitly what it always was in inner intention: a doctrine about God's will for us in *Christ*. A third chapter ends the doctrine of God by telling of his 'commandment'. It is a structural principle of Barth's theology that ethics are integral to dogmatics, that no locus can be carried out without them; thus each part will end as this one, with its specific ethical matter.

It was supposed by many of Barth's critics that this 'dialectical' theologian could have nothing to say about creation; the relative slimness of III/1 – only 488 pages! – was taken to confirm this. In fact, the volume is a key to all Barth's thought and is one of the two or three most influential volumes in the *Church Dogmatics*. It develops one of the most famous – or infamous – of Barthian slogans: the creation is the outer basis of the covenant and the covenant is the inner basis of the creation.[20] God's act of creation makes the covenant possible; and making the covenant is the purpose of creation. This structure will be more fully described in my next section.

The following volumes of Part III make up for skimped space. III/2 develops, at exhausting length, a christological anthropology, in which at every step knowledge of humanity is enabled by knowledge of the one human Jesus. III/3 is a miscellany of topics that have to be covered under 'creation': providence, God's universal rule, evil and the angels. The latter two, each in its own way, are among the most sheerly interesting parts of the *Church Dogmatics*, and provide deep probes into the structure of Barth's thinking. Finally, III/4 brings nearly 800 more pages of ethics, dealing with that aspect of 'special' theological ethics which displays our creatureliness, and in particular our human freedom.

In Part IV, on the doctrine of 'reconciliation', Barth performs what can only be called a *tour de force*. He actually carries out, structurally and materially, what had always been an unfulfilled postulate of Reformation theology: that christology and soteriology be seen as identical. To achieve this, Barth melts the doctrines of Christ's person with the doctrine of his 'states'. Thus in IV/1 the deity of Christ and the descent of Christ to us are one, under the title 'The Lord as Servant'; in IV/2 the humanity of Christ and our elevation to God are one, under the title 'The Servant as Lord'; and in IV/3 the hypostatic union of deity and humanity in Christ is identified with the event of the proclamation of these movements, under the title 'Jesus Christ, the True Witness'. Even to suggest the multifarious problems and possibilities posed in these volumes would entirely burst the bounds of this essay. Let me only hint at them by noting that the concluding *ethics* of this part turn out to be the doctrine of sacraments!

It is likely that no friend or foe of the *Church Dogmatics* has succeeded in appropriating the whole of it, in all its wheels within wheels. The following sections can only claim to seize it from appropriate aspects.

CHRISTOLOGICAL METAPHYSICS

Why, we may ask, did God create the world? It is ecumenical doctrine that the creature does not in itself contain the reason of its existence: whatever I may be in myself, virtuous or vice-ridden, accomplished or failed, nothing of that is a sufficient reason for my existence. But the usual understanding leaves it either a mystery or a banality why then God *does* create. We suppose either that God's motives are obscure and in any case covered over by our fallenness; or that they are adequately described morally, that God wants there to be justice and mercy and love in general, and creates in order to have persons to exercise these virtues. Barth's christological reversal closes off such general answers. God, he teaches, creates in order that there shall be Jesus Christ, just as Jesus Christ is personally concrete in the actual history he has lived and lives.

'Creation,' Barth defines, 'is the . . . external basis of the covenant.' That is, 'It prepares . . . the sphere in which the institution and history of the covenant takes place . . .'[21] If God is to make loving covenant beyond his own triune fellowship, there must *be* others than God. Therefore God creates. Nor is this covenant, this goal of all God's works, a covenant that might have been. It is precisely the covenant that actually occurs, of the reconciliation of sinners in Jesus Christ.[22] 'Because *servatio*, therefore *creatio* . . .'[23]

Thus the content of God's eternal choice is his self-giving in the incarnation of the Son for fallen creatures. This 'eternal decree' is necessarily a 'double predestination', though in a sense very different from that of the Calvinist tradition. God chose eternally that he would live for us and we would live for him. Since we are chosen precisely as fallen, God chose to lose that we might gain. For himself God chose sin and evil, since we were to be sinful and burdened with evil. For us God chose fellowship with himself, in all his blessedness.[24]

So what does God, in good Calvinist 'eternity before all time', first and definitively decree? He chooses to be one with sinful man in the personal existence, exactly as it occurs, of Jesus Christ. This decision *is* the eternal decree. 'In the beginning, with God, i.e., in his decree which precedes the existence, possibility and reality of all his creatures, the primary element is the decision whose carrying out . . . is Jesus Christ.'[25] All his works fulfill this decision, are done in order that Jesus Christ shall exist.[26] 'The reason why God created the world and the purpose for which he created it, and the reason why God set up in the world the office of reconciliation, and the purpose for which he did so, is that he was able, willing and prepared to be one with the creature in Jesus Christ, and that he has in fact done it.'[27] The Incarnation is its own exclusive reason; it 'knows no Wherefore? It is an absolute Therefore . . .'[28]

The content of God's eternal will is the existence of Jesus Christ. The christological reversal will not, however, be carried out fully if we leave that word 'will' in the generality it so far may seem to have. We must ask: what sort of event was/is God's eternal deciding? According to Barth, the event of God's choice to be one with us in Jesus Christ can only be the prevenient reality in God of Jesus Christ himself. For God's choice to be one with us is already a self-determination of God to oneness with us, and just so is itself the chosen state of affairs. But Jesus Christ *is* the chosen state of affairs. Jesus Christ, the God-*man*, happened eternally in that God chose to be God with this man.[29]

Thus Jesus Christ is not only what God chooses, he is also the God who does the choosing. 'Jesus Christ is the electing God.'[30] It is high on the long list of Barth's controversial propositions: between the eternal being of the 'second Person' and the temporal reality of Jesus the Christ there is a 'third' reality, the occurrence of that choice in which the Son is chosen to be and himself chooses to be the man Jesus, and in which the Son therefore *is* the man Jesus.[31] The incarnation, Barth said to the consternation of all standard Protestants, *happened* in God before all time.[32]

The justification of such initially bizarre – and just therefore, in the 'strange new world of the Bible', possibly true! – propositions appears as Barth develops the doctrine of God, in one of the finest volumes of the *Church Dogmatics*. All theology that is not to be *merely* natural theology must stem from trust in the veracity of God's self-revelation in Christ: in trust that God is in himself not different than he is among us as this man. But in the life of Christ we have to do precisely with a *life*, not with a static first Being but with happenings in sequence, with a complex event. Therefore we must acknowledge God's being as in itself an event, an *action*; nor can this event be thought transcended by any depth of deity in which atemporality yet reigns. Barth adapts – or rather, bends – a scholastic formula: God is *actus purissimus*, 'perfectly pure event'.[33] For Barth, this is the same as to say that God is perfectly pure *person*.[34] And again, the purity of God's personhood means that he himself decides what he shall be, that he chooses his own nature.

The final end of this string of analyses – each of them, we must remember, conducted over dozens of pages of careful reflection – is that God's being is his act of deciding. His personal act is based on no merely given being prior to itself.[35] With that we are where we needed to be: God is his own decision.

What has he decided? To be one with us as Jesus Christ. The pre-existence of the God-man Jesus Christ takes place in God's 'eternal self-differentiation from all that is not God and is not willed by God';[36] it is itself 'the living act in which he . . . posits himself and everything that is'.[37]

The more comprehensive statement of the reality of God as these interpretations open it to us, is that God has and is history. It is not we who are innately historical, and God who in fellowship with us adapts himself to historicality; it is God who is himself historical, and we who acquire history as we are taken into him. Barth provides an explicit definition of historical being: 'The history of any being starts, is carried on, and is completed when something other than it . . . encounters it . . . and determines its being appropriately to this other, so that it is compelled and enabled to transcend itself in response . . .'[38] The definition is a standard modern definition. What Barth notices and makes us notice is that it perfectly suits only one reality: the triune God.

In this definition, history is self-transcendence; thus it requires the difference between what is and what is not yet, it requires time. In his triune encounter, God thus *has time*. In his triune encounter, he has beginning and middle and end. The difference between his time and ours is that he rules his no-mores and not-yets, while we are possessed by them. His time therefore *embraces* our time, and just so creates it.[39]

In this definition, history is communion. And the triune God is not solitary; he not only has communion in himself, he *is* that communion. To say that God is love and freedom is to say that the Father and the Son *practice* the love and freedom that the Spirit is.[40]

All God's works are done in the course of the triune history; thus creation too is, derivatively, history. As the union of the one history with the other, as the event in the triune history which posits created history, the eternal decision is pre-eminent history and just so pre-eminent reality, and therefore can be the true pre-occurrence of Jesus the Christ. In God's eternal will God and man meet; they meet as God in Jesus Christ and man in Jesus Christ;[41] and this 'eternal history' is the 'principle and meaning of all else that happens'.[42] If we want to understand the basis in God of any reality other than himself, 'We must look to where the eternal God not only foresees and predestines this person (Jesus the Christ), but as the presupposition of this person's revelation in time *is* this person'.[43]

It is time, though these paragraphs present but a fragment of their matter in Barth's text, to draw out their implication for my purpose. In Barth's interpretation of reality, the life-history of one human person has taken the place held in the West's traditional metaphysics by – to use perhaps familiar language – the Ground of Being. The *Church Dogmatics* casts a metaphysical vision of temporal reality bracketed not by Timelessness but by one of the temporal entities it contains, the Crucified and Risen; it casts a vision of Being that achieves its capital letter not by immunity to time but by, in and through time conquering time's tyranny.

It is a fixed axiom of our inherited metaphysics, deriving from their furthest origin as the theology of Olympian religion, that the Ground can be reached only by abstraction from time and its particularities, that even God can function as Being only if sublimated as 'the Divine', and that assuredly no temporal entity can have the role. But why, after all, should we obey this rule, if it is not Olympian deity we wish to worship? Barth simply proceeded to construct an encompassing, flexible and drastically coherent inter-pretation of reality by defying it. The *Church Dogmatics* is the chief instance in modern theology of a reflection that interprets all reality by the rule that Israel's Christ is precisely not a paradigm or image or even 'revelation' of encompassing truth, but *is* the encompassing truth.

THE TRINITY

It is sometimes supposed that the *Church Dogmatics'* christocentrism may be characterized as 'christomonism', and should be countered by a more 'trinitarian' theology. It is not usually made clear what 'christomonism' is or how then to tell whether Barth commits it. This is unsurprising; for christocentrism and trinitarianism cannot coherently be used to balance each other, since they are the same thing.

By pursuing Barth's christocentric understanding of God's will, we thus have already found ourselves deep in Barth's drastically trinitarian doctrine of God. The doctrine of the Trinity, in the classic tradition as in Karl Barth, is the attempt to speak of God under rigorous obedience to a rule: God is in himself precisely what he is in the history between the man Jesus Christ and the One he called 'Father' and us in their Spirit. It is, indeed, from Barth that twentieth-century theology has learned that the doctrine of Trinity has explanatory and interpretative *use* for the whole of theology; it is by him that the current vigorous revival of trinitarian reflection was enabled.

Even the doctrine's *location* in the *Church Dogmatics* is arresting: it appears at the beginning, as part of the 'Prolegomena', part of the description of the theological enterprise and its rules. For the first matter we must settle, before we can even know how theology as a discipline works, is which God we intend to speak about.[44] And the 'question which the doctrine of the Trinity is to answer' is '*Who* is God?'[45] According to Barth, 'the doctrine of the Trinity is . . . an explanatory confirmation'[46] of God's proper name 'Jahweh'.

By *beginning* with this doctrine, Barth reverses the order not merely of nineteenth-century theology but of the Western theological tradition generally. Traditional theology has begun with what we could say about God in at least methodological abstraction from his actuality in the saving history between Jesus and his 'Father' in their Spirit; only in the second place has it then moved to describe that actuality. Thus it has mitigated the Trinity-doctrine's ability to fulfill its function of stipulating the *identity* of the God of whom the gospel's theology is to speak; the way has been opened to the unnoticed intrusion of alien identifications. Barth unabashedly gives the Trinity-doctrine the place appropriate to its theological function; then, to the contrary of traditional procedure, he will evoke God's 'being' and 'attributes' by subsequent analysis of the sort of reality he must have to be triune.[47] Only so can we be sure to state the being and attributes of the particular God of the gospel.

The fundamental identification of God is, according to Barth, that he is the one '*who has revealed* himself in Jesus Christ'. Thus the doctrine of Trinity is 'analysis of the concept of revelation'.[48] Barth does not mean that we come to the doctrine of Trinity by analysis of a general concept of 'revelation'; the doctrine results from analysis of the way in which Scripture describes the particular historical event Jesus Christ, as in fact revelation of God.[49]

The 'root' of the Trinity-doctrine is the way in which the scriptural witness of revelation poses three questions – with this we come to one of the *Church Dogmatics'* most notorious moves. Scripture, according to Barth, asks us: *Who* reveals himself? It poses this question in that it will not let revelation be understood otherwise than from its agent; it is not our religious concern to know God that is to determine the reflection. And Scripture thus also elicits the answers: *God* reveals himself. But revelation demands to be ultimate also as the sheer fact of the event, and so asks: *What* does God do to reveal himself? And again the answer can only be: he exists among us as *God*, and so is unveiled to us. And finally, to the mandated question, What *results* among us from this event, the scriptural witness will allow only the answer: *God* with and in us is the result. Barth provides an – again notorious – summary: 'God reveals himself. He reveals himself *through himself*. He reveals *himself*.'[50] 'This God is not only himself, but is also his act of self-revelation. . . . He is not only himself, but what he thus creates among us. . . . It is God himself, in intact oneness the very same God, who by biblical understanding of revelation is the God who reveals *and* the event of revelation *and* its work among us.'[51]

Our answers to each of these questions must in this fashion repeat our answer to the others because otherwise our identification of God will be merely the reflection of our religious quest. If the event of revelation and the effect of revelation are not each simply God himself, then our knowledge of God's identity must be the result of our concluding *back* to God from revealed data at hand; then it is a religious projection even if the source of its enabling data is the Bible or the historical Jesus or experience of the risen Christ. If, then, the gospel *so* reveals God as to thwart our religious quest, this circumstance alone teaches us how to answer the questions posed to us by the fact of revelation.

Or we may understand the matter so. Were the answer to the second and third questions in any way mitigated from the answer to the first question, we would arrive at the otherwise universal position of religion: that God in revelation is depotentiated over against God straight, that God in revelation is God at a level *between* God and us. It is exactly this middle realm which the biblical revelation evacuates, and whose evacuation Barth evoked in *The Epistle to the Romans*.

Yet neither can we reduce the three questions to one *question*.[52] And the reason is exactly the same: that then the structure of God's revelatory act would not be taken seriously as the shape of God's own reality, and we would be back with the religious quest for the 'real' God behind revelation.[53]

As Barth moves to develop the three questions and their one answer, which he calls the 'root' of the doctrine of Trinity, into a developed doctrine, it is not so much the resultant formal doctrine of Trinity that is interesting, since this turns out to be a fairly standard

Augustinian doctrine, as it is the patterns and argumentative modes of the development itself. Barth's move is always the same: from the formal structure, the plot, of the historical revelation to the content of revelation, that is, God. Or rather, his move is refusal here to separate form and content at all. What God reveals about himself is that he is Lord. But that he is Lord means precisely that he can reveal himself in the specific way Scripture describes. *What* is revealed is no more and no less than that revelation *does* occur and therefore *can* occur.[54]

Barth initially develops the second of the trinitarian questions – since, of course, it is the one which compels us to think of God in trinitarian fashion. 'Revelation,' he lays down, 'means in the Bible the self-unveiling to us of the God who essentially cannot be unveiled to us.' God takes a specific place in our historical reality; he makes himself the *object* of our intention and language; he makes himself addressable by us. Since this unveiling is of the one who cannot be unveiled, it is 'God's distinguishing himself from himself', a new departure for God, a new 'mode of being' for him.[55] And then the trinitarian move follows: since God in fact thus reveals himself, it must – unless the revelation is a mere clue offered to our religious quest – be 'appropriate' for *this* God thus 'to distinguish himself from himself, to be God hiddenly in himself and at the same time to be God in another way . . ., to be God *again*, a second time'.[56]

And now we know what it means that God is *Lord*. It is 'God's very freedom that he can distinguish himself from himself and still remain the same . . .'[57] What God reveals about himself is that he is free to be *our* God, that he is not bound to be veiled essentially.

But then, revelation means in Scripture also the self-unveiling to us of the One who essentially *cannot* be unveiled to us. That God is ineffable is not a general presupposition of revelation, it is precisely this that is revealed. And thus also as he lives in our history, God remains free to reveal or not reveal himself; that he does reveal himself remains his free act.[58] 'Therefore even in that God takes on form, no middle-thing results, no third between God and us . . .'[59] The polemic is familiar, and Barth makes the target specific with fervor worthy of *The Epistle to the Romans*: 'the "beautiful Lord Jesus" of mysticism, "The Saviour" of pietism, Jesus the teacher and humanitarian of the Enlightenment, Jesus the essence of elevated humanity in Schleiermacher, Jesus as the embodiment of the Idea of religion in Hegel'.[60] What the true revelation teaches is precisely that revelation results in no figures in which the line between God and creature is blurred. Just so, labor to understand the revelation leads to the doctrine of Trinity, to recognition of the Lordship also of the *Father*, of 'God as the free origin and free power of his being God also in the Son'.[61]

And third: 'Revelation means in the bible the self-unveiling to *man* of the God who essentially cannot be unveiled to man.'[62] That is to say, revelation occupies a stretch of our history; and that in turn is to say, revelation is contingent, it happened and might not have happened. Precisely because the relevation happens to particular persons in particular situations it is not our creation, it is beyond our control as no general principle or universal fact can be; its occurrence can only be registered.[63] This too is God's lordship in his revelation. And the move is again the same: 'That God *can* do this . . . , that he can not only assume form, and not only remain free in this form, but in this form and freedom become the God of this one and that one – this is the third meaning of his lordship in his revelation.'[64]

Thus the principle is maintained with rigor: what is revealed is that revelation can occur, that God is such a God as to reveal himself. Alternatively: what is revealed is God's Lordship, and that God is Lord means that he is free to reveal himself. It may well seem that in this circularity nothing is revealed. But in fact we have before us Barth's form of the classic doctrine that God's 'essence' is unknowable also in revelation, that as the recipients of revelation we do not know *what* God is but can only unpack the knowledge *that* he is. And no more than the classic doctrine does Barth's doctrine empty revelation. For if God's Lordship means that he can be and is *our* God, that, for example, he allows us to pray to him, then the biblical promise of God-with-us is fulfilled.

What is revealed is that revelation can happen. But the revelation whose possibility is thus grasped as the reality of God himself is not any revelation, it is *that* event of which the Scripture tells as revelation – it is precisely in order to insure that this is not burked that Barth puts the doctrine of Trinity at the beginning. The event of revelation has a plot: it is Jesus' birth, work, crucifixion and resurrection. That what God reveals about himself is that he can reveal himself as he *has* revealed himself, means concretely that God is a life with this plot and no other. Barth's doctrine of Trinity *identifies* God as the one whose being is the occurrence among us, and so for us, of Jesus' death and resurrection. It is with this material content that the doctrine then functions as a hermeneutic key throughout all the developments and new starts and windings of the *Church Dogmatics*.

LESSONS

It is time to stop and pose a final question: what then should English-speaking theology, now twenty years after Barth's death, finally learn from him? I suggest it is not so much that we need to adopt his theological results – though we could usually do much worse – as that we need to be brought through the overturnings and reversals he experienced and made.

The normal theology of England and North America has never gone through the shock which elsewhere initiates specifically twentieth-century theology. There is regularly a decidedly antiquarian air about our reflections; 'new' and 'radical' theologies among us usually turn out to repristinate some nineteenth-century German expedient. We will not be able indefinitely so to continue. As confidence in bourgeois culture evaporates also among us, our continuing theological neo-Protestantism becomes more and more apparently a play of illusions. It does not matter *how* our theology is belatedly initiated into the twentieth century, but there could be none better to do it than Barth.

A decisive determinant of specifically twentieth-century theology is the critique of religion. As both Scripture and the Reformation should anyway remind us, it is not at all clear by Christian lights that religion is a good thing. Christianity is surely a religion, but perhaps one of its specificities among the religions is that it must be suspicious of just this characteristic of itself. Again, it need not be Barth who initiates us into the critique of religion, but there have been no more decisive practitioners.

As Barth reversed the pattern of neo-Protestantism, inquiring not into Jesus' place in our story but into our place in his, he created the first Western christological metaphysics on an intellectual and spiritual par with the magnificent Eastern creations of Gregory Nazianzus or the Confessor Maximus. The *Church Dogmatics* is in fact a huge doctrine of being, which offends against the previous tradition of Western thought by putting an individual, the risen Jesus Christ, at the Ground of reality. One need not approve this system in its entirety to find it exemplary. It is doubtful that English-speaking theology can much longer survive its supine acceptance of whatever version of Enlightenment mechanism fashion happens from one time to the next to propose.

Finally, in Barth himself the theological incorporation of all these dynamics is a decisively trinitarian theology, after centuries in which trinitarianism was in Western reflection a problem rather than a resource. It can fairly be said that the chief ecumenical enterprise of current theology is rediscovery and development of the doctrine of Trinity. It can also fairly be said that Barth initiated the enterprise. The doctrine of Trinity is Christianity's identification of its God; as Christendom disintegrates we cannot continue to assume that all know which God the gospel means – surely we cannot make that assumption with such sheltered confidence as that with which dominant North American and English theology makes it. Yet again, it need not be Barth from whom we learn, but why not from the pioneer?

NOTES

1 Karl Barth, 'The Strange New World within the Bible' (1916), *The Word of God and the Word of Man*, pp. 28–50.
2 Extensively available in the volume *The Word of God and the Word of Man*.
3 Karl Barth, *Der Römerbrief* (*The Epistle to the Romans*). All citations in this chapter are translated from *Der Römerbrief* (Munich, 1922).
4 Karl Barth, *Die Protestantische Theologie in 19. Jahrhundert* (*Protestant Theology in the Nineteenth Century*) (Zürich, 1952), p. 19.
5 Karl Barth, *Die Kirchliche Dogmatik* (*Church Dogmatics*), IV/1: 395. All citations in this chapter are translated from *Die Kirchliche Dogmatik* (Zürich, 1932–67).
6 Barth, *Protestantische Theologie*, pp. 49ff.
7 Friedrich Schleiermacher, *Über die Religion: Reden an die Gebildeten unter ihren Verächtern* (Berlin, 1799), translated as *On Religion: Speeches to its Cultured Despisers* (New York, 1958).
8 Perhaps I may, instead of endlessly citing, refer to my study: Robert W. Jenson, *God after God: The God of the Past and the God of the Future, Seen in the Work of Karl Barth*, pp. 2–48.
9 Barth, *Der Römerbrief*, p. 7.
10 Ibid., p. 13.
11 Ibid., p. 16.
12 Ibid., p. 96.
13 Ibid., p. xiii.
14 Karl Barth, *Fides quaerens intellectum: Anselms Beweis der Existenz Gottes im Zusammenhang seines theologischen Programs* (*Fides Quaerens intellectum. Anselm's Proof of the Existence of God in the Context of his Theological Scheme*).
15 To this single assertion, the entire 1,000 pages of the *Kirchliche Dogmatik*'s volume I/2 are devoted.
16 For comprehensive presentation of this central point, Robert W. Jenson, *Alpha and Omega: A Study in the Theology of Karl Barth* (New York, 1963), pp. 65–140.
17 Ibid., passim.

18 Barth, *Kirchliche Dogmatik*, I/1: 1.
19 Ibid., II/1: 288.
20 Ibid., III/1: 103, 258.
21 Ibid., III/1: 107.
22 Ibid., III/1: 418–76.
23 Ibid., III/3: 91.
24 Ibid., II/2: 175–85.
25 Ibid., II/2: 171.
26 Ibid., III/2: 173.
27 Ibid., II/1: 579.
28 Ibid., II/2: 20.
29 Ibid., II/2: 109.
30 Ibid., II/2: 110–11.
31 Ibid., II/2: 114–18.
32 Ibid., IV/1: 66, 145.
33 Ibid., II/1: 294–6.
34 Ibid., II/1: 296–300.
35 Ibid., II/1: 305.
36 Ibid., II/2: 152.
37 Ibid., II/1: 661–2.
38 Ibid., III/2: 189.
39 Ibid., II/1: 685–722.
40 Ibid., II/2: 192.
41 Ibid., II/2: 192–7.
42 Ibid., II/2: 201–2.
43 Ibid., II/2: 116.
44 Ibid., I/1: 311.
45 Ibid., I/1: 316–17. Emphasis added.
46 Ibid., I/1: 368.
47 Ibid., II/1: 288–361.
48 Ibid., I/1: 32.
49 ibid., I/1: 329.
50 Ibid., I/1: 311–15.
51 Ibid., I/1: 314–15.
52 Ibid., I/1: 315.
53 Ibid., I/1: 402–3.
54 Ibid., I/1: 323–4.
55 Ibid., I/1: 332–3.
56 Ibid., I/1: 334.
57 Ibid., I/1: 337–8.
58 Ibid., I/1: 338–9.
59 Ibid., I/1: 339.
60 Ibid., I/1: 341.
61 Ibid., I/1: 342.
62 Ibid., I/1: 342.
63 Ibid., I/1: 342–50.
64 Ibid., I/1: 350.

BIBLIOGRAPHY

Primary

Barth, Karl, *The Word of God and the Word of Man* (Weston, W. Virginia, 1928).
—, *The Epistle to the Romans* (London, 1933).
—, *Church Dogmatics* (New York, Edinburgh, 1936–69).
—, *Community, State and Church* (Garden City, NY, 1960).
—, *Fides quaerens intellectum: Anselm's Proof of the Existence of God in the Context of His Theological Scheme* (Richmond, Virginia, 1960).
—, *The Humanity of God*, (Richmond, Virginia, 1960).

Secondary

von Balthasar, Hans Urs, *The Theology of Karl Barth* (New York, 1971).
Berkouwer, G. C., *The Triumph of Grace in the Theology of Karl Barth* (Grand Rapids, Mich., 1956).
Bloesch, Donald G., *Jesus is Victor! Karl Barth's Doctrine of Salvation* (Nashville, Tenn., 1976).
Bouillard, Henri, *Karl Barth* (Paris, 1957).
Busch, Eberhard, *Karl Barth: His Life from Letters and Autobiographical Texts* (Philadelphia, 1976).
Ford, David F., *Barth and God's Story. Biblical Narrative and the Theological Method of Karl Barth in the Church Dogmatics* (Frankfurt-am-Main, Berne, New York, 1981).
Gunton, Colin E. *Becoming and Being: The Doctrine of God in Charles Hartshorne and Karl Barth* (Oxford, 1978).
Jenson, Robert, *God after God: The God of the Past and the God of the Future, Seen in the Work of Karl Barth* (Indianapolis, 1969).
Jüngel, Eberhard, *The Doctrine of the Trinity: God's Being is in Becoming* (Grand Rapids, Mich., 1976).
Jüngel, Eberhard, *Karl Barth: a Theological Legacy* (Philadelphia, 1986).
McLean, Stuart D., *Humanity in the Thought of Karl Barth* (Edinburgh, 1981).
Sykes, S. W. (ed.), *Karl Barth: Studies of His Theological Method* (Oxford, 1979).
Torrance, Thomas F., *Karl Barth: an introduction to His Early Theology, 1910–1931* (London, 1962).

2

Dietrich Bonhoeffer

John D. Godsey

INTRODUCTION: LIFE

Dietrich Bonhoeffer, a German Lutheran theologian, was born in Breslau on February 4, 1906. He and his twin sister were the sixth and seventh of eight children of Karl Ludwig and Paula (née von Hase) Bonhoeffer. In 1912 the family moved to Berlin, where Dietrich's father, a prominent neurologist, occupied the chair of psychiatry at the university. Dietrich was reared in this capital city, with all its cultural advantages, and in the bosom of an academic family that embodied the finest liberal traditions of pre-World War I Germany.

From his scientifically oriented father Bonhoeffer learned the importance of empirical reality and the requirement of intellectual honesty in dealing with it. His pious mother imbued him with a sensitivity to others and awakened his interest in God. Life in a large family, with three older brothers and four sisters, afforded ample opportunity for personal growth in a supportive milieu that encouraged individuality within the constraints of interdependency. Over the years he became a sturdy athlete who enjoyed competition, a scholar with an inquiring mind, and a gifted pianist who accompanied the others at family musical occasions. He liked the outdoors, especially summer vacations at their cottage in the Harz Mountains.

What had been a rather idyllic upbringing was suddenly shattered by the First World War and the tragic death in 1918 of Dietrich's brother Walter, the second eldest child, as a result of wounds received during military service. The loss was devastating for the parents, especially the mother, and the family trauma may indeed have played a role in Bonhoeffer's subsequent decision to study theology – a decision that came as a surprise to a family in which the other males had entered the professions of medicine, physics, or law, and in which the Christian festivals were celebrated more at home than in the church.

The theological education of this talented young German began in the fall of 1923 at the university of Tübingen, where he heard, among others, Adolf Schlatter, Karl Heim, Wilhelm Heitmüller, Paul Volz, and Karl Müller. After a year he returned to Berlin, where he studied with Adolf von Harnack, Karl Holl, Hans Lietzmann, Ernst Sellin, and Reinhold Seeberg. Under the latter he wrote his dissertation in systematic theology on *Sanctorum Communio: Eine dogmatische Untersuchung zur Soziologie der Kirche* (*Sanctorum Communio: A Dogmatic Inquiry into the Sociology of the Church*), on the basis of which he was awarded his Licentiate of Theology in 1927 at the age of twenty-one.

Through the teachings of his professors Bonhoeffer became well acquainted with liberal theology and its critical historical method, but what excited and challenged him much more during his university experience was his introduction to Luther in Holl's seminars and his reading of the dialectical theology of Karl Barth and his friends. Bonhoeffer never studied under Barth, but Barth's influence is evident in his first dissertation as well as in *Akt und Sein: Transzendentalphilosophie und Ontologie in der systematischen Theologie* (*Act and Being: Transcendental Philosophy and Ontology in Systematic Theology*), the habilitation dissertation which qualified him to lecture in theology at the University of Berlin beginning in 1930. Between these academic writings Bonhoeffer spent a year as an assistant minister in a German-speaking congregation in Barcelona, Spain where he lectured and preached often.

Travel outside Germany broadened Bonhoeffer's theological perspective. A trip to Rome in 1924 with his brother Klaus had awakened his interest in Catholicism and in the church in general, and the experience in Spain deepened that interest. But even more important for his budding ecumenicity was his fellowship to study at New York's Union Theological Seminary during 1930–1. Here he studied with Reinhold Niebuhr and John Baillie, explored the black church in Harlem with fellow student Frank Fisher, and traveled around America with friends Erwin Sutz, Jean Lassère, and Paul Lehmann.

Back in Germany, Bonhoeffer visited Barth at Bonn in the summer of 1931, and this sparked a lasting friendship. That fall Bonhoeffer began his lecturing in the theological faculty at Berlin, became chaplain at a technical university, and served as a youth secretary of the World Alliance for Promoting International Friendship through the Churches. Three of Bonhoeffer's lectures series from 1932–3 have been published: *Schöpfung und Fall: Theologische Auslegung von Genesis 1 bis 3* (*Creation and Fall: A Theological Interpretation of Genesis 1–3*) appeared in 1933, whereas his lectures on 'The Nature of the Church' and on christology, both of which were reconstructed from student notes, have been published posthumously.[1] Bonhoeffer's ecumenical activities led to his dramatic call for peace at the Fanö Conference in 1934 and subsequent co-option as a member of the Universal Christian Council for Life and Work, headed by George Bell, Bishop of Chichester.

Two tumultuous events mark the remainder of Bonhoeffer's life: Adolf Hitler's assumption of political power on January 30, 1933 and the onset of the Second World War on September 3, 1939. The first thrust him into the Church Struggle on the side of the 'Confessing Church' that opposed the Nazi attempt to control the Protestant churches, whereas the latter caused him to enter the underground resistance movement dedicated to the overthrow of Hitler, even if it meant tyrannicide.

From the very beginning the entire Bonhoeffer family was opposed to National Socialism because of its racist ideology and totalitarian aims. Only two days after Hitler became Chancellor of the Third Reich, Bonhoeffer delivered a radio address warning against the danger of an idolatrous 'Führer-principle', and in the spring of 1933 he published an article clarifying the church's responsibility regarding the 'Jewish question'. As a staunch member of the Confessing Church he opposed the Nazi-supported 'German Christians' at every turn. When in the late summer of 1933 his own Church of the Old Prussian Union adopted the 'Aryan Paragraph' that forbade anyone with 'Jewish blood' to hold office in the church, Bonhoeffer requested and received an assignment as pastor of two German-speaking congregations in London. There he was able to gain support for the Confessing Church among ecumenical church leaders by interpreting the true state of church affairs in Germany.

While in England Bonhoeffer made plans to visit Gandhi in India to study his nonviolent way of resistance, but he abandoned these when in the spring of 1935 he was called by Confessing Church leaders to return to Germany to establish and lead a special seminary for training its vicars. In April he met his first class at Zingst on the Baltic Sea but soon moved them to the village of Finkenwalde near Stettin. Here began an unusual experiment in theological education, one that combined the practice of spiritual discipline with rigorous study and practical application. At Finkenwalde he wrote and published *Nachfolge* (*Discipleship*),[2] and after the seminary was closed by the Gestapo in 1937 he penned

Gemeinsames Leben (*Life Together*). Except for a small booklet on the Psalms, these were the last publications allowed by the Nazis during his lifetime.

Needing a break from the struggle, Bonhoeffer, with the help of Reinhold Niebuhr, left Germany in June 1939 to lecture at Union Theological Seminary in New York. Soon after his arrival, however, he felt he had made a mistake in leaving when war seemed imminent. In early July he sailed back to England and then on to a deteriorating situation in Germany. Hitler's army invaded Poland on September 1, and England declared war two days later.

For a while Bonhoeffer resumed a make-shift arrangement for teaching ordinands of the Confessing Church in Pomerania, but in 1940 even this was stopped by the Gestapo. His license to teach at the university had been rescinded in 1936, and now he was forbidden to publish or to speak in public. Moreover, conscription into the army seemed likely. At this time he entered the resistance movement through the auspices of his brother-in-law Hans von Dohnanyi, chief counsel in the *Abwehr* (Military Intelligence Office), the heart of military resistance. He was made a civilian employee of the *Abwehr* and assigned to the Munich office.

During 1941–2 Bonhoeffer made three trips to Switzerland and one to Norway and Sweden on behalf of the *Abwehr*, using his ecumenical church connections to relay messages to the Allies. During the same period he worked sporadically on a book on *Ethics*, the fragments of which were published posthumously under this title. In January 1943 he became engaged to Maria von Wedemeyer, the daughter of a prominent family he had known in Pomerania, but for family reasons the engagement was not announced until after his arrest and imprisonment.

The Gestapo imprisoned Bonhoeffer and Dohnanyi on April 5, 1943 on the suspicion that they had been involved in a scheme to help some Jewish employees of the *Abwehr* escape to Switzerland. During the next eighteen months spent in Berlin's Tegel Military Prison he underwent repeated interrogations but also managed to read and to write extensively. His censored letters to his family and uncensored letters and poems to his friend Eberhard Bethge were published in 1951 under the title *Widerstand und Ergebung* (*Resistance and Submission*)[3]. Fragments of a drama and a novel written during the same period were published in 1978 as *Fragmente aus Tegel: Drama und Roman* (*Fragments from Tegel: Drama and Novel*).[4]

An attempt on Hitler's life by the resistance movement on July 20, 1944 failed. This immediately exposed many resisters, and by September the Gestapo had discovered documents that implicated the conspirators within the *Abwehr*. On October 8 Bonhoeffer was moved to the Gestapo prison on Prinz-Albrecht Strasse and then on February 7, 1945 to Buchenwald concentration camp. In April, together with a group of international prisoners, Bonhoeffer was removed to Regensburg and then to the village of Schönberg in Bavaria. Following orders from Hitler to annihilate all resisters, the Gestapo tracked down Bonhoeffer and took him to Flossenbürg concentration camp, where, after a mock trial, he was hanged on April 9, 1945, shortly before the American army liberated the area. Dohnanyi was executed the same day in Sachsenhausen, Dietrich's brother Klaus and brother-in-law Rüdiger Schleicher on April 23 in Berlin.

SURVEY AND CONTENT OF MAIN WORKS

Bonhoeffer's two books, *Sanctorum Communio* (*The Communion of Saints*) and *Act and Being* were both academic dissertations written for the theological faculty of Humboldt University in Berlin, and they exhibit the compact writing style and extensive footnoting that mark such endeavors. Moreover, the subject-matter of each is difficult, requiring for comprehension a familiarity with the theology, philosophy, and sociology of the time. Nevertheless, these dissertations, completed when he twenty-one and twenty-four, respectively, are foundational for everything that follows in Bonhoeffer's developing thought and are probably his most brilliant and intellectually sophisticated achievements.

Sanctorum Communio discloses from the outset Bonhoeffer's commitment to a theology of the concrete as opposed to the abstract. Thus he began with the concept of the church as the unique community in which divine revelation both occurs and takes form. The sub-title, 'a dogmatic inquiry into the sociology of the church', declared his intention; the work is basically theological but at the same time uses social philosophy and sociology to illuminate the peculiar social structure of the Christian church. Thus Bonhoeffer brings together in dialogue and mutual correction the social concern of Berlin's liberal theological tradition from Schleiermacher and Hegel to Troeltsch, and the revelational concern of the so-called dialectical theology of Barth, Bultmann, and Gogarten. Already by 1927, then, Bonhoeffer had forged his own brand of theology that started with divine revelation but insisted on showing the social intention of every basic Christian concept.

Although he could affirm liberalism's interest in social relations,

Bonhoeffer believed its underlying idealistic philosophy prevented its development of an adequate concept of 'person' and thus of God. In his judgment, idealism's subject–object epistemological framework meant that the knowing 'I' remains enclosed in itself and never really encounters the 'alien I' of another subject. Idealism is finally a philosophy of the immanence of the mind which fosters individualism as well as abstract, timeless thinking. The 'person' of idealism is the reasoning person or the personified mind, but not a particular living person.

In contrast, Bonhoeffer set forth a Christian view of person based on the interrelationship of 'I' and 'Thou'. 'Person' arises when an 'I' in a particular moment is confronted by the moral claim of a concrete 'Thou' and is moved to respond with a responsible decision. Decisive for Bonhoeffer was his conviction that the transcendence of the Thou is not epistemological but moral. The Thou of the other presents a 'barrier' that cannot be overcome or absorbed by the process of thought, as in idealism. But why should the Thou of the other make a demand which is absolute for the I? Bonhoeffer answered this by reference to God. Every human Thou is an image of the divine Thou, and it is God who comes and makes the other a Thou for me. Since behind every human Thou is the divine Thou, whose will is love, the I–Thou relation is the basic social category, and the person, God, and social being are intrinsically related. For Bonhoeffer, this meant that the problem one faces in knowing another human is parallel to that of knowing God: the other must reveal itself. In this way, through an act of self-revealing love, the one who confronts us as a Thou becomes known as an I. This understanding of basic social relations leads Bonhoeffer to the concept of the church.

Barth's polemic against liberal theology's focus on 'religion' rather than 'revelation' is evident in Bonhoeffer's view of the church as a God-willed reality of revelation which can only be believed or denied. The church is grounded and consummated once-for-all by and in Jesus Christ, the Word of God's active love that brings reconciliation to a broken and sinful humanity. It is a new community of love characterized by a structural 'togetherness' of its members and by the life-principle of vicarious action for one another.

Bonhoeffer's favorite definition of the church in *Sanctorum Communio* is 'Christ existing as community', by which he meant that the church is where Christ, through the work of the Holy Spirit, takes form among humans. The church that is 'realized' once-for-all in Christ is 'actualized' in time by the work of the Spirit, who calls individuals to faith, brings them into the new community under the rulership of God's will-to-love, and unites them as the Body of Christ.

This theological view of the church raises the question of the empirical church, and here Bonhoeffer warned that the empirical church is not identical with the religious community. Because it has his Word, the empirical church is indeed the Body of Christ, the presence of Christ on earth. But the church can also be analyzed sociologically as a religious fellowship, in which human imperfection and sin are evident. The church, according to Bonhoeffer, is not to be confused with this religious fellowship nor with the eschatological Kingdom of God. Because the Holy Spirit is constantly working to actualize the church in the face of the imperfection and sin of the religious community, the history of the church is hidden in the midst of world history.

In analyzing the church sociologically Bonhoeffer employed Toennies's distinction between a community (*Gemeinschaft*), which is a 'life-community' and an end-in-itself, and a society (*Gesellschaft*), which, as a means-to-an-end, is where people band together for a rational purpose. The church, claimed Bonhoeffer, fits neither type perfectly but manifests aspects of both. In its ministry to the world, which involves proclamation by Word and sacrament, it functions as a means-to-an-end, namely, the attainment of God's will; but, on the other hand, it is an end-in-itself in that the Spirit-effected communal life of love and service is precisely the fulfillment of the will of God.

Of signal importance is Bonhoeffer's view that divine revelation is related not only to the functions of preaching and administering the sacraments of baptism and the Lord's Supper, but also to the being of the church itself. The church *is* a form of revelation, *is* 'Christ existing as community'. To be sure, it is this only as it lives a life of faithful obedience to the rule of God. And, Bonhoeffer emphasized, God rules by serving.

In *Act and Being* Bonhoeffer applied his concept of the church to solve the difficult problem of 'act' and 'being' as they have been related to the theory of knowledge, especially the knowledge of God. Is there revelation of God only in the immediate act of faith, or is there discernible some 'being' of the revelation that perdures? In the first instance, revelation never becomes 'objective', because as soon as one reflects on faith, God disappears into the non-objective sphere. In the second, revelation becomes an object which humans can control – whether it takes the form of orthodox doctrine, infallible Bible, religious experience or an institution of salvation.

In moving toward his own interpretation, Bonhoeffer began by analyzing the problem of act and being as it appears in recent philosophy and theology. In philosophy it is the problem between Kant's transcendentalism, where thinking is always 'in relation to' transcendence but is never able to reach the 'thing in itself', and post-Kantian idealism, which ignored Kant's limitation and drew reality into the thinking self. In theology, Bonhoeffer examined the actualism of revelation as it was manifested in the dialectical theology of Barth and Bultmann, and the objectivism still prevalent in the many forms of orthodox, experiential, or institutional Christianity.

At stake in the act–being controversy is the contingency and the continuity of revelation, that is, God's freedom on the one hand and God's presence on the other. In a significant departure from Barth, who wished to protect God's freedom *from* humankind, Bonhoeffer argued that God's freedom must be understood less as a 'freedom from' than a 'freedom for' us; God's very being is given and 'haveable' in the Word which is Christ. Bonhoeffer's own solution to the act–being problem is found in the concept of the church, which draws together the concerns of both traditions. The contingency of revelation is preserved by the present proclamation of Christ's death and resurrection, which constitutes the church as a community of persons whose being is in Christ. But the continuity of revelation is also assured, because in this community of persons someone is always hearing the Word and responding in faith. Thus the community is entered by the *act* of revelation/faith, but precisely the believer recognizes that the *being* of the community is prior to his or her act of faith.

In light of the above, Bonhoeffer differentiated three forms of knowledge in the church. 'Faith knowledge' is an existential knowing that occurs when, through the hearing of the Word, one is grasped by the person of Christ; this is an *actus directus* inaccessible to reflection. 'Preaching knowledge' is what the preacher knows about what he or she preaches: Jesus Christ the Crucified and Risen One. The preacher is the bearer of the preaching office of the congregation and has full authority to proclaim the gospel to those who listen. Whether the preacher speaks 'rightly' depends finally on 'theological knowledge', the churchly knowledge that is preserved in the memory of the Christian community – in its Bible, its prayers, its liturgy. What differentiates theology from other types of thinking, according to Bonhoeffer, is its commitment to the church and its willingness to submit itself to the judgment of the Christian community.

Bonhoeffer ends *Act and Being* with a discussion of what it means to be 'in Christ'. 'Being in Christ' means bearing the new humanity by believing, praying and proclaiming, but it also means knowing oneself borne by the community, by Christ. One loves, because one is already loved. Being in Christ also means knowing the truth about one's former existence: the sin and guilt and loneliness of 'being in Adam'. For Bonhoeffer, 'conscience' represents the sinner's attempt to overcome inner anxiety by self-justification, and only Christ can unmask this ploy. Conscience is a determination of one's life by the past in Adam; being in Christ through faith is having one's present determined by the future, which, according to Bonhoeffer, is the eschatological possibility of the child of God.

After writing these two dissertations, Bonhoeffer began his university teaching. Two of his lecture series are especially important. In *Creation and Fall* he presented a theological interpretation of Genesis 1–3. Creation, he stated, comes to be through God's Word; God speaks, and it is so. Thus creation, as an utterly free divine act, is 'out of nothing', and what is created is pronounced by God to be good and remains dependent upon God's ongoing preservation.

Bonhoeffer found the uniqueness of humans in their being created in the image of God, which he interpreted to mean that they were similar to God in being created free. But freedom, insisted Bonhoeffer, is not something one has for oneself but only for others; it occurs between two. Thus God created humans male and female, and their creatureliness consists in their being dependent upon God and one another. The analogy between God and humans, then, is one of relationship (*analogia relationis*) and not of being (*analogia entis*). That is, Bonhoeffer proposed that humans are like God, not because of anything they possess (reason, soul, etc.), but because their relationship to each other reflects God's relationship to them. A second meaning of creation in the image of God, according to Bonhoeffer, is humankind's freedom *from* the world in that they are to rule over it as God's representatives.

When Bonhoeffer reached Genesis 3, he interpreted the 'fall' of Adam and Eve to be not simply a fanciful myth but a poetic expression of our own story. The temptation of the serpent, one of God's good but clever creatures, consists in questioning the truth of God's Word. God had prohibited eating of the fruit of the tree of the knowledge of good and evil on penalty of death. The serpent suggested that if they ate, they would be 'like God'. 'And they ate!' The fall, stressed Bonhoeffer, is totally inexplicable, because it occurs out of freedom. We can only point to the fact that it happened and continues to happen. In 'Adam' the whole human race falls.

Adam and Eve transgress their limit, and in doing so lose access to the tree of life. The consequences, stated Bonhoeffer, are disastrous: alienation, shame, loneliness, bondage, death – life under the curse. But this is not the end of the story, cautioned Bonhoeffer. God graciously clothes them and preserves them and directs them toward Christ, whose cross becomes for humankind a new tree of life.

A second set of lectures dealt with christology, the doctrine of the person of Christ. If Bonhoeffer in his dissertations focused on ecclesiology, by 1933 he had moved to a comprehensive christology. Now Jesus Christ, who is still present with us in the form of Word, Sacrament, and church, is proclaimed by Bonhoeffer to be the center not only of human existence but also of history and of nature. Just as Nazism began to assert its claim on the German churches, Bonhoeffer deepened his concentration on Jesus Christ, the one Lord of the church.

For Bonhoeffer, the basic christological question is not *how* Jesus Christ can be both God and man, but *who* Christ is. Jesus confronts us with his claim to be the Word of God in person, and we are forced to decide who he is. Faith declares, 'This man is God for me'. Bonhoeffer also emphasized that the question of christology (person) is theologically prior to that of soteriology (works), because the works of a person are always ambiguous. Who Christ is will dictate the significance of what he does. For Bonhoeffer, christology has to do with the whole, historical Jesus Christ who is present in the church as the crucified and risen One.

Bonhoeffer divided his lectures into three parts: the present Christ, the historical Christ, and the eternal Christ. Unfortunately, the semester ended before he reached the third part. The only place to begin in christology, according to Bonhoeffer, is with the living Christ who is present in the church and whose ontological structure is 'being *pro me*'. That is, Christ can only be thought of existentially as one who is not Christ in and for himself but Christ for me.

For Bonhoeffer, like Luther, the God-man Jesus Christ is hidden in 'the likeness of sinful flesh', which means that the offence of Christ is not his incarnation but his humiliation. It is not that God is hidden in man but that the whole God-man is hidden in the likeness of sinful flesh. Thus Bonhoeffer carefully distinguished between the humanity of Christ and the humiliation of Christ, because Jesus is man both as humiliated and exalted, but only the humiliation presents an offence. Today the offence continues as we meet the risen and exalted Christ only in the humiliated form of proclamation.

Against liberal theology, Bonhoeffer refused to separate Jesus from Christ. Instead, he reaffirmed that the present Christ *is* the historical Jesus of Nazareth. That Jesus really lived and died is of fundamental significance for the church, declared Bonhoeffer, but historical research can never absolutely deny or affirm his existence or the dogmatic statements about him. Faith receives its certainty only from the witness of the risen one to himself – in history, here and now.

Considering that the time of these lectures coincided with the rise of Hitler to power, it is significant that Bonhoeffer not only continued to teach that the church is 'Christ existing as community', but now also taught that Christ – and thus the church – is the hidden center of the history made by the state. The church is both center and boundary of the state, he declared, justifying and judging its fulfillment of the law and its ordering activity from the standpoint of the cross.

The Cost of Discipleship and *Life Together* were both written during the Church Struggle of the 1930s and are clearly responses to the challenge of those times. But they are more than that, for they also represent Bonhoeffer's deeply personal wrestling with what it means to be a Christian – not just an academic theologian but a committed follower of Jesus Christ. Already in the early 1930s he was drawn to the commanding Christ of the Sermon on the Mount and was troubled about the submission of his own will to Christ's dominion. Thus these writings are as much concerned with spiritual discipline within the life of the church as they are a clarion call to responsible discipleship in the face of the Nazi-supporting German Christians' anti-Semitic perversion of the gospel and the state's attempt to control the churches. For Bonhoeffer, discipleship and spirituality went hand in hand.

At the heart of *The Cost of Discipleship* stands Bonhoeffer's interpretation of Jesus' Sermon on the Mount (Matthew 5–7), the demands of which he believed must be taken seriously today. For him, they are not 'interim ethics' (Schweitzer) or, as many Lutherans taught, impossible demands of the law that drive one to the gospel. They are rather the call of Jesus to the 'extraordinariness' of the Christian life.

Bonhoeffer's constant polemic in this book was against 'cheap grace', the grace we bestow on ourselves as we calculate how cheaply we can be Christian. Over against this, he advocated 'costly grace', which he said is *costly* because it calls us to follow but is *grace* because it is Jesus Christ whom we follow. Discipleship leads us in the way of the cross, he declared, but this is the only way to attain joy and peace in living. In opposition to those who argue that all that is required of the Christian is faith, Bonhoeffer insisted that there is no true faith without obedience; only those who obey believe, and only those who believe obey. Although he agreed that, theologically speaking, salvation is by faith alone, he insisted that faith and obedience cannot be temporally separated.

What Bonhoeffer intended in *The Cost of Discipleship* was to show that the underlying meaning of the discipleship language of the gospels is carried over without loss into the churchly language of the Pauline and other New Testament epistles, and therefore into the language of the church today. For example, when the gospels speak of Christ's calling disciples and their following him, Paul speaks of being baptized and participating in the Body of Christ. Bonhoeffer emphasized that the church is *in* the world but not *of* it. He also reminds his readers that, because of the incarnation, *all* human beings receive the dignity of the image of God. Attack on the least of Christ's brothers and sisters is an attack on Christ himself – undoubtedly a reference to the Nazi attacks on the Jews.

If *The Cost of Discipleship* is a sustained wrestling with the relationship between justification and sanctification in the Christian community, *Life Together* probed the spiritual life of that same community. In accord with his experience at Finkenwalde, Bonhoeffer emphasized that Christian life is life through and in Jesus Christ – no more and no less. It centers around Word and sacrament, and it follows a rhythmic pattern of being together and being alone. Bonhoeffer insisted that both are necessary for the Christian. The communal activities of prayer, Scripture reading, and praise are balanced by solitary meditation on Scripture, prayer, and intercession – and all of this surrounding the work of the day.

After pointing out that self-justification and judging others go together, just as justification by grace and serving others go together, Bonhoeffer proposed a number of ministries to be practiced within the Christian community. the ministries of holding one's tongue, meekness, listening to others, active helpfulness, bearing the burden of others, freely speaking God's Word to another when the moment is right, and exercising authority based on loving service. Finally, Bonhoeffer proposed the reinstitution of aural confession among Protestants in preparation for the eucharist – not a confession of lay to clergy, but the confession of one Christian to another as each attempts to live under the cross.

Bonhoeffer wrote his fragmentary *Ethics* during 1940–3, the years of his conspiratorial activities. Considerable discussion has ensued over how the various fragments should be arranged,[5] but there is little doubt that the whole centers around the theme of 'Christ, the church, and the world'. Bonhoeffer is no longer just interested in how Christ is related to the church, but how Christ and the church are related to the world – an interest that is already present in his earlier theology but which is largely underdeveloped during the Church Struggle. Bonhoeffer's perspective is most clearly expressed in these words: 'The more exclusively we acknowledge and confess Christ as our Lord, the more fully the wide range of His dominion will be disclosed to us.'[6] Bonhoeffer not only wanted to emphasize the worldliness of Christian faith but to claim for Christ whatever is good and whatever is humane, regardless of where it is found.

Just as Bonhoeffer's theology had always been penetrated by ethical concerns, so his ethics are thoroughly theological. Eschewing all other approaches, Bonhoeffer claimed that Christian ethics has to do with one thing: the realization of the revelational reality of God in Christ. Since the incarnation, he claimed, the world should not be thought of without God nor God without the world. Indeed, since the world and God have been 'polemically' united in Jesus Christ, Christians should relinquish all ethical thinking that divides the world into two spheres, one sacred and the other secular.

Instead of thinking in terms of two spatially discrete spheres, Bonhoeffer urged Christians to think in dynamic, temporal terms, namely, of how the whole world is related to Christ, whether it knows it or not, and how that relatedness assumes concrete form in certain mandates of God in the world. Bonhoeffer believed that the Bible named at least four: labor, marriage, government, and church. Bonhoeffer used 'mandates' instead of 'orders of creation', arguing that in our fallen state God's original orders of creation can no longer be known. Moreover, he wished to distinguish his view from that of the 'German Christians', who proclaimed the rise of Hitler and the policies of National Socialism to be historical manifestations of God's 'orders of creation'.

It is important to note that, according to Bonhoeffer, God has imposed the mandates on all human beings and that all the mandates are equally 'divine'. Moreover, ethical decisions are to be made as the claims of the various mandates interact with one another, that is, as one simultaneously assumes responsibility as a worker, a family member, and a citizen. The mandate of the church is to proclaim to the world what God has done in Christ and to call it to responsibility in the light of this reality.

Because of its richness and complexity as well as its unfinished condition, *Ethics* defies easy summarization. In his thinking about ethics, Bonhoeffer attempted several approaches, but the unifying element in all of them was his understanding of Jesus Christ. Ethics can mean the conformation of humanity to the servant-form of Christ. Ethics can involve the preparing of the way for Christ in the realm of the penultimate – feeding the hungry, housing the homeless, freeing those in bondage, providing justice for the downtrodden – just because of the penultimate's relation to the ultimate, namely, the justification of the sinner by grace. Ethics can denote a recovery of the rights and duties of the natural life, when this is understood as the form of life that is preserved by God after the fall and directed toward the coming of Christ. Ethics can be interpreted as the command of God, when it is seen as the total and concrete claim laid upon humankind by the holy and merciful God in Christ, and when its content is understood not only as obligation but as permission – the setting free for life. In all these approaches the center is the incarnate, crucified, and risen Christ: the one in whom humanity is loved, judged, and renewed.

Above all, Bonhoeffer's ethics is an ethics of responsibility, evoked by God's Word and characterized by deputyship. Christian ethics involves a willingness freely to accept the role of deputy for others when a concrete occasion arises; it means doing whatever seems pertinent according to the facts of the situation and accepting guilt if the action turns out not to accord with the will of God disclosed in Christ. Responsibility is the Christian's vocation, urged Bonhoeffer, and this means obeying the call of Christ by responding with one's total being to the whole of reality.

Bonhoeffer's own sense of responsibility led him into the conspiracy against Hitler, which resulted in his imprisonment. His final thoughts on theology are found in his *Letters and Papers from Prison*. While in solitary confinement at Tegel Prison, he was able to read and think and take stock of Christianity in the modern world. He came to affirm that the world had undergone a process of secularization since the Middle Ages and that humans had gradually 'come of age', in the sense that they no longer look to God to solve their personal and societal problems but assume responsibility themselves. They no longer call on 'God' as a stop-gap or *Deus ex machina*. To this extent, argued Bonhoeffer, the modern world has cast off the garment of 'religion', by which he meant the individualistic concern for one's own soul or the metaphysical interpretation of a 'God' beyond the world who can be called upon and used when convenient.

As a matter of fact, argued Bonhoeffer, the 'religious' view of God deserves to be discarded because it does not accord with the Bible, which depicts God as suffering with us in the midst of everyday life and helping us by becoming weak in the world (the cross!) in order that we might become strong. In his words, 'Before God and with God we live without God'.[7] Thus Bonhoeffer called for a 'nonreligious interpretation' of the great biblical and theological concepts so that modern people could understand how to participate in the being of Jesus (and thus of God) by 'being there for others' in the joys and sorrows of their mundane life. In this way, asserted Bonhoeffer, they would learn that the transcendence of God is not epistemological but social, that God is as close to us as the nearest neighbor.

Until the church can communicate its message and mission in nonreligious, this-worldly language, concluded Bonhoeffer, it should perhaps remain silent and limit itself to two things: prayer and righteous action. In this way it would renew the ancient practice of an 'arcane discipline' and at the same time enter fully into the midst of earthly life to be there for others.

In his final theology Bonhoeffer compared the Christian life to the polyphonous music of a fugue: so long as the *cantus firmus* (love of God) is clear and firm, the counterpoint (all the other melodies of life – our earthly affections) can be developed to the full.

SOME KEY IDEAS

The attraction of Bonhoeffer for all kinds of Christians and for many non-Christians has been the coherence of his life and thought. His actions exemplified his beliefs, and his beliefs illuminate his actions. The integrity of his witness, which ended in martyrdom, gives weight to his theology. In an extraordinary way he brought together personal piety and political responsibility, faith and works, freedom and obedience, justification and sanctification, church and world, sacred and secular.

To find the key to Bonhoeffer's theology, one must look to the God-man Jesus Christ. Bonhoeffer eschewed speculative ideas of a God beyond the world and pious ideas of a God within us, centering his whole theology on the God concretely revealed in Jesus Christ, the Word made flesh. In Christ, God graciously acted to reconcile the world to God's own self; in Christ, God's being is revealed as a 'being for others', that is, as vicarious suffering love. The incarnation declares God's love for the world, the crucifixion is God's judgment on sin and evil, the resurrection reveals God's will to renew the world. For Bonhoeffer, Christ defines the true and the real and the good – once-for-all.

The distinctiveness of Bonhoeffer's theology is not just its Christ-centeredness but its accompanying sociality. Because Christ's being is a being for others, neither God nor humans can be conceived in isolation but only in relationship to others. Bonhoeffer's polemic against religion is to be understood in this light. For him, religion is the product of sin. Sin, the desire to be for oneself, breaks all relationship. Religion participates in this self-centered destruction of sociality to the extent that it removes the 'otherness' of God by interpreting God individualistically as 'within us' or metaphysically as totally 'beyond us'. In Bonhoeffer's judgment, neither interpretation accords with the God of the Bible, who is the 'beyond' in the midst of our worldly life.

Christ, for Bonhoeffer, brings the restoration of relationships by fulfilling what it means to exist in the image of God; he lived and suffered and died for others, and by doing so he became the new Adam, the new humanity. But Christ is never alone. Here Bonhoeffer's understanding of the relationship between the church and the Holy Spirit emerges. Since the resurrection and until his visible return in glory, Christ is hidden in the form of the church, the community of persons called and formed by the Word through the work of the Holy Spirit.

The church is the church, according to Bonhoeffer, only as it exists for others. To live in Christ is to overcome the world by loving it. The Christian views the world under the mandates of God and joins God's suffering in its midst. Bonhoeffer had no use for a false piety that ignores the world or a false worldliness that ignores God. His plea for a nonreligious, this-worldly faith is based solely on God's relation to the world in Christ. Such faith neither idolizes the world nor writes it off; instead, faith engages it freely on behalf of all God's mandates, working to actualize the unity and reconciliation that is already real in Christ. Thus, declared Bonhoeffer, the Christian life is one of proclamation and praise, of prayer and doing right: opening the mouth for those who cannot speak and risking acts of liberation on behalf of the oppressed. Only a life so lived avoids 'cheap grace' and witnesses to the love of God for the world.

THE DEBATE OVER BONHOEFFER'S THEOLOGY

Letters and Papers from Prison was published in German in 1951 and in English translation in 1953. During the 1950s it caused excitement among many theologians who were looking for a 'third way' beyond the controversy between Barth and Bultmann, but it was not until the publication of Bishop John A. T. Robinson's *Honest to God* in

1963 that Bonhoeffer's name became widely known to the general public. Robinson popularized Bonhoeffer's ideas of a 'religionless Christianity' for a 'world come of age' in which Christians would live 'as if there were no god'. Without knowing the background of these ideas in Bonhoeffer's earlier thought, a few theologians declared that 'God is dead' and advocated a theology of secularity. The debate about whether God is dead raged for several years, and the resulting distortion of Bonhoeffer's theology was not corrected until his 'prison theology' was examined in relation to the entire corpus of his writings. Then it became evident that Bonhoeffer's interest had never been in necrology but in where God is to be found in the modern world.

Barth and Bonhoeffer were friends and allies in the Church Struggle, so it is little wonder that Barth was upset by Bonhoeffer's charge in the prison letters that Barth's commendable criticism of religion had been replaced by a 'positivism of revelation' that ended, especially in the Confessing Church, in a restoration of orthodox doctrines that had to be accepted as a whole or not at all. Bonhoeffer felt that such a positivism ignored the degrees of knowledge and degrees of meaning found in the Bible and turned what was, through the incarnation, Christ's gift to us into a 'law of faith'. What worried Bonhoeffer was the fact that this 'law of faith' made it too easy for the church to go its own way and neglect its obligation to the world. Barth, on the other hand, considered Bonhoeffer's charge to be 'enigmatic' and certainly unjustified. For his part, Barth stated, at the appropriate places in his *Church Dogmatics*, his unmitigated praise for Bonhoeffer's superb treatment of the church in *Sanctorum Communio* and of discipleship in *The Cost of Discipleship*.[8]

Other questions have been raised about Bonhoeffer's theology. Does his emphasis on obedience lead to a works-righteousness inimical to the Reformation understanding of salvation by faith alone? No careful reading of Bonhoeffer will substantiate such a claim. Is Bonhoeffer's view of Christianity too aristocratic, preserving hierarchical models of authority? There is some truth to this, but his prison experience helped him see things 'from below', namely, from the perspective of those who suffer from oppression. Moreover, he consistently took his view of human rulership from that of God's lordship, in which God rules by serving. Does Bonhoeffer's christocentricity lead to a christomonism rather than trinitarianism? Although Christ is clearly at the center of Bonhoeffer's thought, Christ is the Word and Son of the Father whose presence is made possible by the work of the Holy Spirit. What marks Bonhoeffer's doctrine of the Trinity is its non-speculative character; for him, the economic Trinity (God-for-us) is, as such, the ontological Trinity (God-in-God's-self).

Probably the greatest skepticism has been raised about Bonhoeffer's assumption that the modern world has 'come of age' and that religion is not an innate but an historically developed phenomenon that humanity had more or less outgrown. Here close attention has to be given to Bonhoeffer's definitions: 'maturity' does not mean 'better' but 'accountable'; 'religion' denotes an inward or other-worldly God, not the God of Jesus Christ who suffers in the world's midst.

A further question has to do with whether the convictions, decisions and actions of Bonhoeffer's life are more attributable to the influence of his family, its events and values, than to his Christian beliefs. Such psychological queries can never be answered with certainty. Probably the best answer is that both are influential – but the latter more so.

A final issue concerns Bonhoeffer's participation in the movement to overthrow the Nazi government, even in the plot to kill Hitler. For Bonhoeffer, the question was not whether to participate but whether, as a Christian, he could afford *not* to participate in overthrowing an outlaw 'government' that was perpetrating such atrocities against humanity. He condoned the plot against Hitler only as an *'ultima ratio'*, an extreme solution to be pursued in these extraordinary circumstances.

ACHIEVEMENT AND AGENDA FOR THE FUTURE

Bonhoeffer died in 1945 at the age of thirty-nine. At the time, he was a relatively obscure German theologian from whom no one expected anything more. Only gradually, through posthumous publications and the telling of his story, did the public realize that this martyr was also a thinker worthy of mentioning in the same breath with Barth, Bultmann, and Tillich. What is so unusual about Bonhoeffer is that his rare combination of spiritual depth, sound doctrine, and social concern has made him attractive to a broad spectrum of Christians: Protestants and Catholics, evangelicals and liberals, pietists and liberationists. He seems to have helped the church turn to the world without losing the essence of its own life.

Although Bonhoeffer's influence has for a quarter century pervaded much mainline ecumenical, evangelical, and Catholic theology, it is particularly evident in certain movements and theologians. Most obvious is Bonhoeffer's connection to the theology of secularization, whether in the 'God-is-dead' theology of T. Altizer and W. Hamilton or in the secular theologies of P. van Buren and H. Cox.[9] On the other hand, in the atheistic Marxist regimes of Eastern Europe the churches have found Bonhoeffer's theology of discipleship to be a mainstay, as have churches which are fighting apartheid in South Africa, where John de Gruchy has been a spokesman.[10]

Bonhoeffer's theology of a God who suffers on behalf of the oppressed has found a positive response in liberation theology, as exemplified, for instance, in the Latin American theology of Gustavo Gutierrez, in the North American black theology of J. Cone, and in the feminist theology of Dorothée Soelle.[11] Two European theologians who teach in Tübingen are strong proponents of ideas from Bonhoeffer: J. Moltmann was early influenced by Bonhoeffer's doctrine of the church and has since brought Bonhoeffer's (and Luther's!) theology of the cross into the heart of his doctrine of the triune God;[12] E. Jüngel, on the other hand, has utilized Bonhoeffer's notion of the crucified God in his debate with modern atheism. Like Bonhoeffer, Jüngel wants to probe the paradox that the God who allows himself to be pushed out of the world on to the cross is the one who precisely thereby relates himself to the world.[13]

How Bonhoeffer's ethical theology will influence future developments is hard to predict. His thought is rich and multi-faceted, and, although to some extent shaped by the traumatic times in which he lived, it continues to provide fertile insights and provocative ideas for the thinkers of today and tomorrow. During his last years Bonhoeffer himself was troubled by two burning questions: how the coming generation is to live and who Christ really is for us today. Perhaps the challenge of these questions and the way he answered them with his own life constitute his most enduring legacy.

NOTES

1 *Das Wesen der Kirche*, ed. Otto Dudzus (Munich, 1971) and *Wer ist und wer war Jesus Christus?* (Hamburg, 1962). Texts of both publications are also found in Dietrich Bonhoeffer's *Gesammelte Schriften*, vol. 3 and 5 (Munich, 1960, 1972).

2 'Discipleship' or 'following after' is the literal translation of *Nachfolge*; the title of the English translation is *The Cost of Discipleship*.

3 The English translation is entitled *Letters and Papers from Prison*.

4 The English translation is entitled *Fiction from Prison: Gathering up the Past*.

5 See Clifford J. Green, 'The Text of Bonhoeffer's *Ethics*', in *New Studies in*

Bonhoeffer's Ethics, ed. William J. Peck (Lewiston, Maine, 1987), pp. 3–66.

6 Dietrich Bonhoeffer, *Ethics*, p. 58.

7 Dietrich Bonhoeffer, *Letters and Papers from Prison*, p. 360.

8 For an interpretation of the difference between Barth and Bonhoeffer, see John D. Godsey, 'Barth and Bonhoeffer: The Basic Difference', in *Quarterly Review*, 7 (1987), pp. 9–27.

9 See, for example: Thomas J. J. Altizer and William Hamilton, *Radical Theology and the Death of God* (New York, 1966); Paul van Buren, *The Secular Meaning of the Gospel* (New York, 1963); Harvey E. Cox, *The Secular City* (New York, 1965).

10 See John W. de Gruchy, *Bonhoeffer and South Africa: Theology in Dialogue* (Grand Rapids, Mich., 1984).

11 See, for example: Gustavo Gutierrez, *The Power of the Poor in History* (Maryknoll, NY, 1983), ch. 8; James H. Cone, *Black Theology and Black Power* (New York, 1969); Dorothée Soelle, *Christ the Representative* (London, 1967).

12 Jürgen Moltmann, 'The Lordship of Christ and Human Society', in Moltmann and Weissbach, *Two Studies in the Theology of Bonhoeffer* (New York, 1967), pp. 21–94; *The Crucified God* (London, 1974).

13 Eberhard Jüngel, *God as the Mystery of the World* (Grand Rapids, Mich., 1983), especially pp. 57–63.

BIBLIOGRAPHY

Primary

Bonhoeffer, D., *Life Together* (London and New York, 1954).

—, *Act and Being* (New York, 1961; London, 1962).

—, *The Cost of Discipleship.* (New York, 1963; London, 1964).

—, *Sanctorum Communio* (London, 1963); US title *The Communion of Saints* (New York, 1963).

—, *Ethics*, rearranged edn (London, 1964; New York, 1965).

, *Creation and Fall. Temptation* (London and New York, 1966).

—, *Letters and Papers from Prison*, enlarged edn, ed. Eberhard Bethge (London, 1971; New York, 1972).

—, *Christology* (London, 1978); US title *Christ the Center* (New York, 1978).

—, *Fiction from Prison*, ed. Renate and Eberhard Bethge, with Clifford Green (Philadelphia, 1981).

Secondary

Bethge, Eberhard, *Dietrich Bonhoeffer. Theologian, Christian, Contemporary*, ed. Edwin Robertson (London, New York, 1970).

Burtness, James, *Shaping the Future. The Ethics of Dietrich Bonhoeffer* (Philadelphia, 1985).

Feil, Ernst, *The Theology of Dietrich Bonhoeffer* (Philadelphia, 1984).

Godsey, John D., *The Theology of Dietrich Bonhoeffer* (Philadelphia, 1960).

Godsey, John D. and Kelly, Geffrey B. (eds), *Ethical Responsibility: Bonhoeffer's Legacy to the Churches* (New York and Toronto, 1981).

Green, Clifford J., *The Sociality of Christ and Humanity. Dietrich Bonhoeffer's Early Theology 1927–1933* (Missoula, Montana, 1975).

Kelly, Geffrey B., *Liberating Faith. Bonhoeffer's Message for Today* (Minneapolis, 1984).

Klassen, A. J. (ed.), *A Bonhoeffer Legacy. Essays in Understanding* (Grand Rapids, Mich., 1981).

Peck, William J. (ed.), *New Studies in Bonhoeffer's Ethics* (Lewiston, Maine, 1987).

Rasmussen, Larry L., *Dietrich Bonhoeffer. Reality and Resistance* (Nashville, Tenn., 1972).

3

Thomas F. Torrance

Daniel W. Hardy

POSITIVE THEOLOGY AND SCIENCE

Thomas Forsyth Torrance, born in China in 1913 and educated at the University of Edinburgh in philosophy, classics and divinity and at the University of Basle with Karl Barth, is an outstanding churchman and theologian. After two years as Professor of Church History, he was Professor of Christian Dogmatics at the University of Edinburgh from 1952 to 1979, when he retired following the conferral of the Templeton Prize in Religion. A minister of the Church of Scotland, he was its Moderator; he has also been much engaged in ecumenical discussions.

Both a theologian and a philosopher of science, he is virtually unique amongst theologians in the depth of his knowledge of the philosophy of the natural sciences. But the distinctive character of his work arises from the positive position which he adopts about what is proper to the content of Christian theology and that of science. This is

> the conviction that we must allow the divine realities to declare themselves to us, and so allow the basic forms of theological truth to come into view and impose themselves on our understanding. Theology is the positive science in which we think only in accordance with the nature of the given.[1]

> Theology and every scientific inquiry operate with the correlation of the intelligible and the intelligent.[2]

It is both the fashion in which he develops this correlation, and his use of modern views of science in doing so, that makes his work particularly interesting. For that reason, we shall concentrate particularly on these here, to understand how far his approach has enriched theology and its relation to the sciences.

For Torrance, theology rests on the given provided by the self-presentation of divine reality, and when it does, it is scientific. But the natural sciences also think in accordance with the given, in their case the given of contingent reality. In his view, theological science and natural science are a posteriori activities, conditioned by what is given. What human beings need, then, is to be conformed to the given which is present, and to be freed of a priori conceptions through a 'struggle with the habits of mind which [they] have formed uncritically or have acquired in some other field of knowledge and then seek with an arbitrary self-will to impose on other subject-matter'.[3] Interestingly enough, therefore, Torrance is as critical of culturally formed notions as are many more liberal theologians, but – unlike them – he is so because this is conducive to thinking in accordance with the self-presentation of reality.

The tension between conformation to reality and uncritical habits of mind makes Torrance concerned with the *reality* grasped in each, as distinct from the *conventional* content of theology and the natural sciences. Not content with what could be called a 'surface' view of the realities with which theology and the natural sciences are concerned, he attempts to probe as deeply as possible into the constitutive factors of these realities, to discover what makes each what it is and how the two are related. This shows itself in two 'sides' of his work, a pursuit of the *substance* of evangelical theology and of modern science, and a search for the *means* by which each must be pursued. This is why, on the one hand, he gives so much attention to the reality with which theology and the natural sciences are concerned, while also, on the other hand, carefully attending to what he calls the 'philosophy of theology' (or more accurately the 'philosophy of the science of theology') and the philosophy of science.

But there are two things which should be noticed at this point. (1) He is convinced that there can be no sharp distinction between what we have called 'substance' and 'means'. The means to understanding must be in accordance with the substance of what is sought; epistemology must follow ontology, just as form and being are inseparable in what is known. (2) And for him, there is no ultimate separation between theology and the natural sciences, even if each has its own distinguishable subject-matter. The two are ultimately to be coordinated in a unified view; the two assist each other. A truly Christian notion of reality supports the natural-scientific notion of reality; and the latter presumes features of the former without attempting to trace them to their sources. (*a*) Investigation of the intelligible reality of the triune God in his creation of the contingent and orderly universe, and in the depth of his relation to the universe in his Son, provides for the natural sciences the vertical and horizontal coordinates for the integration of the universe.[4] (*b*) The work of the natural sciences enables theology to understand the nature of scientific method; both require a scientific method which in many respects is the same even if the demands of their respective subject-matter makes their work distinctive. (*c*) The natural sciences enlarge understanding of the structure of created reality, the spatio-temporal world with which God is so directly involved in his creative and redemptive work. (*d*) The more profound scientific inquiry into the universe becomes, the more it faces cosmological questions and is forced to adopt a fundamental attitude to the universe as a whole.[5] These conclusions support Torrance's concern to 'evangelize the foundations . . . of scientific culture' in such a way 'that dogmatics can take root in that kind of structure'.[6]

HISTORY OF THEOLOGY AND HISTORY OF SCIENCE

For reasons which we will see, Torrance is convinced that an intelligent grasp of the reality with which theology and the natural sciences are concerned is not only possible in principle, but has been achieved in the decisive periods of theological and natural-scientific advance. He shows much more trust for tradition and the methods of the past than do 'modern' thinkers whose understanding of what is possible in theology and science sets a question mark over the work of previous ages; he works comfortably within the medium of the past and present history of theology and the history of science. As a Christian theologian he carries on a dialogue with major areas of the history of the Christian tradition, while his work as a philosopher of science is conducted through deep engagement with major figures in the history of science.

He is not uncritical of traditional knowledge and methods. He proceeds by *reflecting critically* upon the knowledge which has been achieved in the past and the means by which it has been achieved, in order to discriminate between achievements and distortions in the work of past centuries. Moreover, his reflection is guided by the positive position which he develops and employs; it is not a presuppositionless approach, if such a thing is possible. The two – positive position and historical reflection – are subtly interrelated: his positive position is established by reference to his historical work, while he judges what history is important, and interprets it, with criteria which employ his positive position.

The circularity thus apparent in his approach is not a naive one. It is directed to the discovery of the active truth of God present in history through human understanding past and present. The theories (for Torrance is most concerned with empirically-charged theories, not events as such) found in history are properly 'transparent "disclosure-models" through which . . . the truth in the creation as it has come from God . . . shine[s] through'.[7] Such theories need therefore to show their truth again, to be coordinated with other theories of later times in which the truth also shines forth, in a unitary view of truth. The approach thus undertaken is in self-conscious opposition to most modern biblical and historical interpretation, which supposes that theories are the product of autonomous human grasping for truth in a fashion which is relative to their culture.

Torrance's hermeneutic provides a deep correlation between the truth of the past and the truth of the present; the correspondence which he finds develops this correlation of truth. Moreover, his continuous use of a realist method (the notion that truth shines through transparencies) reinforces the method itself. Hence his historical work provides a powerful argument for the normalcy – as against alternatives – of both the content and the method which he advocates in theology and science. It must be recognized at this point, however, that there is a direct confrontation between Torrance and many others about the implications of modernity. Others base their historical work in a 'modern' worldview drawn from phenomenology or sociology. But Torrance considers this obsolete; their 'modern' ways have been undermined by rigorous scientific work, and radical catharsis in their understanding will be necessary if reality, divine and natural, is to be deeply understood.

The characteristics of Torrance's positive engagement with the past and present can be illustrated by two examples. One is his appropriation of the theology of John Calvin and Karl Barth. Because of Torrance's Reformed background and his early association with Barth, his editing of translations of Calvin and Barth and his various books and essays on the two,[8] he is sometimes simply dubbed a 'Calvinist' or a 'Barthian' as if that excused the reader from any further attempt to understand him. But such claims considerably underrate him. Neither Calvin nor Barth as such attracts Torrance. He is attracted by the possibility for theology which their approaches exemplify, the possibility of a *scientific theology*. For Calvin maintained just that, in contrast to medieval thought. He saw that knowledge was objectively derived from God as 'active', 'through modes of knowing imposed on us from the nature of God and from his self-manifestation through the Word'; it was not 'factive' through ideas or 'images of our own forming'. The ideas or language formed by human beings could only be related to such knowledge through the Spirit of God; 'the Spirit provides *transparence* in our knowledge and language of God.'[9] The great virtue of Barth, as Torrance sees it, was that he recalled theology from 'Calvinism', that logicized version of Calvin which is so frequently mistaken for Calvin's own position, to the recognition that knowledge of God comes by the free and graceful activity of God in a dynamic 'analogy of grace'.

Two things are particularly interesting about Torrance's appropriation of Calvin and Barth, neither of them the characteristics of a simple repeater of the two. One is his freedom to develop the possibility which they recognized in response to the modern scientific context. Even Barth had not fully developed the possibility for scientific theology which he recognized, largely because of his ignorance of the implications of science. The other is his capacity, aided by the positive position thus developed, to penetrate the inner character of the theology of these Reformers, thereby laying aside the 'scholasticizing' tendency of most commentators to immerse themselves in the one or the other. It has recently become common to distinguish between Calvin and Calvinism, but Torrance was aware of the distinction long before. Here in fact we see the dialectic of positive position and historical medium which was mentioned before.

The other illustration comes from Torrance's long-standing concern with patristic theology.[10] In a fashion more typical of ecumenical conversation than of the Reformed tradition, Torrance finds in fourth century Patristic theology the primary elucidation of 'the evangelical and apostolic faith'. As with Calvin and Barth, he finds there a kind of theology which is of the utmost importance because it is grounded in the constitutive factors of reality itself, following 'biblical patterns of thought governed by the Word of God and the obedient hearing of faith'.[11] And while he intends to let the fathers speak for themselves, he is also concerned with rethinking what they had achieved in order to 'bring to light the inner theological connections which gave coherent structure to the classical theology of the ancient Catholic Church'.[12] Here is the same combination of a positive position in theology with the interpretation of the history of the Christian tradition.

The result is impressive particularly in three ways. First of all, unlike so many histories of the period which are essentially humanist in explaining patristic thought as the product of developing human opinion, Torrance attempts to determine the intellectual vision demanded by Christian faith itself, as this was being worked out in the early centuries of the Christian era. Secondly, by contrast with other accounts of the period whose bias towards cultural relativism leads them to explain the notions of the fathers by their affinity to others of the time, Torrance sees the fathers as moving beyond alien views of the time. He shows the ways in which the fathers' appreciation of the implications of the gospel enabled them to resist distortions which had arisen under the influence of Hellenism and Hellenized Judaism. Thirdly, in place of historical accounts of the patristic period whose bias towards history of ideas produces a compartmentalized, linear-developmental treatment of notions of God, man, sacrament, etc., he provides a very rich analysis of the interconnection of doctrines as this develops under the requirements of Christian faith and practice. Where else in current patristic study can one find a discussion of the implications of Christology for sacramental theology? In short, Torrance finds the intellectual heart of Christian faith developing its own internal logic, informing the life of the Church and resisting threats posed to it.

REALISM IN THEOLOGY AND SCIENCE: CONFORMITY TO THE GIVEN

Let us return now to the positive position in theology and science which Torrance finds exemplified in the fathers, Calvin, and Barth, and which he himself develops, in order to understand it more fully. We shall look at the correlation of reality and human activity, and the possibility of rational knowledge of reality which they afford.

Torrance sees reality as disclosing itself to the various sciences, theological and natural, in such a way as to make human beings capable of understanding. Hence, the way forward is to start from the self-presentation of reality, from reality making itself known to us, recognizing that theology and science are always a posteriori and *realistic*: their business is to think in relation to the reality which presents itself as known, and to find the deep structures – the order or interconnectedness – which is intrinsic to that.[13] This is no easy achievement, and it must not be confused with substitutes. For example, it is not to be confused with 'swallowing' a great deal of conventionally accepted material. What is required is a conviction or trust in reality as it presents itself, joined to a continuing struggle to allow thought to be conformed to this reality. The result is a deepening intelligence of the inner relations of reality.

It is possible to *know* such things because the nature of the reality prescribes the mode of rationality which is appropriate to it. One does not start with the question, 'how can this be known', and move to the question, 'how far do we know it'; how, and how far, it is known must be determined by the way in which it is actually known.[14] We actually do know reality, because reality affords us the means by which we know it; scientific knowledge is simply (!) the refinement of that knowledge. God is the paramount cause of this: both by having created us and also by his oneness with us in our created existence, he sustains our knowing of him. But it is also true of contingent reality, because it has been given its intelligibility by God.

The view does not suppose an analogy between nature and the human mind, if by that we mean an automatic correlation between reality and thought. Instead, there is an active self-presentation of reality for the knower to which the knower must respond – a 'grace-giving' by the one and a 'gracefulness' for the other. It is for this reason that the term 'realist' must be used with some caution for Torrance. If realism means a *necessary* correspondence between reality and thought, such as medieval theology asserted by the 'analogy of being', he is not a realist. But, in another and quite precise sense, he is. His realism suggests that there is an *actual correspondence between reality and thought or language if* the thinker is conformed to the mode of rationality afforded by reality; there is a 'gracing' of knowledge when the knower is 'graced'. Scientific knowledge might therefore be described as proceeding within a '*double activity*', wherein reality actively gives itself, together with the appropriate mode of knowing it, and we actively respond by knowing it in the fashion it provides. Only under such circumstances is there a genuine correspondence (or transparence) between reality and thought or language. But when these conditions are met, there is a coordination of what we are given to know and our knowing of it.

SCIENTIFIC INTUITION: THE HUMAN RESPONSE TO THE GIVEN

What is the appropriate response on the part of the human being? Just as intelligible reality meets us and gives us the mode of knowing it, so the human response required is a kind of openness to this gift. Knowledge does not arise a priori outside the relation to the reality being confronted, but through an insight which

> takes shape in our understanding under the imprint of the internal structure of that into which we inquire, and develops within the structural kinship that arises between our knowing and what we know as we make ourselves dwell in it and gain access to its meaning . . . Far from being, therefore, an a priori conception, or preconception, the foreknowledge with which scientific inquiry operates is an intuitive anticipation of a hitherto unknown pattern, or a novel order in things, which arises compellingly in our minds under the surprising disclosure and intrinsic claim of the subject-matter.[15]

In a sense, therefore, the task of the knower is to remain (in Einstein's words) 'helpless . . . until principles he can make the basis of deductive reasoning have revealed themselves to him'.[16] But there is more that can be said than Einstein allowed, and it is at this point that Torrance finds the thinking of Michael Polanyi on the logic of discovery helpful.[17]

Polanyi analyzed the 'tacit power' of the human mind to discern *Gestalten* or patterns in experience through a heuristic leap from parts to a whole in which patterns of coherence could be seen. The problem is a familiar one. What is it that enables us to move from a jumble of discrete, perhaps disorganized bits of experience, to a pattern which enables us to fuse these bits into an integrated whole? For example, what is it that enables us to move from the range of notions which Torrance uses to an integrated view of his work? It is an intuitive leap in which 'clues' are united in a single pattern. Polanyi likened it to looking at a pair of stereoscopic pictures; seeing the two slightly different pictures in a viewer produces a single three-dimensional picture; it is equally apt to use the analogy of a court of law in which two advocates making passionate pleas are necessary in order to arrive at a verdict.[18] In much the same way, 'foreknowledge' or 'scientific intuition' unites the recognition of disparate elements in a whole in which they are interrelated. As Polanyi argues, this is a *personal* and *informal* integrative process, 'the insight of a mind informed by intuitive contact with reality'. It is not limited to the initial moment of discovery, but persists in scientific work and – through its alternation with analytic and deductive procedures – produces a deepening awareness of the object. It is never displaced by logico-deductive or hypothetico-deductive procedures as others have suggested. But it is not the less intelligent for that: there is an inseparable connection between theoretical and observational factors both in the reality known and in the human knower. In that sense the human being is the 'priest' of nature, because in him or her the latent intelligibility of the world can come to be known.

This, then, is the activity by which human beings respond to the self-presentation of reality, the one activity matching the other in the 'double activity' mentioned earlier. Properly speaking, the activity of scientific intuition always involves a movement of thought away from the knower to what is independent of him or her. Such a movement is always personal, but part of a controlled inter-action with the external world in which its 'legislative authority' is recognized:

> the scientist allows the reality he investigates in its own internal structures to impose itself on his apprehension, so that in his contact with it he is committed to a boundless objectivity beyond himself together with an unceasing obligation to let himself and all his preconceptions be called radically into question in face of it.[19]

REALITY, REALISM, AND BELIEF

We may now ask the question 'why?' of all this, and by doing so move to another level of Torrance's discussion. Why must things be as he supposes they are? What is it that sustains such scientific activity? Where others may proceed with scientific knowledge in a more pragmatic fashion, sustained by the recognition that 'it works', Torrance suggests that the basis of scientific activity, whether theological or natural, is actually belief, which plays 'a normative role in the gaining and developing of all scientific knowledge'.

There is a sense in which the structure of belief duplicates that of scientific activity; in the case of the latter, reality gives the modes by which we know it, where in the case of the former, the object of belief commands our belief. This structure is seen in the following general definition of belief:

> a prescientific but fundamental act of acknowledgement of some significant aspect of the nature of things, or an epistemic awareness of the mind more deeply grounded than any set of scientific evidence, without which scientific inquiry would not be possible.[20]

Such belief is integral to knowledge and its establishment. It is not to be contrasted with knowledge, after the fashion of Locke or Hume, as if it required rational demonstration; instead, a belief is to be seen as integral to knowledge and its establishment. Belief of this ultimate kind is actually irrefutable and unprovable: it would have to be invoked in any attempt to prove or disprove it, and it cannot be put into a form by which it could be proved or disproved. In other words, faith is integral to reason; the two cannot rationally be contrasted, 'for faith is the very mode of rationality adopted by the reason in what it seeks to understand, and as such faith constitutes the most basic form of knowledge upon which all subsequent rational inquiry proceeds'.[21] Even when seen in such a way, belief or faith may seem – as it was for Locke – a maximal act of judgment or the ultimate resort of a human being desiring to sustain the possibility of knowledge. But for Torrance it is more like an act of repose, 'the resting of our mind upon objective reality . . . that which really is, the nature and truth of things'.[22]

As we suggested a moment ago, the structure of belief duplicates that of scientific activity; in the case of belief, the object of belief commands our belief. But the situation is more complex. Both beliefs and their 'objects' are differentiated in levels. Properly speaking, beliefs should be proportioned to the *nature of the truth* to which they are directed, to the kind of truth to which they respond, ranging from the truth which is God's to the truth of natural things to the truth of human knowledge. The misplacement of beliefs and truths is the origin of false attributions of authority, by which something is believed in a way which is beyond the truth which it actually has (for example, human beings, their culture or their rationality, or scriptural, doctrinal or scientific statements).

Beliefs, furthermore, are not 'subjective' in the usual modern sense, but personal recognitions of what is objective. Again, there are different *kinds of objectivity*, ranging from the objectivity of God (which is the objectivity of a personal subject who is with humankind[23]) to the objectivity of natural things to the objectivity of human beings, and beliefs sustain our dialogical relation to such objectivities. All forms of scientific activity, whether theological or natural, are sustained by such beliefs. Correspondingly, there is the objectivity of God's truth for humankind in Jesus Christ which sustains scientific theological activity. Likewise, there is the objectivity of the truth of nature which sustains natural science.

If beliefs are proportioned to different levels of objectivity and truth, the theological and natural sciences would end up stratified, each responding in belief to its own truth and objectivity. If that is the case, there would be no unity of the theological and natural sciences after all. Certainly no unity of this kind is available within the natural sciences, even if there may be some unity within those sciences. But ultimately there is a theological basis for a unity of the theological and natural sciences. The different 'levels' of truth and objectivity, divine and natural, are both differentiated and unified by God's self-giving action in creation and Jesus Christ. And the belief which responds to this is one which also derives from God's action, here the action of the Holy Spirit. Such belief has its ground in its response to God's action, and it cannot therefore be validated 'from outside'. The task of scientific theology is to unfold this belief in a fashion which is appropriate to the 'truth' and 'objectivity' to which it is a response, just as the task of natural science is to unfold the belief by which it operates.

Of course, human beings are not simply 'belief-machines', even if they are sometimes treated that way in modern thought. The beliefs we have been discussing are irreducibly personal. Torrance was assisted in the development of his views on belief by Michael Polanyi's consideration of personally-held 'fiduciary frameworks' as the basis of scientific activity. Polanyi thought that human beings 'indwell' frameworks of belief, and that these frameworks form the 'tacit dimension' (which is incapable of full explication) from which they work in intuition and scientific knowledge. Such frameworks are not to be likened to the unalterable categories found by Kant, or to the structures of consciousness discussed by Bernard Lonergan; they are far less consciousness-centered, and far less bound by the limits of rational accounts of the conscious mind. They are more personal, though not the less intelligent for that, and as such capable of modification in response to a reality which is a 'boundless objectivity'. Nor are they inert; precisely because they are a response to reality itself, they exist under the pressure of a depth in objective reality which carries them beyond what the human mind itself can conceive. Therein lies the possibility that the mind can be expanded to meet the fullness of reality, and avoid reducing reality to its own scale.

In being personal in their believing, human beings are also responding to an objectivity which constitutes their personhood. The God to whom their belief is ultimately directed is 'a coinherence of . . . three divine Persons in the one identical being of God'.[24] And this not only unifies their believing, but also personalizes it and them. The personalization of their believing is not a pragmatic construct of theirs, but derived from God's own nature as Trinity.

What then is to be made of the difference in personal believing?

While maintaining that, as the basis of scientific activity, beliefs should be proportioned to truth and objectivity and to the personhood of God, Torrance's view of beliefs allows for the deep difference between people's beliefs or fiduciary frameworks. He recognizes that such disagreements are not trivial, because these frameworks are 'indwelt' – 'we are accustomed to live in our frames of reference; we and they belong together'.[25] There is, so to speak, a logical gap between the frameworks of different people, not simply a difference of opinion. Since such frameworks concern the existence of the believers, gaps between them could not be overcome by compulsion; they can only be changed by persuasion from which results a radical conversion (*metanoia*) from old frameworks and reconciliation to the new. That is not simply a human persuasion from one set of human beliefs to another, however; properly it occurs under the claim of divine truth.

THE 'NEW OBJECTIVITY' OF SCIENCE

Torrance is encouraged in his views by what he finds in modern science. Einsteinian physical science has, he says, rediscovered what we may call the 'sovereign' character of reality, one which transcends all human concepts. The universe is now seen as *intelligible* but *mysterious*, with an infinite depth of comprehensibility which precludes any final notion of physical reality of the sort claimed by physicists at the turn of the century. The intelligibility of the universe is found by the physical and natural sciences in an 'astonishing revelation of the rational structures that pervade and underlie all created reality'. But this comprehensibility also stretches out beyond what we can comprehend. One analogy for this apparent paradox is that of a statue whose front one can see, but whose sides stretch backward out of sight.[26]

> There now opens up a dynamic, open-structured universe, in which the human spirit is liberated from its captivity in closed deterministic systems of cause and effect, and a correspondingly free and open-structured society is struggling to emerge.[27]

What are the implications of these discoveries for scientific knowledge? What mode of rationality is presented by the reality thus known? It seems that the objective referent of natural scientific knowledge is a *constant* or invariant with inherent intelligibility; but as transcendent and mysterious it none the less relativizes the concepts through which it is understood.

So far as physics is concerned, and indeed so far as Einstein's own theory of relativity is concerned, this means that the more profoundly we penetrate into the ultimate invariances in the space–time structures of the universe, we reach objectivity in our basic description of the universe only so far as relativity is conferred upon the domain of our immediate observations. It is precisely because our thought finally comes to rest upon the objective and invariant structure of being itself, that all our notions of it are thereby relativized. This means that knowledge is not gained in the flat, as it were, by reading it off the surface of things, but in a multi-dimensional way in which we grapple with a range of intelligible structures that spread out far beyond us. In our theoretic constructions we rise through level after level of organised concepts and statements to their ultimate ontological ground, for our concepts and statements are true only as they rest in the last resort upon being itself.[28]

The transcendent referent simultaneously confers objectivity and revisability, order and multi-dimensionality, on our concepts.

What kind of concepts are appropriate to this mode of rationality? To be adequate to reality in all its depth, what is necessary are concepts with what we can call an economic 'concentration' through which there can be achieved 'a complete and unitary penetration into things in such a way as to grasp them as they are in themselves in their own natural coherent structures'[29] But at the same time, such 'concentrations' cannot simply be read off from the universe by a process of deduction. Why, after all, is the finding of the structure of the universe so elusive, requiring struggle and experiment? Plainly its order is also a contingent order, the order of an open, moving system which requires movement of thought. So the natural sciences must proceed on the basis of belief in a contingent universe, in order to attempt to grasp its change by thought and experiment.

As we saw before, the structure of belief corresponds to that of scientific activity; in the case of the latter, reality gives the modes by which we know it, where in the case of the former, the object of belief commands our belief. So we would expect to find the same correspondence here.

Belief in an orderly universe and the contingent universe are the two main 'ultimates' which are employed in the natural sciences. And with them, the natural sciences are concerned with the investigation of the ordered, contingent world in its own right; and their interest is in establishing the structures which determine its order, and the vectorial character of its change, including its ultimate origins and ultimate ends. It is no part of their purpose to establish the source of contingent order, or the rational basis of these 'ultimates'. But their research reaches 'limits set . . . by the initial conditions of nature which, though they cannot be accounted for within the frame of our physical laws, are nevertheless essential to the rational enterprise of science'.[30] There are, in other words, theoretical and empirical limits to the enterprise of science; and these are necessary for science to be what it is. They serve to reinforce the contingency of the universe; the openness of the order of the universe does not abolish these limits.

ORDER AND CONTINGENCY AND THEIR SOURCE IN GOD'S CREATION

With such a transformation in the scientific understanding of reality, there comes to light 'a hidden traffic between theological and scientific ideas of the most far-reaching significance for both theology and science . . . where [they] are found to have deep mutual relations.'[31] It is clear that there is a very close link between the new objectivity of the natural sciences, with the beliefs which sustain it, and the truth and objectivity of the Judaeo-Christian tradition, with the ultimate beliefs which sustain it.

The understanding of the order and contingency of the universe (together with the movements of empirical-theoretical thought which are necessary to grasp it) is not generated by natural science, even if it is supposed in – and reinforced by – its work. It derives from the Judaeo-Christian theological tradition. By contrast, Greek philosophy posited a necessary and timeless relation between the world and God which made the world the embodiment of eternal forms, thereby confining it in a rigid pattern of relations which determined the essence of all natural objects; the way to grasp this was to make rational deductions from these essences. On this view, contingency, whether of being or of thought, had to be disallowed as irrational.

The Judaeo-Christian view, however, combines many elements within one view to provide a more suitable basis for the new understanding we find in the natural sciences today. First, there is the Old Testament view of the transcendent Lord God who freely created a world distinct from himself and constituted its nature; its order and the place of human beings are therefore properly understood as distinct from him, but as related to him. Secondly, there is the recognition that he is faithful in his creative act, and thus unceasingly operative in preserving and regulating his world. Thirdly, there is the still more radical understanding of the world, both its matter and its form, 'as equally created out of nothing and as inseparably unified in one pervasive contingent rational order in the universe'.[32] Fourthly, the incarnation of the Son of God, Jesus Christ, as it is fully understood by Christian theology, reveals the full relation of God to the natural world, and how the self-giving action of God differentiates and unifies divine and natural order. Fifthly, the incarnation shows the depth of God's relation to the actual structure and dynamic of the universe: spatio-temporal existence as such is real even for God. Sixthly, the incarnation reveals the depth of the relation between the inner constitution of the Trinitarian God and the inner constitution of the world, and the means by which God continually sustains the order and contingency of the world.

All of this adds up to a 'peculiar' interlocking of the independence of the world from God with its dependence upon him, an independence which gives the world its nature and movement (and requires the self-contained attempt of natural science to know it) and yet refers the nature of the world (and natural-scientific understanding) beyond itself to its freely intelligent and creative source (which requires scientific-theological understanding).[33]

So, in Torrance's view, there is a profound coincidence, so far as it may be, of the metascience which clarifies modern natural science with the metascience of Christian theology. This has the effect of directing each to its proper object, natural science to the contingent order of the universe, thereby to grasp its fundamental structure, and theological science to the source of the contingent order of the universe in the self-presentation of the triune God.

TORRANCE'S ACHIEVEMENT AND ITS PROBLEMS

Torrance's work constitutes a striking and powerful response to a highly defined notion of the demands of modernity. Most of the 'rigor' of the natural sciences as he understands it is the rigor of a certain kind of physical science. There is no doubt that his use of physical science is highly illuminating. But even if we set aside the question of whether he is not developing the implications of this physical science beyond what its practitioners would wish (and there are important questions today about what are the implications of modern physical science), there is still the wider question of whether physical science can be equated with 'the natural sciences' as he does. At the least, such an approach leaves undecided the question of the productive value of the biological and social sciences for the natural sciences and for theology; it also causes Torrance to sidestep difficult questions about the diversity of creation which appear when one considers the implications of the biological sciences, or those of human diversity which appear in the social sciences.

Narrowly based though it may be, Torrance's position is the most highly developed version of realism, the realism both of scientific activity and of scientific belief, which is available in (and perhaps outside) modern theology, one conceived with the utmost strictness. If it has not made as wide an impact as one might expect, it may be due to the fact that those Christians most inclined to realist views (those of a conservative disposition in theology) do not give a high priority to 'science' in theology, or if they do, tend to underrate the use of reason in faith. If it has not attracted theologians, it may be because those who are interested in a rational response to the scientific context prefer a 'soft' version of science which accounts for scientific activity by reference to 'paradigms' and for scientific development by social explanations; they are not likely to agree to Torrance's severely realist approach.

Regardless of the value of his position, Torrance is at times obscure, perhaps himself the victim of the difficulty of his subject-matter, not to mention the diversity of situations in which he lectures. Even for those who appreciate succinctness and know the importance of theory in and beyond theology, his accounts of positions – his own and others – and their relations are sometimes terse to the point of unintelligibility. There are many times when the ideas which he cites need more explication. But, so vast is the terrain upon which he works and so anxious is he to interconnect ideas, to enable people to see the relations between aspects of reality and knowledge, that he often lapses into overcompressed exposition.

It may be that the problem of the intelligibility of his account of his position is connected with the nature of the position he adopts, which verges on the private and publicly inexpressible. To discuss this, we must briefly recount Torrance's view. His concern is to argue for the actuality of knowledge of and from reality, and the knowledge with which he is concerned is 'empirical-theoretical'. He thereby avoids the naïvety of those who disjoin the two. (He is rightly alarmed by those who try to deduce theories from observation or experience, as when people deduce a doctrine of the incarnation from observational data.) The empirical-theoretical knowledge with which he is concerned, therefore, is to operate from the internal correspondences of reality, such as those of being and form. And that, he says, is what actually occurs in knowledge: 'we know as we are known', and we thereby participate in the self-knowing of God through and in the natural world. Furthermore, we are sustained in that by belief that truth and objectivity meet us thus. The relation of knower and known, of empirical-theoretical knowledge to the being and form of the known, cannot be verified from outside the fact that it actually occurs. In other words, it is known to occur by those to whom it occurs. And the best they can do for others is to speak in such a way that their words and ideas are transparencies through which others may see.

The means by which Torrance speaks is to call attention to structures of reality and belief, and their validation of the relation between knower and known; the world *is* ordered this way. And that, in turn, is validated by another structural relationship, that which is made by God, as it is seen in his active deeds of self-giving in creation and incarnation. Were it not for his insistence that these structures present themselves for knowing by human beings, we might be driven to the conclusion that Torrance was too much concerned with a logical account of structures, with a 'Christ-idea'[34] by which the full relatedness of God and mankind is established.

The problem which arises from this statement of structures, however, is a tendency to remain at the level of what we could call 'occurrence' (which is, to be sure, the occurrence of a dynamic), remaining content with the *fact* that these relations *occur*. Torrance's great contribution lies in his extremely careful statement, supported by evidence drawn from Christian and natural-scientific views, of the fact that they occur in theology and the natural sciences, and occur in such a way as to have brought knowledge of the reality with which they are concerned. That, in the end, is what distinguishes his position from those much less certain that they occur or occur in such a way as to yield knowledge. Compare his position with (say) existentialists who at the most will admit that something salvific happened, but not in such a way as to provide knowledge; for them there is no 'factuality of relation' and no authorization of knowledge – only 'something' and human 'interpretations'. Maintaining the occurrence of this 'fact' enables a full appreciation of the positive achievements of the theology and natural science of the past and present, which the others are inclined to treat either negatively or much more tentatively. As was indicated much earlier, he finds depths and correspondence, both in traditional and modern material and between theology and the 'hard' sciences', which other more skeptical people do not find.

Within the struggle to stay within the 'fact' of knowledge (which for Torrance is a struggle to purify available knowledge by reference to its inner structure), there are three other issues. One is the privileged position which it accords to those who live in the 'occurrence', the metascience by which they understand their position and the knowledge which they achieve. Of course, the privilege which is theirs is not, in a sense, theirs at all. It is the product of the deep relation in which they participate; they and the statements by which they express the fruits of this relation are 'transparencies'. None the less, in the history of theology or science, they are taken to provide true knowledge. But, even with all the safeguards which Torrance builds in to prevent intellectual pride, can they be taken so unquestioningly as the bearers of knowledge? There are times when it seems in Torrance's view that human beings are given such a high 'intuitive intellectual judgment'[35] as to be put in the place of angels. That is precisely the question which many would raise about such realism today.

Remaining within the factuality of knowledge provided by reality also makes for an exclusivist and 'occasionalist' tendency in Torrance's theology. In most of his work, there is a very sharp distinction between those who respond properly to truth and those who do not, between when they do and when they do not. On the one hand, in the 'fact' of proper response to truth, human beings achieve knowledge. On the other hand, outside the 'fact' of proper response to truth are those who impose 'self-willed', 'distorting idealisation[s]'[36] on reality. It seems similar to the words of the nursery rhyme, 'when they were up they were up, and when they were down they were down'. That seems to exclude all but that which conforms very strictly to the conditions of the reality which provides the rationality by which it is known, and does so unswervingly. In Torrance's later work, there is more recognition of the contingency of knowledge, though still within the 'fact' of proper response to truth: a 'multi-dimensionality' is conferred upon us by the 'range of intelligible structures which spread out before us', and we rise through the 'levels of organised concepts'.[37] This welcome emphasis on the richness of reality and conceptualities opens the way for a more positive notion of ideas and practices which the earlier view seemed to eliminate. It is not less exclusivist; what is permissible is wider, but it must – and must always – be authorized by reality. This leaves the question of whether the many mundane devices which human beings use in their life and work, from sacraments to technology, are not still too much discounted; contingent structures though they are, they may constitute proper response to an ineffable reality.

There is one final issue that arises from Torrance's concentration on the 'fact' of the relationship between truth and knowledge'; it concentrates so much on the occurrence of empirico-theoretical knowledge, that it produces a restricted view of history. It is admirable to defend and explain the position of space and time in relation to God, and therefore to recognize the contingency of human knowledge, whether theological or natural-scientific. But while this justifies the categories which will be useful in considering history, it is not sufficient for the task of providing a historical account of theology. As we saw, Torrance has produced fascinating and valuable accounts of the history of theology and natural science, evaluating the basic decisions taken by major figures in the past and present as correct responses to truth, but it remains a question whether his is a fully historical account. The truth of history may be more than the achievement of correct accounts of truth.

NOTES

1 T. F. Torrance, *Theology in Reconstruction*, p. 9.
2 T. F. Torrance, *Reality and Scientific Theology*, p. xiii.
3 Ibid.
4 T. F. Torrance, *Divine and Contingent Order*, p. 24.
5 Ibid., p. 1.
6 I. J. Hesselink, 'A Pilgrimage in the School of Christ – An Interview with T. F. Torrance', *Reformed Review*, Autumn 1984, vol. 38, no. 1, p. 59.
7 Ibid., p. 63.
8 For example, Torrance's *Calvin's Doctrine of Man* (London, 1949), *Karl Barth: An Introduction to his Early Theology* (London, 1962), and such essays as those included in *Theology in Reconstruction*.
9 Torrance, *Theology in Reconstruction*, pp. 90–4.
10 The most interesting sustained presentations of Torrance's analysis of Patristic theology are *Theology in Reconciliation* and *The Trinitarian Faith: The Evangelical Theology of the Ancient Catholic Church*, but his work in the period started with one of his earliest books, *The Doctrine of Grace in the Apostolic Fathers* (Edinburgh, 1948).
11 T. F. Torrance, *The Trinitarian Faith*, p. 69.
12 Ibid., p. 2.
13 T. F. Torrance, *Theological Science*, p. 186.
14 Ibid., p. 9.
15 T. F. Torrance, *Transformation and Convergence in the Frame of Knowledge*, p. 113ff.

16 Ibid., p. 115.
17 As found particularly in Polanyi's works *Personal Knowledge; Science, Faith and Society; The Tacit Dimension* and *Knowing and Being*.
18 Torrance, *Transformation and Convergence*, pp. 116ff, p. 121.
19 Ibid., p. 133.
20 Ibid.
21 Ibid., p. 194.
22 Ibid., p. 195.
23 Torrance, *Theological Science*, pp. 37–43.
24 Torrance, *The Trinitarian Faith*, p. 199.
25 Torrance, *Theology in Reconstruction*, p. 29.
26 Torrance, *Reality and Scientific Theology*, p. 135.
27 Ibid., p. ix.
28 Ibid., pp. 135ff.
29 Ibid., p. 134.
30 Torrance, *Divine and Contingent Order*, pp. 27ff.
31 Torrance, *Reality and Scientific Theology*, pp. ix–x.
32 *Divine and Contingent Order*, p. 31.
33 These are matters to which *Space, Time and Incarnation* (Oxford, 1969) and *Space, Time and Resurrection* are devoted.
34 This was a term applied by R. Niebuhr to K. Barth: 'How do we know that this Christ-idea is absolute and not subjective: we do not know. This is simply dogmatically stated'. R. Niebuhr, *Essays in Applied Christianity* (New York, 1959, p. 144).
35 R. Hooker, *Of the Laws of Ecclesiastical Polity* (Cambridge, 1977), p. 84.
36 Torrance, T. F., 'Divine and Contingent Order', in A. R. Peacocke (ed.), *The Sciences and Theology in the Twentieth Century* (Stocksfield, 1981), p. 93.
37 Torrance, *Divine and Contingent Order*, pp. 27ff.

BIBLIOGRAPHY

Primary

Torrance, T. F., *Theology in Reconstruction* (London, 1965).
—, *Space, Time and Incarnation*, (Oxford, 1969).
—, *Theological Science*, (Oxford, 1969).
—, *Theology in Reconciliation* (London, 1975).
—, *Space, Time and Resurrection* (Edinburgh, 1976).
—, *Christian Theology and Scientific Culture* (New York, 1980).
—, *The Ground and Grammar of Theology* (Charlottesville, 1980).
—, *Divine and Contingent Order* (Oxford, 1981).
—, *Reality and Evangelical Theology* (Philadelphia, 1982).
—, *Transformation and Convergence in the Frame of Knowledge* (Belfast, 1984).
—, *Reality and Scientific Theology* (Edinburgh, 1985).
—, *The Trinitarian Faith: The Evangelical Theology of the Ancient Catholic Church* (Edinburgh, 1988).

Secondary

Palma, R. J., 'Thomas F. Torrance's Reformed Theology', *Reformed Review*, Autumn 1984, vol. 38, no. 1.

4

Eberhard Jüngel

J. B. Webster

One of the most potent reminders of the continued fruitfulness of Barth's theological agenda is the work of the Tübingen theologian and philosopher of religion, Eberhard Jüngel. Of East German origins, Jüngel (1934–) studied with some of the leading figures in German-language theology in the 1950s, including Barth and Ebeling. He began his teaching career at the *Kirchliche Hochschule* in East Berlin, moving from there to Zürich in 1966 until taking up his present post in 1969 as Professor of Systematic Theology and Philosophy of Religion in the Protestant Faculty in Tübingen, where he is also Director of the Hermeneutical Institute. Over his time in Tübingen, Jüngel has established himself both as a severely professional theologian whose academic writing makes the greatest demands of its readers, and as a lively and often controversial commentator on issues of religion and politics.

Jüngel shows enviable command of a wide range of theological and philosophical idioms. Much of his best work, indeed, has taken the form of close exposition of texts from classical and contemporary thinkers; from this, something of the variety of influences on his work can be gleaned. The commanding figure has been and remains Barth. Jüngel is one of the most able contemporary interpreters of Barth, partly because of the thoroughness of his acquaintance with the texts, and partly because of his capacity to enter into their inner structure and sense both their cohesion and their real shifts in emphasis. Most of all, Jüngel has assimilated into his own dogmatic work the Christological direction of the *Church Dogmatics*, developing this particularly in the areas of the doctrine of God and of Christian anthropology. Furthermore, he has taken from Barth a resolute theological realism – a sense, that is, of the antecedence, graciousness, and sheer weightiness of the realities with which the theologian is concerned, and which are hostile to neat resolution into patterns of human speech, thought or action. Alongside Barth, Jüngel's chief early mentor was the New Testament theologian Ernst Fuchs, from whom he gained first-hand acquaintance with problems of hermeneutical theory. Fuchs, moreover, gave Jüngel a preoccupation with a set of questions clustering around two concepts: time and language. The former emerged, for example, in his work on the eschatology of the New Testament, where he tried to uncover how New Testament interpreters often work with implicit philosophical doctrine about the nature of temporality. The latter has remained a constant theme. In the tradition of Heidegger and Gadamer, he rejects 'instrumental' theories of language which regard words as essentially dispensable external signs of ideas 'behind' language. More generally, he has given close attention to the dogmatic issues contained within questions of analogy, metaphor, and anthropomorphism. Other twentieth-century figures who have shaped Jüngel's work include Gerhard Ebeling, both in his work on hermeneutics and in his studies of Luther; the Berlin dogmatician Heinrich Vogel, most of all in his work on Christology and the theology of substitution; and Bultmann, especially his earlier dialectical writings. Clearly, the dominant figures are German: Jüngel's writing shows little interaction with contemporary British or North American theological work.

From earlier epochs, Hegel, Luther, and Aristotle are especially important conversation partners. His interest in both Hegel and Luther stems in part from a sense that our perception of the centrality of the incarnation and the cross for a Christian doctrine of God as trinity has often been clouded by inherited metaphysical presuppositions, to which both Luther and Hegel point a challenge. Luther has also, this time in connection with Aristotle, enabled Jüngel to probe a set of issues about human agency and its metaphysical background. Jüngel's knowledge of both Plato and Aristotle is first-hand and detailed, and he has maintained an especial interest in the pre-Socratic philosophers since his early study *Zum Ursprung der Analogie bei Parmenides und Heraklit* of 1964. In the modern era, he is particularly concerned with Descartes, with the idealist tradition in Germany, and with Feuerbach and Nietzsche – all key figures for one whose philosophical landmarks are largely set by Heidegger's reading of the history of metaphysics. Heidegger's more general influence upon Jüngel may also account for his comparative neglect of the traditions of social, political, and psychological theory stemming from Durkheim, Marx, and Freud, as well as of the analytical traditions of modern philosophy.

Despite the range of its scholarly reference, Jüngel's work is by no means simply eclectic or lacking in focus. Certainly it is not easy to characterize his writing in a straightforward manner. Partly this is because he has written extensively in a number of fields – dogmatics, New Treatment studies, philosophy, the theory of language, ethics – as well as engaging in a good deal of editorial work (notably of Bultmann's early lectures and of parts of the Barth *Gesamtausgabe*). Moreover, much of his best work takes the form of shorter studies, densely argued and requiring close familiarity with the texts with which he is interacting. Indeed, it is arguable that his most lengthy study to date, *God as the Mystery of the World*, labors under some problems of organization, which suggests that works of smaller compass, such as those collected in *Unterwegs zur Sache* and *Entsprechungen* suit him better than the comprehensive surveys of theological topics to which many established German theologians devote their energies. For all this, however, a brief chronological survey indicates how a number of interlocking themes have pervaded his theological development.

His earliest publications focused on hermeneutical issues, and in particular on appropriate ways of understanding the language of the New Testament. His doctoral dissertation *Paulus und Jesus* sought to define the relation between the synoptic parables and the Pauline doctrine of justification. Over against dominant models of that relation which focused on tradition-history or the history of religions, Jüngel found their coherence to lie in their character as 'speech-events'. This term, derived from Fuchs, proposed that the language of the New Testament is not simply an information-bearing sign, but rather the actual occurrence, the 'real presence', of the realities to which it refers. However rash its exegesis and uncritical its indebtedness to Fuchs (and through him to the later work of Heidegger), the work was greeted as something of a *tour de force*, already demonstrating Jüngel's considerable skills in dissecting theological and philosophical argument as well as his forcefulness in constructing his own position. The centrality of the category of 'the Word' is evident here and throughout his early writings. It functions partly as a shorthand term for convictions about the origin of certain traditions of Christian language in divine revelation. But it also acts as a focal metaphor in warranting the move from exegesis to dogmatics (a central concern in German-language Protestant theology in the 1950s and 1960s when biblical scholarship and systematic theology seemed to be tugging in different directions). Exegesis and dogmatics cohere in their concern with the divine Word as it 'captures' human language, though they have different tasks with regard to the traditions of language of which revelation takes hold.

Jüngel himself first made the move to dogmatics through an intense engagement with Barth, of which the most important expression was the fine early book *Gottes Sein ist im Werden* (*The Doctrine of the Trinity*), a remarkably acute analysis of Barth's doctrine of God. This study laid the ground for much of Jüngel's future work in trinitarian theology. In essence, he took up Barth's affirmation that God's 'being-for-himself' and his 'being-for-us' are identical. Jüngel developed this theme through applying it to questions of our knowledge and speech of God, but most of all by trying to develop an account of how it is that God can suffer without collapsing into contingency and finitude. This last theme was worked at by Jüngel with increasing frequency in the 1960s in a series of highly-charged reflections on the cross of Christ as the 'death of God'.

Towards the end of the 1960s, Jüngel began to publish on the metaphysical and anthropological corollaries of the doctrine of justification by faith. As a result, Luther came to occupy an increasingly significant place in the circle of his theological authorities. Jüngel's essays from this first decade of theological activity were collected together as *Unterwegs zur Sache*. At the same time, his work moved out in a number of different directions. The publication of Barth's mature thinking on Christian baptism in *Church Dogmatics* IV/4 stimulated wide debate in German-language church and academic circles. Jüngel's contributions to that frequently acrimonious debate were especially important in interpreting Barth's strategy, but also in stimulating his own work to greater concentration upon anthropological issues. His book *Death*, published in 1971, formed the centrepiece of a number of studies of the relation between the cross and the resurrection, and of the nature of eternal life. More importantly, his work on language took on an increasing sophistication, moving away from the somewhat imprecise category of 'the Word', and inquiring more closely into the operations of a variety of types of language. Alongside this, Jüngel became increasingly absorbed in issues of theological anthropology, ethics, and natural theology. In his writings in these areas (many of which are collected together in *Entsprechungen*) Jüngel showed that his primary interest was shifting towards characterizing divine grace in such a way that it is supportive of the freedom and agency of the human creation. In amongst these writings, Jüngel has continued to produce a steady stream of interpretative studies of Barth, (collected as *Barth-Studien*, partially translated as *Karl Barth: A Theological Legacy*), Luther and Heidegger, as well as a larger number of published sermons and other occasional pieces.

Many of these preoccupations found their way into his study *God as the Mystery of the World*, first published in 1977. This – from some perspectives rather diffuse – book is best read as a series of prolegomena studies to a contemporary Protestant doctrine of God: Partly it attempts to trace the fate of Christian thought and speech about God since Descartes, who represents for Jüngel the attempt to base certainty of God on certainty of the self-conscious knower. Its main counter-proposal is twofold. At the level of fundamental theology, it recommends a 'realist' account of our knowledge of God, in which human thinking about God is brought about not so much by human inventiveness as by an initiative beyond itself. That initiative is primarily articulated in the form of language 'transformed' by the coming of God to the world. 'Thinking' follows this astonished transformation of our language by the 'advent' of God in Christ. At the level of dogmatic substance, the book argues through some themes first identified in the 1960s, notably the freedom of God as a trinitarian act of suffering focused on the cross of Jesus, and attempts to show the persuasiveness of this account of God over against both 'traditional' theism and its atheistic shadow.

CONTENT: CHRIST, GOD, HUMANITY, NATURAL THEOLOGY, RELIGIOUS LANGUAGE

From the range of issues which have occupied Jüngel's attention, five emerge as of particular importance.

First, christology. So far, Jüngel has not published a treatise on christology; it is abundantly clear, however, that christology is fundamental to his entire theological activity, both formally and materially. The central dogmatic concept in this area is that of God's 'identification' of himself with the man Jesus. The notion of identification emerges initially as a way of speaking about the judgment which faith in Jesus' resurrection makes about his death. Faith in the resurrection is not concerned with the temporal continuance of Jesus' career beyond Calvary; rather, it is a discernment of 'God's relation to the death of Jesus of Nazareth'.[1]

Hence 'the meaning of the death of Jesus, which is revealed in the resurrection of Jesus Christ, comes to speech in the identity of God with the crucified man Jesus'.[2] Two things are important to note here. First, as always, Jüngel envisages Calvary as the central moment of the incarnation, so that all Christian theology is in one sense 'theology of the crucified'. Second, language about the resurrection points backwards, qualifying Jesus' past by disclosing its ontological grounds in God's relation to Jesus.

This dogmatic proposal is partly rooted in Jüngel's understanding of the literary form of the gospels. As post-Easter confessional narratives of the history of Jesus, they offer an account of Jesus' past as it is refracted through the Christian confession of him as 'Lord', as one who shares in the absolute life of God. This confession integrates and interprets Jesus' past. One consequence here is that Jüngel can adopt a positive attitude towards features of the gospel tradition which often appear to obscure our knowledge of Jesus (such as the creativity of the early church in their transmission of tradition about him). But it also enables him to affirm the divinity of Jesus without having to seek for warrants for that affirmation in explicit statements on the part of the historical Jesus. In rather more abstract terms, Jüngel makes the point by appealing to the patristic language of 'anhypostasia' and 'enhypostasia'. In his historical career, Jesus' existence is defined by the Kingdom of God, which forms the centre of his proclamation and so of his being: his was a 'being in the act of the Word of the Kingdom of God'.[3] His existence is thus 'anhypostatic', in the sense of having no centre in itself. This existence is revealed at the resurrection to be 'enhypostatic' – to have its centre in the Word of God. Jesus' existence is thus '*ontologically* grounded in the fact that his humanity is enhypostatic in the mode of being of the Logos'.[4]

The ramifications here for a theology of incarnation and atonement remain to be explored by Jüngel. Perhaps one of the reasons why this exploration is at present unfinished is the way in which for him christology is not a self-contained locus. As with Barth, a great deal about Jüngel's christology is to be gleaned not so much from explicit treatments of the topic as from observing the way in which he uses it as an explanatory key for other parts of Christian doctrine. Moreover, this goes some of the way towards explaining why he tends to focus on the revelatory rather than the soteriological aspects of christology and the theology of the cross. For it is out of God's identification of himself with the crucified that 'theological thinking has to let it be said what may properly be called God and man'.[5] Jüngel abides by this methodological principle with great tenacity, and it is this which gives his work both a sharpness of profile and a hostility towards styles of theology which, on his reading, reduce Christian theology to religious commentary on concepts and themes not derived from the highly specific center of the Christian faith.

Second, the doctrine of God. Jüngel's handling of this area is markedly impressed by christological considerations. Like many others, he has been deeply affected by the revival of Luther's theology of the cross in post-war German theology, and by accompanying dissatisfaction with received accounts of divine transcendence, immutability, and impassibility. In a characteristically unqualified statement, he proposes that 'the crucified is as it were the material definition of what is meant by "God" '.[6] In constructing its doctrine of God, that is, Christian theology does not presuppose a generally-agreed notion of the character of divinity, but rather, taking its rise from reflection upon God's self-identification with the death of Jesus, seeks to fashion an account of what God is like if he reveals himself in such a way. For much of his career Jüngel has sought to clarify a number of issues here, often by thinking through the meaning of the 'death of God'. *God as the Mystery of the World* offers an extensive review of possible meanings, focusing especially on Hegel, and arguing that in theological usage the 'death of God' ought not to refer to an event in cultural history such as the displacement of God as a significant explanatory factor in metaphysics or cosmology. Rather, it seeks to specify God's being by reference to the godforsakenness of the cross. Jüngel's theology is thus in one sense richly theopaschite, affirming that God suffers. However, he has his own particular emphasis to bring to bear upon the discussion. Much recent writing about Calvary has been directed by apologetic concerns: defending the Christian faith against atheistic critique, developing the theme of God's suffering as a new path in theodicy. Whilst Jüngel shares some of these concerns (*God as the Mystery of the World* contains lengthy debates with representative Western atheist texts), he is equally concerned to work out the *ontological* dimensions of the issues, to try to state how language about God's suffering and death contains 'a deep insight into the peculiar ontological character of the divine being'.[7]

Jüngel is distinctly uneasy with much language about impassibility and transcendence because it appears to run counter to the conviction that God *expresses* rather than *denies* his being at the cross. But this does not lead him to jettison the notions of God as self-caused and as absolutely free: 'God's self-surrender is not his self-abandonment.'[8] Here Jüngel is generally guided by Barth's recasting of the notion of divine sovereignty as the inner possibility of loving action

– a theme presented with rare penetration in *Gottes Sein ist im Werden*. God's aseity is his freedom to love and spend himself in identification with the crucified Jesus. Language about God's freedom, therefore, does not propose some putative capacity in God to be other than he is in Jesus Christ. It speaks of God's capacity to suffer death in such a way that it can be a mode of his life and not the occasion of its collapse. Jüngel has worked hard to construct ontological categories to state this identity between God's self-affirmation and his self-surrender. Such categories include the notions of God's presence-in-absence, of God's involvement in transience as 'the struggle between being and non-being',[9] and above all of God as 'the unity of life and death in favour of life'.[10]

This last category is bound up with trinitarian language about God. Jüngel makes use of such language in trying to state what must be true of God as he makes himself known through Bethlehem and Calvary: the doctrine of the trinity recasts the gospel narratives in conceptual form. More particularly, the concept of God as trinity is closely allied to the further notion that God is love, since both attempt to state how God's unity embraces differentiation. For 'love is structurally to be defined as – in the midst of ever greater self-relatedness – even greater selflessness, that is, as self-relation going beyond itself, flowing beyond itself and giving itself'.[11] Love is neither negative, uncreative self-loss nor pure self-positing; it is self-fulfillment in a freely-chosen act of self-renunciation. To say that God is love is thus to affirm that as a triune being he embraces freedom and self-surrender. Whilst it is not always clear how this issues in language about a threefold differentiation within the being of God, Jüngel is appealing to the doctrine of the trinity to state that it is of the essence of God *a se in nihilum ek-sistere*, to exist from himself in nothingness.[12] The basic setting here again owes much to Barth; but an equally pervasive if less easily detected influence is that of Hegel. In their different ways, both offer a means of stating how God is supremely himself in giving himself as the *human* God.

Third, anthropology. 'What God intends for the human person is only discovered through the *one* man, Jesus Christ.'[13] Christian anthropology, that is, takes its orientation from the humanity of Jesus Christ which is able to function as a determination of true humanness because it is God's humanity. Such an approach clearly raises a host of issues not simply about the place of the human sciences in human self-understanding but also about the dignity and freedom of human persons. Does the grounding of our humanity in the humanity of the one man Jesus Christ reduce us to mere shadows of a prior divine reality? Jüngel is keenly aware of the question, and some of his best writing over the past decade has been undertaken in response. When touching on anthropology in his earlier writings, he tended to lay stress on the definition of human persons from outside, by the gracious activity of God. Here he again frequently made use of the category of 'the Word', this time understood as God's interruption of the settled continuity of human identity. The Word in this context is the 'justifying Word', which 'recognizes' the person and creates value independent of the person's acts. This sharp distinction between person and works evidently draws upon classical Lutheran discussions of the nature of justifying grace and its relation to sanctification, merit, and the ethical life of the Christian. But behind this also lies a deeper discussion of the metaphysical background of how we are to think of our actions and their significance. The discussion focuses on Aristotle and Luther. Aristotle, Jüngel argues, understands the human act as that which realizes the person: a just person is called 'just' because he or she does just deeds. This is tightly bound up with the 'ontological priority of actuality', in which '*work* comes to have an unsurpassable significance'.[14] Being is realized in act. In Luther, by contrast, Jüngel finds an affirmation that human existence is not self-realized but is properly 'existence out of the creative power of the justifying God'.[15] This creative power of God effects what Jüngels calls the 'possibilities' of the human person, granted by God in Christ. These possibilities are more primary than any human self-realization, definitive of the human person in a way which exceeds our self-conscious projects of self-determination.

All this constitutes a vigorous affirmation that Christian – and, indeed, human – existence is 'generated' by an external agency. More recently, Jüngel has pondered the way in which such an affirmation may corrode the substance of the human self and its acts, and has begun to move towards significantly different statements. Once again, the impetus lies in Barth, in part in his theology of covenant in which human partnership with God as his fellow-worker is stressed, but above all in *Church Dogmatics* IV/4, both the fragment on baptism and the posthumously published lectures on *The Christian Life* which Jüngel co-edited for the Barth *Gesamtausgabe*. In these last works, Barth laid stress on the responsive human action which is evoked by God's grace. Jüngel has written widely in commentary upon Barth here, focusing especially on the notion of the 'correspondence' (*Entsprechung*) between God's act and the venture of human agency. Here in the late Barth, 'the human person appears as an agent who *corresponds* to the *active* God'.[16] In effect, then, two rather different accounts of christology in relation to anthropology are found alongside one another in Jüngel's writings. One, derived primarily from Luther, highlights 'Christ in our place' as the one who is vicariously human, and emphasizes imputed righteousness over against human self-realization. In polemic against the excessive focus on human agency which he finds in much 'political theology', Jüngel still appeals to this model as intrinsic to any responsible theology of grace. The second account, taking its cue from Barth, allows more space to human action, and implies an understanding of the history of Jesus as evocative as well as substitutionary.

Fourth, natural theology. Jüngel's interest in this topic, like his anthropological writing, shows how wide of the mark are characterizations of the Barthian tradition as hostile to the natural order. His work here starts from a critique of natural theology conceived as the search for evidence of God in the natural order which can be discerned without the aid of revelation. Such a search (of which Pannenberg is for Jüngel the most distinguished contemporary representative) is criticized because it compromises the particularity of the Christian revelation, making it a specific instance of a more generally-available knowledge. But more importantly, it leaves the created order undisturbed: in searching the fixed structures of creation for signs of God, it lacks alertness to the creation's capacity for renewal, to what under God it might *become*. Jüngel, by contrast, envisages natural theology as concerned, not with a universal basis for Christian assertions but with the universal implications of the highly specific event of revelation. In effect, his natural theology is a 'theology of nature', and does not locate itself in the area of foundations, apologetics or the justification of belief.

Once again, the distinction between 'actuality' and 'possibility' surfaces. The model of natural theology which Jüngel canvasses is not oriented to the actuality of nature or human experience, but to their possibilities, to the gift of enhanced meaning through the self-relevation of God. 'Revelation' is a 'critical comparative'; it discloses a world of new possibilities, which call into question the self-evident actuality of the world and demonstrate its capacity for enhancement. It 'sets in a new light that which has hitherto been self-evident'.[17] Because of this, human experience is not a second source of knowledge of God beyond revelation; rather, revelation brings about an 'experience with experience', a critical appraisal and renewal of human experience of self and world.

What is most important here is the underlying dogmatic scheme: God and creation are not irreconcilably opposed (as, on some readings, they are in Barth), nor are they points on a continuum (as

Jüngel believes they threaten to become in some accounts of natural theology). Rather, each is substantial in its own right, with the natural order becoming newly interesting through the event of revelation.

Fifth, religious language. Here Jüngel often frustrates English-language readers familiar with a very different idiom. His approach tends to be prescriptive rather than descriptive, preoccupied with dogmatic concerns more than with observation of actual linguistic usage. Like his anthropology, his theology of language moves from an insistence on the disjunction between God and creation towards a sense of differentiation in relation. Earlier work appealed to the notion (derived from Fuchs) of God's 'coming-to-speech' in a highly eschatological manner: language about the reality of God remains tangential to worldly language. His interpretation of the parables in *Paulus und Jesus*, for example, presents those narratives as strange intrusions upon the world's language. On this basis, language about God becomes a miracle, going against the grain of our natural linguistic resources, its possibility resting wholly in the event of divine intervention, 'coming-to-speech'.

Later work, especially some important essays on metaphor and anthropomorphism along with the treatment of analogy in *God as the Mystery of the World*, softens this eschatological contradiction into a distinction in relation. Language about God is just that – *language*, a structured system which as a human project has to be understood with reference to the speaker and his or her world, and not simply thought of as something created immediately by God. The most crucial development is Jüngel's discovery of 'tropic' language (such as metaphor and analogy). He is attracted to these language forms because of the way in which they embrace two systems of reference: one system of their regular usage, and a new system to which they refer as that habitual usage is extended without being displaced. Metaphor and analogy testify to what might be called the 'historicality' of language – to the fact that language is a process of becoming rather than a fixed set of referential relations. Certain fundamental kinds of language refer to more than 'actual' states of affairs; in this way they articulate that which is possible. And so, for instance, the parables of Jesus refer both to ordinary worldly states of affairs and at the same time, without abolishing that ordinariness, also refer to the Kingdom of God which 'comes to speech' in them.

All of this is undergirded by a dogmatic conviction that God's coming to the world does not dispossess the world of its reality but grant it further possibilities. As the one who makes us and our world 'interesting in new ways', God is the 'mystery of the world'. By 'mystery' here, Jüngel does not mean a mute reality which will not yield to inquiry, but an 'open secret' – the hidden reality of God made manifest in Jesus Christ. A mystery is that which communicates itself and so makes it possible for us to speak of it. God is the mystery 'of the world' because his self-communication is that which brings about the renewal of that world by disclosing its possibilities. Like his whole theology, Jüngel's theology of language is about the conversion of created reality, recalling our attention to the way in which the event of God's self-manifestation transforms the world and so is to be spoken of in a language which itself bears the marks of convertedness.

DEBATE

So far a substantial body of critical appraisal of Jüngel's work has not emerged, to some extent because he has eschewed popularization and theological fashion, and has not sought to establish and defend a 'position'. That being said, where might debate about Jüngel's work begin?

To many British and North American readers, most at home in a self-consciously pluralist theological environment, Jüngel seems to fall very quickly into the framework and idioms of classical Christian theology. Unlike many inheritors of the 'liberal' traditions of Western Christianity over the past 200 years, Jüngel has focused his imagination on trinity and incarnation as basic theological reference-points within which to develop convictions about the nature of God and his relation to the world. In one sense, of course, this accounts for some of the solidity and attractiveness of what he has to say, especially when harnessed to his considerable technical prowess in metaphysical analysis. But at the very least it leaves him – like any other thinker working within the classical framework – exposed to the need to develop justifications of that framework in the light of persuasive alternative readings of the Christian tradition. His handling of the New Testament, for example, assumes the primacy of the Pauline 'word of the cross', and is often inattentive to the pluriform nature of the New Testament texts and the variety of theological constructs that they might warrant. Or again, Jüngel frequently interprets the history of Jesus through incarnational and trinitarian categories which, without further argumentation, do not necessarily command assent.

Questions of the pluriform nature of Christianity emerge particularly in his treatment of language. The sophistication of what he has to say can hardly be denied – especially when taken in conjunction with, for example, the work of Paul Ricoeur. But there is a certain narrowness in the way in which it construes appropriate Christian speech. By focusing on 'tropic' language, it omits attention to other linguistic expressions of faith (discursive, propositional, hortatory, etc.) or other non-linguistic expressions such as ritual. Furthermore, for all his more recent emphasis on the worldly horizon from which the language of faith is drawn, Jüngel has not undertaken close analysis of the social and political context of Christian speech. Religious language, like any language, is embedded in a set of social structures and power relations which may, in part, be sustained by authoritative discourse. At this level, at least, Jüngel's strong emphasis on revelation appears to make him inattentive to the human context of religious activity.

On the whole, Jüngel has skillfully avoided some of the idealist traps into which a more careless student of Barth might have fallen. This is most obviously so in his anthropology, where he has mounted a spirited defense of christologically-grounded anthropology against the charge of lack of attentiveness to the orders of nature and history. To make his defense more persuasive, however, Jüngel might usefully inquire into the character of divine grace, and especially into its imperatival aspects. He most naturally speaks of grace as a gift which presents us with an undertaking accomplished on our behalf. Barth's final writings have certainly tabled for Jüngel some serious reservations about the imagery of dependence, and pushed him into a deeper interest in the moral world. Some more detailed work in this area would be useful in giving greater resonance to the notion of 'correspondence' between the human God and the human creation, by looking at, for example, the role of moral deliberation or by discussing character and virtue. Above all, this might help lift theological reflection upon the relation of God to human persons out of the idiom of 'consciousness' into which it was set by the German idealist tradition and which Jüngel (like Barth) still to some degree shares.

ACHIEVEMENT AND AGENDA

At the very least, Jüngel's work mounts a serious challenge to easy dismissal of some central Christian problems about trinity, incarnation, and God's action in the world. He has given sustained attention to central dogmatic issues, without being deflected into mere faddishness and without any lack of confidence about theoretical construction. Combined with a remarkable fluency in substantial tracts of the theological and metaphysical traditions of the West, this has made him into one of the most serious-minded and perceptive theologians in the contemporary scene.

His central theological achievement is that of exploring the complementarity of God and the world. As part of this, he has sought to defend 'christocentrism' from the charge of 'christomonism', most of all in pressing a series of questions (about human ethical agency, and about the substance of the natural order) commonly thought to lie outside the agenda of those in the school of Barth. Where he has been most successful in this regard is in developing an account of the being of God to support this sense of complementarity, arguing that it is only on the basis of a specifically Christian understanding of God as the human God that the world's reality may be truly affirmed. His work on the ontological categories which such a task demands is of particular significance, though its oblique and nuanced style of argument, and its dialogue with largely-forgotten classical philosophical texts, do not make it easy of access.

Any reflection on God concerned to engage in serious conversation with its cultural and intellectual milieu needs at least two things. It needs sufficient confidence in its own language and ideas so that it can marshal them with fluency, vigor and imagination. And it needs genuine attentiveness to its conversation partners. For at least the past 200 years, most of Christianity's conversation partners have insisted, sometimes fiercely, that language about God is simply irresponsible if it does not in some way support our human flourishing and expand our vision of ourselves as subjects of and agents in our own history. Jüngel's work is a demonstration that Christian theology has much to contribute to the conversation: 'The essence of the Christian faith is the proper distinction between God and humanity, that is, between a human God and a humanity becoming ever more human'.[18]

NOTES

1 E. Jüngel, *Tod* (Stuttgart, 1971), p. 131.
2 E. Jüngel, 'Das Sein Jesu Christi', in *Entsprechungen*, p. 282 thesis 11.
3 E. Jüngel, 'Jesu Wort und Jesus als Wort Gottes', in *Unterwegs zur Sache*, p. 129.
4 Ibid.
5 E. Jüngel, *God as the Mystery of the World*, p. 231.
6 Ibid., p. 13.

7 Ibid., p. 62.
8 E. Jüngel, 'Säkularisierung' in *Entsprechungen*, p. 289, thesis 57.
9 E. Jüngel, *God as the Mystery of the World*, p. 217.
10 Ibid., p. 299.
11 E. Jüngel, 'Das Verhältnis vom "ökonomischer" und "immanenter" Trinität', in *Entsprechungen*, p. 270.
12 E. Jüngel, *God as the Mystery of the World*, p. 233.
13 E. Jüngel, 'Der königliche Mensch', in *Barth-Studien* (Gütersloh, 1982), p. 234.
14 E. Jüngel, 'Die Welt als Möglichkeit und Wirklichkeit', in *Unterwegs zur Sache*, p. 210.
15 Ibid, p. 219.
16 E. Jüngel, 'Anrufung Gottes als Grundethos christlichen Handelns', in *Barth-Studien*, p. 321.
17 E. Jüngel, 'Extra Christum nulla salus – als Grundsatz natürliche Theologie?', in *Entsprechungen*, p. 188.
18 'E. Jüngel, 'Was ist "das unterschiedend Christliche"?', in *Unterwegs zur Sache*, p. 299.

BIBLIOGRAPHY

Primary

Jüngel, E., *Paulus und Jesus* (Tübingen, 1962).
—, *Unterwegs zur Sache* (Munich, 1972).
—, *Death* (Edinburgh, 1975).
—, *The Doctrine of the Trinity* (Edinburgh, 1976).
—, *Entsprechungen* (Munich, 1980).
—, *God as the Mystery of the World* (Edinburgh, 1983).
—, *Karl Barth – A Theological Legacy* (Edinburgh, Philadelphia, 1986).
—, *Theological Essays* (Edinburgh, 1989).

Secondary

Wainwright, G., 'Eberhard Jüngel', *Expository Times*, 92 (1981), pp. 131–5.
Webster, J. B., *Eberhard Jüngel: An Introduction to his theology* (Cambridge, 1986).

Part II

Existentialism and Correlation

Rudolf Bultmann is unique in this volume in being a major New Testament scholar as well as modern theologian. Robert Morgan pays close attention to these two aspects, and explores Bultmann's relationship to Luther, Barth, nineteenth-century theology and, above all, existentialism. Morgan weaves in a critical dialogue with Bultmann and concludes with a constructive suggestion designed to open a way for Bultmann's theology to continue to be fruitful.

Paul Tillich's theology is also existentialist, though less exclusively so than Bultmann's. David Kelsey describes his lifelong concern for Christianity and culture, and his method of correlating the two. His systematic style is a striking contrast to Bultmann's New Testament interpretation, and Kelsey shows both the conceptual coherence of the *Systematic Theology* and also its method's flexibility and openness.

Robert Schreiter identifies the interrelation of church and world as the leading theme in the theology of Edward Schillebeeckx. He describes how Schillebeeckx developed it by both a critical recovery of historical sources (he was a student of Congar, discussed in chapter 11, below) and engagement with modern thought and life, especially its problematical aspects. Schillebeeckx was influenced by existentialism, but the thrust of his work recently has been more social and political, and in many ways he carries out the program suggested by Morgan.

Hans Küng's method is seen by Werner Jeanrond as one of 'mutually critical correlation' between Christian sources, especially the Bible, and the wealth of human experiences in our world. But whereas Schillebeeckx is mainly concerned to address those struggling to live a life of Christian faith, Küng has recently moved into the dialogues of 'global ecumenism', especially between the world religions. He and Schillebeeckx also represent some of the serious problems posed by modern theology within the Roman Catholic

Church, and Jeanrond gives a concise account of the conflict between Küng and his church authorities.

The four theologians in part II are only loosely related to each other, and they embrace far more than can be summed up by the covering title 'Existentialism and Correlation'. Yet existentialism is important to all (even Küng, whose emphasis on individual decision in faith is seen by Jeanrond as pivotal in his theology), and, with the possible exception of Bultmann, they also practice what Tillich defined as a method of correlation.

5

Rudolf Bultmann

Robert Morgan

INTRODUCTION: LIFE AND THEOLOGICAL DEVELOPMENT

Rudolf Karl Bultmann (1884–1976) was born near Bremen in north-west Germany, the eldest son of a Lutheran pastor.[1] As with all German theologians, before specializing and earning the right to teach in a university, Bultmann had first to receive a thorough grounding in the different disciplines that the subject requires. His studies at Tübingen, Berlin, and Marburg therefore involved philosophy and history as well as theology. His teachers included at Berlin Hermann Gunkel for Old Testament and Adolf Harnack for History of Doctrine, at Marburg Adolf Jülicher and Johannes Weiss for New Testament and Wilhelm Herrmann for Systematic Theology.

This impressive list associates Bultmann with several different strands of liberal Protestantism. His theology was shaped above all by the pious neo-Kantianism of his teacher Herrmann (1846–1922), a devout follower of Ritschl (1822–89). But most of his biblical teachers came from the opposite wing of Ritschlianism, known as the 'history of religions school', whose radical historical criticism had undermined that modern churchman's theology. Bultmann always suspected their representative, Troeltsch, of reducing religion to a human phenomenon, but his biblical scholarship was decisively influenced by this group of young scholars who had qualified in Göttingen around 1890.

This was a high-water mark of the historical critical movement within Protestant theology. In his attempt to resolve the tension between Christian faith and historical reason Ritschl had turned against the historical criticism of Baur. Some of his last pupils reacted against this residual biblicism and supernaturalism, and became key figures in twentieth-century biblical study. Gunkel (1862–1932) advanced history of religions research on the New as well the Old Testament before pioneering a history of traditions approach to the latter and becoming the father of form criticism.[2] There was also William Wrede (1859–1906), whose history of traditions work, and William Bousset (1865–1920) whose history of religions research, were particularly important for Bultmann. Johannes Weiss (1863–1914) rediscovered the centrality of eschatology in *Jesus' Preaching Concerning the Kingdom of God* (1892) and Wilhelm Heitmüller (1869–1926) investigated the Hellenistic antecedents of baptism and Lord's Supper.

All these giants were more consistent historians of intertestamental Judaism and early Christianity than Ritschl. But they seemed barely to be doing *theology* at all. Their application of critical historical methods to the New Testament provided a more secure knowledge of the human past. Whether it also contributed to a knowledge of God was less clear. This question of faith and history has now haunted Christian theology for more than 200 years. It provides the central focus of all Bultmann's work.

One answer is that modern rational methods, including historical research, cannot themselves provide a knowledge of God. They can contribute to this only when associated with some religious, theological, or philosophical framework which licenses talk of God. Without that, history is theologically dumb. Liberal Protestants saw that the traditional religious and metaphysical framework within which the Bible had once been studied conflicted with their new scientific and historical knowledge. Convinced that all truth is of God, and that the Bible must be understood with the help of the best available rational methods, they adopted alternative philosophical theories of religion and reality, and combined their historical research with moral and religious reflection on the Absolute, or divine Spirit in history. This idealist terminology was not quite how the Bible spoke of God, but the ancient and the modern ideas seemed broadly compatible. The main philosophical alternatives (materialism and positivism) were clearly unacceptable to the religious mind.

The liberals' metaphysical foundations were looking shaky by the turn of the century, and the theology constructed upon them decidedly weak. Two letters written by Bultmann in 1904 comment on the religious poverty of Bousset's *Jesus* (1903), and show that even as a student he was concerned about the sad state of contemporary theological liberalism. He subsequently studied Schleiermacher, and Otto's *The Idea of the Holy* (1917). His slow maturation as a theologian can be traced in private letters, reviews, and articles, through some twenty-five years of discussion with the theology of his teachers and contemporaries. The decisive breakthrough came in 1922, when he accepted, with reservations, Barth's critique of liberal protestantism and his Kierkegaardian interpretation of Paul.[3] The confidence with which Bultmann developed his own theology over the next five years suggests that it had only needed this catalyst.

Barth's *Epistle to the Romans* offered a new solution to the problem of speaking of God in the modern world. The old metaphysics had succumbed to the criticisms of Hume and Kant, and the nineteenth-century idealist alternatives seemed bankrupt in the conflagration of Europe. Barth spoke of God's judgment and grace by interpreting Paul. He aimed to speak *with* Paul, as Calvin had done, only in a new cultural situation. This 'hermeneutical' style of theology – theology through the interpretation of texts – corresponded to Bultmann's aim: to do theology as a New Testament scholar. He accepted Barth's theological criticism of the liberals' historical exegesis, and was soon arguing that the main thrust of the neo-Reformation 'theology of the Word' was true to the New Testament itself.[4] That was different from what as a loyal follower of the history of religions school he had written in 1920. The same historical scholarship was arranged in new configurations.[5]

But Bultmann's association with Barth and Gogarten in the 'dialectical theology' of the 1920s did not involve any sharp break with his past. He saw Barth, like Schleiermacher and Otto, as attempting to preserve the independence and absoluteness of religion. What Barth and Paul called 'faith' was what Herrmann and Schleiermacher had called 'religion'. In his own way Herrmann had preserved the 'otherness' of God too. His metaphysical agnosticism prepared Bultmann for Barth's theological modernism, which put God off the cognitive map. But the concept of 'religion' had opened the door to a cosy cultural Protestantism whose day was past. Bultmann was therefore willing to accept Barth's subversion of the liberals' talk of 'religion' by a new Pauline emphasis upon revelation through the Word proclaimed (the kerygma) and accepted in faith.

What Bultmann gained from Barth's theological interpretation of Paul was the impulse to develop a kerygmatic theology which would do better justice to the 'subject-matter' or *Sache* of the New Testament than the historical exegesis of his teachers had done. He could learn from Barth, but not imitate him. In speaking *with* Paul, Barth had failed to recognize that this fallible human author may not always have given adequate expression to the theological *Sache*. In Bultmann's opinion *Sachexegese* (theological exegesis) would have to include *Sachkritik*, or theological criticism, challenging particular formulations in the light of one's understanding of what they were getting at.

This initial reservation marked the limits of their agreement, and a parting of the ways in modern theology. Barth's attempt to speak of God by speaking *with* the biblical author demanded 'utter loyalty' and led to a *Church Dogmatics*. Bultmann refused to identify the Word of God with the words of Scripture, and sought to express the theological content of the New Testament in other ways. The five years 1922–7 were decisive for his integration of theological conviction and biblical scholarship. The synthesis preserved Herrmann's stress upon the non-objectifiability of God. It agreed with Barth that 'the subject of theology is God', and added with Luther that it 'speaks of God because it speaks of man as he stands before God. That is, theology speaks out of faith.'[6] For Bultmann, 'speaking of God . . . is only possible as talk of ourselves.'[7]

Bultmann oriented his historical scholarship and theology to human existence through a theory of both history and human existence drawn first from Herrmann's proto-existentialist theology, then clarified by reading Dilthey and Graf Yorck, and perfected in long discussions with Heidegger. It first surfaces clearly in 'The Problem of a Theological Exegesis of the New Testament' (1925)[8] and the introduction to *Jesus and the Word* (1926). The theory is that historical sources are not merely data for reconstructing accounts of the past. These voices from the past challenge modern hearers and may transform our understanding of ourselves. They mediate an encounter with reality in a way that is structurally similar to the effects of Christian proclamation. This is surely more plausible as a theory of literature than of history, but it allowed Bultmann to see historical study as a theological task, and so to contribute to the 1920s debates about both the intellectual integrity of theology, and the methods of the humanities or *Geisteswissenschaften*.

Twentieth-century biblical scholars rarely mature as theologians before 40, if ever, because they have so much else to learn. From 1907 Bultmann's time was mainly spent establishing himself professionally. He completed his doctoral dissertation on *The Style of the Pauline Cynic-Stoic Diatribe* in 1910 under Heitmüller, and his second qualifying book, on *The Exegesis of Theodore of Mopsuestia* (1912) also reveals the theological scholar rather than the creative modern theologian. A physical handicap made military service impossible and in 1916 he became assistant professor for New Testament at Breslau. Recognized as the standard bearer for the history of religions school in the new generation he became in 1920 Bousset's successor at Giessen, and in 1921 succeeded Heitmüller at Marburg, where he taught until his retirement in 1951. He died in 1976: a street was named after him in 1984.

SURVEY

The appropriate introduction to Bultmann the theolo⌐ian is through his New Testament scholarship. But these two sides to his work cannot really be separated. Though a consummate biblical scholar in a period when the ruling paradigm in this discipline was consistently historical, he engaged in historical research for the sake of theological understanding. Though well informed on philosophy, history of doctrine, and dogmatics, he did his own twentieth-century theology as 'New Testament theology', not as systematics.

Accepting that traditional phrase, and resisting Wrede's attempt to reduce New Testament theology to the history of early Christian religion and theology, Bultmann combined the critical heritage of liberal Protestantism with 'the latest theological movement'. His own theology is therefore best distilled from his accounts of the theologies of his two favorite New Testament writers. But these reflect his historical and exegetical judgments, as well as his theological perceptions, or pre-understanding of the subject-matter. No exegesis is without presuppositions, but the biblical scholar's critical judgments are (or should be) relatively independent of theological preferences. It is therefore appropriate to begin this survey with some account of the linguistic, literary and historical research with which his own theology is fused in a theological interpretation of the New Testament.

Bultmann's direction and stature as a New Testament scholar were made plain in 1921 with the publication of *The History of the* ✓ *Synoptic Tradition*. Together with Dibelius's *From Tradition to Gospel* (1919) this remains the classical form-critical analysis of the synoptic gospels.[9] It was foreshadowed in the gospel criticism of Wrede and Wellhausen and stimulated by Gunkel's form-critical analyses of Genesis and the Psalms. Gunkel had been driven to investigate the pre-literary history of the Old Testament traditions in his efforts to understand the history of Israelite religion, and Bultmann also combined the two operations, drawing upon rabbinic and other analogous material to illuminate the synoptic tradition.

This double-headed historical approach has dominated most twentieth-century New Testament research. But whereas that is now frequently pursued for its own sake, out of a purely historical interest, Bultmann found a theological relevance in history of traditions work, as his liberal teachers, with their interest in religion, had seen theological relevance in their history of religions research. His form criticism lacks the Lutheran kerygmatic emphasis upon preaching which colors Dibelius's book, but when shortly afterwards he espoused the new Pauline-Lutheran 'theology of the Word' advocated by Barth and Gogarten, it made a neat fit with his earlier synoptic criticism. The evangelists and their predecessors were evidently interpreting the tradition as they transmitted it, and doing so in order to enable their hearers and readers to hear the gospel or Word of God through their proclamation. What the New Testament scholar described, the New Testament theologian was himself doing.

The same double-headed historical approach guided Bultmann's next scholarly step as he undertook the preparatory work for his monumental commentary on *The Gospel of John* (1941). The history of religions head was more prominent here, but it was its combination with history of traditions hypotheses which again made possible a link with Bultmann's own kerygmatic theology.

Although the history of religions school began by illuminating the Jewish context of the New Testament, it is best remembered for drawing upon hellenistic and oriental parallel material. Bultmann followed Reitzenstein and Bousset in their search for a pre-Christian gnostic redeemer-myth which might explain the fourth Gospel's peculiar religious language. He recognized that Jewish Wisdom speculation lies behind the Prologue[10] but shortly afterwards emphasized 'the significance of the newly discovered Manichaean and Mandaean sources'[11] for understanding this gospel.

However, the Fourth Evangelist was no gnostic, in Bultmann's view. He interpreted his gnostic source in a Christian direction, historicizing it and transforming its metaphysical dualism into a dualism of decision. He also interpreted the earlier Christian tradition, making its mythical eschatology speak more directly of the human existence of the individual believer. Bultmann was thus able to argue later that the evangelist 'demythologized' his tradition and anticipated his own existential interpretation of the New Testament. It now seems unlikely that the later gnostic documents used by Bultmann justify the hypothesis of a pre-Christian gnostic redeemer-myth. There are certainly some connections between Johannine Christianity and emerging gnosticism, but the Fourth Gospel probably represents a stage in the development of that myth, rather than a reaction to it. Neither the sources of the gospel, nor its subsequent editing into its present canonical shape by a supposed 'ecclesiastical redactor' can be established beyond doubt, and

Bultmann's hypotheses are contested. But history of traditions research does show the evangelist interpreting his tradition critically. It is this general point which endorses Bultmann's way of doing theology, not the details of his reconstruction.

The 'theological exegesis' or interpretation of the New Testament, which flowered in Bultmann's masterpiece *The Gospel of John* (1941), came to final fruition in *The Theology of the New Testament* (1948–53). What followed, during a long and active retirement, and in posthumous publications, drew upon work done earlier in an extremely productive professorial career. Thus his 1955 Gifford Lectures, *History and Eschatology: The Presence of Eternity* (1957), which expound a Dilthey–Collingwood theory of history, are present *in nuce* in the very important introduction to *Jesus and the Word* (1926). The Meyer commentary on *The Johannine Epistles* (1967) builds on essays published in 1927 and 1951, and the torso on 2 Corinthians (1976) on an article from 1947. Most interesting of all, his *Theological Encyclopedia* (1984), a mapping of theological study, was mostly written between 1926 and 1936. Also important for any study of Bultmann's thought are his essays on 'The Problem of Hermeneutics' (1950)[12] and his later essays relating to 'demythologizing' and to the 'new quest' of the historical Jesus (see below).

The Theology of the New Testament, like the commentary on John, has its roots in decisions made by Bultmann in the 1920s. Even its innovatory interpretations of Paul's theology had been published in outline form in 1930 (*Existence and Faith*), and the opening decision to relegate the teaching of the historical Jesus to the presuppositions rather than to the content of New Testament theology was implicit in several earlier writings. The brilliant Johannine section summarizes and systematizes the interpretation worked out in the 1941 commentary: the incarnation is understood in the Kierkegaardian language of paradox as both historical and eschatological event; and in the language of gnosticism (modified and corrected by the Pauline-Reformation emphases of the dialectical theology) the Revealer confronts the world, calling for the decision of faith.

Bultmann's own theology is surely closer to John's than to Paul's. His fusion of first- and twentieth-century horizons is therefore more convincing historically at that point. But a hand is more in evidence where the glove fits less well. When measured against some recent interpretations of the data, Bultmann's Lutheran-existentialist interpretation of Paul looks historically most questionable where it is theologically most profound. But that throws Bultmann's own emphases into clearer relief and makes this the best key to the 'content' of his theology.

CONTENT

When Bultmann writes of 'content' (*Sache*, better translated 'subject-matter'), it is not the content of his own theology that he has in mind, but the essential theological subject-matter of the New Testament: the saving act of God in Christ that Paul calls the gospel of or from God. This 'event' has a point of contact with past history, for Jesus was crucified under Pontius Pilate, but Paul's emphasis falls on the theological interpretation of that history, namely God's inauguration of the new age. This in turn throws the emphasis upon the present actualization of the 'Christ event' in Christian proclamation, and on the faith-response to the 'kerygma'.

As a good Lutheran, Bultmann follows the verbal 'proclamation and response' emphasis in Paul and John, in which revelation 'happens' (when and where God wills) as the gospel or Word is preached through Scripture (or early Christian traditions) being interpreted. It is therefore more appropriate to focus on this hermeneutical 'form' of his kerygmatic theology, i.e. his actual existentialist interpretation of the New Testament, than on its doctrinal 'content'. Bultmann is interested in faith and understanding, not in a system of truths about God and the world. As he explains in the appendix to *The Theology of the New Testament*, vol. II:

> *Theological propositions* – even those of the New Testament – can never be the object of faith; they can only be the *explication* of the understanding which is inherent in faith itself. . . . But the most important thing is that basic insight that the theological thoughts of the New Testament are the unfolding of faith itself growing out of that new understanding of God, the world, and man which is conferred in and by faith – or, as it can also be phrased: out of one's new self-understanding.[13]

This account of faith and theology reflects the pastoral concern which also motivated the demythologizing essays. Only if theological statements are interpreted in a way that clarifies their understanding of human existence will they offer to new hearers the possibility of understanding themselves in the same new way. This takes place in obedient response to God's Word proclaimed today on the basis of the biblical witness. New Testament theology is not identified with preaching, and Bultmann is more detached and analytic than Barth. But his theological interpretation of the Bible is equally concerned to guide and direct actual preaching. Hence the importance of grasping its hermeneutical form.

Some important methodological discussions aside, Bultmann's theological concerns are most apparent in his interpretations of Paul and the Fourth Evangelist. As an exegete and a historian of early Christianity he wrote more extensively, and theology is never far from the surface, but his concentration on these two authors is significant.

It is also at first sight puzzling. A 'Theology of the New Testament' must surely offer an interpretation of *all* the writers or writings, if not of Jesus himself. It is arguable that modern historical re-constructions of Jesus' life and teaching do not belong within this genre, however important they may be for Christianity. But all 27 writings of the New Testament should surely be interpreted.

Bultmann's point, however, is that only Paul and 'John' count as *theologians*, because only they (in the New Testament) explicate faith's self-understanding. 'Matthew', Mark, Luke, John of Patmos, the authors of Hebrews, the catholic, and the deutero-pauline epistles, are all discussed by Bultmann the biblical scholar. But they do not provide a model or criterion for the modern theologian. Unlike Luke[14] and Cullmann[15] who think in terms of 'salvation history', enlightened Protestant theologians must articulate their existential faith in Christ, through a theological understanding of human existence, not assent to some ideology about history which idolizes the visible church.

All Christian theology relates to human existence. Bultmann's is 'existential' in the further sense of being exclusively oriented in this direction, and 'existential*ist*' in the specific philosophical con-ceptuality it uses. Heidegger was in Marburg from 1923 to 1928, and *Being and Time* appeared in 1927. By 1930 Bultmann is having to defend his use of Heidegger's conceptuality, especially in his essay on 'The Eschatology of the Gospel of John' (1928).[16] But the true father of Bultmann's existentialist theology, echoed throughout the all-important 1925 essay on theological exegesis,[17] is Herrmann, who (like Kierkegaard) responded to the collapse of classical metaphysics with new philosophical reflection on human existence. Herrmann not only took critical account of Kant's epistemology and ethics. He was also impressed by the epistemology of his Marburg neo-Kantian colleagues, Cohen and Natorp, and constructed an original philosophical framework for theology based on what he called the 'historical' character of human existence.

Bultmann accepted Herrmann's contrast between the past history researched by historians, and a personal, inner, existential 'history'

(*Geschichte*), which is said to be the locus of faith, genuine religion, and human meaning. This implied lack of religious interest in the social, historical world, and its concentration in ethics on the individual subject rather than on institutions and cultural values, is why many theologians today prefer Troeltsch to Herrmann, and are uneasy about Bultmann. But even Troeltsch, Lagarde, and Overbeck found their religion in a private inner world. Unlike the scholars Lagarde and Overbeck (and many others), theologians such as Herrmann, Troeltsch, and Bultmann, all tried to relate this piety to *Wissenschaft*. But they did so in very different ways, Troeltsch through idealist metaphysics, Herrmann and Bultmann in an anti-metaphysical account of faith, which echoes Luther's hostility to scholastic theology and tends to hold the inner realm of religion separate from the natural, social, and historical world.

The adequacy of this modern theological proposal is clearly open to question. But it provided Bultmann with a framework through which to offer penetrating, profound, and above all *theological* interpretations of Paul and John. They can be challenged by criticism of their philosophico-theological framework, and perhaps falsified by further historical and exegetical argument. But unlike a New Testament scholarship which resists philosophical and theo-logical reflection, they represent a serious attempt to express what Christians claim to be the essential subject-matter of these writings: God.

Bultmann's claim that 'John' provides a theological interpretation of human existence is not self-evident. The Fourth Gospel seems to contain more christology than anthropology. But it retells the story of Jesus in a remarkable way, to assert that the Word was made flesh, and 'to the evangelist these stories taken from tradition are symbolic pictures which indicate that the believer feels himself searched and known by God, and that his own existence is exposed by the encounter with the revealer'.[18] Jesus reveals nothing about himself except that he is the Revealer. The point is not *what* is revealed but *that* the hearer is challenged by the Word to understand himself (or herself) in a new way, no longer dependent upon the world for security, but dependent upon God. The historical event of Jesus is preached as the eschatological event in which God reveals himself to individuals. Both the evangelist and his modern interpreter call for the decision of faith, in which true 'life' or authentic existence is found. All the key Johannine concepts are shown to refer to human existence, understood in relation to God's eschatological self-revelation in Jesus. For example, the 'true light' of the Prologue is 'the state of having one's existence illumined, an illumination in and by which a person understands himself, achieves a self-under-standing, which opens up his "way" to him, guides all his conduct, and gives him clarity and assurance'.[19]

Bultmann has rearranged and edited the text to give it a higher degree of consistency than it possesses in its canonical form. But he can claim to have gone to the heart of what the evangelist is getting at. One defense of Bultmann's own theological position is that if some such critical reduction to bare essentials was good enough for the Fourth Evangelist, why should it not suffice a modern Christian?

The orthodox reply would be that John alone, especially John as reconstructed by Bultmann's elimination of what he considers later additions by an 'ecclesiastical redactor', or even John plus Paul, will not provide an adequate account of Christianity. The synoptic gospels certainly, and perhaps even (despite Luther in 1523) all the rest of the New Testament, contribute something essential to a true understanding of Christianity. Neither Bultmann's 'canon within the canon' (to borrow an unfortunate phrase of his pupil Käsemann), nor Barth's 'biblicism', or rationally indefensible overvaluation of the canon, is satisfactory. A theology based on an understanding and amalgam of two biblical authors has both systematic attraction and historical and doctrinal weaknesses. These are clearest where the textual glove fits less well – in Bultmann's interpretation of Paul.

Abstracting Bultmann's own theology from his account of Paul's is possible because 'doing theology as scriptural interpretation' (following Barth's *Epistle to the Romans*) allows Bultmann to identify with the biblical author and speak *with* Paul. But in disagreement with Barth, Bultmann insists on the theologian's duty to engage in occasional theological criticism (*Sachkritik*) of Paul, where the latter fails to say what he really meant (or what he should have meant – there is some ambiguity here).

What Bultmann finds in Paul and John corresponds to his own convictions, as one might expect in a Protestant theologian finally dependent on Scripture alone. But what he finds is also inevitably the result of an act of interpretation, and this is justified by a theory of interpretation. The theory owes much to Schleiermacher and Dilthey, who thought it possible to understand an author better than he understood himself. In Bultmann's practice the theological *Sachkritik*, justified by appeal to Luther and the Fourth Evangelist, is as important as the hermeneutical 'pre-understanding' (*Vorverständnis*) for which he is better known.

All interpretation (says Bultmann) presupposes some prior under-standing, by the interpreter, of the subject-matter of the text. This *Vorverständnis* is then confirmed or challenged in the course of reading. That account of the 'hermeneutical circle', which also involves reading a part in the light of the whole and vice-versa, is surely correct. So is Bultmann's claim that interpreters can sometimes detect where authors fail to say what they mean and may correct what is said in the light of what is meant.

But Bultmann's prior understanding of what Paul is getting at is not derived purely from reading Paul. It is derived from his own understanding of the Christian gospel, which depends partly on Paul but partly also on other sources, all fused in the crucible of his own experience. Bultmann does not only correct Paul in the light of Paul, as he claims he is doing in *The Theology of the New Testament*, vol. I. He also understands Paul in the light of his own understanding of Paul's *Sache*, which is derived in part from other sources. He in effect distils and *corrects* Paul, as the Fourth Evangelist corrected his sources where (in his view) they failed to express the gospel adequately. This is the *Sachkritik* that caused Barth to protest.

It may well be that like allegory, all theological interpretation does this. Bultmann's response was that Barth also engages in *Sachkritik* of Paul, only without admitting it. But the question remains whether the combination of the interpreter's *Vorverständnis* of the *Sache*, with the right to *criticize* the biblical author for failing to express the *Sache* satisfactorily, gives the interpreter too much power. Does it leave the text with sufficient power to challenge the interpreter's *Vorverständnis*? Will not any such challenge be dismissed by the interpreter as failure to do justice to the *Sache*? Even if Bultmann's basic axiom, that talk of God has to be understood at the same time as talk of human existence, is accepted, there is a danger that Bultmann's prior understanding of the structures of human existence will determine what he can hear the New Testament saying.

Whether Bultmann's theory of interpretation leads to distortion in practice is the critical question in considering *The Theology of the New Testament*, vol. I, pp. 187–352. Bultmann here interprets Paul's concepts in two long chapters entitled respectively 'Man prior to the revelation of faith' and 'Man under faith'. In other words, Paul's whole theology is set out in terms of human existence. That does not mean that the revelation of God in Christ, which is decisive for Paul, is any less decisive for Bultmann. Both theologians find that event actualized in the Christian proclamation which confronts the hearer and calls for the obedience of faith. The 'kerygma' (Paul's word for preaching) brings a new self-understanding and thus bisects the hearer's human existence. Paul himself contrasts these two alternative self-understandings in ways that allow them to be analyzed in terms of his anthropological and soteriological concepts.

This new mapping-out of Pauline theology gives prominence to several concepts which are clearly important in the epistles. Paul is the one New Testament writer who may be said to have a theological anthropology, since the concepts of flesh, body, conscience, heart, sin, world, and death are clearly important for him. Again, much of Paul's theology is unfolded in soteriological images and concepts which describe redeemed human existence. But if Bultmann's presentation of Paul's theology as a 'doctrine of man' is guided by his judgment about which of Paul's concepts are theologically important, that judgment is itself shaped by a prior decision about what theology is.

The controlling theory that theological statements concern human existence is stated with admirable clarity at the outset of Bultmann's interpretation of Paul's theology: 'Every assertion about God is simultaneously an assertion about man and vice versa. For this reason and in this sense Paul's theology is at the same time anthropology.'[20] The same applies to christology. Paul does not speculate about the 'natures', but 'speaks of him as the one through whom God is working for the salvation of the world and man. Thus, every assertion about Christ is also an assertion about man and vice versa; and Paul's christology is simultaneously soteriology.'[21]

Bultmann is surely correct to connect both theology with anthropology, and christology with soteriology. But despite his 'vice-versa' there is some reduction of one to the other. There is surely more to theology than anthropology, and more to christology than soteriology, important though it is to ground them in the reality of human existence. 'Existential interpretation' of the New Testament rightly aims to address the hearer personally, and 'existentialist' terminology may be an appropriate vehicle. But reducing everything to this procrustean bed is likely to eliminate much that is essential to Christianity. That is the main criticism of Bultmann which surfaced in the demythologizing controversy. Before considering some other problems about Bultmann's theology which are visible in his account of Paul we turn to the word with which Bultmann is most indelibly associated.

DEBATE

Early skirmishes aside, the wider discussion of Bultmann's theology begins with the demythologizing controversy initiated by his lecture on 'The New Testament and Mythology' (1941). The word 'myth' was deliberately provocative, intended to draw attention to the 'hermeneutical' problem of interpreting the Christian gospel meaning of the New Testament, in an age which no longer accepts the pre-scientific picture of the word it presupposes.

This problem had been faced by earlier liberal Protestants, but Bultmann objected to the loss of the kerygma in their elimination of myth. Like Barth, he insisted on theological interpretation of scripture, including its mythological elements. Given his pre-understanding of God-talk, that meant existential interpretation. It also meant (as we have seen) *critical* interpretation (*Sachkritik*) Bultmann again expounds this in terms of the distinction between what a text *says*, and what it *means*. The formulations of the biblical writers can be criticized in the light of what, according to Bultmann's pre-understanding (to be confirmed in his exegesis), they were getting at. The mythological formulations *must* be criticized, lest modern readers misunderstand their existential message as information about God and the world.

The '*de-*' (*ent-*) of 'demythologizing' thus implies the removal or elimination of myth in the act of interpreting, i.e., understanding and communicating, the essential meaning of the Bible. The gospel, Bultmann insisted, is not myth – and does not require mythical expression. In the modern world that is inevitably misleading.

The ensuing controversy ranged widely over the nature of Christianity, modernity, and myth. By posing the hermeneutical problem so provocatively, Bultmann drew attention to the general issues. But his essay was largely a summary of his own theology, oriented as this was to the hermeneutical problem. If his specific solution was widely misunderstood, the reason is that not many of those who responded were familiar with Bultmann's philosophical and theological assumptions. The controversy was sometimes perceived as simply another round of the conservative–liberal dispute between supernaturalism and anti-supernaturalism. Despite Bultmann's rejection of the liberals' simple elimination of myth (and with it what this had enshrined), his negative sounding slogan concealed the positive intention of his critical existential interpretation.

For much of the present century Bultmann was seen by religious conservatives as the bogey-man whose form criticism had denied the historicity of the gospels and whose demythologizing reduced the doctrinal content of Christianity to an arbitrary and subjective decision of faith. The hermeneutical form of his theology hindered its discussion by doctrinal theologians accustomed to more systematic forms of elucidating their faith. Even Karl Barth's contribution, 'Rudolf Bultmann, an attempt to understand him' (1952), was uncomprehending, though in his *Church Dogmatics* he also provided some more penetrating discussion. Anyone who gave doctrinal statements more than just existential meaning and value was bound to find Bultmann's approach reductive. Other theologians, who remained convinced about the possibility of metaphysics and its necessity for theology, were inevitably impatient with a Reformation-inspired theology that dispensed with this, and those for whom the hermeneutical question was peripheral had little time for a theology which seemed interested in nothing else.

Less biblically-based theologians still think that despite his rejection of Barth's uncritical loyalty to scripture, and his remarkably bold treatment of even Paul and John, Bultmann's own dependence on the New Testament is itself biblicistic, that is, it accords to these human documents more authority than is rationally justifiable. Bultmann would reply with Barth that as a Christian he does not have to apologize for supposing that the Bible mediates a revelation of God not accessible to human reason alone. That is part of the self-definition of Christianity. But they go further, claiming that rightly understood and received in faith, the Bible mediates a revelation of God not accessible to purely rational historical investigation (such as Pannenberg's) of even the Bible itself. There is something miraculous about revelation as understood by kerygmatic theologians, and that is why theological rationalists dislike it, even though the concept of miracle involved does not involve breaking laws of nature.

The underlying issue here, the main divide in modern theology, is *where* knowledge of God is to be found. Bultmann sides with confessional theologies since Schleiermacher, and against the rationalism of Enlightenment and liberal philosophical theology. Like traditional catholicism and protestantism, he locates saving truth in the religious community responding with heart and mind to a foundational revelation event whose power is experienced in the present. The New Testament is central to Christian theology on account of its roles in protecting and mediating that decisive event to which it bears witness. Any study of the Bible as nothing but a collection of historical sources is destructive of Christian faith in God because historical research alone cannot provide what Christians have always found in it: support and clarification of their religious community's faith in God in Christ. They have brought their own experience to the respected text, and understood each in the light of the other. This is *theological* interpretation because it is guided by the question of God, which has already received an answer in the community, but must constantly be reappropriated and purged of error.

The rationalist temper in theology is rightly suspicious of finding truth behind the closed doors of a specific religious community. Theology is committed to the truth, not to providing ideological support for special interest-groups; and truth must be available to all, on the basis of reason.

'A religion which rashly declares war on reason will not be able to hold out in the long run against it,' wrote Kant in 1794, and even if the counter-evidence is strong, theologians must by definition and in faith and hope agree. Their first loyalty to truth includes a commitment to rationality. However, forms of reasoning are partly relative to particular cultures, and there is in any case more to human life than reason. Some truths and·values may only become accessible by living within a moral community and sharing its discourse. So long as the doors of the community are open to all knowledge, and due weight is given to the self-critical role of reason within it, confessional styles of theology are rationally defensible. They are also demanded if knowledge of God is located in the appropriation of some contingent historical revelation, such as the Torah, the incarnation, or the Qu'ran. In objecting to finding revelation in a contingent historical event interpreted by a specific community, European rationalism parts company with that 'foolishness to the Greeks' which has always been the heart of Christianity. As a fairly orthodox Christian theologian, Bultmann (like Schleiermacher) parts company at this point with the European rationalism he in other respects shares.

In the polemical situation of the 1920s and 1930s he made this break without doing justice to other religious traditions, even Judaism. It is not necessary to deny all other claims to revelation in order to affirm one's own. It is impossible to *affirm* them without participating in their respective religious traditions and communities, and any opinion of their claims will naturally be made from the standpoint of one's own knowledge of God. But it is apparently possible to affirm the reality and nature of God only from within a religious system; and doing so involves claiming a kind of absoluteness for the revelation through which God is known (though not for any particular account of it). But it is impossible to deny the existence and value of other religious systems. It is also impossible to judge them all from some superior rational standpoint, since stepping outside one's own religious practice would be to lose the relationship to God which this mediates. Bultmann's confessional stance is therefore legitimate, but does not exclude a more positive attitude to other traditions, and to the social scientific study of religion. Troeltsch, for example, could appreciate the believer's and confessional theologian's talk of authority, revelation, and miracle, without which Christianity would fade, and yet insist on the preliminary philosophical tasks which Barth affected to despise.

Bultmann sided with the new confessionalism without abandoning the rational methods of his liberal teachers, or denying the importance of philosophy for theology. Unlike Barth he stressed the importance of the 'natural theology' task[22] of making talk of God intelligible in the modern world. But he did not mistake this 'permanent accompaniment of dogmatic work'[23] for the properly theological task of explicating the understanding contained in faith itself. Christian theology begins with the kerygma, and that means within the religious community, wide though its doors are open to knowledge from any quarter.

Christian talk of God has always been the 'property' of the Christian community which draws on a specific tradition and lives within its system of symbols. Its claim to truth about the all-encompassing reality of God requires that this be related to all known truth; and as this changes, theology develops. But the gospel it seeks to clarify and communicate is prior to any theology and inseparable from the scriptural witness, and the justification for doing 'theology as the interpretation of scripture' is this dependence on a specific and contingent revelation. The gospel gives rise to thought, including rational analysis of the foundational texts. But Christians are, as a matter of self-definition, those who find the decisive self-revelation of God in Jesus. To abandon that claim, even to substitute his divine teaching for the crucified and risen Lord of faith, is to part company with what from the beginning has constituted Christian identity.

The christological heart of Christianity is thus the justification for this confessional biblical style of theology. It even requires *critical* theological interpretation of the bible, as Luther insisted when doubting whether the Epistle of James preaches Christ. But Bultmann's negative reading of the Old Testament[24] takes this to extremes, and we have already questioned his particular attempt to hold the balance between loyalty to the traditional text and openness to contemporary experience.

His proposals, however, can be challenged from within his own frame of reference. The most intensive discussion of this theology took place among those who shared its approach. If its weaknesses could be (or can be) corrected from within, using the methods he himself advocated, that should provide the strongest support for the soundness of this whole approach. This contemporary theological debate is simply a part of the Christian community's ongoing conversation with its scripture. It struggles to become clearer about the meaning of the gospel today while preserving the strong continuity with past expressions of Christianity, which is intrinsic to any claim that a unique, decisive, and (so far as we are concerned) final revelation of God has been given in Jesus, normatively witnessed to in scripture, and preserved (however imperfectly) in the church. Bultmann and his closest theological relations re-introduced a direct theological interest into New Testament scholarship, addressing the expectations of a religious community that lives from the theological interpretation of its scriptures. They shared an interest in the religious (including theological) *use* of the Bible today, but disagreed about the master's carrying through of his program.

Those of Bultmann's pupils who had also learned from Barth the centrality of christology and had experienced the trans-subjective power of evil in Nazi Germany were uncomfortable with the certainly one-sided and probably reductive anthropological or existential orientation of his theology, its individualism, and its detachment from the real world. These elements in the New Testament had been heightened in Lutheranism (including Kierkegaard), and given an epistemological twist by Kant and Herrmann. Bultmann radicalized them in his existential theological interpretation.

But the felt needs of the present century point to other emphases, also present in the New Testament. Since it was to this that Bultmann appealed, he could best be challenged on that common ground. For a short period in the 1950s and 1960s the most stimulating Protestant theology was done by New Testament scholars. It seemed possible to dispense with systematic theology, along with metaphysics, and simply do theology as hermeneutics of the Christian tradition. Bultmann's actual interpretation of the New Testament, and so his understanding of Christianity, was challenged, but challenged in its own terms by pupils and colleagues who shared his way of doing theology.

Criticism centered on Bultmann's reduction of christology to a contentless 'kerygma'. Whereas most theologians would remedy this defective doctrine of God, and of God's relation to the world, by metaphysics, Bultmann's pupils sought a corrective within biblical interpretation by re-opening in various ways the quest for the historical Jesus. Clearly Jesus is of central importance for the New

Testament writers, and some at least of these had recourse to the historical traditions by which he could be identified. It was neither historically true to the New Testament, nor theologically true to Christianity, to reduce interest in the historical figure of Jesus to a mathematical point – the 'mere that' of his historical existence and crucifixion.

Several different motives and standpoints ran through this debate and the issues have never been fully resolved. The historical portrait of Jesus remains disputed, and Bultmann's placing him firmly within Judaism is now receiving strong non-theological support, whereas Käsemann's seeing him in the light of Paul appears most questionable in the matter of his attitude to the Jewish law. But the value of this recourse to the historical Jesus in christology remains disputed. Some of Bultmann's disciples, notably Schubert Ogden, were critical of his retention of any such link. Ever since the christological debate was driven by historical criticism into thinking in terms of a contrast between the 'historical Jesus' and the 'Christ of faith', or kerygmatic Christ, attempts to reunite these terms by talk of continuity and discontinuity have proved unsatisfactory. This is an area where the terms of the whole discussion need revising.[25]

Bultmann's critics were more successful in challenging his Pauline interpretation and with it those aspects of his theology which largely depended on that. The opposition was divided, and neither Käsemann's emphasis upon 'apocalyptic' nor his interpretation of 'the righteousness of God' in Paul were widely endorsed. But they pin-pointed the weaknesses of Bultmann's individualistic inter- pretation of Paul. This is now widely agreed to under-emphasize the importance of the historical church, sacraments, salvation history, and the future hope. It is thus arguably more Johannine and certainly more Bultmannian than the historical Paul. 'Body' (*soma*) is suggestively referred to the whole person ('man does not *have* a *soma*, he is *soma*'), but when this is specified as a person's 'being able to make himself the object of his own action . . . as having a relationship to himself',[26] the influence of Heidegger has led Bultmann beyond what is historically persuasive; the interpreter's attempt to link ancient and modern thought fails. Other interpreters rightly see in 1 Cor. 6 evidence that *soma* for Paul is more physical than Bultmann claims.

Underlying this exegetical implausibility is Bultmann's own philosophical account of human 'historical' existence (learned from Herrmann before Heidegger), as essentially detached from the physical world. It was to oppose this residual idealism that Käsemann interpreted Paul's *sōma* as referring to humanity as 'a bit of world'. The same distance from the world is evident when Bultmann understands Christian freedom in terms of the 'as if not' (*hōs mē*) of 1 Cor. 7: 29–31. Paul's eschatology is interpreted in terms of detachment from the world.

Käsemann responds by stressing Paul's insistence on concrete obedience to a living Lord in everyday life, and by taking more seriously Paul's cosmological statements, which Bultmann's existential interpretation had dismissed as myth. No doubt they are mythological in form, but they are saying something about the Creator coming to his *world* which cannot be reduced to a matter of self-understanding without damaging consequences for ethics.

It is important to recognize that within these historical and exegetical arguments over the interpretation of Paul a modern theological argument about the correct understanding of Christianity today was taking place. The texts acknowledged by both sides as authoritative provided an arena. Generalized objections to Bultmann's use of a particular philosophy were answered with the retort that Heidegger simply provides conceptual clarification for what the New Testament (or part of it) is saying. Only specific challenges to his reading of Paul and John could meet him on his own ground. Because he put all his theological eggs in this basket, exegetical defeat could in theory dispose of his theology.

But that suggests that there is something wrong with the theory. Bultmann's theological interpretations of Paul and John remain illuminating even when successfully challenged exegetically. That implies there is more to this hermeneutical activity than unearthing the authors' historical situation and message. The ongoing conversation of the Church with its scripture, mediating the reality of God in Christ, may be more like the moral reflection generated by a national community's ongoing reading of its classic literature.

One inadequacy of the inner-Bultmannian discussion has been that critics such as Käsemann and Bornkamm themselves share in what to non-Lutherans is most problematic about Bultmann's ✳ theology, namely its punctiliar and decisionistic view of faith. Faith comes from hearing the Word preached, and that requires some understanding of what is said. But Bultmann's 'act' of faith is not a reasoned judgment, and sounds suspiciously fideistic. On the other hand, those who criticize it on these grounds seem so out of tune with Bultmann's whole project of combining theology with exegesis, and are also so unrealistic in their own expectations of natural theology, that there has been little fruitful engagement. Bultmann's disciples and his theological and philosophical critics have needed each other; in isolation neither has contributed much to the discussion of his 'biblical theology' since the 1960s. This has been continued by those who maintain the centrality of the Bible for contemporary Christianity without artificially limiting the roles of reason and tradition: Roman Catholics who have rediscovered the Bible, and evangelicals who have learned to value biblical criticism.

The loss of Bultmann's legacy by his more natural heirs is explicable in terms of the vulnerability of any theology which borrows from the prevailing culture in order to make the biblical message intelligible. What illuminated the experience of a generation in the 1920s, and remained persuasive through the 1950s, no longer addressed the concerns of a new generation: 1967–8 was the year in which Bultmann's hermeneutical theology lost the dominant position it had held in the liberal wing of German Protestant theology since the demythologizing controversy. Existentialism faded and a new generation, hoping to change society, briefly found more help in the Marxist tradition, until economic pressures restored power and influence to ecclesiastical conservatism.

Bultmann's theology was most avidly discussed in the 1950s and early 1960s by students who still broadly identified with it. The issues which were not resolved have continued to receive attention, and for twentieth-century theology Bultmann's positions still function as markers. But they do so now as part of the history of modern theology, a resource from which many different constructions draw, rather than as providing the focus for a school. Bultmannian ghosts still haunt a few theological faculties, but religious and theological vitality is to be found elsewhere. The way in which theological liberalism might recover and be renewed by its Bultmannian legacy is the subject of our final section.

ACHIEVEMENT AND AGENDA

The immense prestige of Bultmann within New Testament scholarship today is not focused where he would have wished. Though second to none in exacting scholarly standards, these for him served a theological aim. But it is this dimension of his work (like Baur's) which has proved most vulnerable to a changing cultural climate. His achievement was and is a theological synthesis relative to its mid-twentieth-century European cultural base. If the theology which emerged from this combination of history, literary criticism, and philosophy is in some respects flawed and in other respects dated, it nevertheless recalls the church to an agenda that confronts it afresh in every generation: to interpret its scriptures in ways that communicate its gospel message.

The hermeneutical task of interpreting Scripture theologically is crucially important for the religious community. But it cannot provide everything the community needs. Freed from its unrealistic expectations of replacing systematic theology it can be developed in new ways. The most interesting question in rethinking Bultmann's heritage two generations on, is whether this might be developed by loosening its attachment to the historical paradigm which guided his New Testament scholarship.

The notion of 'interpretation' belongs more within a literary than a historical frame of reference. Historical methods are normally directed towards reconstruction. Bultmann combined his theological interpretation with the historical paradigm which still dominates biblical scholarship by appealing to an 'existentialist' theory of history that saw the historian's task as grasping a text's understanding of human existence. He also engaged in the more usual historical task of trying to reconstruct the development of early Christianity. Even his interpretations of Paul and John involve ordinary historical scholarship. But here his main interest was in the existential interpretation in which 'history' and theology coincided.

Recent New Testament scholarship has abandoned Bultmann's theological synthesis, taking from him only history of traditions and history of religions research. But theologians who value existential interpretation have their own agenda. If Bultmann's interpretations of Paul and John are read as literary criticism, i.e. as brilliant modern interpretations of classical texts, they can survive the modern biblical historians' loss of interest in philosophy and theology.

The theological interpreter who identifies with the literary critic can also afford to make a less strong claim to reflect the author's intentions. But here Christian theologians would be unwise to follow, since they must (on account of the given revelation fundament) maintain a strong continuity with the classic expressions of Christianity. They require some continuity of meaning, and this is best preserved by maintaining the importance of authorial intention. They also look for agreed or shared interpretations of their community's normative texts and these can best be achieved if authorial intention is preserved as an ideal norm or critical control for rejecting arbitrary and implausible interpretations. Accepting a literary paradigm for New Testament studies need not involve a particular literary theory that advocates total textual indeterminacy – i.e. interpretative anarchy.

This respect for authorial intention, so far as it can be known, means that even when working as literary critics theological interpreters of the New Testament still have to be schooled in linguistic and historical methods. But they will be free to introduce whatever philosophical and theological perspectives are needed to articulate the texts' theological meanings in a new age. That is to preserve Bultmann's approach, which is that of all the great theological interpreters, without being committed to a conceptuality which seems inadequate to the theological and ethical tasks confronting a later generation. When Kierkegaard is supplemented by Marx, and Heidegger by Freud and Bloch, Bultmann's framework will allow theology's concern with human existence to include a more positive relationship to real history and society.

NOTES

1 Cf. Rudolf Bultmann, 'Autobiographical Reflections', (1956), in *Experience and Faith*, p. 335.
2 All the scholars mentioned here, including Bultmann, are discussed at greater length in R. Morgan with J. Barton, *Biblical Interpretation* (Oxford, 1988).
3 A translation of his 1922 review article appeared in J. M. Robinson (ed.), *The Beginnings of Dialectial Theology 1920–1926* and is excerpted in R. Johnson, *Rudolf Bultmann: Interpreting Faith for the Modern Era*.
4 See Rudolf Bultmann, 'The Concept of the Revelation in the New Testament' (1929), in *Existence and Faith*, 'The Concept of the Word of God in the New Testament' (1933), in *Faith and Understanding*.
5 Contrast Rudolf Bultmann, 'Ethical and Mystical Religion in Early Christianity' (1920), in Robinson, *The Beginnings of Dialectical Theology*, with the essays in *Faith and Understanding*.
6 Cf. Rudolf Bultmann, 'Liberal Theology and the Latest Theological Movement' (1924), in *Faith and Understanding*, pp. 29, 52; 'The Significance of "Dialectical Theology" for the Scientific Study of the New Testament' (1928) and other essays in *Faith and Understanding*.
7 Bultmann, *Faith and Understanding*, p. 61.
8 Robinson, *The Beginnings of Dialectical Theology*, excerpted in Johnson, *Rudolf Bultmann*.
9 It is conveniently explained in Rudolf Bultmann, 'The New Approach to the Synoptic Problem' (1926), in *Existence and Faith*.
10 Rudolf Bultmann, 'The History of Religions Background of the Prologue to the Gospel of John' (1923), in J. Ashton (ed.), *The Interpretation of John* (London, 1986).
11 The untranslated essay of this title appeared in 1925 and was reprinted in *Exegetica* (1967).
12 New English translation in Rudolf Bultmann, *New Testament and Mythology and Other Basic Writings*, ed. S.M. Ogden.

13 Rudolf Bultmann, *The Theology of the New Testament*, II, pp. 237ff, 239.
14 Ibid., pp. 116ff, 126.
15 Bultmann, *Existence and Faith*, pp. 268–84.
16 English translation in Bultmann, *Faith and Understanding*.
17 In Robinson, *The Beginnings of Dialectical Theology*, and Johnson, *Rudolf Bultmann*.
18 Bultmann, *Theology of the New Testament*.
19 Ibid., II, p. 18.
20 Ibid., I, p. 191.
21 Ibid.
22 Rudolf Bultmann, 'The Problem of "Natural Theology"' (1933), in *Faith and Understanding*.
23 Ibid., p. 330.
24 'The Significance of the Old Testament for Christian Faith', in B.W. Anderson (ed.), *The Old Testament and Christian Faith* (London, 1964).
25 See G. Ebeling, *Theology and Proclamation* (London, 1966, first published 1962); C.E. Braaten and R.A. Harrisville (eds), *The Historical Jesus and the Kerygmatic Christ* (New York, 1964). Also my contribution to the memorial volume for G.B. Caird, *The Glory of Christ in the New Testament*, eds L.D. Hurst and N.T. Wright (Oxford, 1987).
26 Bultmann, *Theology of the New Testament*, I, p. 195.

BIBLIOGRAPHY

Primary

Bultmann, R., *Jesus and the Word* (New York, 1934, London, 1958, first published 1926).
—, *The Theology of the New Testament*, 2 vols (London, 1952, 1955, first published 1948, 1953).
—, *Kerygma and Myth*, 2 vols, ed. H. W. Bartsch (London, 1953, 1962).
—, *Essays Philosophical and Theological* (London, 1955, first published 1931–55).
—, *History and Eschatology* (Edinburgh, 1957).
—, *Jesus Christ and Mythology* (New York, 1958).
—, *Primitive Christianity in its Contemporary Setting* (London, 1960, first published 1949).
—, *Existence and Faith*, ed. S. Ogden (London, 1961, 1964).
—, *The History of the Synoptic Tradition* (Oxford, 1963, first published 1921; 2nd edn 1931).
—, *Faith and Understanding* (London, 1969, first published 1924–33).
—, *The Gospel of John* (Oxford, 1971, first published 1941).
—, *The Johannine Epistles* (Philadelphia, 1973, first published 1967).
—, *New Testament and Mythology and other Basic Writings*, ed. S. Ogden (London, 1985, first published 1941–61).

Kittel, G. and Friedrich, G. (eds), *Theological Dictionary of the New Testament* (Grand Rapids, Mich., 1964–76), including 27 articles by Bultmann.

Jaspert, B. (ed.), *Karl Barth–Rudolf Bultmann. Letters 1922–66* (Grand Rapids, Mich., 1981).

Robinson, J. M. (ed.), *The Beginnings of Dialectical Theology 1920–1926* (Memphis, Tenn., 1968).

Secondary

Braaten, C. E. and Harrisville, R. A. (eds), *Kerygma and History* (Nashville, Tenn., 1962).

Hobbs, E. C. (ed.), *Bultmann, Retrospect and Prospect* (Philadelphia, 1985).

Johnson, R. A., *The Origins of Demythologizing* (Leyden, 1974).

—, *Rudolf Bultmann: Interpreting Faith for the Modern Era* (London, 1987).

Kegley, C. W. (ed.), *The Theology of Rudolf Bultmann* (London, 1966).

Macquarrie, J., *The Scope of Demythologizing: Bultmann and His Critics* (London, 1960).

Macquarrie, J., *An Existentialist Theology: A comparison of Heidegger and Bultmann* (London, 1970).

Malet, A., *The Thought of Bultmann* (Dublin, 1969, first published 1962).

Morgan, R., *The Nature of New Testament Theology* (London, 1973).

Ogden, S., *Christ without Myth* (London, 1962).

Painter, J., *Theology as Hermeneutics* (Sheffield, 1987).

Schmithals, W., *An Introduction to the Theology of Rudolf Bultmann* (London, 1968).

Thiselton, A. C., *The Two Horizons* (Exeter, 1980).

6

Paul Tillich

David H. Kelsey

INTRODUCTION: LIFE

Paul Tillich's principal goal was to make Christianity understandable and persuasive to religiously skeptical people, modern in culture and secular in sensibility. He came to be extraordinarily effective in that role; getting there involved two wrenching turns in his life.

The first was World War I. When he entered the German Army in 1914 as a chaplain Tillich's life had been fairly sheltered and his views, except in theology, conventionally conservative. Born in 1886, he was raised in a conservative Lutheran pastor's home. He studied at the universities of Berlin, Tübingen, and Halle. In 1910 he received a PhD from the University of Breslau for a thesis on the nineteenth-century philosopher Friedrich Schelling whose thought was to remain deeply influential on Tillich. He was then ordained and served a few years as an assistant pastor. However, four years spent sharing the carnage and suffering of war with working-class men utterly transformed him. As his biographers, Wilhelm and Marion Pauck put it, by the time he left the army in 1918, 'the traditional monarchist had become a religious socialist, the Christian believer a cultural pessimist, and the repressed puritanical boy a "wild man". These years represented *the* turning point in Paul Tillich's life'.[1] Tillich believed the change in himself reflected a change in Western civilization.

That experience gave focus to his vocation. The title of his first public lecture in Berlin named the topic that was to remain central to his theology for the rest of his life: 'On the idea of a Theology of Culture'. The Berlin to which he returned in 1919 to begin his academic career was a major center for radical politics and avant-garde art. His fairly chaotic personal life there while teaching theology at the University of Berlin was deeply involved in a bohemian world of artists and political agitators. Thereafter, with the exception of three apparently unhappy terms at the University of Marburg (1924–5), Tillich's appointments were not to theological faculties but to 'religious studies' (at the Dresden Institute of Technology (1925–9), or in philosophy, (at the University of Frankfurt, 1929–33). In both cases he rejoiced at being 'on the boundary', at the point of intersection between a religious tradition and major movements in secular culture. In his years at Frankfurt Tillich became nationally known in German academic circles. There, at the height of his powers, a second wrenching turn was forced on to his life.

In 1933 the Nazi authorities suspended Tillich from his academic position at Frankfurt because his book *The Socialist Decision* attacked Nazi ideology. When it became clear that the Tillichs had to flee Germany, American friends arranged an appointment to the faculty of Union Theological Seminary in New York City. In the fall of 1933, at the age of forty-seven, Tillich began a second academic career in a culture and language with which he was entirely unfamiliar.

For the next fifteen years Tillich taught at Union in relative obscurity which was not much dispelled by the publication in 1936 of autobiographical reflections, *On the Boundary*. He was widely respected within small circles of academic theologians, but few of his writings were available in English. He came to write effectively in English, but he spoke in so heavy an accent that he was difficult to understand. Then, in 1948 a small volume of sermons he had preached in the Seminary chapel was published as *The Shaking of the Foundations* and, against all expectations, it became a bestseller. Three years later the first volume of his *Systematic Theology* was published. It immediately became the subject of vigorous discussion in both academic and church circles. The press gave him considerable coverage, and suddenly this relentlessly complex Germanic thinker became something of an intellectual super-star in America. Tillich retired from Union in 1955, accepting the post of University Professor at Harvard University. There he published the second volume of the *Systematic Theology* in 1957. In 1962 he accepted a second post-retirement appointment at the University of Chicago where the third volume of the *Systematic Theology* was published in 1963. Tillich died in 1965, perhaps the most widely known academic theologian in American history. In the years since his death there has also been a vigorous rediscovery of Tillich in German theological circles.

SURVEY: WORK, APPROACH, AND THEMES

Of the more than 500 works in Tillich's bibliography, the writings available in English fall into four rough groups: (i) the three volumes of his *Systematic Theology*; (ii) writings outside the system dealing with individual theological topics that are also discussed within the system, notably *Biblical Religion and the Search for Ultimate Reality, Love, Power and Justice, The Protestant Era* and*Theology of Culture*; (iii) three volumes of sermons, *The Shaking of the Foundations, The New Being, The Eternal Now*; and (iv) essays in the philosophy of religion, notably *The Courage to Be*. In our discussion of Tillich's theology we shall focus on his *Systematic Theology*.

All of these writings may be viewed as variations on the same approach in theology: to *mediate* between contemporary culture and historical Christianity, to show that faith need not be unacceptable to contemporary culture and that contemporary culture need not be unacceptable to faith. That is, they are all exercises in the theology of culture. For Tillich, that means that making a case for Christianity ('apologetics') is not a specialized branch of theology but rather is one dimension of every sub-section of theology.[2]

In his *Systematic Theology* Tillich undertakes this mediating task by exhibiting a *correlation* between religion and culture.[3] The relation between the two, he suggests, is like the correlation between 'questioning' and 'answering' in a conversation. Or, it is like the correlation between 'form' and 'content' (or 'substance') in a work of art. Indeed, it is possible to correlate them because in concrete reality 'religion' and 'culture' are always a single whole of which 'the form of religion is culture and the substance of culture is religion'.

Tillich suggests that the human condition always raises fundamental questions which human cultures express in various ways in the dominant styles of their works of art and to which religious traditions offer answers expressed in religious symbols. Accordingly he organizes his *Systematic Theology* in five Parts. In each Part a major biblical religious symbol is correlated as 'answer' with a major human question as expressed by modern culture. Part I correlates the symbol 'Logos' with modern culture's form of the skeptical question: How can we know with certainty any humanly important truth? Part II correlates the symbol 'God as Creator' with modern culture's expressions of the question of finitude: How can we withstand the destructive forces that threaten to disintegrate our lives? Part III correlates the symbol 'Jesus as the Christ' with modern culture's secular expressions of the question of estrangement: How can we heal the alienation we experience from ourselves and from our neighbors? Part IV correlates the symbol 'Spirit' with modern culture's expressions of the question of ambiguity: How can our lives be authentic when our morality, religious practices and cultural self-expressions are so thoroughly ambiguous? And Part V correlates the symbol 'Kingdom of God' with the question: Has history any meaning?

CONTENT: ESSENTIAL NATURE, EXISTENTIAL DISRUPTION, AND ACTUALITY

These five pairs of correlated questions and answers are the main themes in Tillich's theology. They resolve into three major sub-divisions that deal with what he abstractly calls, respectively, the 'essential nature', the 'existential' disruption and the 'actuality' of our lives and of every reality. We will follow this trinitarian structure in our discussion of the content of Tillich's theology.

Essential Nature

The first two parts of the system deal with questions concerning our 'essential nature'. 'Essence' refers to what something most fundamentally *is*. In Tillich's view, anything whatever that is actual (as opposed to merely ideal) exhibits three very general features: (i) it is itself an integral whole, perhaps we might say, a 'system'; (ii) it is part of more inclusive integral wholes with whose other members it is engaged in various kinds of transactions; (iii) it is 'finite', that is, inherently vulnerable to dis-integration of itself and to separation from the whole to which it belongs. Tillich analyzes these three features of our essential nature in considerable detail at a high level of abstraction. Part I deals with our essential nature as 'knowers'. Part II deals with our essential nature as 'creatures'. It may make his analysis clearer if we take the Parts in reverse order.

Part II of the system addresses the question raised by experience of the threatenedness of our lives. Incidentally, taking this as his central focus, and drawing here on Kierkegaard and Nietzsche, earned him the label 'existentialist'. There are moments when we experience our lives on the edge of being overwhelmed by meaninglessness, guilt, and death. Put abstractly, 'being' is threatened by 'non-being'.[4] What is equally important for Tillich is that we also have the experience of continually resisting this threat. Put abstractly, we experience the presence of the 'power of being'. Out of this rises the question, 'Whence comes the power to resist the threat of non-being'? The answer is provided by the Christian symbol 'God as Creator'.

Before we can get clear about that, Tillich thinks, we need to ask what it is about us that leaves us so vulnerable to the threat of 'non-being'. Here we encounter Tillich's celebrated ontology.[5] 'Ontology' is thought (in Greek: *logos*) about what it is to *be* (in Greek: *ontos*). It is a topic many philosophers have taken up. Tillich borrows from a great many of them and was, perhaps, especially influenced by Heidegger. Note that while some philosophers hold that careful analysis of what it is 'to be' will demonstrate the reality of God, Tillich is not among them. His ontological analysis is confined to showing our *finitude*, i.e. that we are inherently threatened by non-being and that we are not ourselves the source of the power of being which resists the threat. Tillich suggests that all our interactions with the world exhibit the same basic structure. The structure consists of three pairs of 'polar elements'. In every transaction with the world we have to strike a balance between 'individualization' and 'participation', between preserving and nurturing our own individuality and sharing in community and communion with others. The balance is not a given. We have to strike it again and again, and it is always possible that we shall fail. Obviously, many psychological and social problems can be understood as situations in which these two poles have come into conflict with each other. In every transaction, secondly, we have to keep a balance between 'dynamics' and 'form'. Without rules (form), interactions become unreliable and chaotic. But without creativity and novelty (dynamics), they become rigid. Many political revolutions may be understood as situations in which these two poles have come into conflict with one another. Finally, in every transaction we have to keep 'freedom' and 'destiny' balanced. At the moment of any transaction with the world we are deeply conditioned by the immediate situation and by the entire history of what we have done and undergone to that point. That is our 'destiny', determining who we are at that moment and setting us on a certain trajectory into the future. At the same time we must exercise our freedom, deciding what to do and taking responsibility for it. On this analysis, then, to *be* is necessarily to be *finite*. It is to be inherently, and not just accidentally, vulnerable to interactions with the world in which individualization separates from participation, dynamics separates from form, destiny separates from freedom.

Yet we never totally fall apart. Whence comes the power to resist the threats of non-being? That is the question about our 'ultimate concern'. Now, says Tillich, whatever concerns us ultimately is our 'god'. So this is a question about god. The answer is provided by Christian symbols of God.[6] They are images and stories about God, especially as Creator, that express the experience of the presence of the power of being in a specially appropriate way. 'Creator' does not name a theory about the origin of things. Rather 'God is creator' expresses an experience of a state of affairs: the power of being is present actively ('God lives'), continuously ('God sustains'), grounding our being in the very midst of the threat of non-being ('God creates out of chaos'). At the same time the symbol is nuanced to express another feature of the experience: the presence of the power is experienced as 'inexplicable and uncanny' ('God is holy'). As the ontological analysis has confirmed, this power is not an element in the structure of being. Nor is it just another name for the structure of being, taken as a whole. Tillich rejects that as a form of pantheism. Nor can this power be a 'supreme being'; for by definition *any* 'being' is finite. Hence Tillich refuses to speak of the 'existence' of God. No, the power of being or 'ground of being' is 'being-itself', utterly unconditioned by anything else while being present to everything ('God is Lord').

Part I of the system applies this same pattern of analysis to one type of transaction with the world, *viz.* cognition. It addresses the skeptical question raised by our persistent frustrations in trying to know humanly important truth. Tillich adopts a very rich concept of knowledge.[7] Knowing covers every type of transaction with the world in which we both grasp and shape it. Our capacity to do this is the structure of the mind, which Tillich calls 'ontological reason'. It is much richer than mere 'technical reason', or problem-solving capacities. We constantly find our efforts to grasp and shape reality threatened either with meaninglessness or with uncertainty. And yet we do know enough to live on. The question is, 'How can it be that the threat is overcome?' The answer is provided by the Christian symbol 'Logos'.

We need to ask *why* our efforts to know are threatened before we can get clear about how 'Logos' addresses our skepticism. Our rational efforts are threatened, of course, because ontological reason is finite. Three pairs of polar elements must be kept in balance in our grasping and shaping of reality, and they theaten to conflict. Rational grasp of reality involves both formal and emotional dimensions. However, the formal and emotional roles of our cognitive transactions with the world threaten to conflict and we yearn for some kind of knowing in which they are united. Rational grasp of reality must also hold static and dynamic aspects in balance. These aspects constantly threaten to conflict. Stress on static principles looks from the other perspective like conservative 'absolutism'; stress on concrete changes looks from the other perspective like rootless 'relativism'. The tension between 'absolutists' and 'relativists' is common enough. We yearn for some kind of knowing in which absolute and concrete are held together.

There is a third tension in reason that makes it inherently vulnerable to skepticism. We experience a conflict between relying on ourselves as the final authority in cognition ('autonomy': self [Greek: *autos*] as law [Greek: *nomos*]) and relying on another, perhaps a tradition or an established 'authority-figure' ('heteronomy': other [Greek: *heteros*] as law [Greek: *nomos*]). The conflict is rooted in a polarity between what Tillich calls the 'structure' and the 'depth' of reason. The 'structure' of reason is that which makes it possible for us to grasp and shape reality. But grasping and shaping always involve making judgments about what is more (or less) true, good or beautiful than something else. In making such judgments we employ standards. Furthermore, Tillich holds (borrowing, he thinks, from Plato)[8] we must all, at least implicitly and unself-consciously, rely on the same ultimate standards or we should never be able to agree. The 'depth' of reason refers to the fact that we engage in rational transactions in the light of those standards even when we are unaware of doing so. The presence of these ultimate standards ('truth-itself'; 'beauty-itself; 'goodness-itself') to reason *is* the presence of the power of being ('being-itself') to the mind. Because we are unaware of its presence, however, we alternate between relying on something outside us (a tradition or a powerful personality) and relying on ourselves. Neither is adequate and we yearn for some kind of knowing in which the standards are not simply dependent on our own opinion and yet are not imposed on us as something alien to us. In short, the very possibility of there being reliable meaning to our lives seems to depend on a type of knowing which is at once formal and emotional, absolute and concrete, and in which the structure and depth of reason are united. Where do we ever know in that way?

That, says Tillich, is a question about 'revelation'. The answer to be correlated with it is the Christian symbol, Jesus as 'the Logos'.[9] It is a question about revelation because it is a question about disclosure of our ultimate concern: that which grounds meaning in life. The disclosure is a revelatory event with two sides. The 'receiving' side is a group of persons who are totally grasped by the event, emotions and intellect united in an integral wholeness. This is 'faith'.[10] Tillich also calls it 'ecstasy'. It is a state in which reason transcends itself in a self-conscious grasp of the depth of reason, the ground of meaning. The 'giving' side of a revelatory event Tillich calls 'miracle'. It is some particular concrete object, event or person that functions as a sign-event or religious symbol *through which* the ground of meaning in life makes itself present to persons. In the world's religions various sorts of things have filled the role of medium. For Jesus' disciples it was Jesus himself who was 'miracle' or symbol mediating the ground of meaning to the disciples who received it in their ecstasy. That was what Tillich calls an 'original' revelatory event. The disciples *expressed* the fact that it had occurred by using a variety of stories and verbal images for Jesus which are preserved in New Testament writings. Central to them is the image 'Jesus is the Logos'. 'Logos' (Greek: reason, word) expresses Jesus' function as concrete instantiation of the presence of the ground of meaning in life.

But just what is known in a revelatory event? Ontological analysis of finite reason has shown independently that the ground of meaning is *constantly* present to all human reason as its 'depth', just as the ground of being is constantly present to every life as its 'power of being'. Just as the ground of being is not simply one more item in the world which it 'grounds' so the ground of meaning is not one more object to be known. It transcends the structure of finite reason. It is inherently 'mystery'. It cannot cease to be mystery even in revelation. What then can be known of it through Jesus? Tillich stresses that while the ground of meaning may be present to reason constantly, in fact we are not aware of it apart from revelation. The concreteness of the medium (for Christians, the man Jesus) makes self-consciousness possible about the presence of the absolute or unconditioned ground of meaning. It is crucially important that the mystery whose presence is mediated not be confused with the finite medium itself. To confuse them is idolatry, treating something finite as though it were itself ultimate. We may rank the central symbols of various religions with respect to how clearly they make this distinction. Tillich holds that on such a scale Jesus is 'final revelation', the standard by which all others must be measured, because central to Jesus' functioning as mediator of the ground of meaning is his absolute transparency to the unconditioned. His total self-emptying, as expressed in the crucifixion, is a built-in reminder that he is not what is to be known, but only its medium. What is known of mystery through Jesus is, first, its reality and, second, in the midst of our unawareness, that we are indeed related to it. In short, the revelatory event in which the man Jesus is 'the Logos' is a 'knowing' that answers our skeptical question. It is awareness of the unity of the structure and depth of reason that overcomes the tension between autonomy and heteronomy. In its receiving side, or faith, the emotional and formal are united, overcoming their tension. In its giving side, or miracle, the concrete and absolute are united without being confused, thereby overcoming the tension between relativism and absolutism.

Existential Disruption

Part III of the system deals with the questions arising from our 'existential disruption'. Existence means 'standing out' of non-being. For Tillich the 'non-being' out of which each of us stands is our potentiality which, until it is realized, is simply a possibility. It is our essential nature. To exist is to be distanced, standing-out from, our essence. Hence for Tillich 'existence' and 'existential' have the sense of 'estranged from essence'.[11] Our existential situation is a state of estrangement from ourselves, others, and the power of being. Ontological analysis of our essential nature showed why we are inherently threatened by non-being. Description of our existential situation shows that the threat is actively being actualized. Estranged from the power of being, we are in fact unable to hold individualization and participation, dynamics and form, destiny and freedom in balance in our transactions with our world. As a result our transactions or relations with others break down and our 'world' becomes progressively chaotic. At the same time, our relations with ourselves are disrupted and we become progressively dis-integrated.

We experience all of this as deep guilt, loneliness, and meaninglessness. The Christian symbols for this situation are 'Fall' and 'Sin'. The story of the 'Fall' of Adam and Eve is not an account of an event long ago. Rather it expresses how the transition from essential nature to existential disruption is a result of our freedom and our destiny. On the one hand the transition is not a natural or rational development. It is an absurd discontinuity, an inexplicable leap which freedom makes possible. It is actualized by each individual person. 'Sin' is the religious symbol that expresses this personal responsibility for estrangement. On the other hand, each person does this as a participant in a society of persons who are already estranged. Fallenness is our destiny. Out of this rises the question, 'Where can we find power for new being?' The Christian symbol for this 'where' is 'Messiah' or 'Christ' (both mean: the anointed one). These symbols express the filling of a *function*: the one who functions to represent or manifest the power of being to finite human essential nature in the midst of its estrangement. The question about the power of new being is a question about the 'Christ'.

The answer to be correlated with this question is expressed by the Christian symbol 'Jesus the Christ as the power of New Being'. Here Tillich develops his christology.[12] Explanation of who Jesus is follows from explanation of what he did to 'save' us.[13] Furthermore, 'salvation' and 'revelation' name two aspects of the same reality.[14] 'Salvation' means 'healing'. Healing of existential estrangement comes by reconciliation with the power of being and, along with that reconciliation with others and oneself. That is precisely what happens in a revelatory situation. The power of meaning that is given through Jesus as Logos is, of course, none other than the power of being. Its reception in faith is a moment of insight in which one experiences one's unity with the depth of reason, that is, with the unconditioned mystery that is ground of being and meaning. As in the moment of therapeutic insight in psychoanalysis, in that insight one is healed of one's ontological disintegratedness. It is only a momentary event, fragmentary and ambiguous. It does not eliminate the situation of existential disruptions. What is mediated through Jesus is the power of New Being in the midst of continuing estrangement. The event of mediation always needs to be repeated. But for that moment of the event it is genuine: Participation in the power of New Being is 'new birth' or 'regeneration'. In one way this is our being accepted by the power of being ('God') despite or in the midst of our estrangement, or 'justification'; in another way this is our transformation by the power of being, or 'sanctification'. These are simply different aspects of reconciliation with 'God', or 'atonement' (that is, at-one-ment; reunion). As the ontological analysis showed, the presence of the power of being is inexplicable. It is gift or 'grace'. It is the presence of the power of New Being in the midst of our estrangement from it: God participates *in* our existential situation of disruption. The power of New Being is supremely present in Jesus precisely because Jesus' crucifixion concretely manifests the presence of this power in the midst of an event of the most profound estrangement of persons from one another and from God. Jesus' death is not substitutionary punishment of human sin in the name of divine justice but rather a manifestation of divine love. Divine removal of our guilt and punishment is not accomplished by overlooking their depth but by entering into them in love so deeply as to transform us.

Who Jesus is follows from what he did. What traditional christology expressed by talking about the human and the divine 'natures' of Jesus Christ needs, in Tillich's view, to be reformulated today in order to make basically the same points but in less misleading ways. To say that Jesus is 'human' is to say that the entire analysis of 'essential nature' applies to him too, including vulnerability to dis-integration and its underlying estrangement. To say that Jesus is 'divine' is to say that the power of being which is constantly present to all persons is mediated to others through him as the power of New Being in the midst of estrangement from essential nature. To say that they are one in Jesus is to say that this one life fully actualized without existential disruption (i.e., 'without sin') the eternal God-man-unity which characterizes our essential nature too (recall the ontological analysis' exhibition of the in-explicable but universal presence of the power of being to finite lives; recall the analysis of reason's unity of 'structure' and 'depth'). Faith thus has a large stake in the historical facticity of Jesus' life. Only if existential disruption is overcome in *one* point – a personal life, representing existence as a whole – is it conquered in principle, which means in 'beginning and in power'.[15] Our question about where we can find the power to heal our existential disruption is answered by pointing to the particular man Jesus who actualized essential human nature but without existential disruption and hence can mediate to us the power of New Being that heals or saves.

Actuality

The final two parts of the system deal with questions concerning our 'actuality'. 'Actuality' is Tillich's technical ontological concept for concrete life – 'life is the "actuality of being"'. 'Essence' designates one main qualification of being, taken in abstraction from any particular life in its concreteness. 'Existence' designates the other main qualification, also taken in abstraction. 'Actuality' refers to your life precisely *in* its concrete uniting of 'essence' and 'existence'.[16] This is a key point. 'Uniting' is a *process*, the process of actualizing potentiality or 'essential nature' (here Tillich borrows from Aristotle). It is the dynamic process-character of 'actuality' that makes it alive, *a* life. Beyond its organic and inorganic dimensions, human life has the dimension of 'spirit'. 'Spirit' denotes 'the unity of life-power and life in meanings'.[17] In addition to sheer vitality ('life-power'), human life involves capacities to regulate ourselves according to ideas, purposes and plans ('meanings') which we intensely love and freely choose for ourselves. The spiritual dimension of human actuality includes not only reason but also 'eros, passion, imagination'.[18]

With this brace of observations in place, Tillich can offer an ontological analysis of the process that constitutes life with a spiritual dimension. Such life has three functions. Your life process involves *self-integration*, a circular movement out from what you have been into new experience and back to integrate them into your centered self. You engage in self-integration in moral life, not that you are necessarily morally pure but rather that as self-integrating you are inescapably morally accountable both for integrating yourself as 'centered' and for your choice of norms and goals to guide your interactions with others. However, the moral life is thoroughly ambiguous. No matter how 'moral' an act may seem in some respects, we are aware that it cost the sacrifice of other acts through which we might have been more richly integrated, and that it involved some loss to some other person. Because our lives inherently drive toward self-integration we ask whether there is any way to achieve it through unambiguous morality.

Secondly, your life process involves *self-creation*, a horizontal movement through time as you constantly make yourself up and deeply change. You engage in self-creation in work that produces the meaningful artifacts, symbols and styles of both art and behaviour which comprise a culture and are significant because they express 'meanings' in which a human life 'participates'. However, we experience ambiguity in all elements of culture, from individual artifacts to the way a society is organized and led, finding them both nurturing new life and oppressing it. Because our lives inherently drive toward self-creation, we ask whether there is any way to achieve it through an unambiguous culture.

Finally, your life process involves *self-transcendence*, a vertical movement in which one is 'driving toward the sublime'.[19] You engage in self-transcendence in religious activity. This function intersects and units the other two. It is always moral and culturally creative lives that self-transcend. Hence, there is a religious dimension inherent in all moral and cultural acts. However, the ways in which the drive for self-transcendence expresses itself in ritual, myth and institutional structures are inherently ambiguous. They are all finite things functioning religiously to express the unconditioned, that toward which one 'transcends' oneself. At the same time, they invite for themselves the ultimate concern appropriate only to the unconditioned. Thereby they become 'demonic', powerfully destructive of the life trying to 'transcend' itself. Because our lives inherently drive toward self-transcendence, we ask whether there is any way to achieve it through unambiguous religion.

The answers to be correlated with the questions about unambiguous morality, culture, and religion are expressed in two Christian symbols. In Part IV Tillich correlates the symbol 'Spiritual presence' with the question of the ambiguity of every society synchronically. In Part V he correlates the symbol 'Kingdom of God' with the question of ambiguity diachronically in the entire history of morality, culture, and religion.[20]

'Spiritual Presence' is the Christian symbol expressive of the 'revelatory experience of "God present"'[21] in, precisely, spiritual (human) life. 'Spirit' (with upper-case S) is the most completely adequate symbol for the unconditioned, because it expresses that the unconditioned is *living*. 'God as creator' expresses the presence of the unconditioned power of being to us in regard to our essential finitude, and 'Jesus the Christ as the power of New Being' expresses its presence to us in our existential estrangement, but 'Spirit' expresses its presence to us precisely in our concrete reality as spiritual (lower-case s) lives actualizing our potentiality. In our self-transcendence we reach for this presence. But we cannot grasp it, unless we are first grasped by it. When it does grasp us, we are drawn into its 'transcendent unity of unambiguous life' and it creates unambiguous life in us.[22]

In this experience of 'the reunion of essential and existential being, ambiguous life is raised above itself to a transcendence that it could not achieve by its own power'.[23] Tillich stresses that such experiences are always social and fragmentary. To be sure, they have a subjective dimension which Tillich calls 'mystical'.[24] As the state of being *grasped by* the 'transcendent unity of an ambiguous life', it is called the state of 'faith'. As the state of being *taken into* that transcendent unity, it is called the state of 'love'. However, this always occurs in a communal setting, creating what Tillich calls a 'Spiritual Community'.[25] It is not identical with the Christian churches. The Spiritual Community is not one group beside others. It is 'a power and a structure inherent' in some groups, making them religious groups.[26] Spiritual community is real but immanent in many 'secular' communities outside the church and it is manifest sometimes in the churches.[27] Now, given the ontological analysis of life, this means that when spiritual community 'happens' the ambiguity of our religious enactments of self-transcending has been overcome. Because the ambiguity of self-integration and self-creation follows from the ambiguity of self-transcendence, this means that the experience symbolized by 'Spiritual Presence' is also a moment of unambiguous cultural self-creativity and unambiguous moral self-integration.[28] In those moments cultural and moral activity themselves become self-transcending, that is, religious. Here Tillich's theology of culture has its theological center and context. Tillich calls such moments 'theonomous'[29] – living social moments whose norm (*nomos*) comes, not from ourselves nor from an alien 'other', but from the 'transcendent unity of unambiguous life' (*theos*) which precisely in its transcendence is none the less immediately present to us. 'Spiritual Presence' express those moments when our questions about the possibility of unambiguous religion, culture, and morality are answered. Tillich insists that such moments in social life are fragmentary and paradoxical, but actually do occur in all societies. His favorite examples come from Medieval European culture.

'Kingdom of God' is the religious symbol expressive of Christian answers to the question about the possibility of unambiguous life in its historical rather than social dimensions: is there any meaning to history?[30] In Tillich's view groups, not individuals, are the bearers of history.[31] The three movements comprising any life comprise history also: history drives self-integratingly toward the centeredness of groups in a harmony of justice and power, self-creativity toward the creation of new and unambiguous states of affairs, and self-transcendingly toward unambiguous fulfillment of the potential of being.[32] 'Kingdom of God' expresses the occurrence of this in two ways: as something inner-historical and as something trans-historical.[33]

In one way, 'Kingdom of God' expresses that occurrence *in* the life of any one group which is the decisive and normative instance of 'Spiritual Presence' in the group's history. It is the event which serves the group as the 'center of history', the one particular point in history which is of universal significance for all groups at all times because it is the *most* adequate overcoming of the ambiguities of human life.[34] Tillich calls such a moment the *kairos* (Greek: 'fulfillment of time').[35] In such moments a group's experience of *un*ambiguous self-integration, self-creativity, and self-transcendence in a *kairos*, is its experience of the meaning, the point of history.

'Kingdom of God' also expresses a trans-historical actualization of unambiguous historical life. Here it correlates with the question 'is there anything of permanent value or meaning in the flow of history?'. The same question is often expressed personally as a question about immortality: 'will anything of me survive this life?'. Ontologically, this is a question about the relation of time to eternity.[36] 'Kingdom of God' expresses how the 'inner aim' of created time is the elevating of the finite into the eternal.[37] For the creature this means that 'nothing which has been created in history is lost, but it is liberated from the negative element with which it is entangled within existence'.[38] Following Schelling, Tillich calls this 'essentialization'.[39] It amounts to an unambiguous and permanent participation of finite life in the very life of Divine Spirit, for which the Christian symbol is 'Eternal Life'.[40] Tillich says that this is not a dateable temporal event but rather what is going on all the time.[41] On the other hand, viewed as it were from God's perspective, it is a cosmic process. Tillich calls that process 'eschatological pan-en-theism'. In it Divine Life realizes itself by a movement through self-alienation and engagement in creaturely existential disruption and then back to self-reconciliation, bringing the creaturely realm with it so that, fully reconciled, the creaturely realm is at the end, ('eschatologically') wholly 'within' the Divine Life (*pan* – 'everything' – *en theōs* – 'within God').[42]

CONTROVERSY AND CONSEQUENCES

Tillich's influence on theology has largely come through controversies his proposals generated. He has added a religious term to the English language: 'Ultimate concern' has become a common term in secular discourse to designate 'the religious dimension' as vaguely as possible. There has been considerable controversy whether the related term 'religious symbol', as Tillich understands it, has cognitive import.[43] However, subsequent thinkers have attempted to reformulate the notion to meet objections, and the controversy is no longer on Tillichian grounds.

The system's christology has been controversial. A major objection[44] has been that the structure of Tillich's argument makes the historical facticity of Jesus largely irrelevant to theological claims about his significance. However, the focus of christological debates has shifted and Tillich's proposals do not seem to have influence on current christological discussions.

Tillich's doctrine of God has been more influential. It has been the focal point of controversies about whether Christian understanding of God must be biblically 'personal'. Tillich's description of God emphatically is not personal. A strong case for the opposing view requires that the notion of God 'acting' in history can be shown to be intelligible. Efforts to show that it is intelligible have been highly controversial. Theologians like Gilkey[45] and Ogden[46], who believe it to be an impossible case to make, tend to turn to Tillich as a guide toward formulating an alternative doctrine of God. Zahrnt represents an early and popularized version of a similar view in German theology.

Even more influential has been the related doctrine of grace in which 'sin' and 'redemption' are explicated dynamically in terms of 'estrangement' and 'reconciliation'. That suggested the possibility of integrating theology with dynamic psychology. Especially in the United States, this side of Tillich's theology has deeply stamped theological reflection on pastoral care, with its yearning to combine the Christian message and the techniques of secular counseling. Controversy turns on the question whether Tillich's doctrine of redemption truly yields a correlation of theology and psychology or only offers a pious language in which to make entirely naturalistic psychological remarks.

Perhaps the most important controversy Tillich's theology has generated, and its most widespread influence in systematic theology, has had to do not with its content but with its 'method of correlation'. Tillich's intent was to mediate between the faith and the culture.[47] Controversy turned on whether such 'correlation' does not finally result in translating the content of Christian faith without remainder into the deepest convictions of the secular culture it attempts to address. Karl Barth, Tillich's polar opposite in this debate, insisted that revelation did not answer questions, it posed them. Indeed, he insisted, the question/answer scheme is inherently misleading. Revelation brings unheard of news which totally changes the way everything looks, so that what had looked like important questions now appear trivial or deceptive. However, many theologians are persuaded that Tillich was right to think Barth's route led to the isolation of Christian thought from the intellectual and cultural life of our time. Hence several current theological proposals employ some variant of Tillich's method either explicitly, as in David Tracy and Gilkey, or implicitly, as in Pannenberg.[48]

NOTES

1 Wilhelm and Marion Pauck, *Paul Tillich, His Life and Thought*, vol. I, Life, p. 41.
2 Paul Tillich, *Systematic Theology*, I, pp. 59–66.
3 Ibid., pp. 1–6, 66–8.

4 Ibid., pp. 163–8.
5 Ibid., pp. 168–86.
6 Ibid., pp. 211–89.
7 Ibid., pp. 71–100.
8 Cf. Paul Tillich, *Theology of Culture*, pp. 10–30.
9 Tillich, *Systematic Theology*, I, pp. 106–59.
10 Cf. Paul Tillich, *Dynamics of Faith*.
11 Tillich, *Systematic Theology*, II, pp. 19–96.
12 Ibid., pp. 97–180.
13 Ibid., II, p. 150.
14 Ibid., p. 166; I, pp. 144–6.
15 Ibid., II, p. 98; cf. p. 114.
16 Ibid., III, pp. 11–12; II, p. 28.
17 Ibid., III, p. 22.
18 Ibid., p. 24.
19 Ibid., p. 31.
20 Ibid., pp. 107–10.
21 Ibid., p. 111.
22 Ibid., p. 112.
23 Ibid., p. 129.
24 Ibid., p. 242.
25 Ibid., pp. 149ff.
26 Ibid., p. 162.
27 Ibid., pp. 152ff.
28 Ibid., p. 157.
29 Ibid., p. 266.
30 Ibid., p. 349.
31 Ibid., p. 312.
32 Ibid., p. 332.
33 Ibid., p. 357.
34 Ibid., p. 367.
35 Ibid., p. 369.
36 Ibid., p. 397.
37 Ibid., p. 399.
38 Ibid., p. 397.
39 Ibid., p. 400.
40 Ibid., p. 401.
41 Ibid., pp. 399–400.
42 Ibid., pp. 421–2.
43 Cf. Sidney Hook (ed.), *Religious Experience and Truth*.
44 Cf. John P. Clayton in *Christ, Faith and History*, ed. John P. Clayton and Robert Morgan; and David Kelsey, *The Fabric of Paul Tillich's Theology*.
45 Langdon Gilkey, *Naming the Whirlwind* and *Reaping the Whirlwind*.
46 Schubert Ogden, *The Point of Christology*.
47 Cf. John P. Clayton, *The Concept of Correlation*, for the best discussion.
48 For Tracy arnd Gilkey see *The Modern Theologians*, volume II, chapter 4; for Pannenberg see chapter 13 below.

BIBLIOGRAPHY

Primary

Tillich, Paul, *The Shaking of the Foundations* (New York, 1948).
—, *The Protestant Era* (Chicago, 1948).
—, *Systematic Theology*, vols. I–III (Chicago, 1951, 1957, 1963).
—, *Love, Power, and Justice* (New York, 1954).
—, *The New Being* (New York, 1955).
—, *Eternal Now* (New York, 1956).
—, *Dynamics of Faith* (New York, 1957).
—, *Theology of Culture* (New York, 1959).

Secondary

Clayton, John P., *The Concept of Correlation* (Berlin, 1980).
Clayton, John P. and Morgan, Robert, *Christ, Faith and History* (Cambridge, 1972).
Gilkey, Langdon, *Naming the Whirlwind* (Indianapolis, 1969).
—, *Reaping the Whirlwind* (New York, 1976).
Hook, Sidney (Ed.), *Religious Experience and Truth* (New York, 1961).
Kelsey, David, *The Fabric of Paul Tillich's Theology* (New Haven, Conn., 1967).
Ogden, Schubert, *The Point of Christology* (New York, 1982).
Pauck, Wilhelm and Marion, *Paul Tillich, His Life and Thought*, vol. I (New York, 1976).
Tillich, Paul, *Biblical Religion and the Search for Ultimate Reality* (Chicago, 1956).

7

Edward Schillebeeckx

Robert J. Schreiter CPPS

INTRODUCTION

The Flemish Dominican Edward Schillebeeckx may certainly be described as a genuinely twentieth-century theologian. He was born at the time of the outbreak of the First World War, and his career and thought have been shaped by events and movements typical of the twentieth century. Moreover, his continuing preoccupation as a theologian has been the expression of the gospel and Christian tradition in categories intelligible to twentieth-century Western Christians. His first published articles in 1945 dealt with the challenge of humanism to belief in post-war France, and his concern in the latter 1980s has been for defining how people experience the salvation coming from God in Jesus Christ in their personal lives and in their societies.

Schillebeeckx was born on November 12, 1914, the sixth of fourteen children, to a middle class accountant and his wife in Antwerp. The family had been evacuated to Antwerp from their home in Kortenberg before the advancing German army. After the war, they returned there. Schillebeeckx received his secondary education at a Jesuit boarding school in Turnhout. Upon leaving school, he entered the Dominican Order at Ghent in 1934. His philosophical and theological training for ordination took place at the Dominican house of studies in Louvain, where he came under the influence of Dominicus De Petter, a philosopher who combined the Neo-Thomism of the day with an interest in contemporary phenomenology. Schillebeeckx was mobilized briefly at the beginning of the war, but then returned to Louvain and was ordained a priest in 1941. His superiors appointed him to teach dogmatic theology to the seminarians, since the outbreak of the Second World War made the continuing of his theological education impossible.

After the war he was sent to Paris to study at the Dominican faculty Le Saulchoir, working especially with Yves Congar and M.-D. Chenu. He also attended lectures at other major institutions in Paris, and met Camus and Merleau-Ponty. In Paris, he was schooled in the *nouvelle théologie* with its emphasis on historical research as a counterbalance to the deductive and propositional approach to theology still prevalent in the Scholasticism of the time. The discussions about existentialism and personalism also influenced him profoundly.

He returned to Louvain in 1947, and completed his dissertation, a patristic and medieval study of the sacraments as a basis for a renewed understanding of them, in 1951. It is now seen as a major study in that area, but its publication only in Dutch limited its circulation.

In 1957 Schillebeeckx was called to the chair of dogma and the history of theology at the University of Nijmegen in the Netherlands, a position he was to hold until his retirement in 1983. He quickly came into prominence as an advisor to the Dutch bishops, and accompanied them as their advisor to the Second Vatican Council. He was denied the status of *peritus* to the Council by the Roman Curia (the Dutch were already suspect at that time), but exercized influence through the theological lectures he gave outside the sessions to the bishops. Through this he gained international attention. Schillebeeckx has been closely identified with the reform movement inaugurated by the Second Vatican Council since that time. In 1965 he launched, along with others, the journal *Concilium* as a forum for continuing the dialogue which had been begun at the Council.

His first trip to the United States came immediately after the Council, and this experience coincided with a decided change in the style of his theology. Heretofore he had been concerned especially with the sacraments; now he moved into larger issues of Church and world. To deal with these more adequately, he schooled himself extensively in Heideggerian hermeneutics, Anglo-American philosophy of language, and the social critical theory of the Frankfurt School.

Schillebeeckx's career has been marked by honors as well as challenge to his thought. He has received honorary doctorates from universities in the United States and Europe, and is the only theologian ever to have won the Erasmus Prize for promoting European culture. He also won the quinquennial prize of the Flemish Council of Culture in 1979. He has come into conflict with the officials of his Church: in 1968, 1976, and 1981, the Vatican

Congregation of the Doctrine of the Faith raised questions about his orthodoxy. All three occasioned protracted exchanges, but none has resulted in a condemnation of any part of his theology.

SURVEY

An abiding interest of Schillebeeckx throughout his career has been how the Church relates to the world. He had originally hoped to write his doctoral dissertation in this area, but more pragmatic considerations led to a work on the sacraments. In the first part of his career, from the time of the completion of the dissertation until the end of the Vatican Council, the 'Church' part of the equation received primary attention. Central to this was the appearance in 1957 of his *Christ the Sacrament of the Encounter with God* (translated into English in 1963). In this work, Schillebeeckx developed a more personalist and existentialist approach to the sacraments, seeing them as a personal encounter with Christ, the primordial sacrament of God. His intent was to move away from the more mechanistic models for approaching sacraments and grace which had dominated Scholastic theology. Following that book, he prepared a long study on marriage, published as *Marriage: Human Reality and Saving Mystery* in 1963. Later, too, was to come a study on the eucharist (*The Eucharist*, 1967). His theological essays from this period reflect a common tone and style; namely, questions are discussed within the framework of the renewed Thomist theology of the time, but those discussions are enriched with insights flowing from contemporary philosophy, especially phenomenology and existentialism.

The experience of a wider world during and after the Council led to a change both in style and in content in Schillebeeckx's writings. His work from that period onward relied little on Scholastic vocabulary and showed a greater influence of contemporary philosophy. One of the things that has made Schillebeeckx's thought difficult for some readers has been the wide range of philosophical traditions he draws upon to frame his theology. Prior to 1965, one had to understand something of Thomism, phenomenology, French existentialism, and personalism to follow his thought. All these influences were still present after 1965, albeit in a minor key, but were joined by the hermeneutical work of Hans Georg Gadamer, the research into philosophy of language by Ian Ramsey and Ludwig Wittgenstein, and the social critical theory of Max Horkheimer and Jürgen Habermas – to name but the major figures. No twentieth-century theologian (except perhaps for Wolfhart Pannenberg) ranges so widely over the philosophical territory.

Schillebeeckx studied these additional figures most intensively in the years 1965–70 (essays of his researches have been collected in *The Understanding of Faith*, 1972; ET 1974). This combination of resources continues to shape the philosophical underpinnings of his theology. The thorough philosophical training Schillebeeckx had received at the hands of De Petter has given his theology a decided epistemological cast. A number of years ago, Schillebeeckx recalled that he had originally hoped to become a philosopher rather than a theologian, but had acquiesced to the wishes of his superiors in the Order. The concern for philosophical questions remains very much in evidence in his work.

The other element from his background which has shaped his theology throughout his career is the *ressourcement* advocated by the *nouvelle théologie*. His work on marriage in the 1960s, and his work in christology and ministry in the 1970s and 1980s, all bear this clear commitment to exploration of the historical resources for developing a contemporary theology. This has been most widely noted in the two volumes of the projected trilogy in christology to have appeared, *Jesus* (1974; ET 1979) and *Christ* (1977; ET 1980). In these works, he attempts (and largely succeeds) in presenting an exhaustive account of New Testament research into Jesus and the early Christian movement. And in the book on ministry (*Ministry*, 1979; reissued in expanded and revised form as *The Church with a Human Face*, 1985) he explored the first 1,500 years of history of priesthood in considerable detail.

Schillebeeckx has come to even wider attention through these last two projects, dealing with christology and ministry. In the yet unfinished christology project he hopes to lead contemporary men and women to faith in Christ by allowing them to follow the same path to faith and confession of Christ as did the earliest disciples. He does this through an extensive reconstruction of the life of Jesus and the developments in the Jesus movement up to the redaction of the books of the New Testament. The Jesus who emerges is the eschatological prophet announcing the imminent inbreaking of the Kingdom of God. He is a figure deeply rooted in an experience of God as *abba*. Already in *Jesus*, but increasingly so in subsequent writings, Schillebeeckx has emphasized the Jewishness and Jewish context of Jesus. Jesus' message was the 'praxis of the Kingdom of God', i.e., both Jesus' words and his actions point to what the Kingdom of God will be like.

The second volume, *Christ*, moves especially to a soteriological focus in the christology, exploring how salvation is experienced by those who follow Christ. After an introductory reflection on experience and how it relates to revelation, Schillebeeckx explores New Testament understandings of grace. Toward the end of the volume he turns especially to the social dimensions of salvation in the world, and develops outlines of a social ethics.

The Jesus who emerges from the first two volumes can be summed up in a favorite formulation of Schillebeeckx, Jesus as 'the parable of God and the paradigm of humanity'. Who Jesus is and who God is cannot be captured in propositions. One must tell the story of Jesus and live out that story in one's own life, following the praxis of Jesus, to come to know the God to whom Jesus witnesses. Jesus' life, as a parable of God, becomes for us the clearest revelation of the reality of God. Likewise, Jesus' praxis becomes paradigmatic for the achievement of our own humanity. Schillebeeckx is much pre-occupied with the suffering taking place in the world. Humanity is a state toward which we aim. The struggle for the *humanum* (the term is Horkheimer's) means that we anticipate our fullness; we do not now participate in it. This insight was first developed in Schillebeeckx's reflections on eschatology in the late 1960s, and has remained part of his thought to this day.

The work on ministry grows out of a pastoral concern created by the shortage of priests, a shortage which is depriving communities of the Eucharist. Schillebeeckx's basic argument is that Christian communities have a right to the Eucharist, and if present ordination requirements deprive believers of realizing that right, then that right has priority over the requirements. This has been widely misinterpreted (including in Rome) as Schillebeeckx's advocating eucharistic presidency by the non-ordained. His point has been that eligibility for ordination to priesthood should be expanded, and that emergency situations may have to be dealt with in the interim (as was the case at earlier moments in history). He supports his case with an extensive historical study, showing that there was a significant strand in the first millennium of Christianity that placed the needs of the community before the exigencies of church order. He pleads for a reconsideration of this part of the tradition as a way out of the current priest shortage impasse.

Schillebeeckx has published no compendium of his thought, but a helpful summary of his most recent interests may be found in the little book, *On Christian Faith* (1986; ET 1987).

CONTENT

The thought of a theologian who has been active for forty years with more than 400 works published in fourteen languages is not described easily. It was noted above that the relation of the church to the world has been a continuing preoccupation of Schillebeeckx. Yet he has not written a major work on ecclesiology nor a treatise of any length on the Christian understanding of the world. Rather, the church–world problematic has been the arena in which many themes have been played out: how the sacramental life of the church relates to the broader situation, the meaning of salvation in a secularized society, the role of eschatology in understanding human history, and how Christians should conduct themselves in light of the gospel.

It is possible, though, to delineate three insights which weave through the fabric of his thought and give it a coherence through the many themes Schillebeeckx has treated in the course of his career. These insights have to do with the role of experience in belief, the place of suffering in history, and the unbounded love of God.

For Schillebeeckx, human experience is not to be contrasted with divine revelation; it is the vehicle through which such revelation is communicated. Experience is understood here as wider than rationality or even language. It encompasses the full range of human perceptions and activities, and embraces also events. All revelation is mediated to us through the channels of our experience. This does not reduce revelation to another category of our experience, however. Schillebeeckx is at pains to point out that revelation offers its critique of our experience and ends up standing in a dialectical relationship to it. But by putting the discussion of revelation within the context of human experience, Schillebeeckx is able to open up the understanding of revelation as being more than words or propositions. It also allows him to lay the groundwork for showing how events can be revelatory. All of these revelatory experiences come to be mediated by language but are never exhausted by language and concepts.

The root of this insight can be found in Schillebeeckx's early work with De Petter. Like other Thomists of the time, De Petter struggled with how to link reality and concepts in light of Kant's *Critique*. De Petter's response came by way of the influence of phenomenology: we make the link between reality and language by an intuition based on an act of faith. By stressing intuition, De Petter moved beyond the rationalist impasse which dogged so much of the

Neo-Thomism of that time, but he did so without falling into the voluntarist abyss. Intuition seemed a category that could respect and include the complexity of the perceptual and cognitive processes yet transcend the mind–will dichotomy.

How does this work itself out in Schillebeeckx's own thought? First of all, it is evident in his deep reverence for the nature of experience and especially that which is experienced. From early in his writings, Schillebeeckx has emphasized how experience ultimately cannot be captured in concepts and rationality however much concepts and rationality are key to understanding experience. A favorite word of his for describing that before which humans stand is 'mystery'. Mystery is used in a double sense of the unknown and also of the Greek *mysterion*, a path to knowledge that transforms the subject who undertakes it.

This reverence is fundamental for his understanding of God, and the language he employs about the encounter with Christ in the sacraments. It also appears in his eschatology with its emphasis on God's proviso, i.e., that God is still the ultimate transformer in the face of all human efforts to bring about justice and a more humane society. It is especially evident in the perspectival approach that runs through his theology: every perspective contributes to our understanding, but no human perspective can claim absoluteness. Because of that he has been drawn to employ a wide variety of different philosophical frameworks to interpret Christian history and experience. It has also led him to relativize the place of the church in the world when seen in light of the Kingdom of God. This profound sense of the perspectival character of knowledge was a major sticking point in his conflict with the Roman Curia over his christology: they misunderstood his denial of any absolute language as a denial of Nicaea and Chalcedon.

Another major consequence of placing experience so centrally in his thought is a commitment to the concreteness of history. 'Concrete' is one of Schillebeeckx's most used adjectives. It was concrete experiences in his environment which led to the little books on eucharist, clerical celibacy, and ministry: people's experiences seemed to be contradicting church teaching and discipline. it has led, too, to his formulation of 'orthopraxis' as a key concept: rightness of belief must be expressed in a dialectic of theory and action and not just in theory alone.

To commit oneself to the concreteness of history means that one must come face to face with human suffering, sin and injustice. And this leads to the second fundamental insight in Schillebeeckx's thought. Beginning in the late 1960s, the theme of human suffering emerged as a major motif in his thought. Schillebeeckx speaks of what he calls 'contrast experiences', the experience of events falling short of the ideal of human life, the *humanum*. These contrast experiences are the most revelatory of human experiences in that suffering questions all our assumptions about how the world should be. They provide the basis for developing a critical view of the world that does not succumb to one or other ideology, nor to a naively optimistic view of reality that might be deduced from his respect for human experience. That critical view is called by Schillebeeckx at one point a 'critical negativity', emphasizing the need to question any promise of fulfillment ideologies might bring.

Because of their revelatory power, the contrast experiences of those who suffer provide a privileged view of the world. The results of that view become the engine for the struggle for justice and a fuller revelation of the *humanum* in the world. This struggle is joined by all who share these sentiments; it is how Schillebeeckx explains the ability of differing ideologies to work together for the common good of humanity. The *humanum* has not yet been realized; it will be revealed in the coming of the Kingdom of God when that paradigm of humanity, Jesus Christ, is once again among us.

The contrast experience is expressed most acutely in the life and death of Jesus. Jesus went about doing good, yet came to an untimely and violent end. Thus for a Christian to turn to the contrast experience as the basis for critical thought and critical action has its roots in the contrast experience of Jesus.

Reflection on human suffering has led to a greater concentration in Schillebeeckx's later work on the meaning of salvation. He wishes to explore more closely what impact the presence of God has on the suffering world. This leads to the third fundamental insight moving through Schillebeeckx's work.

Throughout his theology, Schillebeeckx emphasizes the primacy of God in all things. Even as his theology has become more anthropological (but not reduced to an anthropology) he has stressed at the same time the importance of maintaining the mystery of God and the sovereignty of God's activity in human history. God is not a human projection. But that sovereign God is also a loving God, a 'God mindful of humanity', a phrase that appears often in *Christ* and in later works. This is the God of unbounded love, who has made humanity's cause a divine cause. God wishes the 'well-being of humanity', to use another of Schillebeeckx's favorite phrases. Schillebeeckx never tires in his later works of emphasizing how close God is to humanity's struggles and sufferings. Jesus, of course, in his ministry and death, is a parable of that closeness. God is present to us in a 'mediated immediacy', i.e., mediated through human history and through creation in such a way as to be made immediate or directly present. This says something about God and about God's creation. God uses the medium of creation and history to be more present to humanity rather than employing it as a barrier to that presence. This implies that creation is an adequate, though not comprehensive, vehicle for divinity. It is this conviction which not only has permitted Schillebeeckx to take human experience seriously, but it also allows a closer connection between communion with God and action for the world, areas Schillebeeckx designates as the mystical and the political. Christians are called to a 'political holiness' that does not separate the inner life of prayer from the worldly liturgy of betterment of humanity's cause.

The three insights, then, depend on one another: experience is grounded in a God who wishes to communicate, the contrast experiences draw us closer to that God, and the experience of God 'mindful of humanity' affirms that act of intuition and faith by making a mediation of the paradoxical experience of the immediate. In doing this, Schillebeeckx achieves a great deal in his hope to make the Christian message of God and the experience of salvation offered in Jesus Christ more available to a secularized society.

DEBATE

A theologian who has written as widely and as creatively as Schillebeeckx is bound to find himself in controverted areas. His position on experience and its role in theology has been perhaps the most controversial of his positions, although it has usually met questioning on one or other specific point rather than on the entire project. Protestants often hear nineteenth-century liberalism when Schillebeeckx begins to speak of experience. That movement (especially as represented in the Erlangen School) ended up succumbing to the culture and diluting the gospel message by their uncritical acceptance of contemporary experience as the frame of reference for theological discourse. Schillebeeckx is well aware of this tradition and would emphasize the critical edge in his theory of experience, represented especially in his understanding of critical negativity.

From the Roman Catholic side, the emphasis on experience seems to undermine authority and some doctrinal formulations. The Vatican Congregation's objections to Schillebeeckx's christology centered on this concern: must not certain things be maintained dogmatically rather than subjected to the test of experience? His attempt to understand the resurrection faith of the first disciples by proposing how their experience of the Lord was shaped has seemed to some to reduce the event of the resurrrection to one interpretation among many. And Schillebeeckx's accentuation of the pneumatological tradition in the development of church ministry seemed to undermine the dominant christological tradition that sees the priest as the *alter Christus* ruling the community.

Schillebeeckx has responded to challenges of this type by noting the importance of linguistic analysis of formulations, and by reminding his opponents of what it means to take history seriously. One cannot profess to being historical in orientation if history must give way to dogmatic statement whenever the situation becomes slightly problematical. This was most evident in the conflict over his book on ministry. There some opponents insisted upon a dogmatic formulation about the origins of ministry – that Christ intended a certain form of ministry for the community and instituted it in that fashion – as the point of departure for reading the historical data, when exegetes have long questioned such a formulation as historical.

But all of this does raise an important issue: what is indeed the relation between history and dogma? History is always informed by theory and interpretive frameworks, and so does not in itself occupy a higher ground than dogma. Schillebeeckx has not answered this thorny question to the satisfaction of his opponents.

In another area of debate, theologians have objected that his *Jesus* and *Christ* are not a christology – they do not deal adequately with the classical questions in this area. Exegetes, on the other hand, have generally applauded his use of their research into the New Testatment as an instance of a theologian actually paying attention to what is happening in the exegetical field. The latter do object to some of his interpretations (notably on his use of the Q source, his understanding of the *abba* experience, and aspects of his treatment of the resurrection), but on the whole have been more supportive of his project than many of his colleagues. Schillebeeckx has responded that his critics are reproving him for a book he has not yet written. *Jesus* and *Christ* are intended as prolegomena to a christology, not the christology itself. What Schillebeeckx has written may appear to call into question how christology as an area in theology is to be organized, but without the full project in hand it is difficult to assess to what extent those fears are warranted.

One other area where his project has met criticism is in his use of the concept of praxis. He does not seem to be always consistent here, at times equating praxis only with action rather than the theory–

action dialectic. Nor has he worked out in a level of detail satisfactory to some of his critics what he actually means by praxis and by orthopraxis.

On the whole, however, Schillebeeckx's work has been received with great seriousness. The historical depth of his work is widely appreciated, and his attempts to articulate Christian faith in frameworks intelligible to contemporary men and women have gained him a wide readership among theologians and Christians in general.

ACHIEVEMENT AND AGENDA

It is dangerous to assess the achievement of a theologian still alive and quite active. But certain features of the theology of Edward Schillebeeckx suggest aspects of enduring achievement whatever may still come from his pen. He has proposed, particularly in his work since the 1960s, a kind of modern apologia for Christian faith. This apologia is not of a polemical variety that tries to demonstrate the validity of the Christian faith in the face of an indifferent or hostile secularism. Nor does it address itself primarily to the nonbeliever in the hopes of bringing about a conversion. This apologetic is aimed at those who struggle to believe, who strive to be faithful to the gospel and its Lord in a world that cannot immediately make sense of the Christian message in its traditional formulation. That has been the clear intent behind the monumental christology project. As he said in his defense of that project before the Vatican Congregation, he saw his christology not so much as providing the crisp answers believers are supposed to have as a *vade mecum* in their own journey toward their confession of Christ. There is an intent on Schillebeeckx's part, therefore, to walk with the struggling believer. This accounts in some measure for the style of his writing, which often looks as though it was a transcription from an oral medium where he is trying to explain – often passionately – his point of view. The long, sometimes meandering sentences are attempts to gather in the many perspectives that are needed to see a complex picture fully.

As a theologian, Schillebeeckx has made a significant contribution in showing how he and his colleagues should utilize the results of biblical exegesis. This is an area still not explored as it might be by theologians, who often continue to adhere to biblical positions long since abandoned by their exegetical colleagues.

As a theologian, too, Schillebeeckx's use of a wide range of philosophical hermeneutical systems is a contribution to the field. He has been a leader in emphasizing the importance of epistemological and interpretive categories in Roman Catholic theology. He still intends to prepare a systematic treatise of this area upon completion of the christology project.

And for the general believer, especially the Roman Catholic, his achievement has been to allow them to take their own experience of faith more seriously. This was especially evident in the outpouring of sentiment at the time of his difficulties with Rome in the late 1970s. A recurring motif in the correspondence he received was that people appreciated how he had liberated them to think more for themselves and not to dismiss their own experience of God outright when it seemed to be contradicting official formulations. To the extent that this is the case, Schillebeeckx is achieving his project of bringing church and world into closer conversation with each other.

BIBLIOGRAPHY

Primary

Schillebeeckx, E., *Christ the Sacrament of the Encounter with God* (London and New York, 1963).
—, *God the Future of Man* (London and New York, 1968).
—, *The Understanding of Faith* (London and New York, 1974).
—, *Jesus: An Experiment in Christology* (London and New York, 1979).
—, *Christ: The Experience of Jesus as Lord* (London and New York, 1980).
—, *Ministry: Leadership in the Community of Jesus Christ* (subtitled in the UK *A Case for Change*) (London and New York, 1981).
—, *The Church with a Human Face: A New and Expanded Theology of Ministry* (London and New York, 1986).
—, *The Schillebeeckx Reader*, ed. Robert J. Schreiter (New York, 1984, and Edinburgh, 1988). Contains a complete bibliography of Edward Schillebeeckx to 1983.

Secondary

Bowden, John, *Edward Schillebeeckx: Portrait of a Theologian* (London and New York, 1983).
Schreiter, Robert and Hilkert, Mary Catherine (eds), *The Praxis of Christian Experience: An Orientation to Edward Schillebeeckx* (San Francisco, 1989).

8

Hans Küng

Werner G. Jeanrond

INTRODUCTION: LIFE

Hans Küng is a unique phenomenon in twentieth-century theology: no other theologian has been published, translated and read so widely in this century; no other theologian has been the focus of such a major controversy; no other contemporary theologian has covered such a broad spectrum of theological themes. Virtually all important theological topics discussed in our time have been addressed by Küng at some stage in his career. His bibliography includes major works on God, Jesus Christ, the church, eternal life, theological method, the world religions, and the contribution of the arts to religion. Yet it was Küng's challenge of post Vatican II ecclesiology and church management which brought him into lasting conflict with the authorities of his Roman Catholic Church. One effect of this controversy has been that Küng's contribution to modern theology has sometimes been perceived to be of a mainly ecclesiological nature and that his other achievements in systematic theology have not been adequately appreciated. Moreover, the conflict between the Roman Catholic priest Küng and some of the members of the Roman Catholic episcopate has occasionally concealed Küng's important contribution to his own Church before, during and after the Second Vatican Council.

This survey of Küng's theological development will therefore emphasize particularly those areas which are often treated too sparingly. However, it will not be possible to discuss all aspects of Küng's rich contribution to contemporary theology; instead I shall concentrate on his major works.

Hans Küng was born in 1928 in Sursee, Switzerland. His studies at the Pontifical Gregorian University in Rome (1948–55) brought him not only into intellectual contact with important philosophers and theologians, but also into personal contact with some of the leading theological and ecclesiastical figures of the time, such as Joseph Lortz, Hans Urs von Balthasar, Yves Congar and Augustinus Bea. After his ordination to the priesthood in Rome, Küng studied in Paris where he earned his theological doctorate in 1957 with his now famous thesis on Karl Barth's doctrine of justification. This work and its ecumenical spirit made Küng known very quickly. His active participation in the preparation for and his presence at the Second Vatican Council (1962–5) as an officially appointed *peritus* brought Küng to the center of the conflict between reformers and traditionalists in the Roman Catholic Church and directed his theological attention to questions of ecclesiology. Already at the young age of thirty-two, Küng was appointed to the chair of fundamental theology at the Roman Catholic Faculty of Theology at the University of Tübingen.

Since the 1970s, Küng's theological work has concentrated on the major articles of Christian faith without, however, neglecting the theme of ecclesiology. His public image has been influenced to a large extent by the discussion of his book *Infallible: An Enquiry* (1970).[1] It has also been mainly this book and Küng's refusal to revoke the challenge of Roman Catholic Church authority expressed in this book which after nine years of controversy led to the withdrawal of Küng's *missio canonica* (the Roman Catholic teaching permission which every Roman Catholic teacher of religion needs in Germany) by Pope John-Paul II and to his subsequent move out of his faculty and into the now independent Institute for Ecumenical Research at the University of Tübingen. Thus, Küng continues to teach theology in the university, but he is no longer considered an officially authenticated representative of Roman Catholic theology by the Vatican authorities.

SURVEY OF KÜNG'S THEOLOGICAL DEVELOPMENT

Küng's theological development to date may be roughly divided into three periods: (i) his concentration on ecclesiological questions until 1970; (ii) his treatment of major articles of Christian faith (God, Jesus Christ and eternal life) during the 1970s; and (iii) his reflection on theological method and the dialogue between Christianity and other world religions and between religion and culture since 1983. However, all of these periods are inspired by a strong commitment both to dialogue with all current religious, political, and cultural forces in the world in general and to Christian ecumenism in particular. Küng's commitment to Christian and then even global ecumenism must not be confused with a new kind of essentialism according to which all Christian traditions or even religious traditions are essentially the same. Rather, Küng wishes to bring Christians of all backgrounds and the different religious traditions of humankind into a mutually critical conversation.

Already in his first book, *Justification: The Doctrine of Karl Barth and a Catholic Reflection* (1957), Küng investigated the foundations for such an inner-Christian conversation. He examined the common ground of Protestant and Roman Catholic doctrine on this central aspect of Christian faith which has divided both traditions for centuries. But he remained critical of Barth's 'dangerous inclinations', such as his denigration of the ontic-creaturely aspect and his overemphasis of human sinfulness, and the resulting anti-Catholic polemics. Küng's study concluded that on the whole there exists a fundamental theological conformity between what Barth and the Roman Catholic Church teach on justification. This insight shaped Küng's further questioning of how all Christian churches will have to change in order to promote the process of Christian unity and of what especially the Roman Catholic Church ought to be doing in order to respond more adequately to the gospel in a new ecumenical age.

In the 1960s, the Vatican Council inspired all leading Roman Catholic theologians to reflect very thoroughly on the nature and structure of the Christian church. Thus, it need not surprise us that fifteen out of Küng's first twenty books deal with ecclesiological questions, among these publications most prominently *Structures of the Church* (1962), *The Church* (1967), and *Infallible?* (1970). *Structures of the Church* was written in response to Pope John XXIII's call for a renewed theological concentration on this topic with reference to the Council; *The Church* offered a systematic study of the nature of the Christian church on the basis of modern biblical exegetical knowledge; and *Infallible?* represented a first critical study of the Roman Catholic Church in view of the increasing disenchantment among Catholics with the slow process of structural renewal in their church after the Council.

Perhaps Küng's aproach to ecclesiology may be best characterized by his insistence on the need for a critical biblical foundation of all ecclesiology and the resulting insight into the essential difference between the church and the Kingdom of God. The church's mission is to serve the gospel of Jesus Christ, to respond to God's call in Jesus Christ, but not to produce God's reign. Moreover, God's reign is proclaimed to sinners as good news. Thus, the church, itself a community of sinners, is called to preach the good news to the world, but not to rule the world.[2] Like the reformers in the sixteenth century, Küng retrieved the biblical image of the priesthood of all believers. Christ's community no longer needs a mediation between the people of God and God, it no longer requires a priestly sacrifice of expiation. *All* Christians are called to proclaim God's word. Accordingly, Küng demands that any consideration of offices in the church must be spirited by this New Testament heritage. This heritage rules out the establishment of a clergy–laity divide in the Christian movement. Therefore, Küng criticizes the formalism which has emerged in the post-biblical church, and he calls for a redefinition of ministry in the church as a service of love. This is not to rule out the special services of priests and bishops, rather it is to describe the proper theological basis of such a service.

The question of authority in the church was to receive yet further prominence in Küng's theological work when Pope Paul VI issued his encyclical *Humanae Vitae* in 1968 against all forms of artificial birth control. Together with a great many Christians within and beyond the Roman Catholic Church, Küng protested against this encyclical. But he went further and criticized the entire Roman Church system which he saw 'still characterized by a spiritual absolutism, a formal and often inhuman juridicism and a traditionalism fatal to genuine renewal that are truly shocking to modern man'.[3] On the basis of his ecclesiological principles, Küng questioned the infallibility of both the Pope and the Roman teaching office, pointed out past errors of both institutions, and described the peculiar context of the First Vatican Council (1869–70) which had formulated the doctrine of papal infallibility. Finally, Küng proposed a reappraisal of the traditional belief that the church as a whole is maintained in the truth in spite of the possibility of errors. He also emphasized that there is no formal guarantee that even a council is infallible. 'Councils do not have authority over the truth of Christ. They can strive to attain it. It is for this that the Spirit of Christ is promised to the bishops and all participants, as it is also to every Christian.'[4]

As we shall see below, the controversy about Küng's ecclesiology continues to divide Roman Catholics, and although Küng's primary theological attention shifted now to the central theological questions of God and Jesus Christ, he never lowered his commitment to the renewal of the Roman Catholic Church in particular, and the church in general.

Küng's turn to christology did not begin with his famous work *On Being a Christian* (1974) as is generally assumed; rather, this turn was prepared already in his less known work *The Incarnation of God* (1970, translated into English only in 1987). In this work Küng had already pursued the most crucial theological question, namely how God could be encountered in history and how God is related to the process of history. In this book Küng also offered a comprehensive introduction into Hegel's philosophy and theology. His main interest in Hegel derived, however, from this thinker's critique of the traditionally static concept of God. Using this critique, Küng wished to explore the foundations for a future christology.

Over against the classical concept of God influenced by Greek metaphysics, Küng – following Hegel – demands a new theological perspective. 'Hegel's philosophy begins by teaching us not to separate God from man and ends by teaching us not to confound them'.[5] Küng, however, does not follow Hegel's lead all the way. Rather, he reinterprets Hegel's speculative identity between the process of history and God as, in fact, not a totally closed system by pointing out that 'at the level of religion – not of philosophy – Hegel himself, for all his unmistakable emphasis on unity, stoutly maintained that there is an ultimate difference'.[6] On this basis of both identity and difference between God and the world, Küng sets out his prolegomena for a future christology. He calls for a christology 'from below' which is 'interested in the Jesus who meets us today, within the horizon of the world, humankind and God, as the challenge to faith which he personally embodies'.[7] This renewed concentration on historical Jesus research is, however, not seen by Küng as a means to present Jesus as he really was, rather it is understood as a critical tool which enables the theologian to scrutinize and verify the faith which has been handed down to us.[8]

Thus methodologically prepared, Küng constructed his christology in *On Being a Christian*. As the title of this book indicates already, Küng's primary concern in christology is not a theoretical one, rather he wishes to establish what it means to respond to Jesus Christ *today*. Therefore, he places his christology in the carefully analyzed context of the contemporary challenges presented by both Modern Humanism and the world religions. In answering the question of what is special to Christianity in this context, Küng states that Christianity must not be equated with everything true, good, beautiful, and humane in this world. 'Christianity does not exist wherever inhumanity is opposed and humanity realized . . . Christianity exists only where the meaning of Jesus Christ is activated in theory and practice.'[9]

In the main part of this work, Küng examines the dimensions of the Christian programme. He discusses Jesus' life and death in the context of religion and culture at the time, Jesus' proclamation of God's cause and Jesus' own identification with man's cause, the conflict which led to the death of Jesus, and the reactions to his life and death by the emerging Christian communities. The book concludes with reflections upon contemporary Christian praxis in the light of the christological dimensions presented earlier. We shall return to Küng's christology in the next section.

As indicated by Küng in *The Incarnation of God*, any adequate theological approach to God will need to examine the relationship between God and human history. Thus, it was only appropriate that Küng should treat of christology before presenting his thoughts on the concept of God in *Does God Exist?* (1978). The title of this book is somewhat misleading. Küng does not wish to follow the particular tradition of proving whether or not God actually exists. Küng's answer to that question is yes. Rather, in this book he examines the rationality of the Christian belief in God today.

The book takes the reader through the history of the contemporary understanding of God. It analyzes the contribution to this under-standing by the atheistic critique while it demonstrates at the same time that none of the leading atheists (Feuerbach, Marx, Freud, and Nietzsche) would have been able to disprove God's existence, as indeed none of the leading theists would ever be able to prove it. Instead Küng begins with the question of how the modern person relates to reality as such.

Since there is no one and absolute standpoint, our perceptions of the world can never be purely objective. Nor is any perception the exclusive product of a lonely subjectivity. Rather when we speak of 'reality', we always mean 'something that combines and embraces subject and object, consciousness and being, self and world'.[10] The decision which every human being faces, then, is a decision between two basic attitudes to reality: fundamental mistrust or fundamental trust. Moreover, this decision is a lifelong task and it concerns all aspects of our living, researching and activity in this world. Although Küng calls for a clear distinction between this 'fundamental trust' on the one hand, and 'faith in God' on the other,[11] he concludes 'that the fundamental trust in the identity, meaningfulness and value of reality, which is the presupposition of human science and autonomous ethics, is justified in the last resort only if reality itself – of which man is also a part – is not groundless, unsupported and aimless'.[12]

On the basis of these insights, Küng examines the traditional Christian approaches to God. He also notes the increasing interest in the question of God in our time. He forcefully rejects any attempt to divide reality into two spheres, a divine and a human. Rather he insists that God can be assumed 'only in a confidence rooted in reality itself'.[13] This in turn means: 'If someone affirms God, he knows why he can trust reality.'[14] Accordingly, there cannot be any outward rationality able to produce an assured security. 'There is not first a rational knowledge and then confident acknowledgment of God.' But there is an 'inward rationality, which can offer a fundamental certainty'.[15] Moreover, Küng stresses that belief in God must be considered 'a matter not only of human reason but of the whole concrete, living man, with mind and body, reason and instinct, in his quite particular historical situation, in his dependence on traditions, authorities, habits of thought, scales of values, with his interests and in his social involvement'.[16]

This need to consider the historical and social context of any belief in God brings Küng back to the specific Christian faith in God. After assessing the history of the Jewish-Christian tradition of believing in God, Küng concludes that the biblical faith in God 'is in itself coherent, is also rationally justifiable and has proved itself historically over many thousands of years'.[17] Finally, the God of the Bible has also a cosmic dimension, that is to say that the history of the entire universe is the area of this God's presence, not only the history of the individual believer. God operates 'in the world process: in, with and among beings and things. He is himself source, center and goal of the world process.'[18] It is this God which Jesus of Nazareth proclaimed in his life, death, and resurrection. Here, Küng's theological and christological reflections merge again.

Although Küng had begun his christology and his examination of the rationality of faith in the Jewish-Christian God by analyzing the horizon of the modern person who is searching for meaning, in 1982 he paid particular attention to this search for meaning in every individual life: his book *Eternal Life?* addressed the whole complex of questions related to the human hope for an eternal future. Küng interprets the various Christian eschatological symbols such as heaven, hell, eternity, and judgment, in the light of the Christian belief in the resurrection of Jesus of Nazareth. 'Jesus did not die into nothingness. In death and from death he dies into that incomprehensible and comprehensive absolutely final and absolutely first reality, was accepted by that reality, which we designate by the name of God.'[19] Thus, to believe in eternal life does not mean to hope to continue living forever. But it does mean 'to rely on the fact that I shall one day be fully understood, freed from guilt and definitely accepted and can be myself without fear; that my impenetrable and ambivalent existence, like the profoundly discordant history of humanity as a whole, will one day become finally transparent and the question of the meaning of history one day finally answered'.[20]

This book concludes Küng's second period of theological work. In this period he attempted to address the major aspects of Christian faith and to correlate them critically with his interpretation of the contemporary cultural and intellectual horizon of theology. The outline here could only deal with the most significant publications of this period. The interested reader will, however, be amazed at discovering a much greater number of theological publications which deal with other issues of Christian faith, such as liturgy, sacraments, and, of course, the church.

The third and continuing period of Küng's theological work shows two distinct, though related moves: (i) Küng's reflection on theological method, and (ii) his studies of the relationship between Christianity and other world religions and of the relationship between religion and the arts. Both of these moves are in response to a changed awareness among many contemporary theologians: namely that the world with its plurality of religious and cultural traditions and movements, with its wealth of human insight and scientific knowledge, and with its ambiguous history demands a new paradigm for theology.

Accordingly, in his book *Christianity and the World Religions* (1984), Küng calls for a global understanding of ecumenism. Ecumenism must no longer be limited to the inner-Christian conversation, but it ought to include the conversation between all great religions. For Christian theology that implies that the traditional Christian self-understanding marked by exclusivity and superiority must be overcome by an admission that none of us possesses the full truth, and that we are all on the way to the always greater truth. Such an understanding of truth demands, of course, that Christians broaden their knowledge and understanding of the other great religious traditions of humankind. Therefore Küng presents in this book introductions to Islam, Hinduism, and Buddhism in co-operation with leading historians of religion. Each of these introductions is followed by Küng's response from a Christian perspective. A dialogue with a Jewish scholar was already published in 1976; and Küng's dialogue with the major Chinese religious traditions appeared in 1988.

The search for a new paradigm of theology demands the close cooperation of scholars of different background and expertise. Thus, it is characteristic of this third period of Küng's work that many of his publications are produced in cooperation with other scholars:

his dialogues with other world religions, his dialogues with literature, and the results of an international conference on the subject-matter of the paradigm change in theology. In addition, Küng presented a collection of his own recent reflections about the debate on theological method in his book *Theology for the Third Millennium* (1987), to which we shall turn in the next section.

KEY ISSUES

Our extensive survey of Küng's work has been necessary in order to draw appropriate attention to the wide range of his theological interests, developments, and contributions and to offer an initial discussion of his major works. There are at least four unifying constants in Küng's theological work in the three periods described in the last section: (i) his ecumenical interest (from originally an inner-Christian ecumenism towards a global ecumenism); (ii) his continuing ecclesiological reflection; (iii) his concern with the christological and theological foundations of Christian faith and with the rationality of that faith; and (iv) his search for an adequate theological method for today. Let us consider these in reverse order in the remainder of this chapter.

Küng's theological method can be studied both by distilling the implicit methodology operative in his major works and by discussing his more recent explicit discussion of theological method, especially in *Theology for the Third Millennium*. Both his implicit and explicit methodology reveal the same strong commitment to the Bible as the source and ultimate norm of Christian theology, a commitment which has been characteristic of most contemporary Roman Catholic theologians (cf. those discussed in this volume: Rahner, Congar, Schillebeeckx and Balthasar). For Küng, the second source of Christian theology is the wealth of human experiences in the world in which we live today. Both sources, Bible and modern world, need to be interpreted, and both interpretations need to be critically correlated.[21] A similar model of critical correlation can also be found in E. Schillebeeckx and D. Tracy's approach to theology. While promoting this model in principle, Küng does, however, point out that this correlation between both sources may at times lead to confrontation, namely when biblical and contemporary experiences contradict one another. In such a situation of conflict, Küng attributes ultimate normative significance 'to the particular Christian experiences, or, rather, to the Christian message, the gospel, Jesus Christ himself'.[22]

In *On Being a Christian*, Küng had shown how he understands this ultimate norm to work. Here he reminds us that 'narrative presentation and critical reflection . . . must be united in Christian theology and proclamation'[23] and offers his own critical narrative and interpretation of Jesus' life, death, and resurrection. Here in *Theology for the Third Millennium* Küng emphasizes that his own interpretation of the principal norm of Christian theology, Jesus Christ, is informed by historical-critical scholarship which he considers to be essential for any appropriate theology today. He warns us, however, not to confuse historical-critical exegesis with a responsibly constructed historical-critical dogmatics.[24] The latter ought to include a systematic reflection on the (occasionally conflicting) results of modern biblical exegesis.[25]

The dimensions of the particularly systematic task in theology are clearly outlined by Küng: as already indicated in our survey of Küng's work, for him good theology must be (i) ecumenical. Furthermore it must be (ii) truthful, (iii) free (that means not authoritarian), and (iv) critical (not traditionalist).[26] Any candidate for an adequate paradigm for contemporary theology must respect these four essential dimensions.

In this context, however, Küng does not make totally explicit all of the dimensions which are operative in his systematic theology. Against the medieval-neoscholastic paradigm he insists that faith is not simply above reason; against the dichotomies of the dialectical theology he emphasizes that faith is not against reason; and against the modern Enlightenment dichotomy he stresses that reason is not against faith.[27] For Küng, all our thinking and doubting, our intuitions and deductions are grounded on an 'a priori act of trust' of which we might not always be aware, but which, once we are, we may consciously affirm or reject.[28]

As we have seen, Küng's approach to God in *Does God Exist?* is based on this fundamental insight. Although Küng is critical of Rahner's theology because it was still part of the neoscholastic paradigm,[29] Küng's a priori act of trust does bear some resemblance to Rahner's transcendental experience. However, there is also a fundamental difference between both approaches to God: while for Rahner the transcendental experience of any human being is always related (though not always thematically) to God, the God of Jesus Christ, Küng's a priori of trust is not simply identified with belief in God. But there exists an essential connection between trust in reality and belief in God. 'If someone denies God, he does not know why he ultimately trusts in reality.' And respectively: 'If someone affirms God, he knows why he can trust reality.'[30] The precise nature of this connection would need to be clarified further by Küng.

Like Rahner, Küng owes a lot to the Cartesian starting point, namely the individually thinking subject. While it is, of course, correct that any decision to believe in the Christian God is ultimately a decision made by an individual, it does, however, not automatically follow from this that the concept of God operative in the Christian movement must be exclusively grounded on individual trust. Rather it seems, and Küng agrees, that there is a rich, but naturally ambiguous heritage of philosophical attempts which relate ontologically God, Christ, the human being, and the universe. Many of these philosophical models are certainly inappropriate, as Küng himself has documented in *The Incarnation of God* with reference to the static concept of God in Greek metaphysics. Yet Küng does not sufficiently discuss his own use of ontological language which may lead to misunderstandings, particularly in christological thinking which has to wrestle with adequate expressions of the relationship between Jesus and God. When Küng writes 'For me, Jesus of Nazareth is the Son of God,'[31] he makes (if not only a value judgment) some kind of an ontological claim though existentially qualified. But even a qualified ontology is still an ontology. Similarly, his reference to 'reality' as the object of human trust has ontological implications.

Reality is always encountered through particular perspectives. These perspectives are always conditioned by all the dimensions of human experience, including the religious dimensions. Therefore the hermeneutical implications of the method of critical correlation between biblical message and human world would need to be discussed in more detail along the following lines: the contemporary human world is already present, of course, in perspectives which guide our reading of the Bible, as indeed the history of effects of the biblical texts is always present in our Western interpretations of the world. Therefore Küng's 'fundamental trust in reality' is already socially and religiously conditioned, a fact which Küng has not yet explicitly stated.

For Küng, the norm of Christian theology is Jesus Christ. He is the center of Scripture. Yet, he can only be reached through our interpretations of the different early Christian interpretations of his life, death, and resurrection. This hermeneutical situation causes a double pluralism: the contemporary pluralism of readings and the pluralism of early Christian 'readings' of Jesus as Christ. Coping with this double pluralism and the heritage of Christian interpretations in a responsible manner must include the risk of saying who Jesus Christ is in relation to God to the best of our knowledge. We have to make tentative ontological statements. Here Küng does implicitly agree. 'Jesus of Nazareth in fact has, in the last resort, no decisive meaning for me unless he is proclaimed as the Christ of God. Nor, anyway, does the divine Christ mean much to me unless he is identical with the man Jesus.'[32]

Therefore, tentative ontological statements must have a place in the new paradigm of theology in order to help us to express our particular faith in God both in terms of our own inner-Christian understanding of truth, and in terms of contributing meaningfully to the much wider search for truth in the conversation among different religious traditions.

THE KÜNG DEBATE

Küng's theological career has almost always been accompanied by controversies with some of the Roman Catholic authorities. He and a great number of other leading Roman Catholic theologians, such as Rahner, Metz, Schillebeeckx, Pohier, Ranke-Heinemann, and Curran, have been attacked by the Roman Catholic teaching office, the Magisterium in Rome, for alleged distortions of orthodox Roman Catholic teaching.

The opportunity for a fruitful dialogue between the theologian Küng and representatives of the Magisterium has been missed because the latter has approached this dialogue from a position of ecclesiastical superiority and has not been willing to promote an open and public debate of the issues at stake. This is most unfortunate since it did not facilitate a learning experience in either party and among their respective supporters. However, the debate has been well documented in the meantime so that the issues at stake can now be carefully studied.[33] Here we must concentrate on three key issues of this debate.

The freedom of the theologian in the church

Küng has always fought for the freedom of theology in the Roman Catholic Church. Only a free theology, he has claimed, will be able to serve the church. Over against this attitude, the Sacred Congregation for the Doctrine of Faith stressed in its declaration of December 15, 1979 that

> The Church of Christ has received from God the mandate to keep and to safeguard the deposit of faith so that all the faithful, under the guidance of the sacred teaching office through which Christ himself exercises his role as teacher in the Church, may

cling without fail to the faith once delivered to the saints, may penetrate it more deeply by accurate insights, and may apply it more thoroughly to life. . . . It is necessary, therefore, that theological research and teaching should always be illumined with fidelity to the teaching office since no one may rightly act as a theologian except in close union with the mission of teaching truth which is incumbent on the Church itself.[34]

Thus, in this declaration which ruled that Küng could no longer be considered a Roman Catholic theologian, the Magisterium insisted that its paradigm of doing theology is God-given and therefore above suspicion and discussion. Küng replied by defending his paradigm of theology: 'As a Catholic theologian, what was and is particularly important to me is the "Catholic" Church, that is, the entire, universal, all-encompassing, and whole Church. Hence, my task has always been and is to teach Catholic truth with Catholic breadth and depth.'[35]

The actual issue which prompted the Magisterium to withdraw Küng's teaching license was Küng's challenge of the dogma of papal infallibility.

The infallibility of the pope

This issue provided the spark for a much deeper controversy, namely a theological controversy on the nature of authority in the church. While the Magisterium and the Popes have considered their authority over the church as God-given and supported by the Holy Spirit, Küng has challenged this view repeatedly in his writings and lectures and has presented a radically different vision of authority and ministry in the church. For him, as indicated in our survey above, the church as a whole is maintained in truth. This indefectibility of the church is 'a truth of faith'.[36] Moreover, Küng has challenged the Magisterium's appeal to the Bible for support of its special authority and pointed out that biblical texts must not be misused in order to support a particular tradition of ecclesiastical authority. Rather, he insists, all claims to authority in the church must be constantly submitted to the scrutiny of critical interpretations of the Scriptures. Thus, Küng is not against leadership in the church. Rather he stresses: 'It is not no Church leadership that we need, but Church leadership in accordance with the gospel. We do not need less authority, but more qualified authority: authority based on service, and capable of subordinating itself to the subordinate if the latter has the gospel and reason on its side.'[37]

For Küng, then, the dogma of papal infallibility is the logical consequence of a highly questionable understanding of the Christian church, whereas for Rome, Küng is to be corrected for not subscribing to its particular understanding of the church. Two models of church are in conflict here.

The change of paradigms

More recently, Küng has joined the discussion of the nature of paradigm changes and of the problems associated with such changes. While some people continue to defend an old paradigm, others live and work already in a different one. Küng warns in this context against thinking that every new paradigm necessarily means progress just by virtue of being new and different. He calls therefore for a critical conversation between defenders of different paradigms.[38] Such a critical conversation would, of course, be desirable, also with respect to the Küng controversy itself. But is such a conversation possible at all as long as the representatives of one way of thinking believe it to be sponsored directly by God? No call for a mutually critical conversation will succeed in moving them from such an a priori. They basically trust in a different reality than those who believe in the necessity of a truly open-ended and critical conversation about truth.

HANS KÜNG'S THEOLOGICAL ACHIEVEMENT

Hans Küng has not only discussed all essential areas of Christian theology, reflected on necessary changes in theological method today, and opened many doors toward a Christian understanding of the world religions, but has also expressed his thoughts in such a way that every intelligent reader can follow them and thus receive the necessary information for entering into the discussion. Küng cannot be praised enough for the attention he has given to the presentation of theological thoughts. Countless people around the world have thus been allowed to nurture their theological interest and to transform their lives.

Perhaps Küng's two most important contributions to theological method so far have been (i) his proposal for a global theology which is aware of the many facets of human life in this world and of the different and often conflicting religious and cultural interpretations of reality; and (ii) his reconsideration of the nature of truth claims in the context of such a global theology.[39]

Küng's call on all human beings to enter into the discussion about

the meaning and truth in our lives and to respect the open-
endedness of such a discussion is inspired by his understanding of
God's revelation in Jesus Christ. The resulting self-understanding of
theology must therefore conflict with any theological paradigm
which advocates a privileged access to truth for some people.
Genuine conversation about truth cannot tolerate such privileged
participants. This applies not only to the Roman Catholic Magisterium,
but to all human bodies in and outside of Christianity which claim
such a special status and access to God and truth. Küng's vision of
the global conversation about truth is based on his understanding of
God's call in Christ that all people are called to relate to God without
intermediary institutions.[40]

Küng's most significant contribution to the discussion of the
central articles of Christian faith lies in his effort to demonstrate the
rationality of this faith and to reflect upon the implications of this
faith for human praxis today. Küng does not only wish to interpret
the world, he wishes to help in transforming it by critically
retrieving the radical humanism of the Christian faith.[41] Even
though Küng has not yet clarified all the philosophical presuppositions of his work, he has already contributed a lot to the
radical transformation of the nature of theology in the twentieth
century.

But he is the first to admit that there is much more to be done. His
work in the area of interreligious dialogue has only begun. But
already he has helped many contemporary people to enhance their
understanding of the world religions and to grasp more sharply
which consequences this conversation may have for our Christian
self-understanding today.

The controversy about Küng's theology, and especially his
ecclesiology, has had a profound effect on Roman Catholicism itself.
Moreover, for many Protestants, especially in the English-speaking
world, Küng is the theologically acceptable face of Roman Catholicism. Thus, Küng's work has already given rise to much critical
thought and transformative action. What more could any theologian
work and hope for?

NOTES

1 The dates given in parentheses in the text refer to the first German
   edition of Küng's works. Citations are from the editions listed in the
   Bibliography. All works cited in the notes are authored by Küng unless
   stated otherwise.
2 Cf. The Church, pp. 96ff.

3 *Infallible? An Enquiry*, p. 22. (My correction of English translation).
4 Ibid., p. 170.
5 *The Incarnation of God: An Introduction to Hegel's Theological Thought as Prolegomena to a Future Christology*, p. 462.
6 Ibid., p. 428.
7 Ibid., p. 491.
8 Cf. Ibid., p. 492.
9 *On Being a Christian*, pp. 125f.
10 *Does God Exist? An Answer for Today*, p. 432.
11 Cf. Ibid., p. 473.
12 Ibid., p. 476.
13 Ibid., p. 570.
14 Ibid., p. 572.
15 Ibid., p. 574.
16 Ibid.
17 Ibid., p. 626.
18 Ibid., p. 649.
19 *Eternal Life?*, p. 145.
20 Ibid., p. 287.
21 Cf. *Theology for the Third Millennium*, pp. 108ff.
22 Ibid., p. 151 – my translation.
23 *On Being a Christian*, p. 418.
24 *Theology for the Third Millennium*, pp. 112f.
25 Ibid., pp. 113ff.
26 Cf. ibid., pp. 101f., 203f.
27 Ibid., pp. 202f.
28 Ibid., p. 201.
29 Ibid., pp. 186ff.
30 *Does God Exist?*, pp. 571ff.
31 Ibid., p. 688.
32 Ibid., p. 687.
33 Cf. Leonard Swidler (ed.), *Küng in Conflict*.
34 Ibid., pp. 384ff.
35 Ibid., p. 398.
36 *Infallible?*, p. 154.
37 Ibid. p. 188.
38 *Theology for the Third Millennium*, p. 223.
39 Cf. ibid., pp. 304ff.
40 Cf. *On Being a Christian*, pp. 481ff.
41 Ibid., p. 31.

BIBLIOGRAPHY

Primary

Küng, H., *Justification: The Doctrine of Karl Barth and a Catholic Reflection* (London, 1965).
—, *The Church* (London, 1967).
—, *Infallible? An Enquiry* (London, 1972, 1980).
—, *On Being a Christian* (London, 1977).
—, *Does God Exist? An Answer for Today* (London, 1980).
—, *Eternal Life?* (London, 1984).
—, *The Incarnation of God: An Introduction to Hegel's Theological Thought as Prolegomena to a Future Christology* (Edinburgh, 1987).
—, *Christianity and the World Religions: Paths of Dialogue with Islam, Hinduism, and Buddhism* (London, 1987).
—, *Theology for the Third Millennium: An Ecumenical View* (New York, 1988).
—, with Walter Jens, *Dichtung und Religion* (Munich, 1985).

Secondary

Häring, Hermann and Kuschel, Karl-Josef (eds), *Hans Küng: His Work and His Way* (London, 1979).
Kiwiet, John, *Hans Küng* (Waco, Texas, 1985).
LaCugna, Catherine, *The Theological Methodology of Hans Küng* (Atlanta, 1982).
Nowell, Robert, *A Passion for Truth. Hans Küng: A Biography* (London, 1981).
Swidler, Leonard (ed.), *Küng in Conflict* (New York, 1981).

Part III

Transcendental Theology

In Roman Catholic theology in Europe between the First and Second World Wars there were two main theological debates. The first was about history, and especially the appropriate use of modern historical methods in theology. Congar (chapter 11) became a leading contributor to that. The second was about a modern philosophical approach to theology. Karl Rahner and Bernard Lonergan contributed mainly to this.

Official theology was dominated by Thomas Aquinas as understood through the scholastic theologians, who continued his tradition, and their modern successors the 'neoscholastics'. Rahner and Lonergan are sometimes called 'transcendental Thomists' because they, along with others, broke with neoscholasticism and tried to integrate the theology and philosophy of Aquinas with post-Enlightenment thought, especially Kant's 'transcendental' idealist philosophy. That was so called because of Kant's attempt to identify, beyond any particular experiencing, knowing, and willing, the 'transcendental' conditions and limitations under which each person can experience or know or will at all. So 'transcendental' here points to the most general and fundamental features of human existence without which we would not be human at all. Thus J. A. DiNoia describes Rahner's attempt to show how God and revelation cohere with the basic dynamics of the human mind and will; and Hugo Meynell argues that Lonergan's 'transcendental precepts' (be attentive, be intelligent, be reasonable, be responsible) are in fact the foundation of all true knowing and good action and are rightly at the heart of Lonergan's theological method.

DiNoia's interpretation of Rahner differs from many others in two respects: his stress on the pluralist, nonsystematic nature of Rahner's theology, and his insistence on Rahner's continuity with Aquinas. Rahner emerges as above all a theologian of the gracious mystery of God and salvation, who offers a model for the creative recovery of the Christian tradition in new contexts.

Meynell by contrast qualifies Lonergan's debt to Aquinas. Lonergan's main achievement, which is compared to a 'paradigm shift', is seen as his theological method. Lonergan has also been the subject of an extended and well-organized debate, especially in North America, and Meynell summarizes and responds to the main critical points that have been raised in that.

9

Karl Rahner

J. A. DiNoia OP

The most influential and widely read Catholic theologian of the twentieth century was fond of describing himself as an 'amateur theologian' – a piece of self-effacing modesty on Karl Rahner's part which in fact affords illuminating perspectives on the work of this thoroughly professional theologian.

INTRODUCTION: LIFE AND INFLUENCES

Naturally, there was nothing amateurish about Karl Rahner in any conventional sense. Over the course of a lifetime of work, Rahner proved himself to be a scholar of the first rank, in full command of the tools of his craft and with interests ranging across the whole field of theology.

Karl Rahner earned his living, so to speak, as a professional theologian. He was a professor of theology for most of his life. Except for the war years and a stint as a teacher of Jesuit seminarians, Rahner was a member of the faculty of theology at the University of Innsbruck from 1937 to 1964. In addition to teaching and writing, he served as editor, lecturer, retreat master, and preacher. His success in these activities gained him the attention of church leaders. In 1962 Rahner became an official theological consultant (*peritus*) to the Second Vatican Council and in 1969 he was named to the Papal Theological Commission. Then, after holding appointments briefly at both the universities of Munich and Munster, Rahner retired from teaching in 1971. By this time he was a theologian of international reputation. During the last twenty years of his life he was the recipient of many academic honors, including several of British and American provenance. He continued to be active almost until the day of his death at Innsbruck on March 30, 1984.

Rahner's preparation for his professional career was typical for Jesuits of his generation. He was born in Freiburg im Breisgau in 1904, joining the Society of Jesus in 1922. He pursued the standard Jesuit course of philosophical and theological studies until 1932 when he was ordained a priest. The Society's plan that he earn a doctorate in philosophy in order to teach the subject in its schools was thwarted when, after two years of work at the University of Freiburg, Rahner failed to win his director's approval for his completed dissertation. As a result he went on instead to secure a doctorate in theology in 1936 at the University of Innsbruck where he began teaching the next year.

Among the influences that helped to shape Rahner's approach to theology, the spiritual and intellectual formation which he received in the Society of Jesus ranks high in significance. His interior life was shaped by the *Spiritual Exercises* of St Ignatius Loyola (1495–1556), who founded the Society and whose work forms the basis of Jesuit religious formation. The mystical bent of Rahner's theology can in part be traced to his appropriation of the spiritual lessons of the *Exercises* with its emphasis upon meditative introspection and direct encounter with Christ in long periods of private prayer. The soul's experience of God in prayer functioned as a kind of paradigm for Rahner's theological account of the whole Christian mystery.

His membership in a religious order helped to give Rahner's theology its characteristic spiritual and churchly orientation. Despite the university setting in which Rahner pursued his professional career he always practiced theology with a view to its impact upon the church's life, its spiritual progress, and its pastoral and social engagement.

Rahner was educated during the period between the wars when the mood of modern Christian theology was one of reaffirmation and revival in the face of the challenges of modernity. During this period, a variety of theological programs emerged to replace the failed accommodationist strategies associated with Protestant liberalism and Catholic modernism. Efforts to reaffirm Christian identity gave added impetus to the revival of the study of the classical sources of Christian thought under way in Catholic circles since the mid-nineteenth century. Renewed study of St Thomas Aquinas (1225–74) and of medieval scholastic thought continued to be an important aspect of this revival. In combination with both favorable and critical readings of modern philosophers, this revival spawned a variety of vigorous neo-Thomistic and neoscholastic movements in Catholic philosophy and theology.

Undertaken in this climate, Rahner's philosophical and theological education favored the development of the ingenious fusion of scholasticism with German idealism and existentialism which is characteristic of his thought. Nurturing a broadly Augustinian construal of Aquinas, partly dependent upon his reading of St Bonaventure (1217–74), Rahner's studies served to confirm the mystical direction of his thought. The primacy accorded to metaphysics and theory of knowledge (over natural philosophy, logic and rational psychology) in Rahner's theological appropriation of Aquinas' philosophy was typical of traditions of interpretation shaped by the great Jesuit scholastic, Francisco de Suarez (1548–1617). The broadly Kantian construal of Aquinas' philosophy – 'transcendental Thomism', as it has come to be called – advanced in the writings of the two Jesuit philosophers Pierre Rousselot (1878–1915) and Joseph Maréchal (1878–1944), had a decisive impact on Rahner's thought. Then, while studying at Freiburg Rahner became familiar at first hand with the developing project of existential philosophy through seminars conducted by Martin Heidegger. Under the influence of such diverse factors, Rahner's own version of transcendental Thomism gradually took shape.

Along with his brother Hugo Rahner S J, and many other theologians of their generation, Rahner was also swept up in the movement to revive the study of prescholastic sources of Christian doctrines and theology. In addition to furnishing resources for renewed Christian affirmation, this *ressourcement* equipped progressive theologians of this period for battle on another front. For, besides its more creative impulses, the scholastic revival had also generated a spate of fairly reiterative and defensive philosophical and theological works, often textbooks or seminary manuals, which blocked creative developments in Catholic thought. By recovering and exhibiting the diversity of theological expression which marks the classical sources, progressive theologians sought to shake the dominance of derivative and unimaginative forms of neoscholasticism in Catholic theology. Such theologians welcomed the application of new critical and historical methods to the study of the Scriptures, the liturgical sources and the Fathers of the Church. Rahner himself undertook a considerable amount of scholarly work along these lines. As a result, his own constructive theology came to be profoundly influenced by patristic sources, especially the writings of St Augustine and of the Greek fathers.

SURVEY

These diverse influences helped to foster the relatively unsystematic approach that would become one of the hallmarks of his theology. This approach to theological topics could be characterized as at once mystical, philosophical, dogmatic, scholastic, pastoral, apologetic, transcendental, anthropological, and ecclesial. Rahner referred to himself as an amateur theologian in part to signal the unsystematic nature of his work.

In Rahner's writings various conceptual frameworks and theological interests intersect. None of them attains an all-encompassing, systematic status in his theology. His approach is experimental, exploratory, even non-technical. His essays represent a series of brilliant, often successful, but relatively unsystematic experiments, intended to advance the state of discussion of particular Christian doctrines by pressing at the boundaries of prevailing neoscholastic formulations. The internal coherence of Rahner's theology arises not from his espousal of a single, unitary conception or methodology, but from a vision of the human reality as being completely embraced and irreversibly transformed by divine grace.

Rahner's preference for the essay as a vehicle for theological construction is indicative of the relatively unsystematic character of his work. His essays were published over a thirty-year period (1954–84) in sixteen volumes, modestly entitled *Schriften zur Theologie* or 'writings in theology' (extending to twenty volumes in the still incomplete English *Theological Investigations*). Also typical of this genre are the more extended essays which Rahner wrote or co-authored in the theological series, *Quaestiones Disputatae* (1958ff), which he founded and edited.

No single volume presents Rahner's entire theological project in a comprehensive or systematic fashion. Like his essays and monographs, his three most significant booklength publications furnish only elements of that project, viz., the substance of his contribution to foundational theology. The two earliest of these works – *Spirit in the World* (*Geist im Welt*, 1939) and *Hearers of the Word* (*Hörer des Wortes*, 1941) – together comprise a complex, extended argument in philosophical theology. The more recent *Foundations of Christian Faith* (*Grundkurs des Glaubens*, 1976), as its title implies, surveys the rational warrants for central Christian doctrines.

In addition to writing numerous shorter works on various topics, Rahner accepted partial or complete editorial responsibility for several major reference works: the *Lexikon für Theologie und Kirche*

(1955–67), the *Handbuch der Pastoraltheologie* (1964–72) and the theological encyclopedia, *Sacramentum Mundi* (1967–9). These collaborative efforts bear the mark of Rahner's distinctive theological perspectives and, like the single volume *Dictionary of Theology* (*Kleine Theologische Wörterbuch*, 10th edition with Herbert Vorgrimler S J, 1976), hint at the outlines of the systematic theology that he never wrote.

Though there is no system here, there is certainly a coherent theological program in the service of an encompassing vision of the Christian faith. Rahner was continually in search of conceptual tools equal to the task of depicting this vision and freeing it from conceptualities which obscure it. Moving across the whole range of individual theological topics, Rahner at each point sought to articulate a vision of concrete Christian and human existence in the world as embraced by God the holy Mystery – not as an impersonal force, but as personal presence. In the modality of self-communication, this holy Mystery presents an inexhaustibly rich object for human contemplation and engagement in knowledge, freedom, and love. Grace enters human reality as something gratuitous though not alien, as something for which the ground is already prepared by creation in the very structure of the human spirit in the world. While faithful to traditional formulations, Rahner sought to express this vision in conceptualities congenial to modernity. For modernity is the present context of historical human experience in which the divine self-communication takes concrete form.

CONTENT: TRANSCENDENTAL METHOD, GOD AND HUMANITY

By referring to himself as an amateur, Rahner maintained a friendly though critical distance from prevailing practices within his craft. He sought alternatives to reigning approaches and conceptions in theology in order to bring his vision of the Christian reality into sharper relief. Still, many of his significant theological proposals about individual Christian doctrines are more nearly intelligible when set in their traditional, usually neoscholastic, contexts. The continuities that obtain between these proposals and the neoscholastic formulations which he sought to correct are as crucial to understanding and appraising his theological program as are the discontinuities.

Rahner's endeavour to recover the vitality and relevance of Christian faith impelled him to probe almost every element of Christian belief and practice. Three topics invite extended consideration here as illustrative of his theological program at work on particular doctrines: the nature and method of theology, the doctrine of God, and theological anthropology.

Rahner's approach to methodological issues shares in common with classical Catholic theology a set of basic convictions about the nature and method of theology. Philosophical analysis and construction play a prominent role in his theological program, particularly as they help to advance the truth claims conveyed by Christian beliefs. In this his work stands firmly within the Catholic theological tradition in its neoscholastic and other forms. Although he exploits modern conceptualities in his articulation of the Christian faith, he resists any tendency to mute the realism of theological affirmation under the pressure of modern philosophical critiques of religion. On this score and despite their contrasting positions on other issues, Rahner's work is akin to Karl Barth's.

Rahner's methodological convictions are likewise typically Catholic in the primacy his work accords to standard Christian idiom in the practice of theology. While several of Rahner's essays seek explicitly to chart the pathways from kerygma to theology, his actual practice of the theological craft reflects a striking fidelity to the full range of the Christian proclamation.[1] For Rahner, the proclamation of the kerygma – shaped as it is by Scripture, tradition, liturgy, doctrine, and ecclesiastical magisterium – provides the original setting for theological inquiry and construction.[2]

A distinctive mark of Rahner's conception and practice of theology is his effort to display the inner unity and intelligibility of the Christian proclamation in its simplicity and richness. His pursuit of this objective led to his rejection of standard neoscholastic theological procedures.

Neoscholastic theologians had, of course, inherited the intellectual ideal of a unified, comprehensive vision of the Christian faith from their study of the *Summa theologiae* of Aquinas. Indeed, they routinely invoked its authority at many points in their own works. But with rare exceptions the practice and literary forms of neoscholastic theology prevented the realization of this ideal for at least two reasons. First, in order to do justice both to the range of materials requiring explication and to the demands of the theological curriculum, the various topics of theology were distributed over a series of loosely connected treatises for manageable presentation in textbook form. The unity and coherence of the Christian faith were more likely to be presupposed than actually exhibited by this division of labor and materials. Secondly, given the cumulative character of scholastic dialectics, the presentation of each topic was saddled with highly compressed reviews of scholastic debates of more historical than contemporary or systematic interest. Relevant modern views could only receive cursory attention. Such expository procedures were unfavorable to the development of an understanding of fundamental issues in theology or of a comprehensive theological vision of the Christian faith. At the same time, the sweeping repudiation of modernity implied by a dismissive and defensive treatment of modern conceptualities inevitably fostered the isolation of the Christian faith and its expositors from the discourse of educated people of the twentieth century.

Rahner saw these deficiencies of textbook theology with absolute clarity and undertook to offset them. In the end, his alternative methods generated a sustained program of unsystematic but largely coherent theological construction, intended to rescue fundamental Christian doctrines and an integral vision of the Christian mystery from the thicket of standard neoscholastic exposition.

A prominent aspect of Rahner's methodology in developing this theological program was his employment of the 'transcendental method'. This expression designates at least two features of Rahner's characteristic methodology. First, it refers to the employment of transcendental arguments which Rahner favored in his effort to overcome some of the defects of neoscholasticism and to advance his own theological proposals. A second and grander meaning of the expression – one which gives rise to the designation of a whole school of 'transcendental theologians' – can best be clarified in connection with a discussion of Rahner's philosophical theology later in this essay.

In its first or logical sense, transcendental method designates a class of arguments which defend the actuality of certain states of affairs by demonstrating that the conditions for their possibility do in fact obtain.[3] Initially, arguments of this kind pose a certain difficulty because their sequence runs in the reverse of what we normally expect from arguments: in effect, such arguments begin rather than end with the conclusion to be proposed. In any case, Rahner's particular philosophical commitments incline him to employ these arguments less to demonstrate the conditions for the possibility of certain states of affairs actually obtaining than to display the conditions for the possibility of our knowing or believing that they obtain. Rahner puts such arguments to many ingenious theological uses and in ways that reflect their peculiar suitability for the exposition of the Christian faith. Since many of the central elements of the Christian faith are known by divine revelation alone, only God posesses an insider's knowledge, so to speak, of the conditions of their actuality. But theologians and ordinary believers can explore the reasons why it makes good sense to hold the truths revelation teaches or try to show how these truths hang together in their entirety. Aquinas made this point by saying that, although theology could seek the inner intelligibility of revealed truths, it could never supply strict demonstrations for them.[4] Transcendental arguments function in somewhat the same way in Rahner's exposition of individual Christian doctrines. The particular sort of intelligibility which Rahner pursues is that which reveals how Christian truths fit with ordinary human experience. What is more, by linking individual Christian truths – for example, about purgatory or the sacraments – with a unifying vision of God's personal presence to human beings in grace, such arguments also fulfill a chief objective of Rahner's theological program.[5]

Like his conception of the nature and method of theology, Rahner's numerous essays on the doctrine of God also illustrate both his ties with and his departures from standard neoscholastic theology. As a whole, Rahner's theological program is typical of Catholic dogmatic theology in placing God firmly at the center of the enterprise.[6] A fundamental concern for him is that theology do justice to the realism of the Christian confession of the universal personal presence of God and of his absolute claim on human minds and hearts. Rahner is impatient with neoscholastic theological accounts of God which give prominence to metaphysical speculation at the expense of explicating the fundamental experience of the presence of God at the very center of human existence. While he does not repudiate any of the classical theology of God (such as might be found in Aquinas), neither does he show much inclination to discuss it in detail. Rahner's theology of God can be characterized as a primarily mystical one which deploys an extended transcendental argument to disclose in the human experience of God the grounds for explicit belief in him and thus for classical arguments for the existence of God.

This transcendental argument is elaborated sequentially in *Spirit in the World* and *Hearers of the Word*. Actually, the argument moves beyond philosophical theology into the domain of fundamental theology in that it considers not only the conditions for the possibility of human knowledge of God's existence but also the conditions of human receptivity to a possibly divine revelation. In so far as this includes receptivity to individual doctrines as well, the project begun in these two early works extends into the more recent *Foundations of Christian Faith*.

Classical arguments for the existence of God take for their starting points regular or persistent features of the natural order like motion, perishability, design, finality and so on. The arguments are then elaborated, usually in connection with some metaphysical scheme, in order to demonstrate that the whole natural order exhibiting such features is brought into existence and preserved in existence by God.[7] Rahner's philosophical theology does not contest the validity of the classical arguments, but rather advances a transcendental argument for their possibility. Its starting point is not some observable or generalizable feature of the natural order, but the structure of human knowledge itself.

In Rahner's philosophical theology, the Kantian cognitional a priori is transformed into a metaphysical a priori. Along with his already noted preference for transcendental arguments, Rahner's reliance here upon a transcendental account of the metaphysics of human knowledge explains why his program is commonly described as an instance of transcendental theology.

According to this account, beyond the transcendental structures of reason which Kant argued make it possible for sense perception to become knowledge, there is the readiness to affirm being which serves as a kind of precondition for the knowledge of anything at all. Ordinary knowledge of particular objects of experience presupposes a prior readiness to affirm their existence – the readiness to affirm the being of things. But there is always more to 'being' than can be comprised by particular beings. A transcendental analysis of this readiness to affirm the being of beings and its inexhaustibility discloses that the human mind is structurally oriented to a horizon or backdrop of being (Rahner's notion of the *Vorgriff auf esse*). Beings appear, as it were, on a backdrop of being. The horizon of being is disclosed as limitless, unrestricted, or Absolute Being. Hence, that to which knowledge is oriented is the Absolute Mystery which all call God – to paraphrase Aquinas' conclusion to his statement of the classical arguments for God's existence. Thus the experience which supplies the starting point for this argument is a transcendental one: not observation and generalizations arising from sense-perception, but a reflexive analysis of the structures of knowledge itself. And the argument advanced on the basis of this experience is a transcendental one – an argument which shows, Rahner contends, that a prior experience of God in knowledge is the condition for the possibility of classical arguments for the existence of God.

Despite the technical difficulty of this argument, it is not hard to see what Rahner has in mind here. But the move from Absolute Being to God as Absolute Mystery seems to represent something of a leap, facilitated by a broadly Hegelian conception of Absolute Being as unrestricted. Since in this conceptuality the causal dependence of beings upon Absolute Being is expressed in terms of differentiation rather than creation, the transition from beings to Absolute Being is a relatively smooth one, despite the complexity of the transcendental argument advanced to show this. Aquinas thought that the uses of the concept of 'being' in describing the many varieties of entities we encounter in experience – not to mention entities which transcend our ordinary experience – turned out upon examination to be irreducibly distinct, and he proposed a theory of analogy to account for the legitimacy of these extended uses.[8] On Aquinas' view of the matter, arguments for the existence of God possess an inferential rather than transcendental structure. In contrast, since Rahner's metaphysics clearly supposes that the concept of being in its various uses has a more nearly univocal sense, the way is clear in his philosophical theology for the extended transcendental argument sketched above.

In its next phase, the argument undertakes to disclose the grounds for the revelation affirmed by Christianity to have occurred. The Absolute Mystery to which all knowledge is oriented and which could have remained silent has in fact spoken. Rahner's argument here is not deductive but transcendental. It answers the question: given that Christians confess by faith that revelation has occurred, what must be true about the structures of human knowledge for such a revelation to be recognized and received? The message of revelation – the divine self-communication – travels air waves, so to speak, which are already in place. Revelation does not invade the human reality as something utterly alien but as something to which human beings are already attuned.

Rahner's stress on the incomprehensibility of God is intelligible in this connection – not as a species of covert agnosticism, but as the reaffirmation of a traditional Christian notion framed in terms of modern German philosophy. God is the Absolute Subject (not, it should be noticed, 'substance'), the absolutely transcendent 'elusive I' whose self-communication beckons the human spirit to respond. God is incomprehensible in the sense of being never fully comprehensible, endlessly knowable, endlessly interesting; always elusive because always surpassing human spiritual capacities; great enough, in the Augustinian sense, to satisfy the longings of the human heart, and greater still. In Rahner's view, the extended transcendental argument sketched above – indeed any argument or discourse about God – can only begin to hint at the immensity of the Mystery that surrounds us.[9]

Generally speaking, Rahner's proposals in theological anthropology are best interpreted in the light of the mystical or relational character of his theological program so clear in his essays concerning God's incomprehensibility and mystery. This is especially evident in his proposals concerning the relationship of nature and grace, or the natural and the supernatural orders. Again, the state of discussion within neoscholastic theology provides the context for Rahner's position on these issues. It can be argued that Rahner endeavored to break the mid-twentieth-century stalemate between neoscholastic and progressive theologians by recovering and reappropriating Aquinas' fundamental insight about the true character of the supernatural.

Augustinian conceptions of the relation of the natural and the supernatural orders decisively shaped Western theological positions on this topic.[10] According to these conceptions, two elements define the specific character of the supernatural. In the first place, whatever is supernatural, properly speaking, surpasses in possibility the innate and acquired capacities of any entity in its natural condition. The supernatural order is transcendent. In addition, whatever is supernatural enters the natural order as an unmerited gift. That human beings now have a destiny in God himself, for example, and that they begin to enjoy in the present the benefits of this future destiny are utterly free gifts bestowed by God on them. This is the sense of saying that the supernatural is gratuitous. Aquinas made a considerable advance on the classical Augustinian conceptions by subordinating these senses of the supernatural – transcendence and gratuity – to what he took to be the most precise, or formal, property of the supernatural: that it involves a participation in the divine life itself.[11] Properly speaking, the supernatural order involves living life at a new level, a life lived in charity with God and others in him. On this account, transcendence and gratuity are functions of divinization.

For various reasons, Reformation and post-Reformation controversial theology on all sides tended to revert to earlier Augustinian conceptions in framing the issues in doctrinal dispute. To the extent that controversial theology prevailed in standard neoscholastic formulations, the significance of the advance represented by the theology of Aquinas was often lost or obscured – even where theology was supposedly being practiced under the guidance of his works. In the climate of post-Reformation polemics, reversion to a definition of the supernatural chiefly in terms of transcendence and gratuity tended to accentuate the discontinuity between nature and grace. 'Nature' came to be conceived as something which *de facto* exists almost in its own right. Aquinas' vision of the concrete order of things as an order of grace and salvation was eclipsed in much neoscholastic theology. The natural and supernatural orders were viewed as coexisting, parallel orders of reality which only subsequently came to be related (the 'extrinsicism' which Rahner deplores). The reaction to the dualism of these conceptions in some twentieth-century progressive theology (the *nouvelle theologie* as it was tagged) risked a conflation of nature and grace.

In this situation, Rahner strove to recover a genuinely Thomistic position on these issues by stressing the participational or relational character of the supernatural order, and therefore the continuity between human nature as divinely constituted in creation and human being transformed by grace. Rahner proposed the much contested category of the supernatural existential as an antidote to both extrinsicism and its contemporary alternatives. Without itself being grace, the supernatural existential confirms the orientation of the human natural order to the supernatural order which God's intention to confer grace presupposes.[12]

Rahner and Aquinas are congruent here in striving to do justice to the concrete order of salvation. 'Nature' or the human natural order is understood properly only when subsumed as an inner moment within the order of grace. Neither Aquinas nor Rahner take 'nature' to be an independent order which at any time exists outside or beyond the order of grace. A key difference between Rahner and Aquinas at this point is that, with the introduction of the supernatural existential conceived in terms of transcendental philosophy of mind and metaphysics, Rahner cannot provide a description or analysis of the natural order at the theoretical level which is not dependent upon, or does not require appeal to the supernatural order. Despite his emphasis on the unity of the two orders in the concrete working out of the plan of salvation, Aquinas can supply such a description and thinks that it is important for certain purposes to do so.

Rahner's proposals about nature and grace afford an insight into the coherence of his theological program. He is at every point concerned to display the continuities between the human order and the divine purposes and activities in its regard, without subverting the confession of their utter gratuity and transcendence as pure grace. The divine purposes and activities are not alien to human well-being, even though surpassing human possibilities and merits utterly.

DEBATE

It is clear that Rahner strove to recover the best elements of the Catholic doctrinal and theological tradition, while avoiding some of the obscurities into which it had fallen in some of its standard versions and popular conceptions. As might be expected, his theological proposals have provoked controversy on various fronts.

On the one hand, there are broad issues of interpretation. The sheer variety and volume of Rahner's essays, reference work entries, monographs and books have fueled the search for some overarching conception under which to organize his entire output. 'Divine self-communication', 'holy mystery', 'theological anthropology', and 'transcendental method' have all been advanced as likely candidates. Another strategy has been to treat the booklength works, individually or *en bloc*, as supplying the interpretative key to his writings as a whole. In this connection, there has been substantive debate about the role of transcendental philosophy in Rahner's thought, and the extent to which interpretation of his theological proposals depends upon his philosophical works. Naturally, his more plainly philosophical works afford a perspective on his theology. But it seems preferable to assess the theological essays on their own merits as unsystematic contributions to particular traditional debates rather than to view them as offshoots of the project adumbrated in Rahner's philosophical and foundational proposals.

In addition to these and other questions of interpretation, there has been controversy about particular aspects of the content of Rahner's theology. Two topics illustrate typical issues raised by his overall theological program: his trinitarian theology, and the universalism of his theology of revelation and grace.

Rahner was sharply critical of a twofold disjunction in standard neoscholastic theology of the Trinity: a disjunction *between* the doctrine of God and the doctrine of the Trinity, and another *within* the doctrine of the Trinity itself. In Rahner's view, this twofold disjunction underlay the practical unitarianism of average Christian thought and piety. He advocated strategies to overcome this disjunction which, despite their advantages, posed difficulties which have generated considerable debate.

One aspect of the disjunction which Rahner perceived in standard trinitarian theology was that between God's being as one and God's being as triune. Following Aquinas and in accord with Western theological traditions generally, standard neoscholastic theological accounts of the doctrines of God and the Trinity addressed the existence and nature of God prior to addressing the processions, relations, and persons in God. But neoscholastic imitators of Aquinas in fact often failed to preserve the integration and the scriptural context which characterize his treatment of these issues in the *Summa theologiae*.[13] Rahner argued that as a result of this disjunction, the Trinity came increasingly to be viewed as a kind mysterious (in the sense of merely puzzling) appendage to the doctrine of God conceived primarily along metaphysical lines. Standard theology thus failed to do justice both to Christian revelation about the Trinity and to the distinctively Christian content of the doctrine of God.

In order to correct this first disjunction in standard trinitarian theology, Rahner advocated a recovery of the Greek patristic account of the divine nature which he took to be better warranted by scriptural usage. In this account, the divine existence and attributes are given a strictly trinitarian setting in the discussion of the doctrine of God the Father. This Greek view was understood by Rahner to respect the biblical account of God according to which the term 'God' (*ho theos*) normally refers to God the Father. A theological procedure along these lines, in Rahner's view, accorded full weight to the distinctive Christian confession of God as trinitarian in his very being.[14]

But against Rahner's construal and use of the scriptural evidence, it could be argued that the strongly monotheistic logic underlying biblical usage is better respected by theological positions (such as that of Aquinas though granting the weaknesses of its derivatives) in which the discussion of the divine nature is constructed in such a way as to address those features of the life of the divine Trinity which are ascribable to the divine persons in so far as together they are the one God. Rahner was right to deplore the covert unitarianism fostered by trinitarian theologies which divorce the doctrines of God and the Trinity. It was entirely appropriate for Rahner to appeal to the Scriptures in order to support his larger argument, but misleading to suggest that the Scriptures rule out alternative accounts. Appeal to the biblical evidence is not likely to settle this old battle in favor of one over the other approach.

More crucial than the biblical evidence here is the long-recognized systematic disadvantage in treating the divine nature as an aspect of the doctrine of God the Father. Lurking in this approach is the danger of subordinationism which can only be overcome by a vigorous subsequent defense of the substantial divinity of the Son and the Spirit against the suggestion that they are only derivatively divine. In any case, it is not clear that a creative recovery of Greek patristic trinitarian theology would necessarily facilitate a spiritual or pastoral retrieval of what might be called trinitarian realism. The sometimes unperceived, although always undesired, tendency toward a subordinationism in some Greek trinitarian theology was to a certain extent surpassed by subsequent developments in the doctrine of the Trinity as elaborated in the Western theology by St Augustine and others. Something is to be gained in intelligibility and breadth by theological accounts (like Aquinas') which link the biblical revelation of the divine being and identity as trinitarian with philosophical reflection about the kind of life which is enjoyed by the one, transcendent cause of the world whom Christians know and worship as Father, Son and Holy Spirit.

Debate has also been generated by Rahner's strategy for dealing with a second disjunction in some standard trinitarian theology. This strategy gave rise to the central axiom of Rahner's theology of the Trinity: the identity of the economic and the immanent Trinity. The axiom is susceptible of a perfectly non-controversial reading. The God who in the activities of salvation appears as triune (the economic Trinity) is triune in himself (the immanent Trinity). Father, Son, and Holy Spirit are not roles which God assumes for the purposes of engagement in the economy of salvation. Father, Son, and Holy Spirit are God in himself. The external missions of the Son and the Holy Spirit are extensions of the internal processions in God himself. The Trinity is not a culture-bound manifestation of the hidden God whom we never know in himself and who employs a number of impersonations. Being the Trinity is being God. Christ's revelation of the nature and intentions of God is definitive and complete. Although, given the limitations of human knowledge and the utter transcendence of the divine mystery, God is never fully comprehensible, God's trinitarian self-description is confessed by Christians to provide the most intimate possible knowledge of God's being. Rahner's axiom should be construed as a strong reaffirmation of this traditional understanding of the doctrine of the Trinity. Rahner advanced this axiom to offset a disjunction between the economic and the immanent Trinity latent in neoscholastic accounts which neglect the trinitarian structure of the divine activity in salvation.[15]

But the conceptuality which Rahner employed to express the identity of the economic and the immanent Trinity has provoked controversy because it involves too tight an identification of the missions and the processions. In this conceptuality, the trinitarian processions and missions are explicated in terms of the concepts of self-expression and self-possession. This conceptuality can suggest that the Trinity really could not be fully itself independently of the orders of creation and redemption.

Central here is Rahner's conception of the nature of symbols which he employed in various contexts in his theological program (e.g., trinitarian theology, christology, ecclesiology, sacramental theology, and exegesis).[16] The so-called 'ontology of the symbol' takes self-involving performative utterances for its paradigm case of what constitutes a symbol. Self-involving performatives are expressions in which *saying* something is tantamount to *doing* something. For example, promising obedience equals committing onself to the performance of particular actions. Generalized and extended to account for symbols, the point would be – not simply that certain actions performed by an agent are symbolic – but that the agent (and events and things as well) is by nature symbolic. As in self-involving performatives, an entity becomes itself (does something) in expressing itself (in saying something).[17]

Rahner applied the ontology of the symbol to his trinitarian theology. The Father expresses himself in the Son in order to possess himself in the Spirit. The processions of the Son and Spirit are thus processions of self-expression and self-possession. Rahner insisted with the tradition that the external missions of the Trinity are extensions of the processions. But in traditional theology, these missions were understood as freely chosen actions, described in terms of efficient causality. Given a description of the processions in terms of the ontology of the symbol in combination with an insistence on the strict identity of the economic and the immanent Trinity, Rahner's trinitarian theology risked a pattern of explanation in which the free actions of creation, incarnation, and grace could be seen as necessary extensions of God's inner self-expression and self-possession.[18]

This tendency also appeared in Rahner's christology. The ontology of the symbol enabled Rahner to make a strong case for the Second Person of the Trinity being the only one who could become incarnate, since only the Son is the self-expression of the Father.[19] The incarnation was for Rahner the supreme instance of the ontology of the symbol. There is no doubt about the great explanatory power of this conceptuality, as can be seen in Rahner's theology of the church and the sacraments.[20] But in Rahner's christology, as in his trinitarian theology generally, it raised the specter of a necessitarian account of divine action.

Another major source of debate concerning Rahner's theology is the universalism of his theology of grace and revelation. To be sure, Rahner was above all else a Catholic dogmatic theologian who, in asking about the conditions for the possibility of this or that aspect of the Christian mystery, endeavored to display the continuities between the natural and the supernatural orders. Rahner's characteristic treatment of these innerly Christian dogmatic issues afforded new perspectives upon the nature of universal features of religious experience and wisdom. For the most part, these perspectives arose as corollaries of Rahner's central theological proposals. But when either critics or defenders of Rahner's theology reverse the priorities here, they applaud or censure his theological program for its subordination of innerly Christian doctrinal concerns to another explicandum, viz., the universal presence of grace. Rahner's theology of revelation provides an excellent illustration of this controversy.

The doctrine of revelation constituted a major focus of attention for Catholic and Protestant theologians throughout Rahner's lifetime. Progressive theologians during this period sought to correct what they saw as the extreme propositionalism of some conservative accounts of revelation which had arisen in response to the seeming subjectivism of liberal and modernist accounts of the doctrine. It was characteristic of progressive positions to frame the doctrine of revelation in terms of categories of interpersonal relations with particular emphasis on some notion of self-revelation. In revelation, God provides not just information about objective states of affairs, but offers personal communion with himself. Revelation invites a response of faith not just as an intellectual assent, but as a complete personal commitment to God.[21]

Rahner was one of many Catholic theologians who sought to correct standard neoscholastic theology by arguing along these lines. His characteristic contribution to this discussion was to give an account of the conditions for the possibility in human knowledge of a recognition and reception of divine revelation. Typically, then, Rahner strove to disclose the structure of the Christian revelation by advancing a transcendental argument which appealed to the general states of human beings who are all embraced in the concrete plan of salvation.

Rahner's proposal concerning the doctrine of revelation parallels his conception of a universal divine self-communication which as uncreated grace transforms the horizon of all knowledge and willing. Since the divine self-communication is universal, revelation is in an important sense universal: it has a history which coincides with the whole history of humankind (in Rahner's technical terminology, the 'universal transcendental history of revelation'). Throughout this history human beings have striven to give expression to their acknowledgment of this universal revelation in a variety of symbols, actions and forms of life some of which have been explicitly religious (and could be studied in the history of religions) and many of which have not been. Hence it is possible to speak of a history of revelation in a second sense, also coextensive with the history of humankind, as the history of the expressions of original and universal revelation (the 'universal categorical history of revelation'). The Old Testament and Christianity have a special place in this history of expressions of revelation because in both cases God manifested himself in a more direct way and furnished the means by which all human beings could respond to him in a relatively undistorted way (the 'special categorical history of revelation'). But the place of Christianity is unique because in Jesus Christ both the divine revelation and the human response to it are perfect and definitive ('the unsurpassable climax of revelation').[22]

Rahner posits transcendental revelation in order to explain the structure of special Christian revelation. By extension, this provides the basis for an account of non-Christian religious experience and wisdom.[23] Classical theology fielded the notion of general revelation – identifiable as a possibility only from special revelation – for similar reasons. But given its identification of transcendental revelation with general revelation, Rahner's argument seems to reverse the order of the classical view. The transcendental argument he advances can be misconstrued to imply that the categorical revelation entrusted to the Christian community is merely an instance, along with other more or less valid instances, of general revelation.[24] Rahner's notorious designation of these extra-Christian possibilities as 'anonymous Christianity' confounds the difficulties here. Although the work of some of his popularizers merits it, the inevitable charge that his theology subverts the traditional claim of the Christian community to be in possession of a definitive revelation seems unjust when pressed against Rahner himself. Perhaps such a misunderstanding of Rahner's theology of revelation is unavoidable given the subtlety and difficulty of the transcendental argumentation in which it is framed.

ACHIEVEMENT AND AGENDA

Rahner's achievements help to define the continuing agenda to which his theological proposals give rise. He successfully challenged the hegemony of a narrow and defensive neoscholasticism in early twentieth-century Roman Catholic theology. With refreshing orig-inality, he broadened the standard treatments of one after another doctrine, exposing anew the depths of intelligibility in the Christian faith and unleashing its power to shape and transform human life and society. Despite the unsystematic character of Rahner's theology, its richness and suggestiveness will undoubtedly stand the test of time and guarantee him a permanent place as an authoritative teacher in the Catholic tradition and beyond.

This achievement sets an agenda for further research. Commentators have devoted considerable attention to questions of the validity of the transcendental reading of Aquinas espoused by Rahner and others. But Rahner's links with scholastic movements in all their diversity have yet to be fully explored. The objective of such study would be to expose the continuities which obtain between Rahner's proposals and typical neoscholastic formulations in order to define more precisely his place in the history of classical and modern Catholic theology.

On a broader front, Rahner's theological program turned out to have a forceful and effective apologetic edge. His presentation of the Christian faith restored its appeal for many who had been swayed by modernity's critique of religion. In the face of this challenge, Rahner's writings embody a strong affirmation of the central elements of the Christian tradition. The requirements of an emerging world church in dialogue with large religious and non-religious movements increasingly attracted his attention in his later essays. But he reaffirmed the importance of institutional commitment in the practice of Christian faith. While critical, his theology remained firmly loyal to the traditions and authority of the Christian community. Through many spiritual writings, Rahner stressed the importance of the interior life for modern men and women, and thus clearly drew many to practices of prayer and meditation.

But Rahner's enthusiastic, if critical, embrace of modernity entwines the fortunes of his theological program with those of specific modern conceptualities which are themselves under attack. It was Rahner's contention that Catholic theology must appropriate the transcendental, anthropological and subjective turns characteristic of modern thought. Thus in an intellectual climate in which postmodern philosophers and theologians are increasingly critical of precisely these elements of modern thought, Rahner's theological program will seem to be wedded to outmoded interests and conceptions. Such a view of Rahner is fostered by disciples and popularizers who typically construe the entire Rahnerian corpus in terms of its foundational segments – commending precisely the modern strategies which are in retreat elsewhere. An important question is whether a relatively unsystematic reading of his works will help to insure the continued appeal and viability of his theological program in an intellectual climate alert to the deficiencies of modern philosophy since Descartes.[25]

Rahner was introduced to the English-speaking world in 1961 with the publication of a translation of the first volume of *Theological Investigations*. Since that time and particularly after the Second Vatican Council, Rahner has had a powerful impact on English-speaking theology, especially in the United States. His theology swept into the vacuum created by the collapse of the neoscholastic synthesis in American Catholic theology after the council.[26] This relatively uncritical appropriation of Rahner's thought has in some circles fostered the emergence of a 'Rahnerian' orthodoxy to replace the neoscholastic orthodoxy which Rahner strove to unseat. In all likelihood, this form of Rahnerian theology will yield to more eclectic appropriations of his program under the pressure of postmodern developments in Anglo-American philosophy and theology. The deeply traditional and scholastic character of Rahner's thought, and the recognition that he cannot be properly assessed apart from the achievements of classical theology will presumably encourage a more balanced appropriation of his theology.

Generally speaking, Rahner's essays furnish a model for recovering the tradition in new contexts. Although the style of these essays is famously dense, their format is admirably free of the technical apparatus which sometimes encumbers academic writing. Surely this was deliberate. Despite their convoluted prose, Rahner's essays are accessible precisely because of the directness and inventiveness with which they approach classical theological themes. While steeped in the scholastic tradition, the essays are remarkably free of its trappings.

Perhaps the greatest achievement of the program of this lifelong 'amateur' theologian was its unfailing testimony to the mystery to which the Christian tradition bears witness. The absence of system in Rahner's theological program finds its final explanation in the nature of this mystery. 'The true system of thought really is the knowledge that humanity is finally directed precisely not toward what it can control in knowledge but toward the absolute mystery as such; that mystery is . . . the blessed goal of knowledge which comes to itself when it is with the incomprehensible one. . . . In other words, then, the system is the system of what cannot be systematized.'[27]

NOTES

1 Karl Rahner, 'Reflections on Methodology in Theology', *Theological Investigations*, 11, pp. 68–114.
2 James Buckley, 'Karl Rahner as a Dogmatic Theologian', *The Thomist*, 47 (1983), pp. 364–94.
3 Stephan Korner, *Fundamental Questions of Philosophy*, (London, 1969), pp. 213–19.
4 Thomas Aquinas, *Summa theologiae*, 1a. 1, 8.
5 Karl Rahner, 'Theology and Anthropology', *Theological Investigations*, 9, pp. 28–45.
6 Karl Rahner, 'Observations on the Doctrine of God in Catholic Dogmatics', *Theological Investigations*, 9, pp. 127–44.
7 Aquinas, *Summa theologiae*, 1a. 2.
8 Ibid., 1a. 13.
9 Karl Rahner, 'The Concept of Mystery', *Theological Investigations*, 4, pp. 36–73.
10 Henri Rondet, *The Grace of Christ* (New York, 1966), pp. 275–348.
11 Aquinas, *Summa theologiae*, 1a2ae. 106–10.
12 Karl Rahner, 'Concerning the Relationship Between Nature and Grace', *Theological Investigations*, 1, pp. 287–317; 'Some Implications of the Scholastic Concept of Uncreated Grace', ibid., pp. 319–46.
13 Aquinas, *Summa theologiae*, 1a. 27–43.
14 Karl Rahner, 'Theos in the New Testament', *Theological Investigations*, 1, pp. 79–148.
15 Karl Rahner, *The Trinity* (New York, 1970).
16 Karl Rahner, 'The Theology of the Symbol', *Theological Investigations*, 4, pp. 221–52.
17 James Buckley, 'On Being a Symbol', *Theological Studies*, 40 (1979), pp. 453–73.
18 William J. Hill, *The Three-Personed God* (Washington DC, 1982), pp. 130–45.
19 Karl Rahner, 'On the Theology of the Incarnation', *Theological Investigations*, 4, pp. 105–20.
20 Karl Rahner, *The Church and the Sacraments* (New York, 1963).
21 Avery Dulles, *Models of Revelation* (New York, 1982).
22 Karl Rahner, *Foundations of Christian Faith* (New York, 1978), pp. 138–75.
23 Karl Rahner, 'Christianity and Non-Christian Religions', *Theological Investigations*, 5, pp. 115–34. For a fuller discussion of Rahner's theology of religions see vol. II of *The Modern Theologians*, chapter 14.
24 J. A. DiNoia, 'Implicit Faith, General Revelation and the State of Non-Christians', *The Thomist*, 47 (1983), pp. 209–41.
25 Fergus Kerr, *Theology After Wittgenstein* (Oxford, 1986).
26 Philip Gleason, *Keeping the Faith* (Notre Dame, 1987), pp. 136–77.
27 Paul Imhof and Hubert Biallowons (eds), *Karl Rahner in Dialogue: Conversations and Interviews 1965–1982* (New York, 1986), pp. 196–7.

BIBLIOGRAPHY

Primary

Rahner, K., *Theological Investigations*, 20 vols (New York, 1961–; London 1961–).
—, *Spirit in the World* (New York, 1968).
—, *Hearers of the Word* (New York, 1969).
—, *Foundations of Christian Faith* (New York, London, 1978).
—, in *The Practice of Faith: A Handbook of Contemporary Spirituality*, ed. Karl Lehmann and Karl Raffelt (New York, 1984).

Secondary

Hill, William J., 'Uncreated Grace: A Critique of Karl Rahner', *The Thomist*, 27 (1963), pp. 333–56.
Marshall, Bruce, *Christology in Conflict: The Identity of a Saviour in Rahner and Barth* (Oxford, 1987).
McCool, Gerald A., *A Rahner Reader* (New York, 1975).
O'Donovan, Leo J., 'A Journey into Time: The Legacy of Karl Rahner's Last Years', *Theological Studies*, 46 (1985), pp. 621–46.
Pedley, C. J. 'An English Bibliographical Aid to Karl Rahner', *Heythrop Journal*, 24 (1984), pp. 319–65.
Vorgrimler, Herbert, *Understanding Karl Rahner* (New York, 1986).

10

Bernard Lonergan

Hugo Meynell

INTRODUCTION: LIFE AND INFLUENCES

Bernard Joseph Francis Lonergan was born in Buckingham, Quebec, on 17 December, 1904. His father was a land surveyor, who had to be away from home for much of the time. At the age of fifteen Lonergan almost died when he underwent an operation for mastoiditis; his mother spent two months almost constantly at his bedside. In 1922 he entered the Society of Jesus, and spent the next two years at the Jesuit novitiate in Guelph, Ontario. He studied philosophy at Heythrop College in England from 1926 to 1929; and after three years of teaching at Loyola College in Montreal he went to the Gregorian University in Rome, where he took a licentiate in theology in 1937, finishing his work for a doctorate three years later.

For the next thirteen years, Lonergan was professor of theology in Jesuit seminaries in Montreal and Toronto; in 1953 he was assigned to the faculty of the Gregorian University in Rome. In 1965 he fell ill with cancer of the lung, and one lung was removed; he was sent after his recovery to Regis College in Willowdale, Ontario, where his relatively light teaching schedule enabled him to concentrate on his writing. In 1971–2 he was Stillman Professor at Harvard Divinity School, and from 1975 to 1978 he was Visiting Distinguished Professor in the Department of Theology at Boston College. He died in 1984, shortly before his eightieth birthday.[1]

Lonergan was taught philosophy from textbooks based on the thought of Francis Suarez, the Spanish Jesuit philosopher of the late sixteenth and early seventeenth century; but he felt deeply critical of this position from the first. A glance at the succession of Lonergan's publications, in the light of the well-known development in Roman Catholic attitudes over the past thirty years or so, is apt to foster the belief that Lonergan started out as a Thomist, and only later became preoccupied with modernity. But such a view of the matter would be quite wrong, as has been shown convincingly by Frederick Crowe.[2] It can be seen from Lonergan's early papers that his basic ideas were solidly in place by 1929, before he had read a line of Aquinas. His conception of 'insight' seems to have been derived from Euclid; his notion of the role of judgment from the work of J. H. Newman, whose *Grammar of Assent* he read through many times. Lonergan's early tendencies towards nominalism were counteracted by a study of Plato, and of Augustine's early dialogues. At Rome he came under the influence of the work of Maréchal, especially in respect of the latter's attempt to refound what was of permanent value in Thomism on a transcendental basis which took Kant's *Critique* into account.[3]

SURVEY

Lonergan's lifelong ambition was to find a method for theology which would take into account modern advances in science and face the objections to the enterprise raised by modern philosophers. Few great minds have matured so slowly; Lonergan was nearly forty when his first large-scale work, a series of articles describing and vindicating Aquinas' account of grace, was published (it was later issued as the book *Grace and Freedom*). A few years later there followed another series of articles on Aquinas' thought, this time on his account of the human mind and his application of this account to the understanding of the doctrine of the Trinity (*Verbum. Word and Idea in Aquinas*). In 1957 appeared Lonergan's largest and probably greatest book, *Insight. A Study of Human Understanding*. Its aim was to lay the groundwork for method in theology by outlining methods for other disciplines, including mathematics, physical and biological science, psychotherapy, political theory, metaphysics, and ethics. It is concluded by a sketch of a natural theology, followed by an outline of what a revelation from God might be supposed to contain. During the late 1950s and early 1960s, Lonergan was lecturing in Rome on the doctrine of the Trinity and on christology; each set of lectures exhibits the development of the doctrine concerned as the ever-deepening understanding of revealed mysteries. In 1972 there appeared *Method in Theology*, which is in some sense the culmination of Lonergan's work. Central to that book is appreciation of the great changes constitutive of the advent of modern culture, to which the theologian must accommodate herself if she is to do her work adequately. To do this she needs a transcultural method, which is to be found by attention to one's own mental operations; these are fundamentally a matter of experience, understanding, judgment, and decision. All of these are to be employed to establish what has been the content of the Christian (or other religious) tradition in the past, and what one is to make of it in the present and for the future.

Quite apart from Lonergan's philosophical and theological achievement stands his work on economics, on which he was engaged in the 1930s and the last decade of his life. The relevant material has not yet been published; but is reckoned by some good judges to be comparable in importance to the rest of his output.

CONTENT: KNOWLEDGE, TRINITY, INCARNATION, AND METHOD

Three topics may be isolated as central to Lonergan's work: (i) the foundations of knowledge in consciousness; (ii) the application of the analysis of knowledge and consciousness to the basic Christian doctrines of the Trinity and the Incarnation; (iii) method in theology.

(i) Anti-foundationalism is becoming a well-established and fashionable view in philosophy; how could Lonergan have opposed it? As he sees the matter, it is self-destructive to deny that one ought to be attentive, intelligent, reasonable or responsible, if one is to get to know what is true on any matter whatever, or to know and do what is good in any conceivable situation. As he pointed out, there are few authorities who explicitly deny that they ever attend to the evidence of their senses, or have ever had the experience of coming to understand what had previously puzzled them. Furthermore, university lecturers seldom admit to their students that they have no inkling of what it is to make a judgment for a good as opposed to a bad reason. And authors of learned books do not generally begin bluntly by assuring their readers that they have never consciously made a responsible decision, least of all in offering this book to the public. The fact is that all rational discussion presupposes that the 'transcendental precepts' (be attentive, be intelligent, be reasonable, be responsible)[4] are being obeyed. However, whole schools of thought are based on the premiss that they are not and cannot be. For example, strict behaviorism and eliminative materialism imply that such conscious acts are not real, but are illusions of primitive folk-psychology, destined to disappear in favor of a truly scientific account of the mind. Thus both these influential philosophical and psychological doctrines are what Lonergan calls 'counter-positions',[5] incompatible with their own being asserted as a matter of reasonable belief or as a result of responsible decision.

It might be objected that the 'transcendental precepts' are simply not applicable to all areas of inquiry. But this objection does not stand up to examination. The physicist, the sociologist and the historian all, in the course of their investigations, have to decide responsibly to attend to evidence, to accept provisionally the account which best fits that evidence, and so on. No more in organic chemistry than in palaeontology does one tend to advance towards the truth by brushing relevant data aside. (One may well create more favorable prospects for oneself; or gratify those in a position to advance one's career; but that is another matter.) In cosmology, just as much as in ancient history, one has to be at once bold and ingenious in formulating hypotheses (intelligent), and stringent in testing them against the available evidence (reasonable).

The fundamental difference between the natural and social sciences is that in the latter, as opposed to the former, the object as well as the subject of investigation may be known as exercizing the transcendental precepts more or less. Furthermore, human individuals or groups may indulge in a 'flight from insight',[6] where inconvenient or uncomfortable acts of understanding or reason are systematically avoided. In the individual, the habit of such evasions will lead to a radical discrepancy between his real self and his conception of himself; if his life is sufficiently disturbed as a result, he will need psychotherapeutic help. In and between groups, the flight from insight gives rise to increasing discontent and social disruption; with each group blackening the image of its rivals in order to preserve its own self-esteem.[7]

As well as the demands of intelligence and reason, Lonergan takes into account the permanent emotional needs of human beings, which are too easily met by the falsifications of myth[8] in modern as in ancient times, in societies which have the benefit of scientific and philosophical sophistication as in those which have not.[9] What would meet both requirements, and so enable human beings to become fully authentic, applying the transcendental precepts in an unrestricted manner, would be a historically true narrative which met the emotional needs catered to by myth without being enmeshed in its falsifications. Granted the existence of God, one might suppose God to have provided just such a solution to the human predicament. The authentic human being who apprehends the human situation, with its vast potentialities and lamentable moral tragedy, for what it is, will seek for that solution, and if she finds it will embrace it, apply it to the reorientation of her own life, and proclaim it to others.[10] However, it is important to note that the truth of one religion (Christianity) by no means implies that one may not be authentically religious within other traditions.[11]

Still, it might be asked whether there are after all sound reasons for believing that there is a God. Lonergan holds that there are. The theory of knowledge outlined above gives rise to a corresponding metaphysics or theory of reality. On the basis of the data presented to our senses, we (intelligently) propound and (reasonably) assess hypotheses and theories about how the world is; the world is in the last analysis nothing other than what is knowable in this way. It is thus intrinsically intelligible; the notion of unintelligible parts or aspects of the world (such as would correspond to no conceivable hypothesis or theory) turns out in the long run to be incoherent.[12] The existence and nature of such a world is to be accounted for fully only if there exists an 'unrestricted act of understanding' which conceives and wills it rather as each human being conceives and wills her actions and products; and such a being is none other than what religious persons call 'God'.[13] It is of course to be acknowledged that arguments of the sort just mentioned rather seldom lead to religious conversion; more commonly, religious conversion comes first, and the soundness of such arguments is recognized subsequently.[14]

(ii) As Lonergan sees it, the solution to the deepest problems of Christian systematic theology is to be found by attending to the nature of human consciousness, and re-expressing the best of the medieval 'metaphysical' achievement in this direction in terms of an 'interiority' more consonant with our own times. If God as creator is remotely to be understood by thinking about our practical consciousness of ourselves as makers and doers, so God as Trinity is to be thus understood in terms of our 'existential' consciousness, our attitude to ourselves. A human being's conception of herself is apt to be distorted, her self-love inappropriate. In God, on the contrary, infinite understanding may be understood to give rise to utterly just conception, and proper self-love to emerge from both. As understanding giving rise to conception, God is Father; as conception so arising, Son; as love emerging from understanding and conception, Holy Spirit. Thus the triune God of Christian belief, three persons in one substance, is to be understood as 'three subjects of a single, dynamic, existential consciousness'.[15] It should be noted – here Lonergan attends to the decrees of the First Vatican Council – that we cannot show that God must be triune just as intelligent cause of the world. But he insists that we can show, by attention to our own consciousness, how God *can* be so; and the hypothesis that God is triune in the manner just outlined accords both with the New Testament and the doctrinal definitions of the Church.

The incarnation of the Son may be regarded as God's conception of self expressed in terms of a human life. Christ as one person in two natures is to be conceived, in terms of 'interiority', as one subject conscious of self as both human and divine. We ourselves, as well as the specifically human consciousness of intelligence, reasonableness, and responsibility, have a sensitive and emotional consciousness of a kind that we share with the higher animals. We may thus remotely conceive of how one Person could be conscious of self as both human and divine; and this conception appears to do justice at once both to tradition and to Scripture.[16]

(iii) Christianity (in common with other religions) comes to us as a message proclaimed at various times and in various situations in the past, which we have to apply to human life in the present and the future. This entails, as Lonergan says, that there are two phases to theology as reflection on religion, the *mediating* (where we retrieve the message from the past) and the *mediated* (where we apply it to our own situation). In the mediating phase we have to fix what the content of the relevant documents is; we have to understand what their authors meant in terms of their own times; we have to weave documents and meanings into an objective account of what was going forward; and we have to make a value judgment about how far the authors and agents concerned were correct or mistaken, in good faith or corrupt, in what they said and did. So we have here the first four 'functional specialities' which are constitutive of mediating theology – *research, interpretation, history,* and *dialectic.* The practice of dialectic in particular, the making of value-judgments about the words and deeds of others, makes ever more pressing the question of questions, 'How far am I a genuinely converted subject, thoroughly in love with what is truly lovable, and committed to trying to know what is true and to know and do what is good?' The clarification and explication of the nature of human authenticity or conversion is the role of the fifth functional specialty, the first of the *mediated* phase, which Lonergan calls *foundations.* It remains to put forward the set of judgments of fact and value to be assented to here and now by the converted subject (*doctrines*); to show how these fit together into a whole which coheres with itself and with the rest of our knowledge (*systematics*); and to communicate the set of doctrines thus systematically understood to each human being in her own situation and cultural milieu, and at her own intellectual level (*communications*). To distinguish 'functional' from 'field specialties' (Old Testament, New Testament, patristics, and so on, with their infinite subdivisions), is to be encouraged to see theology as a dynamic whole, to which each part is necessary, rather than merely an uncoordinated bundle of ever more specialized and mutually unrelated scholarly disciplines.[17]

Lonergan distinguishes two notions of culture; the classical, supposed to be universal and permanent; and the empirical, where a culture is the set of meanings and values which informs a way of life, thus varying very considerably from place to place and from time to time. It is the move from a classical to an empirical notion of culture, very typical of our own time, which demands that theology, consisting as it does of reflection on a faith which is to be preached to every culture, should have a transcultural base; and it is just this which Lonergan's method aims to supply.[18] He further alludes to a number of 'differentiations of consciousness'. First, there is that of common sense, which is the birthright of everyone as a person of her place and time; most human beings of most times have been confined within it. Poets and artists on the one hand, and religious adepts on the other, respectively are characterized by aesthetically and religiously differentiated consciousness. Then there is the theoretical differentiation of consciousness represented by medieval scholasticism and modern science, where persons look for exact definitions of the terms of their discourse; the medieval theological achievement was largely a matter of the re-expression of the content of Christian faith in terms of this. The scholarly differentiation of consciousness, which is the notable achievement of nineteenth-century Germany, is a matter of ability to apprehend the common sense of places and times other than one's own. The application of scholarship to the reading of the bible and of ecclesiastical authorities has brought about something of a crisis in theology, since it is difficult at first sight to comprehend how so many documents from so many backgrounds could amount to the expression of one faith. The problem may be resolved by an entry into the differentiation of consciousness of interiority, represented by philosophers of the phenomenological school and by Lonergan himself, which by attention to acts of consciousness themselves can show how the deliveries of other differentiations of consciousness can be reconciled and coordinated.[19]

DEBATE

Many objections to Lonergan's whole approach to theology have appeared in print, of which one may mention the following:[20]

1 His methodological principles are too restrictive.[21]
2 His appeal to introspection in articulating basic human mental capacities is illegitimate.[22]
3 His treatment of objectivity is inadequate.[23]
4 His preoccupation with epistemology leads to an unsatisfactory metaphysics.[24]
5 He underestimates the discontinuity of cultures.[25]
6 For all his repudiation of 'classicism', he has not outgrown it.[26]
7 His method is not specific enough to theology.[27]
8 His insistence on 'religious conversion' for many phases of theology unduly restricts discussion, for example with atheists.[28]
9 His method is so broadly conceived that it puts everyone in the right.[29]
10 His work pre-supposes the truth of the Catholic faith.[30]
11 It is not clear from this method where among the functional specialities the question of God belongs.[31]
12 His distinction between basic elements in cognition is too vague to be serviceable.[32]

There is no space here to do more than sketch the kind of answer that Lonergan might have given to these objections. It does seem self-destructive to deny that one performs such acts as observing, inquiring, framing hypotheses, marshalling evidence, judging, and deciding; as I have already argued. It is furthermore at least rather odd to claim that we cannot attend to the fact that we perform these mental operations. That it is crudely misleading to suppose that in doing so we take an 'inner look' at ourselves is emphasized at least as strongly by Lonergan as by any of his opponents (cf. 2 above). The basic elements in cognition as distinguished by Lonergan do seem applicable to all topics of inquiry (is there really such a topic where one ought not to aspire to judge in accordance with the available evidence?), and to be distinct from one another (how could one reduce judging to the enjoyment of sense-experience, or deciding to the envisagement of hypotheses? Cf. 12). And for all the enormous diversity of cultures, a person is hardly human except so far as she acts on the basis of some judgments arrived at on the basis of some understanding of some evidence; the 'transcendental precepts' thus do appear to have a transcultural application (cf. 5).

To be 'objective' for Lonergan is nothing other than to apply the first three transcendental precepts in a thoroughgoing way; not just to take a look at what is there to be looked at. This enables one to be objective about what is unobservable – like historical events, the particles of nuclear physics, and the thoughts and feelings of other persons. 'Genuine objectivity is the fruit of authentic subjectivity.'[33] That this is an unsatisfactory account of the matter has not been shown; and it at once avoids the notorious paradoxes of behaviorism and pragmatism, and resolves some knotty methodological problems in the human sciences (cf. 3). And if we come to know the world by means of the basic types of mental act listed by Lonergan, it does not seem implausible to infer that the world is nothing other than what we thus come to know – epistemology in this way giving rise to metaphysics (cf. 4). It is surely a virtue in this view, furthermore, that in accordance with it one can see all the main alternative philosophical positions – empiricist, materialist, pragmatist, idealist, naive realist, and so on – as partial viewpoints, each having a certain merit, but erring through exaggerating one or more basic mental operations at the expense of the rest. Similarly, it seems a hopeful feature of Lonergan's account that virtually all religious positions turn out to have *some* worthwhile feature to contribute to a fully ecumenical consciousness; and that such limitations and oversights as they contain are liable to emerge through discussion with others (cf. 9). The 'religious conversion' with Lonergan specifies as necessary to work in the last five functional specialities amounts rather to a basic and radical good will, than to espousal of any particular set of doctrinal propositions, let alone those of Lonergan's own Roman Catholic Christianity (cf. 8).

It is important to note that Lonergan in *Method* sets out to *describe* what he regards as the fundamental tasks of theology, and to *justify* his claim that they are fundamental; he does not attempt there actually to *perform* these tasks. Lonergan assumes for this book a Roman Catholic readership in the first instance; it is thus convenient for him to take Christian and Catholic doctrines as examples for discussion. But some brand of Buddhism, or even of Marxism, would have done just as well for his fundamental purposes; here are sets of existentially significant beliefs with a bearing on religion, which have been proclaimed in the past, and which one might wish to commend and apply for the present and future (cf. 10). As to the *explanation* or *defense* of specifically Christian or Catholic doctrines, Lonergan undertakes it elsewhere than in *Method*,[34] in the context of which it would have been quite improper. It is true that the eight functional specialities might be applied to any ideology whatever; but Lonergan makes clear enough[35] how their special application is to be made to religion. And short of such generality of application, the theologian cannot seriously raise, as surely she ought to do, the question of whether all religious belief is based on error (cf. 7).

Whatever the limitations of 'classicism', it would be folly to neglect the achievement of those confined to a 'classicist' frame of mind, for example, in systematics; one may applaud the work of a systematic theologian, without insisting on the linguistic uniformity which is an important aspect of classicism (cf. 6). The question of God belongs to *all* the functional specialities – since documents treat of God, authors meant something in writing those documents, they were more or less in good faith in writing as they did, we ourselves have to make up our minds what we are to believe about God, and so on and so on (cf. 11).

ACHIEVEMENT AND AGENDA

Thomas Kuhn has described the haphazard nature of any subject of inquiry until some mastermind proposes a 'paradigm'. That contemporary theology is in a somewhat chaotic state, and that its fundamental principles are in dispute, would hardly be denied by anyone. Lonergan has in effect proposed such a 'paradigm' for theology; this is the fundamental nature of his achievement. The main agenda which he has left us is closely to examine the validity of his proposals, and, so far as they are sound, to apply them to performing the herculean tasks which confront the contemporary theologian.

NOTES

1 I owe this biographical material to the kindness of Fr F. C. Crowe S J.
2 In a talk delivered at the Lonergan Workshop in Boston College on June 15, 1987.
3 Cf. Lonergan's own account of his development in 'Insight Revisited', *A Second Collection*, pp. 263–78.
4 B. J. F. Lonergan, *Method in Theology*, pp. 13–17, 20, 53, 55.
5 B. J. F. Lonergan, *Insight. A Study of Human Understanding*, pp. 387–90, 488–9, etc.; *Method*, pp. 249–54.
6 Lonergan, *Insight*, pp. xi–xii, xiv, 191, 199–203.
7 Ibid. chs VI and VII.
8 The term 'myth' is in some ways unfortunate, as it does not carry the connotation of error in much modern usage. Yet it seems convenient and even inevitable in a brief exposition. See Lonergan, 'Insight Revisited', p. 275.
9 Lonergan, *Insight*, pp. 539–47.

10 Ibid., ch. XX.
11 I attempt to combine here the viewpoint of *Insight*, of which the argument appears to lead to the conviction that Christianity is the one true religion, with that of *Method*, which brings out the positive (and negative) potential of religions in general. Cf. Lonergan, *Method*, pp. 109–12.
12 One may compare the objections of Fichte, Hegel and others to Kant's conception of the 'thing in itself'.
13 Lonergan, *Insight*, ch. XIX.
14 This was emphasized strongly by Lonergan in writings subsequent to *Insight*; cf. *Method*, p. 339. In his later writings, Lonergan distinguishes three types of conversion: intellectual, which is the unremitting pursuit of truth along with radical rejection of the 'cognitional myth', that knowledge is fundamentally a matter of taking a look; moral, which is the replacement of mere satisfactions with real values in the aims of one's living; and religious, which is the fundamental re-ordering of one's life in love.
15 Lonergan, *A Second Collection*, p. 25.
16 Lonergan, *De Deo Trino*, I and II; *De Verbo Incarnato*.
17 Lonergan, *Method, passim*; especially chs 5–14.
18 Ibid., pp. xi, 2, 29, 124, 300–2, 315, 326, 363.
19 Ibid., pp. 302–19.
20 I have treated these objections at much greater length in *The Theology of Bernard Lonergan*, ch. 3.
21 B. Hebblethwaite, *The Practice of Theology* (Cambridge, 1980), p. 19.
22 P. McGrath, in P. Corcoran (ed.), *Looking at Lonergan's Method*, p. 34.
23 Mary Hesse, in Corcoran, *Looking at Lonergan's Method*, pp. 68–71.
24 W. R. Shea, 'The Stance and Task of the Foundational Theologian', *Heythrop Journal*, 1976, p. 278. Cf. J. B. Reichmann, 'The Transcendental Method and the Psychogenesis of Being', *The Thomist*, 1968, pp. 449–508.
25 Nicholas Lash, in Corcoran, *Looking at Lonergan's Method*, p. 127.
26 Shea, 'Stance and Task', p. 275.
27 Karl Rahner, 'Some Critical Thoughts on Functional Specialities in Theology', in *Foundations of Theology*, ed. P. McShane, pp. 194–6.
28 W. Pannenberg, in Corcoran, *Looking at Lonergan's Method*, p. 98; also Hebblethwaite, *Practice of Theology*, pp. 18–19. Lonergan states clearly in fact that a contemporary Catholic theology must address itself not only to all Christians, but to non-Christians and atheists (*Second Collection*, p. 62).
29 E. McLaren, in Corcoran, *Looking at Lonergan's Method*, p. 81.
30 David Tracy, cited in Shea, 'Stance and Task', p. 279.
31 Shea, ibid., p. 281.
32 Hesse, in Corcoran, *Looking at Lonergan's Method*, pp. 60–1, 67, 72.
33 Lonergan, *Method*, p. 292.
34 Lonergan, *Insight*, chs XIX and XX; also *De Deo Trino* and *De Verbo Incarnato*.
35 Lonergan, *Method*, ch. 4.

BIBLIOGRAPHY

Primary

Lonergan, B. J. F., *Insight. A Study of Human Understanding* (London, 1957).
—, *De Deo Trino*, I and II (Rome, 1964).
—, *De Verbo Incarnato* (Rome, 1964).
—, *Collection*, (London, 1967).
—, *Verbum. Word and Idea in Aquinas* (London, 1968).
—, *Grace and Freedom* (London, 1971).
—, *Method in Theology* (London, 1972).
—, *Philosophy of God and Theology* (London, 1973).
—, *A Second Collection* (London, 1974).
—, *The Way to Nicea* (London, 1976).
—, *A Third Collection* (New York, 1985).

Secondary

Corcoran, P. (ed.), *Looking at Lonergan's Method* (Dublin, 1975).
Crowe, F. E., *The Lonergan Enterprise* (Cambridge, Mass., 1980).
Keefe, D. J., 'A Methodological Critique of Lonergan's Theological Method',
    The Thomist, (January 1986), pp. 28–65.
Lindbeck, G., *The Nature of Doctrine* (London, 1984).
McShane, P. (ed.), *Foundations of Theology* (Dublin, 1971).
Meynell, H. A., *An Introduction to the Philosophy of Bernard Lonergan*
    (London, 1976).
Meynell, H. A., *The Theology of Bernard Lonergan* (Atlanta, Ga, 1986).
Reichmann, J. B., 'The Transcendental Method and the Psychogenesis of
    Being', *The Thomist*, (October 1968), pp. 449–508.
Shea, W. R., 'The Stance and Task of the Foundational Theologian',
    Heythrop Journal, 1976.
Tyrrell, B., *Bernard Lonergan's Philosophy of God* (Dublin, 1974).

Part IV

Tradition and Beauty

Yves Congar has probably had more influence on church history than any other theologian in this volume. Aidan Nichols portrays him as a reformer with a dedication to tradition, understood as 'the permanence of the past in a present in whose heart the future is being prepared'. He was a key figure in the *ressourcement* (return to sources) which prepared the way for Vatican II and also in the accompanying ecumenism between Catholics, Protestants, and Orthodox. Very much a church theologian, and not either systematic or philosophical, his historical sensitivity and vast learning were the medium for a wisdom which helped to change the sensibility of the Roman Catholic Church and informed many of the documents of Vatican II.

Hans Urs von Balthasar's main spheres of life were the church, European culture, and the 'secular institutes' which have tried to form a way of lay Christian life in the world. His 'kneeling theology' of prayer and contemplation has as its motto: 'the greatest possible radiance in the world by virtue of the closest possible following of Christ'. John Riches describes the leading theme of beauty in his theology as it connects with his approach to biblical revelation and the saints and theologians of the tradition. The pivotal focus emerges as the death and resurrection of Jesus Christ, with the dark and original theme of the descent into Hell at its center. Riches also gives an account of Balthasar's debates with Barth, Bultmann, and Rahner, thus offering a new perspective on each of the earlier parts of this volume.

Congar and Balthasar both represent a form of orthodoxy which has been suspicious of the theologies discussed in parts II and III above, and both owe much to Karl Barth. They have been uneasy with many 'progressive' developments in their own church since Vatican II. They have also, despite many differences, shared an expository rather than argumentative style (though Balthasar's is also evocative and metaphorical), a deep immersion in the theology of the early church, an appreciation of Eastern Orthodoxy, a certain distance from university-based theology, and a debt to twentieth-century French theology.

11

Yves Congar

Aidan Nichols OP

INTRODUCTION: LIFE AND INFLUENCES

Yves Congar was born on May 13, 1904 at Sedan in the French Ardennes.[1] His family belonged to the lower bourgeoisie. Unusually for the period, his childhood friends were Jewish and Protestant, spreading seeds of an ecumenical vocation. Despite earlier attraction to medicine, Congar decided in 1921 to enter the Parisian seminary known as 'of the Carmelites', where his spiritual director encouraged him to study Thomism, at the time the most sophisticated theological idiom available in the Catholic Church. His mind awakened, he attended the Thomistic courses of the rising philosophical star Jacques Maritain, and frequented retreats given by Maritain's theological mentor, the Dominican Réginald Garrigou-Lagrange. The Neo-Thomist disdain shown by Maritain and Garrigou for the more historically-minded study of Aquinas emerging in the Dominican Order, which they termed 'Palaeo-Thomism', accusing it of antiquarianism, foreshadowed certain conflicts in Congar's later career. Meanwhile, the young ordinand was frequenting the Benedictine abbey of Conques, whence he drew his lifetime love for the Catholic liturgy. He nearly joined the Benedictines, but decided instead for the Dominican noviciate of the Province of France at Amiens, which he entered in 1925.

Congar's serious studies were carried out at the Dominican study-house of Le Saulchoir, then at Kain-la-Tombe in Belgium, where teachers and pupils had sought refuge from the anti-clerical legislation of the French Third Republic. Thanks to the high standards of its 'regent' or president, Ambroise Gardeil, this institute had reached a level of academic attainment comparable with any university. Historical theology was a particular strength. The young friar read deeply in texts, whether classical, biblical, patristic or medieval. His concern to set Thomas within the context of the thirteenth century led to relations with the historian of medieval philosophy Etienne Gilson, but cooled the ardors of his friendship with the Neo-Thomists.

Congar's master, Marie-Dominique Chenu, had communicated an enthusiasm for the infant Ecumenical Movement, now drawing Protestants and Orthodox together, notably at the Lausanne Faith and Order Conference of 1927. Chenu suggested that a suitable model for a sympathetic Catholic contribution to that movement might be the ecclesiologist of the nineteenth-century German Catholic revival, Johann Adam Möhler. Accordingly, Congar selected as the subject of his 'lectoral' thesis (an internal Dominican degree) in 1928 Möhler's favored theme, the unity of the church. On the eve of his ordination to the priesthood on July 25, 1930, he prepared himself by meditating on Jesus' high-priestly prayer for the unity of his disciples in John 17, with the help of the commentaries of Thomas and the contemporary biblical scholar Marie-Joseph Lagrange. This he recognized in retrospect as the true launching of his ecumenical vocation.

During two visits to Germany, he discovered the 'High-Church' movement in German Lutheranism, and, on a tour of the places associated with the career of Luther, intuited in the latter 'depths . . . which demanded investigation and understanding'. Back in Paris, he was allowed to attend lecture courses by theologians of the Reformed Church of France, who were at the time re-discovering the classical dogmatic Protestantism of Calvin, and thereby preparing the way for the French reception of the anti-liberal neo-orthodoxy of Karl Barth. In time, Congar would be deeply affected by Luther's stress on the primacy of grace, and of the Scriptures, though avoiding Luther's accompanying negations of the role of charity, and of tradition. He would also be influenced by Barth's massive emphasis on the sovereignty of the revealing, redeeming and reconciling *Word* of God, whilst regarding Barth's denial that God grants a saving co-causality to creatures as 'disastrous'.[2] Though, at this early stage, Protestantism still meant more to him than did Orthodoxy (a state of things which would later be reversed), he also participated in Catholic–Orthodox 'reunions of Franco-Russian friendship', as these were discreetly called, where he encountered the ideas of Möhler's Orthodox contemporary and counterpart, the lay theologian Alexis Stefanovič Khomiakov.

So far as his own teaching was concerned, he was obliged by Chenu's absence in Canada – for the founding of the Institute of Medieval Studies at Toronto – to take responsibility for a course of theological propaideutics, 'introduction to theology'. As part of his preparation, he looked into the work of the Modernist exegetes and thinkers of the turn of the century. (Alfred Loisy's monumental autobiography had just appeared.) The idea came to him that his own generation should rescue for the church whatever was of value in the approach of the Modernists. In his judgment, this meant two things. First, it meant the application of the historical method to Christian data – though not a restrictively 'historical-critical' method where the dimension of faith was epistemologically blotted out. Secondly, it meant greater attention to the viewpoint of the experiencing subject, whose needs and concerns shift with the contours of history itself. In the course of this work, he discovered the contribution of the highly original Catholic philosopher Maurice Blondel, whose reflections on the relation of history and dogma had tried to chart a course between the Scylla of Modernism and the Charybdis of what he dubbed 'Veterism' – essentially, closed-mindedness to everything that historical study could offer to the better grasp of a revelation which, though supernatural and miraculous, was mediated by the texture of history. Blondel's concept of tradition struck him particularly forcibly.[3]

Congar's lectures on introducing theology, which were the origins of his interest in fundamental theology, were soon supplemented by far more numerous ones on ecclesiology. This was to remain, with ecumenism, the great passion of his life. It gave him the excuse to broaden his contacts, and so extend his sense of the church. This led him to the bi-ritual Byzantine–Latin monastery of Amay, and its ecumenical pioneer founder, Dom Lambert Beauduin, and also to England, where he made Anglican friends and began to acquire a thorough knowledge of the chequered theological history of the Anglican tradition. However, such visits, like his regular excursions to French cities for the preaching of the Christian Unity Octave, were simply punctuations of a domestic round of study and teaching, set within an austere monastic and liturgical framework. This conventual round continued until the outbreak of the Second World War when he found himself first mobilized as a military chaplain, and then immobilized, as a prisoner-of-war at Colditz. There he learned with dismay and stupefaction of the Roman condemnation of Chenu's academic manifesto entitled 'A School of Theology, Le Saulchoir', which had set out the shared theological vision and methods of that house.[4] As late as 1964 he confessed himself unable to comprehend the sense of this action, which he could only regard as based upon informational error. In fact, as later investigation has shown, the charge against Le Saulchoir was 'Semi-

Modernism', a slippery concept indeed. In Rome, voices were raised, not least that of the Dominican 'master of the sacred palace', Mariano Cordovani, protesting that the emphasis of the Saulchoir men on historical context would end up by turning theology into cultural anthropology, deprived of any real hold on its divine subject-matter, revelation.

In the creative ferment which characterized the French Catholicism of the immediately post-war years, Congar made a major literary contribution which will be outlined in the next section. However, the hesitations of more conservative churchmen about his work were increasing. As early as 1947, he was refused permission to publish an article on the position of the Catholic Church vis-à-vis the ecumenical movement which was entering a new phase with the preparation of the first assembly of the World Council of Churches. The Master of the Dominicans warned him against a 'false eirenicism', which might be construed as indifference to specifically Catholic doctrines. Further editions, and any translations, of one of his works were prohibited. Despite these severe vexations, the making of ecumenical links went on, especially among the Orthodox as a result of a lecture tour in the Near East during the winter of 1953–4. In early February of the latter year, he returned to France, to hear the news that, following an article in defense of the 'priest-worker' movement, to which a number of French Dominicans had lent their support, he was forbidden to teach. He was exiled first to the École Biblique in Jerusalem where, however, he managed to write his only substantial essay on biblical theology, and then, in November 1954, to Blackfriars, Cambridge. Only the kindness of Jean Weber, Bishop of Strasbourg, enabled Congar, at the time of his return to France in December 1955, to resume a pastoral and theological ministry. In retrospect, Congar believed that these difficult years had called forth in him an 'active patience', especially fitted to the work of ecumenism, a 'long process of convergence' as this was, bound up with the inner renewal of each Christian communion.[5]

With the coming of Giuseppe Roncalli to the papal chair as John XXIII in 1959 all was changed. Shortly after the new Pope's announcement of the calling of a General Council, Congar was named as theological consultor to the preparatory commission. At the Second Vatican Council itself, he helped write the 'Message to the World' at its opening, and worked on such major documents as *Dei verbum* (the 'Dogmatic Constitution on Divine Revelation'), *Lumen gentium* (the 'Dogmatic Constitution on the Church'), *Gaudium et spes* (the 'Pastoral Constitution on the Church in the Modern

World'), *Ad gentes divinitus* (the 'Decree on the Church's Missionary Activity'), *Unitatis redintegratio* (the 'Decree on Ecumenism'), *Presbyterorum ordinis* (the 'Decree on the Life and Ministry of Priests'), and *Dignitatis humanae* (the 'Declaration on Religious Freedom'). The second Pope of the council, Paul VI, and his successors did Congar no less honor. In 1965 he became a member of the official Catholic–Lutheran commission of dialogue, a recognition of his lifelong erudite interest in the Reformer of Wittenberg. And by way of testimony to his wider theological service, Paul VI added his name to the newly founded Pontifical International Theological Commission, which had been brought into existence in order to lend a broader expertise and vision to the work of the Roman Congregation for the Doctrine of the Faith. John Paul II invited him to attend the Extraordinary Synod of 1985, convened to consider the fruits of the Second Vatican Council, itself deeply indebted to Congar's master-ideas, but his health was by then too poor for him to accept. These post-conciliar years were serene for Congar, though he did not hesitate to speak of a 'crisis' in the church beyond, where 'openness to novelty' had too often been traduced by a 'proposal of rupture'.[6] He himself lived in the fraternal ambience of the Couvent Saint-Jacques at Paris, to which the library of the now defunct Saulchoir had been transferred. There he received a flow of visitors, inquirers, students, and well-wishers, inevitably reduced by his move to the Hôtel des Invalides in 1984 when his paraplegia became too advanced for the brethren to be able to nurse him at home. As a former Colditz internee who was also a luminary of French learning, he had a claim to be housed in the great military hospital, along with the marshals of France.

SURVEY

The following summary survey of Congar's writing must be seen against the background of the history, and influences, charted above. It will emphasize what is most significant, and that in broadly chronological order. Congar's literary activity first received wide attention with a controversial essay of 1934 on the pastoral mission of the church in contemporary society. He ascribed the alienation of French culture from the church to the latter's 'disfigured visage', which made the Catholic community seem too juridically-minded and defensive, and thus a poor expression of the 'incarnation of grace' and the 'humanization of God' found in the person and work of Jesus Christ.[7] In 1936, he launched a series of ecclesiological inquiries under the general title *Unam Sanctam*, a reference to the words of the Creed: 'one holy (Church)'. Their ecumenical inspiration was signalled by his decision to make the first volume his own *Divided Christendom*, which sought, through reflection on the essential nature of the church and its unity, to work out 'principles for Catholic ecumenism' in the light of the different conceptions of unity, and so of ecumenism, among liberal Protestants, Anglicans, and the Orthodox. In the war-time *The Mystery of the Church* he countered the claim that, in his work so far, there was little of the traditional Dominican Thomism by outlining a distinctive approach to Thomas. This took the form of a twofold concern: first, for Aquinas' continuity with the Fathers (something which had an obvious ecumenical import), and, secondly, for what Aquinas might offer by way of materials for the construction of a contemporary theology (highly pertinent to the needs of the 'Mission de France'). The truly breathtaking grasp of theological history he had acquired by the age of forty was revealed in the article 'Theology' which he contributed to the 'Dictionary of Catholic Theology', later published as a separate book under the title *A History of Theology*.

After the war, he wrote his courageous but careful call for ecclesiastical reform, 'True and False Reform in the Church'. This, after distinguishing the senses in which the church must be holy (thanks to her divine origination) but could be sinful (owing to her human composition), pleaded for a reform not of abuses (for there virtually were none) but of the structures of the church, her concrete adaptation, or, more frequently, in-adaptation to the world to which she preaches. Such a reform should, he argues, proceed by way of 'return to the sources', a phrase he took from the poet and social critic Charles Péguy, as well as from the liturgical changes inaugurated by Pope Pius X. Congar laid down the conditions on which it could be 'true', that is, manageable without disrupting the continuity of the church's history, or disturbing the peace and charity of the church's members. He devoted special attention to the making of a theology of the laity, who must mediate between the church and the world, in his *Lay People in the Church*. There he insisted that the laity are not simply the objects of the ministrations of the hierarchy, but are, on the basis of their baptism and confirmation, acting subjects in their own right of the threefold office of Christ as Priest, Prophet, and King. They exercize this threefold office in their own distinctive sphere, which is at the 'suture' of church and world. The laity are responsible for the interchange between the two great histories, sacred and profane. By relating the world to the church, they provide the Kingdom of God with its earthly material. In so doing, they contribute to the *plērōma*, 'fullness', which Christ is destined to have in his total reality, which includes his church-body.

Major church anniversaries gave him the opportunity for further significant contributions. In 1952, for the fifteenth centenary of Chalcedon, celebrated the previous year, he produced *Christ, our Lady and the Church*, an exposé of the theological principles underlying and connecting orthodox Christology, ecclesiology and Mariology. In 1954, for the ninth centenary of the schism of Michael Kerullarios, he published the important study of Catholic–Orthodox relations *After Nine Hundred Years*, thanks to the good offices of Beauduin's monastery, now transferred to Chevetogne, in Belgium. During his exile in Jerusalem, he turned his hand to the wider issues of the God–world relationship as that unfolds in history. *The Mystery of the Temple* outlined a theology of a developing divine– human relationship, whose stages are marked by an ever-increasing interiority of divine presence, whose climax is in Jesus Christ as the God-man, and whose goal as well as terminus is the eschatological 'temple' of the divine presence described in the Johannine Apo- calypse.

In *Tradition and Traditions*, written as the Second Vatican Council was proceeding, Congar's attention began to shift from a Christo- logically oriented picture of the church to one which, though by no means neglecting the dominical determination of the church's life made by the Word Incarnate and Risen, gave greater weight to the mission of the Holy Spirit, by whose agency the gifts of Christ to the church are concretely realized in the lives of believers. Manifesting the vast reading which the hidden years of Le Saulchoir had made possible, there followed two major chronicles of the history of ecclesiology, 'The Ecclesiology of the High Middle Ages' and 'The Church. From Saint Augustine to the Modern Period'. He also offered a more personal synthesis based on these traditional materials in 'The Church: One, Holy, Catholic, Apostolic', which was a contribution to the Franco-German handbook of salvation- historical theology, 'The Mystery of Salvation'. In the course of this research, he learned that the two most important alternative perspectives in which ecclesiology can be approached are by starting from the local church (an 'ecclesiology of communion') or from the church universal (a 'universalist ecclesiology').

In addition to numerous collections of essays on his favored subjects, from Luther and the Ecumenical Movement to church, ministry, and the Second Vatican Council, he also produced in the years 1979–80 a full-scale pneumatology, the three-volume *I Believe in the Holy Spirit.* Beginning from the witness to the Spirit in Old and New Testaments and in various phases of church history, Congar considered the role of the Spirit in the corporate life of the church, as in the personal lives of Christians, with a sizeable section on the 'Charismatic Renewal'. In the last volume of the trilogy, he looked at the theology of the Spirit found historically in East and West; attempted to resolve the delicate problem of the procession of the Spirit (from the Father only, or from the Father *and the Son*), which still divides Catholic and Orthodox; and concluded, after an exploration of the activity of the Spirit in confirmation and eucharist, with a portrait of the church's life as a prolonged *epiclēsis*, or prayer for the Spirit's advent. By his own account, as offered in what he assures his readers will be his final book, 'Autumn Conversations', his own sensibility and reflections have moved, in conformity with the inner movement of the Holy Trinity itself, from Father, through Son, to the Holy Spirit.

CONTENT

In this section, attention will be concentrated on the heart of Congar's theology, his doctrine of the Church. By way of contextualization, however, this will be prefaced by an account of his fundamental theology, seen in his understanding of revelation in tradition.

Congar's account of revelation begins from the concept of the Word of God, a tribute *inter alia* to the influence of Barth.[8] God's Word is the generative element in the history of salvation, the act by which he makes known to humanity his personal mystery and will in converting it to himself. Simultaneously, then, saving action and saving knowledge, the Word of God stimulates words and gestures with a revelatory sign-value among those to whom it is addressed. Through such language and motions, people are brought to understand and affirm a divine meaning by way of human means. Conformably to traditional Catholic and Thomist realism, Congar deems such 'thinking with assent' to be true with the truth of the Primal Truth itself.

This drama of God's self-communication is worked out through a protracted saving history, but its climax is Jesus Christ. He it is who unveils the total design of the covenant relationship between God and man, as that relationship's unconditional realization, its 'Absolute'. As the divine plan unfolds, the noetic conditions for its perception are progressively created. The Son acts as our 'interior teacher', a phrase borrowed from Augustine, while the Spirit, in the language of the First Letter of John, serves as our 'unction', the gracing of our sensibility. The Word of God requires, and thus can receive, its co-responding word from us. The unseen Father is manifested and communicated in the missions of the Son, incarnate in Jesus Christ, and of the Spirit, who is poured out into the world from the Paschal mystery at Pentecost. Of those missions the modifications of our mind and feeling are the internal echoes. In the time between the Resurrection and the Parousia, God continues to restore human persons to himself, and thereby to disclose his own being as the Trinity, and this he does by means of a community, the church, living in communion with the ceaseless consubstantial exchange of the divine persons.[9]

The revelation given once for all, then, is conserved and proposed to all mankind by the church Christ founded. Though the church's mediation of revelation issues in objective determinations of its content, namely dogmas, Congar insists that public doctrine must be contextualized within a wider whole. The church is not only a teacher; she is also 'Mother Church', and her total membership provides, over and above the specific doctrinal contribution of the apolostolic ministry with its teaching office, 'the nourishing and educative milieu of faith'. Though the origin of Tradition lies in the Father's handing-over of the Son to the world, and the Son's subsequent acceptance of betrayal (also, in Latin, *traditio*, a 'handing-over') at the hands of sinful men, this two fold 'productive act', linked to a *masculine* divine symbolism, is received and transmitted in the church's tradition whose ultimate subject is the Holy Spirit and which Congar conceives in essentially *feminine* terms. The entire church, lay and clerical together, is the mediate subject of Tradition which she passes on not just as a teaching but as a reality, the reality of Christianity itself. And in terms drawn from Blondel's *History and Dogma*, Congar insists that tradition constitutes 'the permanence of a past in a present in whose heart the future is being prepared' – thus transcending the limitations of a fixist conservatism or a falsely radical disregard for continuity.[10] In each age, the Church of Tradition puts forth expressive monuments, ranging from a liturgical text to an artwork, from a theological classic to a saint.[11]

Although the content of revelation, the mystery of communion between God and man, carries within itself its own justification, it nevertheless also offers to the mind of man inexhaustible possibilities of reflection. This is the task of theology which must bind itself to seek (without ever fully comprehending) the totality of revelation in its internal coherence. Attempting to unite the characteristic emphases of the two medieval mendicant masters Bonaventure and Thomas, Congar insists that theology must show a continuous reference both to revelation's center, Jesus Christ (hence Bonaventurian 'christocentrism'), and to revelation's term, God himself (hence Thomist 'theofinality').[12]

We now turn to Congar's understanding of the church. As we have seen, Congar's interest in ecclesiology can hardly be separated from his concern with a church reform that will 'return to the sources'. He discerned a crying need, both in missionary outreach and in ecumenical endeavor, for 'a concept of the church which is broad, rich, living, and full of biblical and traditional sap'. To foster such a notion, the theology of the church must live by 'an intimate and organic contact with its own data, its "given"'.[13] It is this desire to restore to the contemporary community its own historic heritage which explains the copious documentation in which Congar's ecclesiological essays seem positively to exult. The chronicling of successive ecclesiologies in Congar's strictly historical works provides the treasury of theological concepts on which he draws for his attempts to reproduce the pattern of this many-faceted reality.

There is no one Congarian ecclesiology. In *Divided Christendom*, however, he shows a characteristic concern to illuminate the rationale of the church's unity by disengaging the basic principles of her life. First and foremost she is 'the Church of the Trinity', the extension of the divine life, itself a unity in plurality. Congar stresses the role of the Spirit as unifier for us as for the divine Trinity. The Spirit is the gracious source of all the supernatural gifts and virtues which orient us towards God's own inner-trinitarian unity. The church is also, secondly, 'the Church in Christ', the Body of the Mediator of the divine self-communication. We enter this Body, and partake of the life it brings, by the sacraments in which faith is expressed and rendered vital. Lastly, the church is 'the Church taken from amongst men', since God's relations with humankind must take a social form and face, appropriate to a polis-dwelling animal. The law of incarnation, adopted by God in the work of our redemption by Christ, from the flesh-taking through Passion to Resurrection, also governs the work of our deification, from Pentecost to the Parousia. It follows that the life of the Church–Body must be served by an institution, for the earthly church must assume the human and social form of any community bound together in pursuit of common ends. Drawing on the principles of Chalcedonian christology, identified as the key to theological evaluation in all realms of a Christianity 're-centered' on Christ, Congar proposes that, like Christ's two natures, the church's mystery and her institutional existence are united inseparably but without confusion. Or again, on the analogy of Aristotle's doctrine of man, he suggests that, as the body is the instrument and manifestation of the soul, so the visible church is the instrument and manifestation of Christ's invisible life.[14]

In a way crucial for both reform and ecumenism, Congar describes the church's catholicity as the 'dynamic universality of her unity'. It is the capacity of her principles of unity to unite with God all human beings and every human value. Trinitarian and christological in its foundations, that catholicity expresses the relation between the unity of God and the manifold of the creature. It is defined simultaneously in terms of unity and diversity. Though it demands on the visible plane a unity, and unicity, in the measure in which interior unity must have institutional and organic expression (and here the 'organs of oneness' for faith, grace, and the common life are given with the apostolic ministry, in its threefold office of teaching, sanctifying, and governing), it also demands, for the vital increase of that oneness, appropriate adaptation to the multiform humanity in which the church's unity is expressed. Variety of language, culture, and custom, manifesting itself in variety of religious temperament and style of theological thought, is a human value, a reflection of the divine image in man. Although diverse values must be integrated into the hegemony of the unity of the Spirit, Catholic unity is capable of incorporating all that is true and good. Here, through the concept of integrable value, Congar first laid out his ideal of a Catholicism maximally polychrome in culture, and enriched by the 'reconciled diversity' of separated Christian churches, whose spiritual, liturgical, and intellectual flourishing witnesses to the evangelical values they have taken with them into schism.[15]

In his attempt to bring lucidity into reflection on the church, Congar, in his post-war writing, introduced a distinction which some found over-schematic, between 'structure' and 'life'. The institutional elements of the church, given directly by Christ and sharing in his changeless holiness, provide her *structure*: the deposit of faith, the sacraments, and the historic threefold ministry. The church's members, on the other hand, determine her communitarian *life*, the quality of operation of her God-given structure. If the first is bound up with the founding activity of the Son, and his continued activity in his signs and offices, the second depends more closely on the Spirit, as Pentecostal distributor of charisms for the life which the work of the Son has structured. Insisting as he did that the charisms of the community can only be fully integrated into the Church of the Incarnate by the action of the ecclesiastical hierarchy, Congar left himself open to the charge that none save the ordained ministry are truly active in the church, all else being a reflection, as in many mirrors, of an image projected by the successors of the apostles. Subsequently, he would prefer to say that in the original Twelve, both hierarchy *and* church were co-founded, so that, within a community itself prophetic, priestly and regal, the ordained ministry acts in the service of what all the church is called to do and be.[16]

Where models and images of the church are concerned, Congar's essays exemplify his belief in the simultaneous employment of many, and his hand can be discerned in the acceptance of such multiplicity in the Dogmatic Constitution on the Church of the Second Vatican Council. The church is, for Congar, at once the people of God and the Body of Christ, the temple of the Holy Spirit and a communion, a society and an extended sacrament. This linguistic generosity does not derive from theological indecisiveness, but from the desire to keep in equilibrium the institutional aspect of the church, linked chiefly with the mission of the Son, and its charismatic side, connected mainly to that of the Spirit. There can no more be ultimate incompatibility between these two dimensions than there can be dissonance between the two divine missions. The humanity of the Word Incarnate is Spirit-filled, just as the Spirit himself is always the Spirit of the Son. The two are, in a phrase of Irenaeus beloved of Congar, the 'two hands' of the Father. No Christology without pneumatology, no pneumatology without Christology.[17]

Congar's post-conciliar ecclesiology does indeed find his own earlier distinction between structure and life too rigorous. The role of the Spirit is found not only in the raising up of prophetic individuals or groups, from Catherine of Siena to Alexander Solzhenitsyn, from human rights movements to the Charismatic Renewal. The Spirit enters into the very texture of the hierarchical society fashioned by the Son, and this on a threefold path of conciliarity, collegiality, and reception, whereby the dominical authority of the Roman Pope (for the universal church) and of the individual bishop (for his particular church) is conditioned by the free play of Christian minds and hearts among the wider episcopate and people. The impulses of the Spirit spread through the church's whole conciliar being, her *sobornost'*, are manifested in councils; the episcopate co-witnesses to them as a college around the Pope who, even when acting 'alone', acts as collegial head; and the determinations of bishops, including the chief bishop, cannot bear fruit in the Spirit save through reception by the whole *laos*.[18] Thus

Congar's ecclesiology, in sharp contrast to that of his original inspiration, Möhler, became less christological and more pneumatic as he grew older. Convinced that Western Catholics have not done justice in recent centuries to the person and work of the Holy Spirit – here his early dialogue with the exiles of the Russian Orthodox diaspora had left a permanent mark – it was understandable that Congar should end his theological career by, at least in appearance, turning away from his great love, ecclesiology, to what was, in fact, its own deepest basis, the doctrine of the Spirit.

DEBATE

Since so much of Congar's theological achievement takes the form of the recuperation of the history of the subject, a fact-finding enterprise, albeit one undertaken with a constant eye to the pastoral needs of the church's life and mission, it is not surprising that there has been less debate about his work than with theologians of comparable influence. Attention has been focused on his ecclesiology – again, understandably enough, since it forms the bulk of his output.

A major critic, T. I. MacDonald,[19] regards Congar's dialectic of 'structure' and 'life' as the key to his work. He argues that, after adopting a 'pleroma christology' with a greater stress on the eschatological finality of Christ's person and work, Congar was able to create a better balance between the two poles of structure and life, seeing the church's structures as means towards the development of her common life, and towards the ultimate fulfillment which is the Kingdom of God. When combined with Congar's discovery of the shift, under the impact of the twelfth-century Gregorian Reform, from a doctrine of the church as a communion of local churches to a universalist ecclesiology, where the many communities stand to the one church as parts to a whole, the same key terms could also be applied to a restored ecclesiology of communion: here they helped Congar preserve a balance between the church as an institution of grace, and as a communion of grace. Less successful, in T. I. MacDonald's view, was Congar's presentation of the church–world relationship; here the dialectical sense which gave such rich equilibrium to Congar's ecclesiology somewhat deserted him: the unity-in-difference of church and world was, as a result, inadequately brought out. The same writer offered to lend Congar's work a philosophical underpinning which Congar was the first to admit it somewhat lacked. This he did in terms of Blondel's categories. The

'supernatural' of Blondel he accommodated to Congar's 'structure' –
the divine saving reality constitutive of redeemed humanity and
present in the church. The 'inexhaustible willing' of Blondel, that
which calls for the supernatural and can receive it, MacDonald
accommodated to Congar's 'life': the spring of action in persons,
giving rise to an unending chain of concrete choices that makes up
the texture of the church's common existence.

Confusingly, Congar's other principal critic to date is of the same
clan, *Charles* MacDonald.[20] His criticisms center on the relation of
Congar's christology to his eschatology – a relation which is through
and through ecclesiological, since the time between the Paschal
event and the final consummation is the time of the church. The
activity of humanity in history, while drawing all from the risen
Christ, is seen as contributing to Christ's plenitude at the Parousia.
Church and world each approach the kingdom in their own way in
the divine plan, but have it in common that both must develop their
fullest potential. Charles MacDonald's criticism of this is that it is
too redolent of an ideology of progress, failing to do justice to the
elements of tragedy and waste in the world, and of loss and
narrowing in the church's memory. In making development a
necessary condition for the kingdom, Congar imperils, MacDonald
believes, the kingdom's gratuity. Moreover, his theology, which
MacDonald regards as essentially a theology of history, would have
been enriched by reflection on the church as the place where the
eschatological destiny of the world is anticipated. In the church's
sacramental life, past, present and future are united; and the free gift
of the kingdom is reflected in the 'uselessness' of her worship.

Such criticisms point in opposing directions, for the first regards
the divine element in the God–man relationship as the provision of
resources for human creativity to work upon, pressing Congar's
theology in the direction of a theological anthropology of the kind
represented by Karl Rahner. The other sees the divine initiative as a
sovereignly free agency which, in its response to the turns of human
history, has surprises in store for us in its script, even though it has
disclosed the final *dénouement* – thus nudging Congar's thought in
the direction, rather, of the theological dramatics of Hans Urs von
Balthasar. All in all, the debate suggests the perennial importance of
reflection on the interweaving mysteries of God's grace and human
freedom.

ACHIEVEMENT AND AGENDA

Congar's achievement is primarily that of a theologically-gifted, historically-minded preacher and pastor, rather than of a speculative or systematic theologian. The Russian Orthodox layman Leo Zander, in an encomium of Congar, called him 'the icon of Saint Dominic', another 'evangelical man' whose concerns were wholly enfolded in the church's life.[21] In evaluating Congar in terms of Dominic of Calaruega rather than of Thomas Aquinas, Zander was surely correct. For whereas Thomas's theology in the *Summa contra Gentiles* is pastoral and missionary in its concern to address different categories of religious man at the points where they are, the *Summa theologiae* marks a decisive shift to a systematic, scientific theology concerned with the rationale of faith in the interconnection of its various aspects. As Marie-Jean Le Guillou has fairly noted, Congar's philosophical equipment as a theologian was inadequate to take him far along the path of a speculative re-construction of Christian tradition.[22] Congar concentrates on an evocation of the divine economy in its richness, rather than an account of its foundation in what both the Greek fathers and the early Scholastics would have called *theologia*. At the same time, he is fully aware that *someone* must produce a renewed theological ontology suitable to Catholic Christianity, since a purely phenomenological description, taken by itself, will not suffice.

Congar's religious impact has been as a reformer who meets the conditions he himself laid down for authentic reformation: prophetic yet traditional. His monument is to be seen in the shifts of sensibility he has helped to bring about in the Roman Catholic Church and beyond: in a return to the sources at once biblical, liturgical, and doctrinal, manifested in ecumenical generosity and a juster sense of the church's communion as a complex of ministries, both lay and ordained.[23] Yet the means whereby he achieved all this can themselves only be termed theological. Probably Jean-Pierre Jossua is right to see Congar as recreating by his practice a more ancient model of what it is to be a theologian than that found, ever since the thirteenth century, in the world of the Western universities.[24] Like many patristic divines, his theology consists in the service of the church's peace and welfare, and of the spiritual life and mission of all its members.

For the future, two questions suggest themselves. First, is not the desire of the human mind, thinking theologically, for intellectual coherence itself a genuine Christian need which it would be pastoral for a shepherd to meet? (Congar's own Bonaventurian–Thomist account of the aim of theology, cited above, implicitly admits this.) Hence the desirability of a more *synthetic* presentation of the multitudinous material Congar has salvaged from the tradition, material present in the form of an embarrassment of riches in much of his writing. Secondly, in an age marked by philosophical, and especially epistemological sophistication in the academy, and by ideological competition in the market-place, can Congar's consciously naive reliance on the language of the Fathers suffice to ground the Trinitarian vision of a world moving, as the church, to its eschatological completion? Is there not a need here for a Christian *ontology*, itself in close touch both with philosophical rationality and with revelation, to ground the synthetic presentation which may emerge from the students of Congar's work? Such an ontology, to be a suitable partner for Congar's theology, would have to be relational, like the 'Church of the Trinity'; Chalcedonian, with the finite and the Infinite in unconfused union, like the 'Church in Christ'; and marked by the dynamic integration of an ever richer diversity into an ever more complete unity, like the 'Church taken from amongst men' on its way to the Kingdom.

NOTES

1 I am grateful to Messrs Chapman for their kind permission to draw on material presented in my book *Yves Congar* (London, 1989). For Congar's life, I have used chiefly J.-P. Jossua OP, *Le Père Congar. La théologie au service du peuple de Dieu* (Paris, 1967).

2 Y. Congar, *Chrétiens en Dialogue. Contributions catholiques à l'Oecuménisme* (Paris, 1964), pp. ix–lxiv.

3 Congar's course of theological propaideutics is substantially present in *La Foi et la théologie* (Tournai, 1968).

4 M.-D. Chenu OP, *Une École de théologie. Le Saulchoir* (Tournai, 1937; Paris, 1985).

5 Congar, *Chrétiens en Dialogue*, p. xxi.

6 Y. Congar, *La Tradition et la vie de l'Église* (Paris, 1963; 2nd edn 1984), p. 5.

7 'Une conclusion théologique à l'enquête sur les raisons actuelles de l'incroyance', *La Vie Intellectuelle*, 37 (1935), pp. 214–49.

8 For Congar's testimony to Barth, see his 'Karl Barth: un homme qui aimait Jésus Christ', *Signes du temps*, January 1969, pp. 13–14.

9 Congar, *La Foi et la Théologie*, pp. 7–17.

10 Congar, *La Tradition et la Vie de l'Église*, 2nd edn, pp. 16–26, 86.

11 Y. Congar, *La Tradition et les traditions* (Paris, 1960–3), Vol. II, pp. 181–213.

12 Congar, *La Foi et la Théologie*, pp. 25–6; cf. 'Le moment économique et le moment ontologique de la *sacra doctrina*', *Mélanges offerts à M.-D. Chenu, maître en théologie* (Paris, 1967), pp. 135–87.

13 Cited from the prospectus to *Unam Sanctam*, included as a separate sheet in *Chrétiens désunis. Principes d'un oecuménisme catholique* (Paris, 1937).

14 Ibid., pp. 59–110.

15 Ibid., pp. 115–48.

16 Y. Congar, *Ministères et communion ecclésiales* (Paris, 1971), pp. 9–30.

17 Y. Congar, *La Parole et le souffle* (Paris, 1984), p. 1.

18 On conciliarity, see 'Structure ou régime conciliaire de l'Église', in *La Concile de Vatican II* (Paris, 1984), pp. 33–43. On collegiality, see 'Synode épiscopal, primauté et collégialité épiscopal', in *Ministéres et communion ecclésiales*, pp. 187–227; on reception, 'La réception comme réalité ecclésiologique', *Revue des Sciences Philosophiques et Théologiques*, 56 (1972), pp. 369–483.

19 T. I. MacDonald, *The Ecclesiology of Yves Congar*.

20 C. MacDonald, *Church and World in the Plan of God. Aspects of History and Eschatology in the Thought of Père Yves Congar, OP.*

21 Jossua, *Le Père Congar*, p. 102.

22 M.-J. Le Guillou OP, 'Yves Congar', in R. van der Gucht and H. Vorgrimler, *Bilan de la théologie du XXe siècle* (Tournai, 1970), vol. II, p. 805. Congar admits as much himself in his 'Reflections on Being a Theologian', New Blackfriars, LXII. 736 (1981), p. 409.

23 That is, these things *at their best*. For Congar's balance-sheet of the post-conciliar period, see his *La Crise dans L'Église et Mgr. Lefebvre* (Paris, 1976), pp. 59ff; *Église catholique et France moderne* (Paris, 1978), pp. 43–71; *Le Concile de Vatican II*, pp. 49–72.

24 Jossua, *Le Père Congar*, p. 53.

BIBLIOGRAPHY

Primary

Congar, Y., *Divided Christendom* (London, 1939).

—, *Vraie et fausse réforme dans l'Église* (Paris, 1950).

—, *Christ, our Lady and the Church* (London, 1957).

—, *Lay People in the Church* (London, 1957).

—, *After Nine Hundred Years* (New York, 1959).

—, *The Mystery of the Church* (London, 1960).

—, *The Mystery of the Temple* (London, 1965).

—, *Tradition and Traditions* (London, 1966).

—, *L'Ecclésiologie du haut Moyen Age* (Paris, 1968).

—, *A History of Theology* (New York, 1968).

—, *L'Église. De saint Augustin à l'époque moderne* (Paris, 1970).

—, *L'Église une, sainte, catholique, apostolique* (Paris, 1970).

—, *I Believe in the Holy Spirit* (London, 1983).
—, *Entretiens d'automne* (Paris, 1987).

A list of Congar's numerous books and articles can be found in P. Quattrocchi, 'General Bibliography of Yves Congar', in J. P. Jossua OP, *Yves Congar. Theology in the Service of God's People*, pp. 185–241, for the period up to 1967; and for afterwards in A. Nichols OP, 'An Yves Congar Bibliography: 1967–1987' in *Angelicum*, 66, 1989.

Secondary

Jossua, J.-P., *Yves Congar. Theology in the Service of God's People* (Chicago, 1968).
MacDonald, C., *Church and World in the Plan of God. Aspects of History and Eschatology in the Thought of Père Yves Congar, OP* (Frankfurt-am-Main, 1982).
MacDonald, S. I., *The Ecclesiology of Yves Congar. Foundational Themes* (Lanham, Md, 1984).
Nichols, A., *Yves Congar* (London, 1989).

12

Hans Urs von Balthasar

John Riches

INTRODUCTION: AND SURVEY

Hans Urs von Balthasar's is not an academic theology. He never held a university post; the circle which surrounded him was drawn as much from the church and the literary world as from that of academia. The most important influence on him during his active life was, in his own view, that of a medical doctor and mystic, Adrienne von Speyr. His own time, since 1948, was divided between running a publishing house, writing, translating and editing, and being chaplain to a new form of religious order, a secular institute, which he founded with Adrienne. His is above all a theology which springs from a sense of his own commission (*Auftrag*) which has linked him to the development of new forms of life in the church with their roots in the Johannine/Ignatian tradition of spirituality.

Born in 1905 in Lucerne, Balthasar was educated first by the Benedictines at Engelberg, then by the Jesuits in Feldkirch. In 1923 he enrolled in the university of Zürich. His studies in philosophy and German literature led him to Vienna and Berlin and culminated in his doctoral work on German idealism, subsequently published in three volumes as *Apokalypse der deutschen Seele* (1937–9). At this point, 1929, he entered the Society of Jesus. Three years philosophy at Pullach near Munich brought him into contact with Erich Przywara whose work on *analogia entis* (the analogy of being) had a foundational influence on him. For his theological studies he went to the Jesuit school at Lyons. Here he encountered Daniélou, Fessard, and Henri de Lubac who gave him his enduring love of the Fathers, which was to lead to his studies of Maximus, *Kosmische Liturgie* (1941), and Gregory of Nyssa, *Présence et Pensée* (1942). It was here too that he met the French Catholic poet Paul Claudel, whose works he was to translate into German. Lyons was the centre of the *nouvelle théologie* which raised deep questions about the Thomist doctrine of grace and nature, with its suggestion that human nature could be conceived of in isolation from its relation to the vision of God. Hence the appeal to the Fathers with their conviction that communion with God is of the essence of humanity. Hence too Balthasar's own conviction that nowhere is humanity ever wholly bereft of the grace of God – and his life-time search for the fruits of such openness in the works of philosophers and poets outside the Christian tradition, notably in the grand tradition of classical antiquity.

After his studies at Lyons he was briefly in Munich as editor of *Stimmen der Zeit*. There then followed a period of eight years as student chaplain at Basle which shaped the pattern of the rest of his life. Here he met Adrienne von Speyr and received her into the Catholic church. Together they conceived the idea of a new form of religious order whose members would continue to exercize their normal professions and occupations in the world. It was on the occasion of the first retreat which Balthasar conducted for this *Johannes-Gemeinschaft*, that Adrienne experienced the first of her visions which were to accompany her for the rest of her life and to provide the central themes of Balthasar's own writing (documented in *First Glance at Adrienne von Speyr* and in the many published transcripts of her meditations and experiences, which Balthasar himself made). And it was in Basle that Balthasar turned his attention to the work of Karl Barth which gave him 'the vision of a comprehensive biblical theology'.[1] His relationship with Barth, at first enthusiastic and friendly, may have cooled, but Barth's theology remained for Balthasar one of the fixed points by which he set the course of his own work.

In 1950 Balthasar left the Society of Jesus which would not allow him to remain a member while he was developing his work with the secular institutes. For long he was in the ecclesiastical wilderness yet it was during this period of isolation and disfavor that his major writings were produced or conceived. He published important studies of literary figures – Bernanos, Schneider; of the saints – Thérèse of Lisieux and Elisabeth of Dijon; and it was at this time that the first volumes of his great trilogy began to appear. His restoration to favor came in the wake of Vatican II. In 1967 he was appointed to the Papal Theological Commission and began now to gain the reputation of a conservative theologian, not least for his pronouncements on the ordination of women and on his fellow Swiss, Hans Küng. However inadequate such a tag may be, there was nevertheless a growing rift between Balthasar and the circles around Rahner, Küng and Schillebeeckx which came to the front in Balthasar's attack on Rahner's notion of 'anonymous Christians' in *Cordula* (1966) and his own establishment of a rival periodical to *Concilium* entitled *Communio*. To this day his work remains a foreign body in the corpus of progressive Catholic theology. And yet there is much that each could learn from the other.

Balthasar died in 1988, a few days before he was due to become a cardinal.

CONTENT: BEAUTY, FAITH, AND THE CHRIST EVENT

Beauty

Balthasar gives us as his theological motto: 'the greatest possible radiance in the world by virtue of the closest possible following of Christ'.[2] Openness to the world, faithfulness to Christ! The formulation is, consciously, both polemical and a reflection of his own deepest concerns. It comes out of his commitment, formed along with those around de Lubac, to open the church to the world, to raze the bastions of fear[3] which had kept it isolated and thereby prevented it from engaging freely and redemptively with the world. But it also reflects his subsequent anxiety over developments in progressive Catholic circles where openness to the world, the readiness to baptise secular and religious movements outside the church as examples of 'anonymous Christianity', can lead to a loss of identity, of consciousness of the specifically Christian call and witness. More of this in the next section.

But how are we to catch sight of that which is distinctively Christian, among all the competing movements of the human spirit? How is such vision to be achieved? How to do justice to the unity and diversity of the Christian tradition and its many 'mediations' of its central glory, the 'revelation-figure' of Christ? How to do justice to the richness of perceptions of *truth and glory* outside that tradition, the poets, the philosophers, the myth-makers, not denying, that is, their originality and freshness nor reducing them simply to inadequate copies of the Christian revelation itself?

The question of method – better of the correct point of departure for his inquiry – long concerned Balthasar: in his engagement with Barth, throughout the first part of his trilogy, *The Glory of the Lord*, in summary form in *Love Alone*. What matters is to set one's goals aright from the start, to sense from the beginning what it is that one is looking for;[4] and for Balthasar this is summed up in the one word, beauty. In this he is concerned with the appearance of, the manner of manifestation of a thing *that reveals its being, its reality*. Balthasar rejects, quite rightly, the charge that such a concern with form and beauty is Platonist. It is not that he wishes to penetrate behind the appearances of things to the enduring, eternal ideas of which they are manifestations only. His whole theological endeavor is directed towards learning to see things as they are in themselves, whole and entire, and in so seeing to perceive the reality of being in all its variety and concreteness.

Balthasar's approach here is contemplative as opposed to critical; it is concrete rather than abstract. Much of Balthasar's work in the first volume of *The Glory of the Lord* is concerned with the notion of the light of faith, with the way of perceiving its object which is peculiar to faith. The biblical writers, Paul and John at least, speak of faith, not simply in terms of modifications of the believers' own self-understanding but as a particular mode of apprehending and entering into relationship with the object of faith: God in Christ. Faith, that is to say, is not sightless faith; it is intimately linked with knowledge and has its own mode of apprehending and growing in the truth. This is as much related to the manner in which the ability of the believer to perceive and understand the object of faith needs to be nurtured, as it is to the inexhaustibility of the object of faith. Analogies from the world of aesthetic appreciation serve to illuminate this point. The appreciation of works of art is something which needs to be cultivated. Youthful enthusiasm gives way to a more mature enjoyment of the work, better informed by an understanding of the artist's mastery of his medium and forms, by comparison with other works. All of this serves to sharpen the eye for the particular beauty of this work, its splendor; just as contemplation of its glory will deepen our understanding, and will continue to do so the more we contemplate.

Such contemplation is above all a contemplation of the object as it is in itself, whole and entire. We may indeed profit from an understanding of its constituent parts, of the influences and circumstances of the artist, of preliminary sketches and of contemporary developments in the medium: none of that will of itself bring understanding unless it enables us to see this painting as a whole, to perceive, as Hopkins would have said, its 'inscape'.[5]

Much of Balthasar's writing is concerned with the working out of the implications of such analogies for the doing of theology. In polemical terms this brings him into sharp conflict with all those who have turned away from contemplation of the object of theological reflection, God in his self-revelation, to a consideration of the conditions of human subjectivity and the manner of our apprehension of that revelation. And this distinguishes his approach as much from Bultmann's programme of existential interpretation as from Catholic transcendental theology. What Balthasar particularly singles out in Bultmann is the combination of critical historical study with an' anthropological reduction of faith to the moment of decision. It is interesting to contrast the very different perception of Bultmann's achievement given by Donald Baillie in *God was in Christ*.[6] For Baillie, Bultmann's achievement was to have brought a very radical gospel criticism 'right into the citadel of positive theological thought'. For Balthasar his demythologization and reductive explanations of the origins of mythological concepts in the biblical texts together with his existential interpretation of those texts both serve equally to dispel the object of faith, leaving only an existential moralism.[7] And there is a recurring polemic throughout his writings against those who choose reductive explanations, historical, psychological or whatever and thereby fail to do justice to the object of their study.[8]

Such a failure to attend to the object is ascribed by Balthasar to the disappearance of the appreciation of beauty in Western culture, fatally in Western theology since the Reformation.[9] Where theology no longer sees the beauty, however paradoxical, of the revelation-figure, it not only loses its power to attract and to convince but it also loses sight of its very center and can listen only to the echoes of the divine word in its own self-consciousness. It ceases to be concrete, attracted to the particular *Gestalt* in which the divine glory is to be seen, and concerns itself with the abstract, that which is perceived as the condition of the possibility of any perception at all.

But how is our sense of the beautiful, of the graciousness of things as they give themselves for our beholding, to be rekindled in an all too functionalist world? Balthasar's answer to that is disarmingly simple. True contemplation is a gift and we must learn it from those to whom it has been given: the saints. His debt is to Ignatius, whose *Spiritual Exercises* he conducted some hundred times, to the Society of Jesus and to his own *Johannes-Gemeinschaft*; above all to Adrienne 'who showed the way in which Ignatius is fulfilled by John, and therewith laid the basis for most of what I have published since 1940. Her work and mine are neither psychologically nor philologically to be separated: two halves of a single whole, which has at its centre a unique foundation.'[10]

It is because Balthasar's work is primarily concerned with the recovery of this vision of the Christian glory that it is at once expository and apologetic. It is expository in the sense that he wishes to open his readers' eyes to the bewildering richness of the forms of glory both inside and outside the Christian tradition, uncovering their particular composition and structures, their inner measure and rightness, their limitations as well as the way in which they manifest the creativity and graciousness of being. It is apologetic not in the sense that he develops a natural theology to support his dogmatic claims; but in a more subtle and, as Noel O'Donoghue has sharply seen, not wholly acknowleged way. In the most obvious sense it is the very demonstration of the beauty of the Christian tradition which has power to convince. Once one has shown the way in which the human and created world is taken up into the service of the divine and now mediates the divine glory what other proof is needed? This was precisely the apologetic strategy of the *nouvelle théologiens* and indeed of the worker priests with whom they were associated. But in another sense Balthasar does begin to develop something closer to a form of natural theology, as can be seen most clearly in his volume *The Realm of Metaphysics*. That which is grasped of the beauty of being in the myths, the poets and the philosphers, awaits its fulfillment in God's self-revelation of his freedom and grace; at the same time that which is grasped *is* grasped and thus the way is opened to 'the return of philosophy as a discipline formally and adequately distinct from theology'.[11]

FAITH AND THE CHRIST-EVENT

Balthasar's theology is expository and this can be seen clearly in his studies of the saints and of theologians, clerical and lay: most notably in his work in *The Glory of the Lord*, volumes 2 and 3. One might be tempted to see this as his best work and certainly such discussions are always illuminating and attentive, recovering as they often do figures from the past whose work has been relegated to the side-lines of present day theological discussion: Denys, Bonaventure, Dante, Pascal, Hopkins, Péguy . . . But this would be to overlook the sense in which such studies stand in the service of Balthasar's own continuing meditations on the mystery of the Christ-event, starting with the christological reflections of *Heart of the World*, and running via his reflections on the *triduum mortis* (Good Friday, Holy Saturday, Easter Sunday), in 'Mysterium Paschale'[12] to his sustained meditation on the drama of the passion and resurrection in *Theodramatik*.[13] It was to Barth, I have said, that Balthasar owed his vision of a comprehensive biblical theology, which is how he would ultimately wish his work to be judged. From Barth he learnt firstly, that theology must stand in the service of the *deus dixit* (God has spoken) which judges all human words and thoughts about God and brings its own word of grace and promise. But if the Barth of the Romans commentary had suggested that this word was so free, so transcendent, that it could not be tied down to any particular historical manifestation, the Barth of the *Church Dogmatics* asserted that the Word of God was not a formless word but one which takes form in a particular human life. And just as in the incarnation Jesus the Logos assumes and transforms human nature as it is brought back into its true relation to the Father, so too in the biblical Word human words and concepts are given their true sense as they are pressed into the service of the 'new' creation in Christ. This demands therefore not that we demythologize the thought of the New Testament but that we discover how the myths have been rescued and transformed in the witness of the Word to itself.

It is this that Barth means by *analogia fidei* (analogy of faith): that human words and concepts find their proper sense in the service of the gospel of reconciliation and that therefore all other senses are – at best – predicated by analogy with this. Balthasar was deeply indebted to Barth at this point; and yet, as we shall see, it was one of the points at which Barth believed there were still deep differences between them.

But if Balthasar's theology is in this sense a biblical theology, do not his studies of the saints of the great tradition of classical theology stand in the way of such an endeavor? Not, certainly, for him. To study the saints is to seek to see the revelation in Christ as it is mediated to them through the Word. And the fundamental test of such theology and spirituality is its obedience to the Word. In this sense Balthasar's theology may be described as Marian: it is out of the believer's obedience to the divine word that the richness and diversity of the many forms of the Christian tradition are born. And one may note here a paradox whose implications for present theological debate deserve far greater pondering: it is precisely in the measure that the believers are open to, that they are faithful to the *one* Word that the Word bears fruit in their life and spirituality and theology, demonstrating in the richness and diversity of such fecundity its own inexhaustible fullness. Hence the lives of the saints and the classical Christian theologians are not to be seen as pale copies which obstruct our view of the unchangeable reality of the biblical Word. Rather, because it is in the nature of the Word to generate new forms of life in so far as people are obedient and faithful to it, so too we may learn in the study of such lives and theologies to catch sight of the divine glory as it has transformed their lives and in so doing to discipline ourselves in the same obedience.

Noel O'Donoghue has drawn attention to the way in which Balthasar's theology hangs as it were between conceiving the obedience of faith as pure passivity ('Barthian "monergism"') and as a creative response to the enabling divine grace (the synergic theology of Scheeben, Adam, Guardini and Pzrywara).[14] What is at stake here is of no small importance for debates about the nature of biblical theology. If the role of the hearer of the divine Word is – ideally at least – one of pure obedience, in the sense of simply allowing the Word to leave its imprint, then – again, ideally – the true understanding of the Word, faith itself, ought to be identical as between Christians of every age and time. Such a notion lies behind orthodox forms of Protestantism which identify the plain sense of Scripture with its original historical sense. This plain sense, though often lost sight of, was, on such a view, at least perceived clearly by some, Augustine, the Reformers, and preserved in the confessional documents of the Reformation churches. And, interestingly, such a notion also lies behind the kind of liberalism which identifies the gospel with some timeless essence, some particular experience of filial relationship with the Father which Jesus himself both exemplified and communicated to his followers. Here again it is allowed that this essence has often been obscured, not least in the metaphysical speculations of the church fathers; nevertheless in such spirits as Luther it is rekindled and again made available to the church.

For Balthasar the encounter with the Word is indeed something which molds the believer, so much so that he can use mechanical metaphors to describe the manner in which the revelation in Christ impresses its character on the soul. Such metaphors serve to underline the sense in which in the encounter with the divine self-revelation all human perceptions of truth, goodness and beauty are superseded, judged. The impersonal language stresses, that is, the sovereignty of the divine grace in its dealings with human nature. But there is also a recognition of the way in which the believers find fulfillment in the encounter with such divine graciousness, of the way in which human freedom and integrity is respected and allowed to flourish and be fruitful. If our ideas of truth, goodness, and beauty are superseded, that is not to deny any continuity between such ideas and the glory of the revelation *Gestalt* of the one crucified and risen.

It is as Balthasar comes to consider the *event* of revelation as an actual drama between God and his creatures that the role of the believer assumes greater importance.[15] Precisely as Balthasar considers divine revelation as a dramatic action through time, so he must attend more to the interrelationships between God and his creatures, to the struggle between them as well as to the sheer diversity of forms to which the encounter with the divine gives birth. The diversity of forms of sanctity within the church is a proof, not only of the inexhaustibility of the divine glory – *deus semper maior* (God is always greater) – but also of the way in which the divine love finds expression in the diversity of human gifts and graces which it assumes and transforms. And in a darker sense, the experience of those who are called in the church to share in Christ's redemptive work is testimony to the appalling reality of evil which Christ bore on the cross. This is a caveat to Barth's doctrine of the unreality of evil.[16]

Through all this Balthasar presses on to the contemplation of the central mystery of the faith: the drama of the passion and resurrection of the eternal Son. It is a drama which for Balthasar reaches its climax in the Son's *visio mortis* as he descends into Hell to experience the absolute God-forsakenness of the dead. The eternal Logos takes upon himself the fate (not only the substance but the condition) of sinful humanity, drinks its cup to the lees, and so embraces that which is wholly opposed to God – and yet remains God. The exploration of this theological motif which has rarely attracted much attention proves surprisingly fruitful. In the first instance it provides the core of Balthasar's most original christological reflection. The kenosis of the Son finds its fullest expression, not in his voiding himself of God-consciousness, but in precisely this willingness to take upon himself the whole condition of sinful human nature, in order to 'live it round'. The full meaning of the burden which he assumes is glimpsed only when we realize that it means the bearing, not only of the pains of dying but of the state of being dead itself. Balthasar draws here on the tradition of Virgil and Dante, more closely on the mystical experience of Adrienne. The passing into the realm of the dead is a passing into the place which is cut off from God, which is beyond hope, where the dead are confronted with the reality of that which is wholly opposed to God. This is the measure then of the Son's obedience to the Father: that he goes into the realm of that which is at enmity with him in order to bring it back under his rule.

And at the same time this casts light on the mystery of the Trinity, in so far as it is nevertheless *God* who thus enters into the realm of that which is opposed to himself – and yet remains God. Such presence of the divine in the God-forsakenness of Hell is possible only on the basis of the trinitarian distinction between the Father and the Son.

> This opposition between God, the creative origin (the 'Father'), and the man who, faithful to the mission of the origin, ventures on into ultimate perdition (the 'Son'), this bond stretched to breaking point does not break because the same Spirit of absolute love (the 'Spirit') informs both the one who sends and the one sent. God causes God to go into abandonment by God while accompanying him on the way with his Spirit.[17]

But equally, reflection on this divine drama discloses the enormity of radical human evil. What the Son has to do battle with, though with arms of a paradoxical kind, is the whole realm of that which is opposed to God. And the measure of that evil is the Son's own death, the fact that nothing less than his taking of the reality of sin and death upon himself will suffice if it is to be redeemed. Donald MacKinnon has written that it is a test of any contemporary theology that it should refuse to turn aside from the overwhelming, pervasive reality of evil, which was manifested in the deliberate murder of six million Jews in the years between 1933 and 1945. In Balthasar's meditations on the Stations of the Cross he wrestles with the enormity of that history and the ultimate questions of its re-demption.[18]

DEBATE

But to return to the sense in which Balthasar's work is expository and the way in which this distinguishes and yet brings his manner of working closer to his contemporaries in Protestant and Catholic theology. As we noticed, his objection to Bultmann was on two counts. It was firstly to the way in which Bultmann reduced the christological and soteriological elements in the New Testament to their sources in first-century mythology; secondly, it was to his anthropological reduction of faith to the sightless decision whereby 'my' existence is transformed. The combined result of these reductions is that the Christ of faith becomes an incognito Christ grasped only in the *pro me* of 'the process of the upturning of all man's natural aims in life'.[19] but it is important to note that these are two very different kinds of reduction. In the first case we have an *explanatory* reduction whereby, true to the program of the History of Religions School, religious beliefs are explained 'out of', that is to say in terms of, their sources in other contemporary – or near contemporary – religious beliefs and systems. In the second we have a *conceptual* reduction: what is being affirmed is that what may have been thought of as statements about the manner of God's action in the world, in certain events in human history, *are really* statements about the manner in which I may experience a change in my existence.

Now it is perfectly true that there is a neat fit between these two reductionisms in Bultmann's historical and theological method. Nevertheless there is a less than adequate acknowledgment in his work of the sense in which he passes from historical exposition of, say, John's Gospel to rational, theological reconstruction of it. What Balthasar wants to affirm is equally two things. First, it is that a proper exposition of such texts must pay due attention, not only to the historical sources of particular doctrines but to the integrity of the synthesis which is achieved by the author when he or she puts such ideas to work. This seems to me a wholly necessary corrective to much of the work which, directly or indirectly stems from the History of Religions School. The second point is quite different: it is that in reading such texts we should be attempting to see the way in which they mediate to us the revelation-*Gestalt*, in which that is to say there appears in them the divine glory for those who have eyes to see. This is properly contentious. Indeed it is an open question as to whether Bultmann is right in his claim that the only way in which we can understand such texts is in so far as they confront us with an existential decision. He might even be right to rejoin that there is no conceptual reduction involved in reading them in this way; that this was indeed how they were meant to be understood by Paul and John.

Much of Balthasar's most original work has been done in and through a sustained engagement with others' work. This is true above all of his relationship with Barth, which has provided a continuing point of reference for all his theology. As with Rahner, his great Catholic contemporary, the relationship has not been without its tensions.

To Barth Balthasar owes above all his vision of biblical theology rooted in the witness to itself of the divine self-revelation. Here it is that human words and language are taken up and given their true sense and that the vision of the divine glory can be sighted most clearly, taking us up into itself and transforming us as we contemplate the image of the Father in the Son (2 Cor. 3). In his study of Barth's theology (originally delivered as lectures in Basle with Barth and his seminar among the audience)[20] Balthasar not

only gives us a perceptive study of Barth's development from his
Romans commentary through into the *Church Dogmatics* but he also
explores the fundamental theological issues that Barth raises in a
long discussion of Catholic doctrines of grace and nature. Balthasar's
position here is carefully sited between Barth's '*Offenbarungs-
positivismus*' (positivism of revelation) on the one hand and
traditional Thòmist apologetics on the other. He does not wish to
deny all validity to the long history of human search for truth and
life outside the Christian faith. He is as open to the religions of the
East as to the rich mythology and philosophy of antiquity. This is all
part of the history of *God's* world which remains God's world
however fallen. But nor does he wish to construct out of such
searching a philosophical or natural theology as a framework around
which to erect a 'revealed' theology. On the contrary the relationship
must be reversed: the revelation of the Word of God, precisely
because that Word is himself the Creator and Logos of the world,
judges and fulfills all human attempts to plumb the mystery of
Being. Christianity is not simply the highest form of religion as
Liberal theology would have it; rather the revealed Word is the
'apex' inserted into it *from above* such that 'the revelation of God in
Christ and its proclamation is not derivable from the "base" of
cosmic and human nature but can be what it is only as the apex of
the base'.[21]

Of course such a position has its dangers; it may easily lead to
reducing theology to a form of philosophy, or to allowing philosophy
to dictate to theology. But such dangers do not undermine the basic
validity of Balthasar's position which is grounded, not in a prior
understanding of truth and Being, but in belief in the identity of the
revealed Word and the Creator. And it is precisely because of
this identity that the revelation does not simply cut across the
world's attempts to come at the truth but both judges and fulfills
them.

Barth was never entirely happy with Balthasar's claim in the
Preface to the second edition of *The Theology of Karl Barth* that the
dispute between them had been resolved. He remained deeply
suspicious of the dangers of a natural theology which would
ultimately control a theology of revelation, a suspicion greatly fueled
by his battles with theologians like Brunner and Althaus who
advocated a doctrine of orders of creation. And Balthasar himself
was fully alive to such dangers. He was to live to see the way in
which the opening up of the church to the world which he and
others had fought for could easily lead to the erosion of that which
was distinctively Christian. Hence his fierce reaction, notably in

Cordula,[22] to Rahner's development of the notion of 'anonymous Christians'.

What Balthasar attacked in *Cordula* was Rahner's emphasis on the sense in which men and women are by virtue of their own inherent spiritual dynamism capable of apprehending the divine, of believing, hoping and loving. If elsewhere Balthasar was sympathetic to Blondel's 'méthode de l'immanence' which attempted to demonstrate from a study of human dynamism the need for divine revelation, he saw in Rahner's identification of such natural spiritual dynamism with the life of faith a fatal blurring of the distinction between men and women's apprehension of the divine and the divine self-revelation. To speak thus was, in Balthasar's terms, to confuse the natural searching of men and women for the truth with that ultimate vision of God which both fulfills and transcends those intimations of the divine which he had himself treated so sensitively in *The Glory of the Lord: In the Realm of Metaphysics*. It was above all to lose sight of the way in which true Christian belief flourishes as a response to the encounter with the revelation *Gestalt* of Christ. Hence his emphasis on the place of martyrdom and witness in the Christian life.

As Rowan Williams has argued,[23] this debate has deep roots and can be traced back to Balthasar's review of Rahner's much earlier work *Spirit in the World*. There Balthasar warns against the attempt to build a theology simply on a study of the human spirit's transcendence of experience in its judgments and actions. Such a move effectively short circuits all attempts to perceive the nature of the divine freedom by contemplation of the world of objects. Should we not rather begin by contemplation of the natural tendency of Being to take *form*? By attending, that is, to the way in which the wonderful diversity of created things speaks of the sheer creativity of Being and points us to a source of creativity and freedom beyond Being itself which is God? It is this that kindled the wondering attention, the *thaumazein*, of the myth-makers and the philosophers of antiquity. Analogously, it is as believers contemplate the divine form of the revelation in Christ, that their eyes are opened to the grace and majesty of God and that that grace generates new forms of life as it is perceived and obeyed.

It is because of this generative power of Being, as it takes form and is contemplated, that Balthasar insists on the particularity of Christian discipleship and witness. This against Rahner's baptizing of other forms of spiritual life as 'anonymous Christianity'. Too ready an equation of such forms of life with Christian discipleship would be to lose sight of the heart of the Christian experience of grace, of 'being changed into his likeness from one degree of glory to another'. Such insistence is not, it should be emphasized, a denial of the spiritual worth or reality of other religious traditions. Nevertheless Balthasar's emphasis on the dialectic between grace and judgment also obliges him to emphasize the normative character of the revelation form, the sense in which, in its light, all other forms of spirituality are not only affirmed but judged.

But what of that which is perceived? What of Balthasar's emphasis on the *triduum mortis* (three days of death) and specifically the *descensus* (descent into Hell)? Here Balthasar's theology is strangely at its most mythological and at its most concrete. It seems most estranged from contemporary thought and attitudes while at the same time it touches most closely the nerve of contemporary theology with its doctrines of the crucified God and of hope and liberation.

It is true, this concentration on the *descensus* appears to be an almost willful act of remythologization of the gospel. It is a motif that receives hardly more than the most fleeting attention in the pages of the New Testament and its development in church tradition is erratic, though, interestingly, it was a theme which engaged some of the Reformers. Why explore and develop something as seemingly un-biblical as this in a biblical theology? Balthasar's answer must, I think, be threefold: one is undoubtedly that it is part of the specific contribution that Adrienne von Speyr's mystical experience (documented most notably in *Kreuz und Hölle*) has made to his theology. Another that this is precisely to draw out the sense of the divine kenosis which is central to the witness of Paul and, most notably, John. The third, that unless the divine act of salvation embraces the reality of Hell there remains that of human evil which is for ever past redemption.

The strength of kenotic christologies, as Donald Mackinnon has often argued, lies not so much in the account which they offer of the mode of the eternal Logos' taking flesh as in the way in which in the humiliation of the Son there is achieved the transformation of our natural perceptions of the divine. What is it to predicate omniscience and omnipotence of the one hanging on the Cross in weakness? Yet that humiliation reaches its term in the death of the Son, his passing into the realm of that which is most wholly opposed to God, into the realm of death and sin. Is it mythology to talk in this way? Or is it one way, perhaps the most effective way, of bringing to expression the concrete reality of death, of betrayal, of the weight and consequence of sin? And equally of bringing out the trinitarian implications of the death of the Son?

It is here that Balthasar comes closest to the best writing of Jürgen Moltmann. Like Balthasar, Moltmann has seen the need for recasting the traditional doctrine of the immutability of God in the light of the relations between the Father who delivers his Son into the hands of wicked men to be killed and the Son who wills to drink the cup that the Father offers him. Strangely, where Moltmann has made the doctrine of the divine immutability the subject of sustained criticism,[24] Balthasar has not, preferring to develop those biblical concepts which enable him to enter more closely into the inner-trinitarian drama of the sending of the Son by the Father into the world of sin and death. But where the differences between the two theologians become most illuminating is in their treatment, precisely, of the death of the Son. Moltmann prefers to speak of the dying which the Son experiences and the Father's experience of the Son's death. Balthasar speaks by contrast, and here he is guided by Adrienne's Holy Saturday visions of Hell, of the *visio mortis* (vision of death) of the Son. Only he could experience the horror of death in all its fullness, because in entering into the realm of death he encounters that which is contrary to his divine nature. And yet even in entering into that realm he does not cease to be God; the Spirit binds him to the Father; God, in the person of the Son, enters the realm of death, gathering in all that has been lost and drawing it back to him.

At the heart of all such theologizing lies the question of theodicy, reintroduced so vigorously into Protestant theology by Moltmann after its banishment by Barth. Yet the 'answers' which are offered are less in the nature of theoretical solutions to the question of the existence of evil as such than pointers to the way in which God has himself acted to right his world. Such pointers in turn shed light on the nature of God himself, as they also draw believers into the very process of the divine reconciliation.

ACHIEVEMENT AND AGENDA

Balthasar, I have tried to show, is an expository, rather than an argumentative theologian. To say that is in no sense to suggest that his work is simply derivative. It is rather to point to the way in which his theology seeks less to analyze, to construct a theology on the basis of rational, natural theological argument than to give creative, imaginative expression to Christian truth. The task he has set himself is to articulate a vision of the Christian mystery, drawing on the great riches of the Christian tradition as that comes again to

life in the meditations of Adrienne, but which above all is rooted
and grounded in the language and imagery of the Bible. His
achievement is to have woven together so many diverse strands into
such a rich tapestry: where always it is the central mystery of the
cross which integrates and provides the key to the complexity. And
it is this central orientation to the cross which ensures that his
theology is never facile, but always mindful of the reality of sin and
death which the Son must confront in the *visio mortis* of the
descensus.

To present Balthasar's theology in this way is to show the extent to
which it is truly church theology. It grows out of his sense of
vocation which is intimately linked to that of Adrienne, and the
founding of the *Johannes-Gemeinschaft*, the secular institute which
has found a wide echo within the Catholic church. It is deeply
indebted, as he readily acknowledged, to Adrienne's mysticism, not
least her experiences in Holy Week. But it also owes a debt to their
literary circle and to his own love of European culture and letters. In
this sense his theology is 'contextual', though it is a context very
different from that in which much church theology has to be worked
out in Latin America, Southern Africa and elsewhere; as it is
different again from the academic context to which much Western
theology has to answer.

Balthasar himself, stressing the roots of his theology in meditation
and prayer, called his theology 'kneeling theology': but this is in no
sense to deny the intellectual rigor of his work. His reflections on the
Christian mystery are schooled in a searching study of the Bible and
tradition. He has the trained eye and sensibilities of the literary
critic who has submitted to a life-long study of the texts, through
which he has appropriated the language and concepts of the
tradition. Thus if his theology remains firmly identifiable as the
work of a cultured and devout Swiss man of letters, it constantly
takes us out beyond that immediate milieu, as his – and Adrienne's
– insights and visions are clarified and elucidated by being given
their place in a comprehensive vision of the Christian mystery.

In this regard Balthasar has bequeathed to those who come after
him the perennial task of any church theology: how, as someone
who is set in a particular time and culture, to create a theology which
is truly catholic, truly universal? In one sense Balthasar's answer to
this is simple. It is in the measure that one is obedient to the
particular vocation that one receives that one is drawn into the
paschal mystery and enabled to see the glory of the Lord: and it is
this vision which enables one in turn to see the world, with all its
grandeurs et misères, as never without grace, always in need of

reconciliation and transformation. Catholic in this sense means seeing things whole: perceiving the inexhaustible fullness of the revealed glory, not reducing or foreshortening it. It means then constantly working to recover those aspects of the tradition which have been lost and obscured. As it means ever greater openness to the world, to its beauties and consolations, its terrors and *longeurs*. In this sense the task of theology is never done. It needs constantly to battle against the tendency to foreclose: to absolutize its own particularities. If for some Balthasar's world seems too far removed from the world of revolutionary Latin America or indeed the sense of impending anarchy of newly independent states, then that should act as a challenge to turn again to the central mysteries of the cross and resurrection, of the bearing and overcoming of human enmity by the Lord of glory, to find there that which may illumine the darkness of their world with all its hopes and fears. And in so doing they may discover that they can turn again to the very different legacy of Balthasar's own meditations on the divine drama and find in it strange insights into the nature of that struggle.

NOTES

1 Balthasar, 'In Retrospect' in *The Analogy of Beauty*, ed. J. Riches, p. 220.
2 Ibid., p. 201.
3 Cf. his *Schleifung der Bastionen. Von der Kirche in dieser Zeit* (Einsiedeln, 1953).
4 See, for example, the opening of *The Glory of the Lord* vol. 1, pp. 17ff.
5 See Balthasar's own study in *The Glory of the Lord*, vol. 3.
6 London, 1948, p. 21.
7 Balthasar, *The Glory of the Lord*, vol. 1, pp. 44ff, 52, 56.
8 See, for example, Balthasar's essay in *Elucidations*, 'A Verse of Matthias Claudius'.
9 Balthasar, *The Glory of the Lord*, vol. 1, pp. 45–79.
10 Riches, *The Analogy of Beauty*, p. 220.
11 Ibid.
12 In *Mysterium Salutis III/2. Grundriss heilsgeschichtlicher Dogmatik*, ed. J. Feiner and M. Loehrer (Einsiedeln/Cologne, 1969), pp. 133–326.
13 Five vols (Einsiedeln, 1973–83).
14 Riches, *The Analogy of Beauty*, p. 4.
15 Cf. the discussion in *Theodramatik* I, pp. 20, 24ff; II/1, Pt II *passim*.
16 Balthasar, 'Christlicher Universalismus', *Verbum Caro*, p. 269.
17 Balthasar, *Elucidations*, p. 51.
18 Balthasar, *The Way of the Cross*.
19 R. Bultmann, *The Gospel of John* (Oxford, 1971), p. 69.
20 Balthasar, *The Theology of Karl Barth*.

21 Balthasar, 'Christlicher Universalismus', p. 262.
22 English translation *The Moment of Christian Witness*.
23 Riches, *The Analogy of Beauty*, pp. 19ff.
24 Most notably in *The Crucified God* (London, 1974), ch. 6.

BIBLIOGRAPHY

Primary

Balthasar, H. Urs von, *Heart of the World* (San Francisco, 1979; first published 1945).

—, *The Theology of Karl Barth* (New York, 1971; first published 1951).

—, *A Theology of History* (New York, 1963; first published 1959).

—, *The Glory of the Lord*, Edinburgh, 1982–; first published 1961–)

—, *Love Alone: The Way of Revelation* (London, 1968; first published 1963).

—, *The Way of the Cross* (London, 1969; first published 1964).

—, *The Moment of Christian Witness* (New York, 1968; first published 1966).

—, *First Glance at Adrienne von Speyr* (San Francisco, 1981; first published 1968).

—, *Elucidations* (London, 1975; first published 1971).

—, *The Christian State of Life* (San Francisco, 1984; first published 1977).

Secondary

Riches, J. (ed.), *The Analogy of Beauty: The Theology of Hans Urs von Balthasar* (Edinburgh, 1986).

Part V

History and Eschatology

In the 1960s Wolfhart Pannenberg and Jürgen Moltmann introduced new ideas and programs to contintental European theology. History and eschatology were their common themes, although, as Christoph Schwöbel shows, they have deep differences in content and method. They are now international and ecumenical theologians both in the scale of their influence and the range of their interests and dialogues.

Pannenberg challenged both Barth and Bultmann on the issue of faith and history. For him the integrity of Christian theology requires that faith be grounded in knowledge which can be rationally established outside faith. It also requires an understanding of the totality of reality which can match atheist and other worldviews. Schwöbel describes Pannenberg's often complex ideas, points to significant developments in the past fifteen years which put *Jesus – God and Man* (for which he is best known) in a new light, discusses the first volume of his systematic theology, and concludes with some probing questions.

Moltmann has always stayed closer to Barth and Bonhoeffer, but his development shows a remarkable openness to further influences. Richard Bauckham describes his dialogical theology, brings out the coherence of Moltmann's theological program, suggests that human rights can be seen as the integrator of his political theology, and discusses some of the criticisms of him.

13

Wolfhart Pannenberg

Christoph Schwöbel

INTRODUCTION

In 1961 a slim volume of essays published by a group of younger academics created a considerable sensation in the somewhat static situation of Protestant theology in Germany. The title of the collection, *Offenbarung als Geschichte (Revelation as History)*, was correctly understood by the theological public as the programmatic statement of a new theological conception. The group of essayists soon became known under the name of their editor as the 'Pannenberg Circle'. It was Wolfhart Pannenberg, the systematic theologian of the group, whose 'Dogmatic Theses on the Doctrine of Revelation' contributed significantly to the programmatic character of the volume and who was soon identified with this theological conception that was widely considered to be a genuinely new approach to fundamental issues of modern theology.

Revelation as History did not only provide the basis from which Pannenberg developed his systematic conception; it can also be regarded as the provisional conclusion of his earlier development in which he gradually achieved an independent position. Born in 1928 in Stettin (now Poland), Pannenberg grew up in the atmosphere of the totalitarian regime of National Socialism, before he began his studies after the war at the University of Berlin.[1] After spending some time in Göttingen and after a short interlude in Basle where he encountered Karl Barth, Pannenberg continued his theological studies at the University of Heidelberg. There he wrote his doctoral dissertation *Die Prädestinationslehre des Duns Skotus* (published in 1954) under the supervision of the Lutheran Barthian Edmund Schlink, and in 1955 completed his *Habilitationsschrift* with an analysis of the role of analogy in Western thought up to Thomas Aquinas. After a few years of academic teaching at Heidelberg as

Privatdozent, in which he discovered the significance of Hegel's thought for the formation of modern theology, Pannenberg was called to become professor at the *Kirchliche Hochschule* in Wuppertal where Jürgen Moltmann was his colleague. In 1961 he was appointed to the chair in systematic theology at the University of Mainz.

Pannenberg has always acknowledged the influence of the theological teachers at Heidelberg on the formation of the new theological program.[2] Gerhard von Rad's reconstruction of the theology of the Old Testament as the history of the transmission of traditions, Günther Bornkamm's insistence on the importance of the historical Jesus for New Testament theology and Hans von Campenhausen's attempt to reinstate a theological interpretation of history in church history coincided in a new emphasis on the theological significance of history for Christian faith. This theological perspective was soon assimilated by the young theologians constituting the 'working circle'. But whereas the teachers were quite content to develop a more positive theological appropriation of history in their respective disciplines, the 'working circle' of their pupils tried to work out a new comprehensive framework for the perennial question of the relationship of faith and history in interdisciplinary dialogue. The original group of Rolf Rendtorff and Klaus Koch (Old Testament), Ulrich Wilckens and Dietrich Rössler (New Testament), which was later joined by Martin Elze (church history) and Trutz Rendtorff (social ethics), represented together with Pannenberg almost a complete faculty, and this interdisciplinary cooperation constituted an effective counter-move against the growing alienation of dogmatic, exegetical, and historical theology.

Although Pannenberg has always attributed the seminal idea of God's indirect self-revelation in history to Rolf Rendtorff (who later abandoned it),[3] his own systematic exposition of this basic idea soon led to the identification of the program of *Revelation and History* with Pannenberg's own theological conception. Even if this is not entirely correct with regard to the initial programme, it is perhaps justified to say that Pannenberg's own theological conception developed in his attempt to hammer out the full implications of the basic ideas contained in *Revelation as History* and to find sufficient strategies for substantiating its claims in response to its critics. The 'working circle' discontinued its regular meetings in 1969 and since then other members have presented theological conceptions, whether in biblical or in systematic theology, which are notably different from that of Pannenberg.

In the course of Pannenberg's development the new conception has been influenced by theological insights from quite different contexts from that of the initial program. Pannenberg's encounter with North American theology is one of the factors that have shaped the systematic structure of his thought. Beginning with an invitation as a guest professor to the University of Chicago in 1963, Pannenberg has lectured widely at most centers of theological learning in the United States, and his continuing dialogue with the leading exponents of process thought has contributed significantly to the development of his theology. He is today at least as widely recognized as a leading contemporary theologian in the United States as in Germany. Pannenberg's involvement in ecumenical theology, which acquired increasing importance after his move in 1967 to the chair in systematic theology at the University of Munich, where he is director of the Ecumenical Institute, has led to new areas of theological reflection in which he attempts to demonstrate the relevance and comprehensiveness of his theological approach. This expansion of themes in Pannenberg's thought reflects the ongoing systematic development of his conception as well as the reception of his theological ideas in different contexts of theological reflection. In 1988 Pannenberg published the first volume of *Systematische Theologie* which presents the synthesis of the various strands of his theological development in a comprehensive dogmatic conception.

SURVEY

What are the main elements of the new approach in *Revelation as History* which provide the outline for the further development of Pannenberg's theological conception? In his analysis of the structure of the concept of revelation Pannenberg starts from the assertion that revelation cannot be adequately understood as the disclosure of truths about God. It has to be interpreted strictly as the self-revelation of God.[4] This assumption, which shows the measure of Pannenberg's agreement with Barth, is traced back to Hegel who is seen as the one who established this principle in modern theology and first recognized its full implications.[5] Divine self-revelation entails that if there is only one God there can only be a single and unique revelation in which God is at the same time author and medium of revelation. It constitutes genuine, though not necessarily exhaustive, knowledge of God. The next step – and here Pannenberg parts company with Barth – is the thesis that according to the biblical traditions God does not reveal himself directly (e.g. in his 'Word'), but *indirectly* through his acts in history. On the basis of the strict understanding of revelation as God's self-revelation this cannot refer to specific historical events or series of events. It can only be applied to the end of history from which every preceding event and, indeed, the whole of reality is illuminated. This eschatological perspective constitutes the universality of revelation.

It is for Pannenberg the distinctive claim of Christian faith that God's eschatological self-demonstration is proleptically actualized in the destiny of Jesus of Nazareth, more precisely, in his resurrection. The preceding history of Israel has to be understood as a gradual universalization of the understanding of God's action in history, reaching its final stage in Jewish Apocalypticism where the end of history is expected as the complete revelation of God. From the end the course of history – now understood in its entirety – can be seen as God's indirect self-revelation. The universality of God's self-revelation as it is pre-actualized in the resurrection of Jesus has the important corollary that it can be accessible not only for a specifically privileged group of people. Since it happens for 'all flesh', it is in principle open for all who have eyes to see.[6]

The crucial point of this rudimentary program is the claim that the end of history as the final self-revelation of God is proleptically realized in the resurrection of Jesus. Pannenberg tackled the task of substantiating this claim in a comprehensive christological conception, published in 1964 as *Grundzüge der Christologie* and translated into English in 1968 under the (somewhat unfortunate) title *Jesus – God and Man*. Because of its impressive synthesis of exegetical and historical research and systematic exposition the book has been celebrated as one of the most comprehensive treatments of christology in this century and soon became one of the standard textbooks in academic theology.

The distinctive and much debated feature of this christological conception is its methodology which follows from Pannenberg's understanding of the task of christology as that of *establishing* the true significance of Jesus as the Christ of God from his history.[7] For this reason – Pannenberg claims – christological reflection must go back behind the New Testament kerygma to the historical reality of Jesus himself and start 'from below'. Pannenberg uses this somewhat ambiguous metaphor to designate the difference of his method from the approach 'from above', starting with the incarnation of the second person of the Trinity which presupposes what it seeks to establish, i.e. the divinity of Jesus Christ. In Pannenberg's view it also neglects the historical particularity of the man Jesus in the religious and cultural context of his time and adopts a humanly impossible epistemic stance.[8] Furthermore, Pannenberg rejects the approach to christology from the question of the significance of Jesus Christ for us, which, in his view, implies that christology becomes, in effect, a 'function of soteriology' (P. Tillich). This procedure runs the risk of being dominated by soteriological interests which all too easily turn into the christological projection of human desires for salvation. What Jesus *means* for us must be grounded in what he *is*, and what he *is* can only be established by starting from the past reality of the historical Jesus.[9]

The starting-point 'from below' does, however, not mean that Pannenberg's christology remains below. Knowledge of the divinity of Jesus is grounded in the resurrection in which his unity with God is established in such a way that the claim implied in his pre-Easter appearance is vindicated. Only on the presupposition that the resurrection is understood against the background of apocalyptic expectation as the proleptic actualization of the end of history is it possible to see Jesus in his person as God's self-revelation, because the vindication of his unity with God in the resurrection extends retroactively to the pre-Easter life of Jesus.[10] This does not mean that the distinction between Jesus and God the Father is blurred at any point in this conception. In the framework of the revelational unity of God and Jesus the divinity of Jesus has to be understood as the unity of the Son with the Father which leads directly to the Christian understanding of God as Trinity.[11] More recently Pannenberg has worked out in detail what this self-differentiation in the triune life of God, implied in the cross and resurrection of Jesus, would suggest for a fully-fledged doctrine of the Trinity.[12]

The resurrection, which Pannenberg attempts to establish as a historical event whose probability is stronger than any alternative explanation,[13] is not only the crucial point for the validation of the claims of Jesus' divinity; it is also the foundation for understanding the true humanity of Jesus as the fulfillment of human destiny. From this anthropological perspective Pannenberg explores the soteriological content traditionally presented as the work of Christ, before turning to the relationship of humanity and divinity in Christ. Deeply skeptical about the adequacy of the traditional Two-Natures Doctrine, conceived in terms of a metaphysics of substance which he sees as inevitably trapped in the dilemma of having to choose between a 'unification' and a 'disjunction' Christology,[14] Pannenberg explores the possibility of asserting that the identity of Jesus with the Son of God is established indirectly through his relationship of absolute obedience to God the Father.[15] In this sense Jesus' eternal Sonship is interpreted as dialectically identical with his humanity, in so far as the relationship of Jesus to God the Father in the historical aspect of his existence mediates the relationship of the eternal Son to the Father. This involves the inversion of the order of knowing and the order of being. While the dialectical identity of Jesus with the Father can only be known from the particularity of Jesus' historical human existence, it is grounded in the ontologically prior relation to divine Sonship as the ground of the existence of Jesus.[16] In this approach Pannenberg sees the possibility of reappropriating the *particula veri* of the logos-christology.[17]

At a number of crucial points the validity of this christological conception rests on the justifiability of its *anthropological* pre-suppositions. The appeal to the resurrection as the foundation for christological statements about the unity of Jesus with God and about the fulfillment of human destiny in him presupposes that the apocalyptic expectation of the end of history as the disclosure of the totality of meaning can be justified on general anthropological grounds. And Pannenberg's thesis that the identity of Jesus and the eternal Son is established indirectly through his humanity pre-supposes that the openness for God which is the hallmark of Jesus' obedience to the Father is the determinative feature of the human condition. In his writings on theological anthropology, beginning with a published series of radio talks (*What is Man?*, 1970; German edition, 1962) and coming to a preliminary conclusion in his magisterial work *Anthropology in Theological Perspective*, 1985 (German edition, 1983), Pannenberg has combined the more specific aim of providing the foundational principles for his exposition of Christian faith with the general task of elucidating the anthropological foundation for Christian truth-claims. After the atheistic critique of religion in the modern era anthropology has become for him the battle-field on which theology has to demonstrate the validity of its claims to universality.[18]

The decisive thesis which has been extensively developed over a period of more than twenty years is already introduced in the first chapter of *What is Man?* The fundamental openness to the world which has been interpreted by modern philosophical anthropology as the key to the understanding of what it means to be human has to be interpreted as a fundamental openness for God.[19] God is the infinite horizon which is implicitly presupposed in every act of human self-transcendence. This fundamental relatedness to God constitutes the irreducible dimension of human religiousness which, according to Pannenberg, underlies all structures of human culture.[20]

Although the universality of all theological claims has to be substantiated by reference to these general anthropological considerations, they do not provide a sufficient platform for developing the specific insights of Christian anthropology. For this task it is for Pannenberg necessary to distinguish between the actuality of human existence and the final destiny of humanity.[21] Actual human existence is characterized by the universality of sin, evidence of which is given in the egocentricity of human behavior which denies the fundamental *exocentricity* of human life. This consists in the fact that human life receives its center from outside itself.[22] In contrast to actual human existence, what it means to be human has to be understood as the destiny of humanity which was essentially realized in Jesus but is not yet effectively actualized for all humankind. The term 'human nature' should therefore be understood as designating the history of the realization of the human destiny.[23]

The claim that the destiny of humanity has been actualized in Jesus and specifically in his resurrection is the ground for the hope that our future resurrection will realize our true being as communion with God in the divine kingdom in which even 'the last enemy', death, is overcome. From this basis Pannenberg offers a theological explanation of the reality of freedom as well as of the communal destiny of humanity. Jesus' resurrection as the foundation of our future resurrection is seen as the warrant for the conviction that the individual human person, as the obedient object of God's love, has infinite value and dignity. This is the ground of freedom which cannot be inferred from the actual existence of humanity. It can only be communicated by reconciliation with God in Christ.[24] On the other hand, Christ's sacrificial devotion to God in giving himself to the world, which is vindicated in the resurrection, pre-actualizes the communal destiny of humanity in the kingdom of God. The eschatological community of humankind in the Kingdom of God finds its anticipatory actualization and symbolic representation in the church which expresses its character most cogently in the eucharist.[25] With this attempt Pannenberg tries to point to the mediation of freedom and community in the Kingdom of God and develops on this basis the constructive task of the church in representing the true 'global village' of the Kingdom of God and its critical task of resisting every denial of freedom in the name of penultimate communities and authorities. This perspective not only provides a basis for the description of the role of the church in society, it also illuminates the motivation for Pannenberg's ecumenical activity. If the symbolic representation of the community of humankind in God's kingdom is the primary character of the church from which all other tasks are to be determined, the separation of the churches must seem theologically scandalous.[26] The awakening of a new eucharistic piety which expresses what Pannenberg sees as the true character of the church appears from this viewpoint as the most decisive sign of hope for ecumenism.

The way in which Pannenberg has tried from the outset to integrate different theological disciplines and to relate theological reflection to various non-theological sciences raises many questions concerning the scientific status of theology and its methodology. Pannenberg addressed these questions in his *Theology and the Philosophy of Science* (1976; German edition, 1973) against the backdrop of a detailed description of the development of the philosophy of science and of an exposition of the different historical attempts to determine the scientific character of theology.

Starting from the traditional definiton of theology as the science of God, Pannenberg immediately qualifies this definition by asserting that God as the subject-matter of theology must be understood as a hypothesis if one is to avoid the twofold pitfalls of religious subjectivism and dogmatic positivism.[27] If the word 'God' can meaningfully refer only to the reality that determines everything, God cannot be directly experienced like an object in the world, but can only become indirectly accessible in the subjective anticipation of the totality of meaning which is presupposed in all particular experiences. Since the experience of reality as a whole finds symbolic expression in the historic religions, a theory of the history of religions is the place where the indirect co-givenness of God in all experience has to be analyzed.[28] The specific claims of Christian theology to a specific revelation of God have to be substantiated against the background of this general reflection which Pannenberg now calls *fundamental theology*.

On the basis of this understanding of the nature of theology, Pannenberg characterizes theological statements as *hypotheses*. While their complete verification can only be expected from the *eschaton*, there are nevertheless specific criteria for their substantiation. Theological hypotheses purporting to state the implications of Christian faith are to be considered as *not* substantiated, if they cannot be shown to present implications of the biblical traditions; if they are not related to the whole of reality in a way that can be validated by present experience and substantiated against the background of contemporary philosophical reflection; if they are not capable of being integrated with the relevant area of experience; and if they are deemed to be inadequate in relation to the present stage of theological debate.[29]

This comprehensive conception of the status of theological theory and of the criteria regulating theological practice summarizes on a metatheological level some of the main elements which have been present in Pannenberg's theological work from the early stage of *Revelation as History*, and which continue to determine the working out of his conception in new areas of theological reflection.

KEY ISSUES: UNIVERSAL HISTORY, FAITH, TRUTH, GOD

The key issues underlying Pannenberg's whole theological conception were first presented in a comprehensive form, when Pannenberg's collected papers were published together in the volume *Basic Questions in Theology* (German edition, volume I, 1967 – English edition, volumes I and II, 1970/71; volume III, 1973 contains the paper 'The Later Dimensions of Myth in Biblical and Christian Tradition' and the essays from *Gottesgedanke und menschliche Freiheit*, 1972; German edition, Volume II, 1980, has not been completely translated into English). This collection brought together papers from the 1950s concentrating on the foundational questions of a theology of history, essays responding to the debate after the publication of *Revelation as History* and focusing on the relationship of faith and reason, and studies concerned with spelling out the implications of the conception and provided an impressive summary of the basic insights of Pannenberg's theological position.

The first issue that is constitutive for Pannenberg's whole theological program is his concept of a *universal history* and its implications for the overall project of Christian theology. History is, as Pannenberg programmatically asserts, the most comprehensive horizon of Christian theology.[30] This claim has its foundation in the development of Israel's faith in which an understanding of history is gradually formed that conceives reality in its totality as history. This view of history which finds its definitive expression in Jewish Apocalypticism is presupposed in the Christian belief that the end of history from which the unity of history can be conceived is anticipated in the destiny of Jesus of Nazareth. Far from abandoning the universal historical outlook of Jewish Apocalypticism, Christian faith had to retain it in order to make sense of its christological claims.[31]

From the viewpoint of universal history the turn to an anthropocentric conception of history in the Enlightenment, which interprets the human agent as the creator of history and conceives the unity of history as constituted from this anthropocentric perspective, must appear as a serious threat to a specifically Christian understanding of history.[32] In contrast to existentialist philosophers and theologians who see the origin of an understanding of history in the historicity (*Geschichtlichkeit*) of human existence and thereby adopt the anthropocentric perspective, Pannenberg tries to show that the experience of reality as history constitutes the historicity of human existence. This leads to important theological conclusions, since the understanding of reality as history, constituted by the fulfillment of God's promises, is established in Israel's belief in Jahwe as the only God. Pannenberg tries to reclaim this theological framework for the Christian understanding of history.

The theological perspective of universal history has a number of implications for the relationship of theology to historical investigation and to hermeneutics. Pannenberg attempts to demonstrate that only on the presupposition of the anthropocentric conception of history do the principles of historical understanding have to be interpreted as implying the uniformity of all events and their interrelatedness in a closed immanent causal nexus which precludes a theological interpretation of history. If historical understanding is interpreted along these lines, it implicitly denies the conditions for its own possibility, since this view excludes the appearance of genuine novelty in history and undermines the conditions for understanding history which always presuppose a comprehensive and unitary framework of the totality of meaning. For the theological interpretation of history, however, God's eschatological self-disclosure in its pre-actualization in Jesus' resurrection provides the conditions for perceiving the unity of history which constitutes a comprehensive horizon of meaning and at the same time establishes genuine and contingent novelty in history.[33] On these presuppositions the antinomy between faith and historical investigation can be overcome and historical research can help to establish the foundations of faith.

The understanding of *faith* demanded by this conception of universal history can be seen as the second key issue of Pannenberg's work. From the very beginning Pannenberg has staunchly defended his contention that faith must be based on knowledge, if it shall not turn into a purely decisionistic and irrational act. The kind of knowledge presupposed in faith cannot be seen as a special kind of knowledge that somehow transcends the conditions of natural knowledge and is only accessible to believers. It is the same kind of 'natural' knowledge that is the object and objective of all scientific inquiry.[34] While consistently denying the necessity of postulating a special knowledge of faith, Pannenberg has, on the other hand, never been content with an a-theological understanding of knowledge, but has instead attempted to uncover the theological presuppositions and implications of the human quest for knowledge and truth.

This attempt rests on the conviction of a fundamental compatibility of faith and reason.[35] Faith is in Pannenberg's interpretation by definition eschatological in character. As trust faith anticipates something that lies in the future. According to Pannenberg, this characteristic has in Christian faith been radicalized in such a way that God is seen as the ground of faith, because he is in the coming of his kingdom the future which faith anticipates. This feature of the anticipation of a final future is in no way restricted to faith. It belongs for Pannenberg to the very nature of reason, which in its attempts at classifying and determining the structure of reality has to presuppose a fore-conception of the final future. By illuminating the whole of reality this fore-conception provides the conditions for determining each of its aspects. Yet, while this future becomes explicitly thematic in faith, it has to be implicitly presupposed in every act of reason. This implicitness can account for the fact that reason can deceive itself about the nature of its absolute pre-supposition and consequently (mis)interpret its relationship to faith as an antinomy.[36]

The fundamental compatibility of faith and reason is anchored in the understanding of *truth* which underlies Pannenberg's entire conception and which could be seen as the third key issue of his theology. Starting from the premiss of the necessary unity of truth, Pannenberg follows Hegel's view that truth has to be understood not as a static givenness but as a process characterized by change which is disclosed in its totality only at the end when history has run its course.[37] He sharply differs from Hegel by asserting that we cannot take our own position to be the end of the historical process, since that would deny the openness of the future. Rather, we have to follow what Pannenberg sees as the early Christian view of history that the end of history is already proleptically realized in the resurrection of Jesus and that therefore this event constitutes the unity of truth without denying the openness of the future and the contingency of events.

In this framework the unity of truth requires a conception of the historical character of truth which Pannenberg attributes to Hebrew thought and in which truth is what will be made evident in the future.[38] In this conception the ultimate coherence of truth is the condition for asserting the correspondence between concepts and reality. Under this condition faith as well as certainty is characterized by the anticipation of the future appearance of the totality of truth in the present.[39]

The emphasis on the anticipation of a future totality of meaning which characterizes Pannenberg's understanding of history, faith, and truth is mirrored in his reflection on the *conception of God* – the fourth key issue of his theology. From the outset Pannenberg's reflection on the question of God is motivated by the attempt to respond to the atheistic critique of theism in the modern era.[40] This starting-point implies for Pannenberg that one should accept the criticism of a concept of God developed in the categories of substance metaphysics or conceived in terms of an anthropomorphic understanding of God as a person. For Pannenberg, the modern atheistic critique turns any attempt to deal with the question of God dogmatically into an exercise in religious subjectivism.[41]

In his own constructive attempts Pannenberg tries to elucidate the understanding of God against the background of anthropological reflection, since he sees the crucial point of the atheistic critique in the assertion that the concept of God is not necessary for a complete and meaningful understanding of human existence. In his earlier work Pannenberg concentrates on the problem to what extent human existence itself can be seen as an implicit quest for God so that human life can be understood as the question which receives its answer only in God. God can be understood as the answer to this question, in so far as the future of his rule makes his Godness ultimately evident in illuminating the whole of history and with it the meaning of every being and event in it.[42] From this perspective, the future is the mode of God's being in so far as it ultimately reveals God's existence and his nature as the reality that determines everything. God is God in the exercise of his rule and since the complete demonstration of his rule lies in the future, God's being and his kingdom have to be seen as identical.[43]

In later years Pannenberg has expanded and modified this approach by concentrating on the problem of human freedom against the background of a general theory of human subjectivity. In this context, Pannenberg claims, God must be conceived as the transcendent ground of the structure of human subjectivity who is encountered in human existence where the exercize of human freedom points to a transcendent reality as the condition for its possibility. If the ground of human freedom is located in human existence itself, personhood becomes something which is completely given in the present, and that contradicts the structure of person-hood as constituted by interaction with others and denies human freedom as the ability to transcend everything that is given in the present. This implies for God as the ground of freedom that he cannot be thought of in categories that would entail his present givenness, but must be conceived as a free person whose coming in the future is the final self-demonstration of his existence and of his true nature.[44]

This approach to the conception of God has a number of crucial corollaries. The futurity of God necessitates, for instance, an eschatological transformation of the idea of God the creator. This means that creation cannot be interpreted as an initial act 'in the beginning', but as the consummation of God's rule 'in the end'.[45] Furthermore, if the notion of the coming God binds together the eschatological self-demonstration of God's existence and nature, then this leads to far-reaching revisions in the doctrine of God's attributes, since the traditional interpretation of divine attributes could be quite incompatible with this conception.[46]

In Pannenberg's conception the futurity of God implies that God remains ahead of every attempt to express his being and nature. This leads Pannenberg to reject all conceptions of discourse about God which are based on the assumption of an analogy between God and the language used in talking about God. He admits only a weaker sense of 'analogy' in which theological language is analogical to ordinary human speech. Pannenberg takes over Edmund Schlink's characterization of the *doxological* character of all language about God which expresses adoration of God on the basis of his works. This, however, implies that in the act of adoration the univocity of speech is 'sacrificed' and language becomes equivocal in the act of transferring concepts which in ordinary discourse have a creaturely content to God. The truth of theological language about God can, according to Pannenberg, nevertheless be substantiated by reference to the proleptic appearance of the divine *doxa*, the glory of God, in the resurrection of Jesus.[47] Pannenberg's critics have intimated that the admission of the equivocity of all language about God is in danger of putting the propositional content and truth-value of theological language at risk, especially when the eschatological self-revelation of God is interpreted in the strong sense suggested by the concept of the 'futurity of God'.[48]

SYSTEMATIC THEOLOGY, VOLUME I

In the spring of 1988 Pannenberg published the first volume of his *Systematische Theologie*, comprising the prolegomena to dogmatics and the doctrine of God. Compared to Pannenberg's earlier writings one distinctive difference becomes immediately obvious. While the earlier works can, at least to a certain extent, be seen as successive steps in the development of the theological conception that was programmatically introduced in *Revelation as History*, this conception is now presented in its full systematic *Gestalt*. The systematic balance that is achieved in this comprehensive presentation also leads to a number of important clarifications concerning some of the more contentious aspects from Pannenberg's earlier work.

Pannenberg starts with a discussion of the truth of Christian doctrine as the organizing theme of systematic theology. This has a number of important corollaries. First of all, Pannenberg rejects the notion that theology can be adequately understood as the expression of human notions about the Divine. It must be grounded in the divine mediation of God in revelation.[49] The dependence of all knowledge of God on God as the ground of its possibility necessitates, secondly, understanding dogma not primarily as an expression of the consensus of the church, but as an 'eschatological concept' (K. Barth), referring to the final disclosure of truth at the end of history which is nevertheless proleptically present in God's self-revelation in Christ as it is presented in Scripture.[50] This implies, thirdly, that dogmatic theology has to presuppose the truth of the tradition of faith grounded in revelation without claiming that this is an already established and self-evident truth. In order to overcome this apparent dilemma Pannenberg suggests that the fact that God's reality and the truth of his revelation remains contentious before the *eschaton* must itself be understood as grounded in God, if God is indeed the creator of heaven and earth.[51] To face up to this contentiousness of God's reality means for Pannenberg that theology cannot claim to rely on an already established truth which is contained in the witness of Scripture, the tradition of the church or in the certainty of religious subjectivity. At the same time, theology is, according to Pannenberg, obligated to hold fast to the belief in the unity of truth which has its ultimate ground in the unity of God.[52]

On the basis of these considerations Pannenberg can now introduce his thesis about the hypothetical character of the statements of faith and theology. This familiar thesis is, however, carefully qualified. Pannenberg insists that this hypothetical status does not in any way diminish the nature of theological statements as real assertions stating genuine truth-claims and that it does not affect the certainty of the act of faith.[53] These qualifications seem to indicate that this thesis has not so much a constructive, but a critical function. It serves to remind the theologian and the believer of the finite, fallible and approximate character of all human knowledge and underlines the dependence of theology on the self-revelation and self-demonstration of God.

In a theological conception where the relationship of 'truth' and 'God' is made the unifying focus of the exposition of the contents of Christian faith, the questions surrounding the concept of God and the possibility and actuality of knowledge of him are – not surprisingly – of central importance. Pannenberg argues against all attempts to analyze 'God' as a proper name and insists that the expression has to be understood as a general designator. The metaphysical concept of God which is expressed by this use of 'God' functions in his view as a general condition for understanding Christian God-talk. It has to be presupposed in order to assert the claim that the God of the philosophers really exists as the God of the Bible.[54]

It was, according to Pannenberg, the original intention of 'natural theology' to examine the adequacy of religious ways of talking about God in any given religious tradition about the 'nature' of the Divine. In his view philosophical reflection on the minimal conditions for an adequate conception of God, as it is exemplified in its classical form in the theistic proofs, has to retain its critical function for contemporary theology, although it can no longer be used as a strategy for establishing conclusive reasons for the existence and nature of God. For Pannenberg the anthropological conception of natural theology in the Enlightenment and the anthropological reinterpretation of the theistic proofs in the philosophy of Kant and Hegel is irreversible. [55] Nevertheless, he argues that Christian theology would be ill advised if it rejects any possibility of 'natural' knowledge of God and adopts a reductionist anthropological interpretation of religion in the form of Feuerbach's projectionism. Against the early work of Karl Barth where Feuerbach's theory of religion is positively appropriated in order to show that there is no viable alternative to a theology of revelation, Pannenberg argues that such a move would in the end be self-destructive, since it would be impossible to demonstrate that Christian faith is an exception from the general verdict that religion is the creation of human imagination. Moreover, such an uncritical embrace of projectionism would prove to be self-defeating on Barth's own criteria, since it would be impossible to interpret religion as the rebellion of human self-assertion against God.[56]

We seem to be left with a very problematical situation: neither the theistic proofs nor the theological critique of natural theology seem to offer a reliable foundation for the justification of theological claims. Is there a possible resolution to this dilemma? Pannenberg thinks that such a solution can be found, if we hold fast to the underlying conviction of natural theology that God has to be conceived as the ground of the possibility of the existence of the world and humanity. Although this does not offer firm ground for developing a *natural theology* by means of reason alone, it neverthe-less indicates the possibility of conceiving of *natural knowledge* of God, not as a human capacity, but as a factual characteristic of human life. Pannenberg thereby shifts the ground of the discussion from the *cognitio Dei naturalis acquisita*, the acquired natural knowledge of God that forms the basis of the formal theistic proofs, to the *cognitio Dei naturalis insita*, the innate knowledge of God. For Pannenberg there is such an awareness of God, a claim that can in his view be substantiated from anthropology, and which is discussed in the history of religious thought with reference to concepts such as 'conscience', 'immediate awareness' and 'basic trust'. These notions express, according to Pannenberg, the fact that human beings live in virtue of the 'excentric openness' of their existence in an unthematic awareness of their own life as being posited into the whole of reality and dependent on the divine ground of reality. Although this awareness is unthematic and can only be identified as awareness of *God* from the perspective of a reflective interpretative framework, it is nevertheless not a human possibility that awaits actualization; it is fully actual in the very fact of human existence.[57] In Pannenberg's view it is this feature of the human condition which Paul refers to in Romans 1:19ff[58] and which provides an essential *Anknüpfungspunkt* (point of connection) for all Christian claims to universality.

Pannenberg frequently emphasizes that in a time when one can no longer expect theistic proofs to provide conclusive evidence for theistic claims, every attempt at finding a universal foundation for religious claims has to be based on the interpretation of reality in the concrete religions. The approach from the phenomenon of religion, which replaced Scripture in many strands of modern religious thought as the foundational principle of theological assertion, is, however, riddled with difficulties. Can a general concept of religion be reconciled with the particular religious perspective of the theologian who employs it? And is it possible to avoid the dichotomy of an anthropological and a theological view of religion? Pannenberg hopes to overcome these difficulties by interpreting the history of religions as the history of the appearance of the unity of God which is the way in which God discloses his truth. This view presupposes the anthropological universality of religion and it requires us to see the divine mystery acting upon reality as the unitary focus of conflicts between religious traditions and disputes within a religious tradition. In Pannenberg's view

Israel's understanding of history as the sphere of the appearance of God's unity provides the key for the theological interpretation of the history of religions. It provides a possibility for resolving the thorny problems of particularity and universality in their manifold forms, because the mediation of particularity and universality is an essential characteristic of divine self-demonstration in history itself.[59] Within the framework of this conception the concept of revelation denotes the origin and basic criterion of knowledge of God.

Within the Judaeo-Christian tradition revelation is therefore also seen as the criterion for the adequacy of a religious relationship. The fundamental ambivalence of this relationship is for Pannenberg a crucial aspect that regulates the use of the concept of religion and the employment of the insights of the phenomenology of religion in Christian theology and philosophy of religion. This ambivalence is rooted in the fact that human beings become aware of the divine ground of being in the context of human experience of the world. This produces the danger that the divine mystery itself is identified with its sphere of manifestation so that the Infinite is turned into something finite. And this applies not only to the conception of God, but also to all cultic activities and to the mythical depiction of the Divine. It is here that Pannenberg locates the *particula veri* of Barth's criticism of religion as human self-assertion and rebellion against the reality of God. If God is identified with the finite context of his manifestation, human religiosity implicitly denies the infinite and absolute nature of God. If God is identified with the finite context of his manifestation, human religiosity implicitly denies the infinite and absolute nature of God. Pannenberg claims, however, that in Christianity the reduction of the Infinite to a finite entity is sublated by the event of revelation which creates the possibility that the fundamental ambivalence of the religious relationship is healed in faith grounded in revelation.[60]

Pannenberg's analysis of revelation is in many ways the center of the exposition in the first volume of the *Systematische Theologie*. First of all, it is the place where it has to be shown that human knowledge of God has its origin and foundation in God's self-disclosure. Secondly, it has to be demonstrated how the unthematic awareness of the divine ground of reality receives a definite content in revelation. And thirdly, it is here that the justification of the claim that the notion of God's self-demonstration in history can mediate particularity and universality in the history of religions has to be developed. At the same time these considerations are also the turning-point for the structure of the argument in the *Systematische*

Theologie. Pannenberg turns from the external perspective where the conception of God and the claims of the history of religions are phenomenologically introduced and analyzed with regard to their function for the view of reality, to the internal perspective of Christian revelation from which a systematic reconstruction of Christian doctrine is developed. This shift of perspective is possible because the concept of revelation appears from the external perspective as the foundational notion for the validation of religious claims.[61]

After a detailed survey of the biblical conceptions of revelation Pannenberg carefully analyzes the factors that led to the central role of the concept of revelation in modern theology. According to his reconstruction it is only with the idealist philosophies of Schelling and Hegel that the concept of revelation acquired this foundational function by being conceived as God's self-revelation. They postulated a strict identity of subject and content of revelation and related it to universal history as presenting the full scope of divine self-disclosure.[62] In spite of this powerful stimulus, subsequent theological developments remained in Pannenberg's view trapped in the difficulties of relating God's manifestation in history to his inspiration acting upon the subjectivity of the believer. In response to that Martin Kähler introduced the notion of the 'Word of God' as the theological concept that would integrate the disparate notion of historical manifestation and subjective inspiration.

Pannenberg interprets his own proposal in *Revelation as History* as an attempt at overcoming the dilemma involved in the dichotomy of manifestation and inspiration by reinterpreting and correcting the idealist conception of universal history as the process of divine self-revelation from the perspective of Christian eschatology.[63] He furthermore claims that the notion of God's indirect self-revelation in history provides a possibility for integrating the pluriform conceptions of revelation in the biblical writings and offers a systematic framework for the clarification of the notion of the Word of God.[64]

Throughout the discussion it is Pannenberg's aim to integrate the legitimate emphases of the Word of God theologies in his own conception and to correct overstatements in his original program. This is especially apparent in the discussion of the thesis that had elicited much criticism when *Revelation as History* was first published, that God's revelation in history is open to everyone who has eyes to see. Pannenberg explains that the thesis of the universal epistemic accessibility of God's revelation refers primarily to God's universal self-demonstration in his kingdom. Only in so far as this is pre-actualized in Jesus Christ can the accessibility of revelation be extended to history.[65] It is precisely this notion of the anticipatory disclosure of God's ultimate purpose in Jesus which leads to the understanding of Jesus Christ as the Word of God in the full sense developed in the doctrine of the Trinity.[66]

Pannenberg's conception of the doctrine of the Trinity is perhaps the most interesting aspect of his dogmatic synthesis which shows a definite advance over his earlier writings, where trinitarian reflection appears to play either a very minor role (as in the essays developing the presuppositions and implications of *Revelation as History*) or is confined to specific *loci* of Christian dogmatics (as in *Jesus – God and Man*). Pannenberg attempts to use the trinitarian perspective, which first came to the fore in his writings from the mid-1970s, as a new approach for the solution of some of the crucial problems of the traditional conception of the doctrine of God. The result is a reversal of the traditional structure for the exposition of the doctrine of God which started from the existence of God, proceeded to the discussion of the essence and attributes of the one God and then added the doctrine of the Trinity. Instead, Pannenberg started from the doctrine of the Trinity and employs this as the interpretative key for the conception of the being and attributes of the triune God.

Pannenberg's proposal is to develop the doctrine of the Trinity from the way in which the relationship of Father, Son and Spirit is disclosed in revelation.[67] This approach from Jesus' relationship to the Father and the Spirit has a number of important consequences for the conceptuality of the doctrine of the Trinity. The classical Western distinction between the processions of the Son (*generatio*) and the Spirit (*spiratio*) from the Father, which constitute the persons of the immanent Trinity, and the sending of the Son and the gift of the Spirit in the divine economy can no longer be seen as adequate to the witness of Scripture where such a distinction between immanent and economic relations cannot be made. Therefore the mutual self-differentiation of Father, Son and Spirit in the divine economy must be seen as the concrete form of the immanent trinitarian relations.[68] The key to an adequate description of these relations is for Pannenberg the fact that Jesus distinguishes himself clearly from the God he calls Father, but in renouncing himself completely he makes room for the action of the Father and the coming of his kingdom. In this way God as he eternally is discloses himself in his relationship to Jesus and this reveals an 'aspect' in the humanity of Jesus which is the eternal correlate to the Fatherhood of God: the eternal Son.[69] The way in which Jesus distinguishes himself from the Father discloses, when it is interpreted as the self-revelation of God, that there is an eternal relationship of Father and Son in God. The self-differentiation of the Son from the Father corresponds to the self-differentiation of the Father from the Son which consists in the fact that the Son receives all power in heaven and on earth from the Father (Matthew 28: 18) until God's rule has become universally victorious, when the Son will return the power to the Father (cf. 1 Cor. 15: 24 and 28). Since God's Godness is not independent of the exercise of his rule, this *motif* enables us to see a mutuality in the relationship of Father and Son which is absent from the traditional language of the 'begetting' of the Son.[70] The mutuality of the relationship of the Father and the Son is for Pannenberg the key for the correct interpretation of the cross of Christ so that an alternative between the view of the death of God on the cross and the suffering of the human nature of the Son which does not affect the eternal trinitarian relationship can be found.[71]

The resurrection is in Pannenberg's view the access to an adequate understanding of the Third Person, because it depicts the dependence of the Father and the Son on the Spirit as the medium of their community. And from this perspective the whole work of the Son in the glorification of the Father can be assessed on the basis of his dependence on the Spirit. From this approach it is not surprising that Pannenberg rejects the addition of the *filioque* to the Nicene–Constantinopolitan Creed by the Western church. The reason is not simply that this one-sided step was uncanonical, but more importantly, that it rests on the mistaken Augustinian view of all relations of the Trinity as originating relations which overlooks the pluriform character of the trinitarian relations and cannot do justice to the Spirit as the medium of the community of the Father and the Son.[72]

The conception of the Trinity that is developed in this way implies with its dialectic of self-differentiation and mutuality that the three persons cannot be understood as three modes of beings in one subject. They have to be understood as three centers of activity. They cannot be reduced to a single relation, but each of them is a focus of a network of relationships. The mutuality of their active relationships implies for Pannenberg furthermore that the *monarchia* of the Father has to be understood as the result of the cooperation of all three persons. The full realization of the *monarchia* of the Father is the kingdom. From this perspective the world as a whole can be seen as the history in which it will be finally demonstrated that the trinitarian God is the only true God. This claim about the eternal Trinity can, however, not be asserted apart from the dynamics of the divine economy in which it finds its eschatological validation.[73]

In the last chapter of the *Systematische Theologie* Pannenberg turns to the issues of the unity of the divine essence and the divine attributes. Following his approach of using the doctrine of the Trinity as the framework for the whole doctrine of God he connects the trinitarian question of the unity of the divine essence with the fundamental questions about God's existence and attributes that are commonly treated before the doctrine of the Trinity. He first identifies the central area where the respective problems of both approaches overlap. For the traditional approach the problem consists in the difficulty of reconciling the unity of the divine essence with the pluriformity of the divine attributes. From the perspective of trinitarian theology the question is how the three persons of the Trinity can be understood as presenting one divine essence without reducing them to moments or aspects of the one essential Godhead and without positing the divine essence as a fourth subject lurking behind the persons of Father, Son, and Spirit. As Pannenberg emphasizes, this is to a large extent a question that is related to the eschatological resolution of the tension between the persons of Father, Son, and Spirit in revelation and the hiddenness of the unity of God in the world.

Pannenberg approaches these problems from the question of the relationship of divine essence and existence. He distinguishes two basic models for determining the divine essence. The first, expressed in exemplary fashion in Thomas Aquinas' thought, is the model of God as the first cause which develops the rules for talking about God's essence from the causal relationship between God and the world. The second, and in Pannenberg's view preferable, model is the understanding of God as Infinite as it was first introduced by Gregory of Nyssa as an alternative to the Arian conception of God as ingenerate being.[74] Pannenberg sees this notion further developed in Descartes' conception of God where the intuition of the Infinite is understood as the condition for all our knowledge of finite objects. The Infinite therefore has a 'transcendental' function for all our knowledge of finite things. Pannenberg is, however, critical of Descartes' immediate transition from the intuition of the Infinite to the concept of God. The identification of the Infinite with God can only be made from the standpoint of a reflective religious consciousness which can then interpret the transcendental function of the Infinite as the mode of God's presence to the human mind.[75]

This Cartesian model is then applied to the question of essence and existence. The concept of essence is in Pannenberg's view always relative to an indeterminate something that is determined *as* something by applying an essence concept. In the same way God's existence has to be understood first as the indeterminate Infinite that underlies our knowledge of finite objects which we gain by restricting and qualifying the notion of the Infinite. The essence of something appears in distinct moments of existence, but only the complete range of the appearance of something is sufficient for the determination of its essence. We can only speak of the disclosure of essence, if we know the complete appearance of something or have a singular appearance that can be seen as constitutive for the full range of appearances. If we apply this conception to the Christian understanding of God we can say that Father, Son, and Spirit are the forms of existence (*Gestalten des Daseins*) of the one divine essence that make it possible to give the notion of the divine essence a distinctive and determinative content.[76] It is, however, crucial for the universality of Christian claims that the determinative forms of the existence of God as Father, Son, and Spirit are ultimately identical with the whole range of his non-thematic and indeterminate presence in his creation.

This reformulation of the traditional problem of the relationship of God's *essentia* and his *existentia* forms the background for Pannenberg's reflections on the doctrine of the divine attributes. He follows the suggestion, first made by Herman Cremer in 1897,[77] to approach this problem not from a conceptual framework wedded to a problematical form of substance metaphysics, but from the concept of divine action. But this notion seems to be inextricably bound up with the notion of a self-conscious agent who is able to determine certain purposes and objectives of his will. This model, however, seems to be inextricably bound up with the agency of a finite agent and becomes immediately problematical when applied to the infinite God. The heart of the matter is for Pannenberg the notion of God as *nous*, understood in terms of a self-conscious mind who is seen as the subject of specific interrelated acts of knowing, willing, and acting.[78] Pannenberg tries to overcome the difficulties of this conception by pointing to the analogies of the biblical notions of God as Spirit with the scientific concept of a universal field of force that is manifested in particular corpuscular constellations. This move enables Pannenberg to retain the notions of energy, dynamic effects, and life without ascribing them to a self-conscious subject. His bold proposal is to understand the divine essence and life on the analogy of the field-model and not in terms of the *nous*-model. The Godhead is in this way understood as the divine Spirit or life that is manifested in the three persons of Father, Son, and Spirit.[79]

This suggestion, however, seems to challenge precisely what Pannenberg set out to develop: a theological conception of divine agency that could provide the foundation for the ascription of attributes. In order to counter these difficulties, Pannenberg insists that the three persons of the Trinity are the primary and immediate subjects of divine activity. At the same time he rejects the view that the three persons are first individually constituted and are only then united by *perichoresis* and in joint action. Since the three persons have to be seen as the forms of existence of the one divine life they are eternally constituted and correlated by its overflowing energy which is mediated through the inner-trinitarian relations.

With this conception Pannenberg still faces two problems. First of all, it must be shown that there is a connection between the relatedness of the divine Triunity and the relationship of the Trinity to the world. The concept of action is in his view eminently suitable for expressing this relationship between the immanent Trinity and the divine economy. In his actions the agent relates to what is outside himself, but in doing so he also relates to himself. In this way God's active presence as Father, Son, and Spirit in his creation is acutely relevant to the eternal identity of the Trinity.[80] Secondly, Pannenberg has to show that it is possible to find a coherent conception of the unity of divine action, because otherwise the ascription of attributes to God would be questionable. He achieves this by reinterpreting the traditional notion of the *monarchia* of the Father in such a way that one can avoid the subordinationist connotations of the traditional view of the Father as source and origin of the Trinity. The *monarchia* has to be related to the Kingdom of God as the ultimate 'objective' of God's action, but this *monarchia* is mediated through the Son who becomes incarnate to make the participation of God's creatures in the kingdom possible and through the Spirit who enables them to participate in the relationship of Father and Son. The *monarchia* of the Father in the kingdom is the unitary focus of all divine activity in creation, redemption and salvation and of the interrelationship of the three trinitarian persons.[81] Pannenberg emphasizes that divine action should not be understood as satisfying a deficiency in God's eternal being. Rather, God's action in relation to the world has to be seen as 'repetition', or perhaps better re-enactment of his eternal Godhead in relation to his creation.[82] The correlation of 'other-directedness' and self-determination in the notion of action and the interpretation of the *monarchia* of the Father in the kingdom as the unitary focus of the immanent and the economic Trinity are the two essential presuppositions of Pannenberg's attempt at reconciling the view of the three persons as primary subjects of all divine activity with the ascription of divine attributes to the one divine essence.

The divine attributes are divided into two groups by Pannenberg: the first set comprises those attributes (like infinity, eternity, omnipotence and omnipresence) that identify the being who is subject of further predications. Their function is to make sure that these attributes are indeed attributes of *God*. The attributes of the second set (like righteousness, faithfulness, wisdom, mercy, patience etc.) are predicated of the being that conforms to the minimal conditions for talking about God laid down by the first set of attributes. Here as in other parts of the *Systematische Theologie* it is Pannenberg's intention to show that the different perspectives of a philosophical conception of God and of a Christian theological understanding of God are ultimately capable of being integrated without losing their respective emphases.

In accordance with the reflections in other parts of the work the concept of the Infinite is presented as the fundamental notion that regulates the entire conception of the divine attributes. It is, however, only capable of performing this regulative as well as integrative role, if it is not understood along the lines of the quantitative notion of the mathematically infinite. Drawing on Hegel's understanding of the Infinite, Pannenberg insists that the truly Infinite cannot simply be understood in contrast to the realm of finitude because that would produce the contradictory notion of a limited infinity. The truly Infinite must comprehend everything finite within itself without blurring the initial contrast of infinity and finitude. In order to underline the religious significance of such a conception of God as infinite Pannenberg refers to the biblical understanding of God's holiness which sees holiness as opposed to the profane, but also comprehends the profane through its inclusion into the sanctifying dynamic of God's truly infinite holiness.[83]

This pattern of opposition and inclusion also determines the conception of the other divine attributes. God's eternity cannot only be understood in contrast to time; it must also be thought of as including time in its totality. In contrast to his temporal creatures, God is not confronted with a future that is different from his present. God is his own future and this implies perfect freedom, a freedom that is not restricted by being bound to a temporally limited present.[84]

Pannenberg's treatment of divine omnipresence follows from his understanding of God's eternity which is interpreted as the way in which everything that was, is and will be is present for God who is his own future. It also shows that his notion of the Infinite as including its opposite corresponds to one of the main implications of the trinitarian conception of God: the mediation of transcendence and immanence. This can be achieved, because the trinitarian conception reconciles the transcendence of the Father with the presence of the Son and the Spirit for the believers which, by virtue of the coequality of the persons and their *perichoresis*, also extends to the Father.[85]

Omnipresence is a condition for divine omnipotence. Perfect omnipotence can only be predicated of God the creator. Seeing God as the creator would imply that God's omnipotence cannot be understood as opposed to the being of his creation. The perfect exercize of omnipotence therefore consists according to Pannenberg in the divine activity that overcomes the alienation between the creator and his creation. For this reason the incarnation of the Son must be understood as the highest expression of God's omnipotence.[86]

This thought leads already to the treatment of the divine attributes that are predicated of God on the basis of his trinitarian action. Here the notion of divine love has the same integrative and regulative function as the notion of the Infinite for the 'metaphysical' attributes of God. On the basis of God's revelation in the story of Jesus, love has to be understood as the concrete form of the unity of the divine essence which is manifested in the relationship of the trinitarian persons. Pannenberg therefore presents God's goodness, grace, mercy, righteousness, faithfulness, patience and wisdom as aspects of the all-encompassing reality of divine love.[87]

The crucial question that is raised by this treatment of the divine attributes from the two perspectives of philosophical reflection and biblical revelation is, of course, whether it can be demonstrated that the God of the biblical revelation is the God who is described by the attributes of philosophical theology. Pannenberg emphasizes that the claim that the God of revelation is the only true God must remain contentious until it is validated through God's action in history. Every attempt at arguing for the unity of God as the identity of the God of revelation and the only true God must therefore be content to show that this claim is coherent. Pannenberg's concluding thesis is therefore that the notion of love conceived in its trinitarian concreteness enables us to form a coherent notion of the unity of God's essence and existence with his attributes which includes the unity of the immanent and the economic Trinity.[88] In this way the trinitarian conception of love becomes the coping-stone of Pannenberg's dogmatic synthesis.

DEBATE

Pannenberg's theology has from the beginning provoked both criticism and approval. After the publication of *Revelation as History*, the two dominating groups of German post-war theology, the Barthian and the Bultmannian schools, reacted vigorously against the criticism of the 'Theology of the Word of God' implied in the new theology of history. While the Barthians emphasized the necessity of interpreting the concept of divine self-revelation as God's *direct* revelation in his threefold Word and rejected Pannenberg's conception as a new version of theological rationalism,[89] Bultmann's followers complained about the misunderstanding of the relationship of Christian kerygma and the historicity of human existence and accused Pannenberg of reconstituting an obsolete speculative metaphysics of history.[90] Both schools accused Pannenberg of making Christian faith dependent on the results of historical investigation and of sacrificing the autonomy of theological reflection in an attempt at establishing its foundations. In contrast, the close relationship between theology and historical research was one of the reasons why Pannenberg's work was greeted with enthusiasm by more conservative Christians who saw in his arguments for the resurrection as a historical event a decisive refutation of modern skepticism concerning the historical foundations of Christian faith.

In the 1960s Pannenberg's work was often seen in connection with that of his former colleague at Wuppertal, Jürgen Moltmann. The superficial similarities in the shared emphasis on an eschatological perspective should, however, not disguise the fundamental differences in their respective approaches to theology. Whereas for Moltmann the predominance of the eschatological perspective is grounded in the *'future of truth'* as it is revealed in the divine promise which is constitutive for the experience of reality as history,[91] the eschatological perspective establishes for Pannenberg the *totality* of reality as history and the comprehensive horizon of meaning which, in turn, necessitates a conception of the future demonstration of truth. For Moltmann's conception in *The Theology of Hope* the *future* of truth is the primary aspect that provides the foundation for his specific view of reality. For Pannenberg the totality of reality and the unity of truth are the primary aspects and these elements lead to the emphasis on the future as the mode of God's being and as the ultimate horizon for his eschatological self-demonstration. Moltmann has consequently interpreted Pannenberg's conception as one which remains wedded to the view of revelation as the epiphany of truth in Greek cosmology so that it cannot accommodate the primacy of divine promise in Old Testament and Christian thought. He therefore accused Pannenberg of seeing the task of the theologian as *interpreting* the world differently, instead of *changing* it in expectation of the fulfillment of the divine promise.[92] Whereas the further development of Moltmann's theology can, at least partly, be explained as a theological reaction to the changing intellectual and political climate in Western Europe, Pannenberg has devoted his theological efforts to the elaboration of his original program in a comprehensive conception which is aimed at integrating all aspects of reality in their changing historical and cultural context. This difference in their general approach to theology is further illustrated by their respective trinitarian theologies. Moltmann's doctrine of the Trinity is aimed at providing an alternative to traditional Western theism, based on the monotheistic principle, which he sees with regard to its theological content as well as with regard to its ethical and political implications as deeply compromised. In contrast to that Pannenberg intends to present his trinitarian theology as an attempt at resolving some of the traditional difficulties of Western theism and emphasizes the necessity of retaining the monotheistic emphasis of the Western tradition.

When one compares Pannenberg's writings from the 1960s with his publications from the past fifteen years one notices a significant shift in emphasis. The early writings stress the objectivity of universal history as the comprehensive horizon for theology and are concerned with the historical verifiability of the prolepsis of the end of history in the resurrection of Jesus. In the later writings Pannenberg emphasizes that this totality of reality and meaning is only given in subjective anticipations that have to be validated intersubjectively. In consequence, the systematic importance of the verifiability of the resurrection for the whole conception appears to be less pronounced. This shift of emphasis is mirrored in the response to Pannenberg's conception, where in recent years the issues connected with the problem of 'natural theology' have become increasingly prominent. That this problem has currently, after Karl Barth's rigorous condemnation of its theological legitimacy, such a high priority on the theological agenda – although the proposals offered for its solution differ radically – is, at least to some extent, due to the long-term influence of Pannenberg's conception on the theological scene. Pannenberg's own contention that, since faith is not constituted by itself, it has to be grounded in knowledge that can be rationally established outside faith, remains, however, as hotly debated as in the first years after the publication of *Revelation as History*.[93]

ACHIEVEMENT AND CRITIQUE

There can be no doubt that Pannenberg's theological conception is one of the major contributions to twentieth-century Protestant theology which has also stimulated considerable debate in Roman Catholic theology. Although firmly rooted in the intellectual traditions of German theology and philosophy, Pannenberg's theology has influenced theological debate in various other intellectual and religious contexts and has, in turn, been influenced by a variety of intellectual currents and traditions in the Western world. It is thus an example of theological reflection under the conditions of cultural contact and scholarly communication after the Second World War.

When one attempts to summarize the achievements of Pannenberg's theological conception three characteristics seem to be most notable. First of all, Pannenberg's theology is an attempt to meet the challenge of the atheistic critique of religion in the modern era without seeking refuge in strategies of intellectual immunization, and on the reflective level that is required by the intellectual standard of the critique and by its pervasive influence in contemporary culture. Secondly, Pannenberg seeks to realize this aim by developing his theology in close contact with the findings of biblical exegesis and against the background of a comprehensive analysis of the Christian tradition. Thirdly, one of the distinctive marks of Pannenberg's theological reflection is the awareness of the necessity for interdisciplinary cooperation with the human science and, to a certain extent, with natural science, in which Christian theology interacts with the intellectual efforts of its time. All three characteristics illustrate the conviction underlying Pannenberg's entire conception that Christian theology will only be able to fulfill its task adequately if it develops a comprehensive view of reality that is authentically Christian as well as intellectually plausible and that provides ethical orientation in the complexities of the modern situation.

It is precisely this view of the task of theology which can provoke a number of critical questions with regard to the conceptual framework in terms of which Pannenberg attempts its execution. The development of a comprehensive view of reality in Christian theology seems to require some kind of ontology which explains what there is and how it is to be interpreted. If the activity of determining how something is to be interpreted is to be capable of resulting in genuine truth-claims, it is necessary to establish that it can correspond to the determination of what there is. Especially in Pannenberg's earlier writings we encounter at this point a twofold *indeterminacy* in Pannenberg's conception: what something *is* is only established in what it *becomes* in the future; and every act of determining how what there is is to be interpreted has an irreducibly hypothetical status. Is this a necessary corollary of Christian eschatology or does it introduce an unnecessary element of indeterminacy into the Christian view of reality which would have to be seen as self-defeating? This problem is further illustrated by Pannenberg's proposal of comprehending both God's creation and his self-revelation in the concept of the futurity of God. If the existence and nature of God are finally determined and made evident only in the eschatological self-demonstration of his kingdom, it would seem that God's relation to the world remains – at least penultimately – indeterminate.

The *Systematische Theologie* does not only document Pannenberg's awareness of these difficulties, it also demonstrates his attempt to overcome its problematical consequences. This is illustrated by the determinative role of the doctrine of the Trinity not only for the understanding of God, but for the entire dogmatic conception. If everything that is, is ultimately grounded in God's trinitarian relation to his creation and if God's relation to the world is the repetition or re-enactment of his eternal being as Father, Son, and Spirit, then the apparent indeterminacy has its limit precisely in the eternal identity of the triune God. What something is and how it is to be interpreted will only be ultimately established in the Kingdom of God where the relationship of creation to the trinitarian God will be evident for all in the self-demonstration of his rule. But since this is the 'repetition' in the relationship to creation of what God is eternally in his triune being, this ultimate disclosure is far from indeterminate.

It does, however, seem questionable, whether the conception of God as Infinite is indeed the most adequate model for understanding the divine essence. One could ask whether this does not reintroduce an element of indeterminancy into the conception of God which the careful description of the relationship of the economic and the immanent Trinity attempted to overcome. It could furthermore be questioned whether the concept of 'the Infinite' is indeed a key model for describing the divine essence or whether it does not function as 'a qualifier' for other models for the description of the God–world relationship and for the concepts employed to express the divine attributes. Pannenberg's own attempts to give content to this purely formal concept by adapting the Hegelian notion of the 'truly Infinite', which comprehends the contrast of finite and infinite in itself, and by developing the analogy with the biblical notion of God's holiness, would seem to point in the same direction. The general question that seems to arise at this point is whether the strong emphasis on God as the Infinite is (in spite of its venerable theological ancestors) really demanded by the contents of Christian faith or whether it is not primarily required by Pannenberg's own conception of the non-thematic awareness of the Infinite which plays such an important role for Pannenberg's religious epistemology.

This leads to the second problem that seem to underlie many of the crucial and much debated features of Pannenberg's theological methodology. Pannenberg has from the outset attempted to find a middle way between the Scylla of a 'dogmatic' exposition of Christian doctrine based on revelation which fails to offer sufficient reasons for its assertions and the Charybdis of a 'rationalist' treatment of theology which only allows such statements that can be justified by means of reason alone. The *Systematische Theologie* presents his most developed attempt to mediate between the internal perspective of faith and the external perspective of reason.[94] His approach to start from the description of religious and theological claims and to identify within this framework the concept of revelation as the irreplaceable foundation of all theological claims from which the reconstruction of the contents of revelation can then proceed, is certainly one of the most interesting proposals for the solution of this thorny problem in modern theology. It documents Pannenberg's insistence that faith is not grounded in itself and can therefore not be treated as self-justifying and it illustrates the determined effort to give reasons for the assertions of faith that are intelligible and rationally plausible within the framework of reason. But at least some would disagree with the conclusions which Pannenberg draws from this for the conception of Christian theology. For Pannenberg it is essential that the theologian can establish certain foundational principles outside the perspective of faith that would support the claims to universality made within that framework. Therefore he attempts to reconstitute the traditional insights of natural theology in his conception of the non-thematic awareness of the Infinite that is given in the factual constitution of humanity. The fundamental problem connected with this approach is *not* the thesis that there is a universal awareness of the Divine which is the basis for the culpability of humanity's attempt at ignoring the reality of God. This thesis only becomes problematical when it is employed as a foundational principle for securing the universality of Christian truth-claims. The use of anthropological and epistemological reflections as a modern *praeambula fidei* would seem to provoke the danger that these considerations are made subject to far-ranging theological reinterpretations that would reduce philosophy to an ancillary role for the constructive theological task. But as the complex history of the relationship of faith and reason documents, this strategy does not only threaten the autonomy of philosophical reflection which, after all, would not have to be the primary concern of the theologian. It would also appear that if the theologian employs non-theological considerations as foundational principles for theology the categories developed from the perspective of reason would have a determinative effect for the conception the theologian develops in the reconstruction of the contents of faith from the perspective of faith. Again, the central role of the concept of the Infinite would seem to provide evidence for this danger.

The problems of Pannenberg's attempt at combining the perspective of reason and the perspective of faith in his theological conception could be summarized in the following question: is it necessary to try to establish the basis for the claims to universality in Christian faith from the perspective of reason, before one turns to the explication of the contents of faith as they are grounded in revelation, or would it be more adequate to treat the universality of theological truth-claims as an implication of the Christian revelation that can only be developed in terms of a rational reconstruction of its contents from the perspective of faith? It is one of the decisive criteria for each of these approaches that a theological conception has to demonstrate its plausibility and coherence by attempting to elucidate the whole of reality and our position in it. In this respect it is necessary to emphasize the premature character of these critical questions, because the comprehensive treatment of the relationship of the trinitarian God to his creation will only be presented in the as yet outstanding second volume of Pannenberg's *Systematische Theologie*. Every theologian interested in fundamental theology has reason to expect much illumination from the completion of Pannenberg's theological synthesis as well as from the debates it will almost certainly provoke.

Is Pannenberg's 'theology of the future' the type of theology that will determine the future of theology? With regard to its conception of the task of theology in presenting an authentically Christian and intellectually plausible view of reality, developed in intradisciplinary theological cooperation and tested in interdisciplinary dialogue with other sciences, it is to be hoped that many theologians will follow the inspiration of Pannenberg's attempt. With regard to the conceptual framework in which Pannenberg attempts to tackle this formidable task, one can only point to the criterion provided by his own conception and leave the answer to the future.

NOTES

All works cited are authored by Wolfhart Pannenberg unless otherwise stated.

1 For a biographical portrait cf. R. J. Neuhaus, 'Pannenberg: Profile of a Theologian', in W. Pannenberg, *Theology and the Kingdom of God*, ed. Neuhaus, pp. 9–50.
2 For a short description of the formative influences on Pannenberg's early theology cf. E. Frank Tupper, *The Theology of Wolfhart Pannenberg*, pp. 19–44.
3 Cf. Epilogue to the second edition', in *Revelation as History*, Supplement 1 to *Kerygma* and *Dogma*, 2nd edn (Göttingen, 1963), pp. 132–148, p. 132 n. 1.
4 Cf. 'Dogmatic Theses on the Doctrine of Revelation', in *Revelation as History*, pp. 125–58.
5 In *Jesus – God and Man*, pp. 127ff. Pannenberg argues for the assumption that Hegel's concept of revelation was mediated to Barth through the Hegelian dogmatician Ph. H. Marheineke.
6 Cf. thesis 3 of the 'Dogmatic Theses' and the response by the Lutheran theologian Paul Althaus, 'Offenbarung als Geschichte und Glaube, Bemerkungen zu Wolfhart Pannenbergs Begriff der Offenbarung', *Theologische Literaturzeitung*, 87 (1962), cols 321–30. Pannenberg replied to Althaus's critique in his paper 'Insight and Faith', in *Basic Questions in Theology*, vol. II, pp. 28–45.
7 Cf *Jesus – God and Man*, p. 30.
8 Ibid., pp. 33–7.
9 Ibid., pp. 38–49.
10 Ibid., pp. 53–114.
11 Ibid., pp. 115–87.
12 Cf. his essays 'Die Subjektivität Gottes und die Trinitätslehre. Ein Beitrag zur Beziehung zwischen Karl Barth und der Philosophie Hegels' and 'Der Gott der Geschichte. Der trinitarische Gott und die Wahrheit der Geschichte', *Grundfragen Systematischer Theologie*, II, pp. 96–111 and pp. 112–28.
13 Cf. *Jesus – God and Man*, pp. 88–106, and the essay 'Dogmatische Erwägungen zur Auferstehung Jesu', *Grundfragen Systematischer Theologie*, II, pp. 160–73.
14 Cf. *Jesus – God and Man*, pp. 283–96.
15 Cf. ibid., pp. 334–49.

16 Cf. esp. ibid., p. 337.
17 Cf. ibid., pp. 166ff and the 'Postscript to the Fifth German Edition', ibid., pp. 409ff.
18 Cf. the introduction 'Theology and Anthropology' in *Anthropology in Theological Perspective*, pp. 11–23.
19 Cf. *What is Man?*, pp. 1–13: cf. also the detailed exposition in *Anthropology*, pp. 43–79.
20 Cf. *Anthropology*, pp. 473–84.
21 Cf. *Human Nature, Election and History*, p. 23ff.
22 Cf. *Anthropology*, pp. 60–74 (esp. p. 64, n. 61) and pp. 80–6).
23 Cf. *Human Nature*, p. 24.
24 Cf. ibid., pp. 24ff.
25 Cf. 'Eucharistic Piety – A New Experience of Christian Community', in *Christian Spirituality and Sacramental Community*, pp. 31–49, esp. 38ff.
26 Cf. also 'The Kingdom of God and the Church', in *Theology and the Kingdom of God*, pp. 72–101.
27 Cf. *Theology and the Philosophy of Science*, pp. 297ff.
28 Cf. ibid., pp. 310ff and pp. 358ff.
29 Cf. ibid., pp. 326–45, esp. pp. 344ff.
30 Cf. 'Redemptive Event and History', in *Basic Questions in Theology*, vol. I, p. 15.
31 Cf. ibid., pp. 16–38, and 'On Historical and Theological Hermeneutic', pp. 137–81, esp. pp. 157–60, pp. 174–81.
32 Cf. 'Redemptive Event and History', pp. 39–50.
33 Cf. ibid., pp. 66–80.
34 Cf. 'Insight and Faith', esp. pp. 32ff.
35 Cf. 'Faith and Reason', in *Basic Questions in Theology*, vol. II, pp. 46–64.
36 Cf. ibid., pp. 63ff.
37 Cf. 'What is Truth?', *Basic Questions in Theology*, vol. II, pp. 1–27, esp. 21ff.
38 For this conception of truth Pannenberg refers regularly to Hans von Soden, *Was ist Wahrheit? Vom geschichtlichen Begriff der Wahheit*. Marburger akademische Reden 46 (Marburg, 1927), esp. p. 15.
39 Cf. 'Wahrheit, Gewißheit und Glaube', *Grundfragen Systematischer Theologie*, II, pp. 226–64.
40 Cf. 'Types of Atheism and their Theological Significance', in *Basic Questions in Theology*, vol. II, pp. 184–200.
41 Cf. 'Speaking about God in the Face of Atheist Criticism', in *Basic Questions in Theology*, vol. III, pp. 99–115.
42 Cf. 'The Question of God', *Basic Questions in Theology*, vol. II, pp. 201–33.
43 Cf. 'The God of Hope', in *Basic Questions in Theology*, vol. II, pp. 234–49, esp. pp. 242ff.
44 Cf. 'Anthropology and the Question of God', in *Basic Questions in Theology*, vol. III, pp. 80–98, pp. 95ff.
45 Cf. 'Theology and the Kingdom of God', in *Theology and the Kingdom*, pp. 51–71, esp. pp. 64ff. Cf. 'The God of Hope', pp. 243ff.

46 Cf. 'Anthropology and the Question of God', in *Basic Questions in Theology*, vol. III, pp. 92ff.
47 Cf. 'Analogy and Doxology', in *Basic Questions in Theology*, vol. I, pp. 211–38.
48 Cf. 'What is a Dogmatic Statement?', in *Basic Questions in Theology*, vol. I, pp. 182–210, esp. pp. 203ff. Cf. on this point the perceptive criticism of D. McKenzie, *Wolfhart Pannenberg and Religious Philosophy*, pp. 23–45.
49 Cf. *Systematische Theologie*, Band I (Göttingen, 1988), pp. 12ff.
50 Cf. ibid., pp. 24ff.
51 Cf. ibid., pp. 59ff.
52 Cf. ibid., pp. 62ff.
53 Cf. ibid., pp. 66ff.
54 Cf. ibid., pp. 78ff.
55 Cf. ibid., pp. 102ff.
56 Cf. ibid., pp. 117ff.
57 Cf. ibid., pp. 127ff.
58 Cf. ibid., pp. 121ff and 131ff.
59 Cf. esp. ibid., pp. 189ff.
60 Cf. ibid., pp. 202ff.
61 Cf. ibid., pp. 214ff.
62 Cf. ibid., pp. 244ff.
63 Cf. ibid., pp. 250ff.
64 Cf. ibid., pp. 266ff.
65 Cf. ibid., pp. 273ff.
66 Cf. ibid., pp. 288ff.
67 Cf. ibid., pp. 331ff. Pannenberg criticizes Barth, who argued programmatically for the same approach for not following his own program, since he develops the doctrine of the Trinity from the formal notion of revelation as expressed in the statement 'God reveals himself as the Lord'. With this approach Barth renews Hegel's conception of describing the three persons of the Trinity as 'moments' or 'states' of the divine self-consciousness by talking about 'modes of being' in the one divine subjectivity. Pannenberg interprets this strategy as a renaissance of Augustine's psychological theory of the *vestigia trinitatis* (which Barth had explicitly rejected), since its interpretative key is the *imago trinitatis* in the human soul. Instead of starting from the formal notion of revelation, Pannenberg proposes to develop his trinitarian conception from the content of God's revelation in Christ.
68 Cf. ibid., pp. 332–35.
69 Cf. ibid., p. 337.
70 Cf. ibid., esp. p. 340.
71 Cf. ibid., pp. 341ff.
72 Cf. ibid., pp. 342–7, esp. pp. 344ff.
73 Cf. ibid., pp. 359ff.
74 Cf. ibid., pp. 378ff.
75 Cf. ibid., pp. 382ff.
76 Cf. ibid., esp. p. 388.

77 Cf. H. Cremer, *Die christliche Lehre von den Eigenschaften Gottes* (Gütersloh, 1897).
78 Cf. *Systematische Theologie* I, pp. 401ff for an exhaustive discussion of this model.
79 Cf. ibid., pp. 414ff.
80 Cf. ibid., pp. 418ff.
81 Cf. ibid., p. 421 and p. 455.
82 Cf. ibid., p. 422; Pannenberg adapts here Barth's concept of the divine 'self-repetition' in his own theological conception.
83 Cf. ibid., pp. 427ff and pp. 430ff.
84 Cf. ibid., p. 441 and p. 443.
85 Cf. ibid., p. 449.
86 Cf. ibid., p. 451 and pp. 454ff.
87 Cf. ibid., p. 461 and p. 464.
88 Cf. ibid., p. 482.
89 Cf. L. Steiger, 'Revelation History and Theological Reason: A Critique of the Theology of Wolfhart Pannenberg', *History and Hermeneutic* (Journal for Theology and the Church 4), ed. Robert W. Funk (New York, 1967), pp. 82–106.
90 Cf. G. Klein, *Theologie des Wortes gottes und die Hypothese der Universalgeschichte* (Munich, 1964).
91 Cf. J. Moltmann, *The Theology of Hope: On The Ground and Implication's of a Christian Eschatology*, (New York, 1967), pp. 74–84.
92 Cf. ibid., p. 69 and p. 74.
93 Cf. E. Jüngel, 'Das Dilemma der natürlichen Theologie und die Wahrheit ihres Problems. überlegungen für ein Gespräch mit Wolfhart Pannenberg', *Entsprechungen: Gott–Wahrheit–Mensch. Theologische Erörterungen* (Munich, 1980), pp. 158–77.
94 Cf. the careful and detailed analysis of this problem in I. U. Dalferth, *Theology and Philosophy* (Oxford, 1988), pp. 61–148.

BIBLIOGRAPHY

Primary

Wolfhart Pannenberg, 'Dogmatic Theses on the Doctrine of Revelation', in Wolfhart Pannenberg (ed.), *Revelation as History* (New York, 1968) also in *Human Nature, Election and History* (Philadelphia, 1977).
—, *Jesus – God and Man* (London, 1968).
—, *Theology and the Kingdom of God*, ed. R. J. Neuhaus (Philadelphia, 1969).
—, *Basic Questions in Theology: Collected Essays*, 3 vols (London, 1970, 1971, 1973). (Volume III is also published under the title *The Idea of God and Human Freedom*, Philadelphia, 1973.)
—, *What Is Man? Contemporary Anthropology in Theological Perspective* (Philadelphia, 1970).
—, *The Apostles' Creed: In the Light of Today's Questions* (Philadelphia, 1972).

—, *Theology and the Philosophy of Science* (London, 1976).

—, *Reality and Faith* (Philadelphia, 1977).

—, *Christian Spirituality and Sacramental Community* (London, 1984).

—, *Anthropology in Theological Perspective* (Edinburgh, 1985).

—, *Systematische Theologie*, volume I (Göttingen, 1988).

Secondary

Carl E. Braaten, Philip Clayton (eds), *The Theology of Wolfhart Pannenberg. Twelve American Critiques, with an Autobiographical Essay and Response* (Minneapolis, Minn., 1988). This contains an excellent bibliography.

D. McKenzie, *Wolfhart Pannenberg and Religious Philosophy* (Washington, DC, 1980).

E. F. Tupper, *The Theology of Wolfhart Pannenberg*, postscript by Wolfhart Pannenberg (London, 1974).

14

Jürgen Moltmann

Richard Bauckham

INTRODUCTION: LIFE AND INFLUENCES

Jürgen Moltmann, born in 1926 and since 1967 professor of systematic theology at Tübingen, first became widely known for his *Theology of Hope* (first published in 1964). This and his subsequent works have made him one of the most influential of contemporary German Protestant theologians, in the non-Western as well as the Western world and in wider church circles as well as in academic theology.

Moltmann himself finds the initial source of his theology in his first experience of the reality of God when he was a prisoner of war in the period 1945–8. This was an experience both of God as the power of hope and of God's presence in suffering: the two themes which were to form the two complementary sides of his theology in the 1960s and early 1970s. Moreover, his sense of involvement, during and after the war, in the collective suffering and guilt of the German nation, set him on the road to his later theological involvement with public and political issues, not least the legacy of Auschwitz.

As a student at Gottingen after the war, Moltmann imbibed the theology of Karl Barth and it was some time before he saw any need to move beyond it. The new directions in which he was to move, while remaining indebted to Barth, were inspired in the first place by his teachers at Göttingen: Otto Weber, Ernst Wolf, Hans Joachim Iwand, Gerhard von Rad, and Ernst Käsemann. From Weber and the Dutch 'apostolate theology' of A. A. van Ruler and J. C. Hoekendijk, to which Weber introduced him, he gained the eschatological perspective of the church's universal mission towards the coming Kingdom of God. Moltmann was one of the first theologians seriously to study Bonhoeffer's work, from which, as well as from

Ernst Wolf, he developed his concern for social ethics and the church's involvement in secular society. The influence of Hegel reached Moltmann in the first place through Iwand: both Hegel and Iwand contributed significantly to the development of Moltmann's dialectical interpretation of the cross and the resurrection. Finally, von Rad and Käsemann helped to give his early theology its solid grounding in current thinking about biblical theology.

The catalyst which finally brought together these converging influences and concerns in Moltmann's theology of hope was the work of the Jewish Marxist philosopher Ernst Bloch, whom Moltmann first read, with great excitement, in 1959. He conceived his *Theology of Hope* as a kind of theological parallel to Bloch's philosophy of hope, and has kept up a continuing dialogue with Bloch throughout his career. Since it was possible for Moltmann to see Bloch's work as, from one point of view, a kind of Marxist inheritance of Jewish messianism, it is not surprising that the most important subsequent influences on Moltmann's thought from outside Christian theology were Marxist and Jewish. In the 1960s he was involved in the Christian–Marxist dialogue and, especially in the early 1970s, he took up important concepts from the critical theory of the Frankfurt School. The influence of Jewish theologians such as Franz Rosenzweig and Abraham Heschel can be found at many points in his work.

While Moltmann remains a recognizably Protestant theologian writing in the German context, his work has become increasingly open to other traditions and movements – Roman Catholic theology, Orthodox theology, and the liberation theologies of the Third World. His experience of the worldwide church – including the sufferings, the charismatic worship and the political commitment of churches in many parts of the world – has also affected his ecclesiology in particular.

SURVEY: WORKS, KEY IDEAS, METHOD

Moltmann's major works comprise two distinct series. In the first place, there is the trilogy for which he is best known: *Theology of Hope, The Crucified God* (1972), and *The Church in the Power of the Spirit* (1975). These represent three complementary perspectives on Christian theology. *Theology of Hope*, probably Moltmann's most original and most influential work, is not a study of eschatology so much as a study of the eschatological orientation of the whole of theology. *The Crucified God* is not simply one of the most important modern studies of the cross, but a 'theology of the cross' in Luther's sense, an attempt to see the crucified Christ as the criterion of Christian theology. *The Church in the Power of the Spirit* complements these two angles of approach with an ecclesiological and pneumatological perspective. The three volumes can be read as complementary perspectives in a single theological vision.

Moltmann now regards this trilogy as preparatory studies for the second series of major works, which is now in progress. This comprises studies of particular Christian doctrines in a planned order, which will resemble a 'dogmatics', but which Moltmann prefers to call a series of 'contributions' to theological discussion. Two volumes have so far appeared: *The Trinity and the Kingdom of God* (1980) and *God in Creation* (1985). Moltmann plans to complete the series with three further volumes on christology, eschatology, and the bases and methods of theology.

The most important controlling theological idea in Moltmann's early work is his dialectical interpretation of the cross and the resurrection of Jesus, which is then subsumed into the particular form of trinitarianism which becomes the overarching theological principle of his later work. Moltmann's dialectic of cross and resurrection is an interpretation of the cross and resurrection *together* which underlies the arguments of both *Theology of Hope* and *The Crucified God*, though the former book focuses on the resurrection and the latter on the cross. The cross and the resurrection of Jesus are taken to represent complete opposites: death and life, the absence of God and the presence of God. Yet the crucified and risen Jesus is the same Jesus in this total contradiction. By raising the crucified Jesus to new life, God created continuity in this radical discontinuity. Furthermore, the contradiction of cross and resurrection corresponds to the contradiction between what reality is now and what God promises to make it. In his cross Jesus was identified with the present reality of the world in all its negativity: its subjection to sin, suffering, and death, or what Moltmann calls its godlessness, godforsakenness, and transitoriness. But since the same Jesus was raised, his resurrection constitutes God's promise of new creation for the whole of the reality which the crucified Jesus represents. Moltmann's first two major books work in two complementary directions from this fundamental concept. In *Theology of Hope* the *resurrection* of the crucified Christ is understood in eschatological perspective and interpreted by the themes of dialectical promise, hope, and mission, while in *The Crucified God* the *cross* of the risen Christ is understood from the perspective of the theodicy problem and interpreted by the themes of dialectical love, suffering, and solidarity. (These themes will be explained below.) Finally, it is possible to see *The Church in the Power of the Spirit* as completing this scheme: the Spirit, whose mission derives from the event of the cross and resurrection, moves reality towards the resolution of the dialectic, filling the godforsaken world with God's presence and preparing for the coming kingdom in which the whole world will be transformed in correspondence to the resurrection of Jesus.

The dialectic of cross and resurrection gives Moltmann's theology a strongly christological center in the particular history of Jesus and at the same time a universal direction. The resurrection as eschatological promise opens theology and the church to the whole world and to its future, while the cross as God's identification in love with the godless and the godforsaken requires solidarity with them on the part of theology and the church.

In *The Crucified God* Moltmann's theology became strongly trinitarian, since he interpreted the cross as a trinitarian event between the Father and the Son. From this point he developed an understanding of the *trinitarian history* of God with the world, in which the mutual involvement of God and the world is increasingly stressed. God experiences a history with the world in which he both affects and is affected by the world, and which is also the history of his own trinitarian relationships as a community of divine persons who include the world within their love. This trinitarian doctrine dominates Moltmann's later work. The dialectic of cross and resurrection becomes the decisive moment within this broader trinitarian history, which retains the eschatological direction of *Theology of Hope* and the crucified God's suffering solidarity with the world but goes further in taking the whole of creation and history within the divine experience.

In addition to these controlling theological ideas, two methodological principles of Moltmann's theology can be mentioned. The first is that it is orientated both to praxis and to doxology. From the beginning a strongly practical thrust was inherent in Moltmann's theology, expressed in *Theology of Hope* in terms of the church's mission to transform the world in anticipation of its promised eschatological transformation by God. It was from this sense of theology's task not merely to interpret but to change the world, to keep society on the move towards the coming kingdom, that Moltmann's political theology derived. But already with *Theology and Joy* (1971) Moltmann became dissatisfied with seeing theology purely as 'a theory of a practice', and began to inject elements of contemplation, celebration, and doxology into his work. Praxis itself is distorted into activisim unless there is also enjoyment of being and praise of God not only for what he has done but also for what he is. And if praxis is inspired and required by the eschatological hope of new creation, contemplation anticipates the goal of new creation – enjoyment of God and participation in his pleasure in his creation. This rejection of the *exclusive* claims of praxis in theology enables Moltmann also, in his later work, to distinguish theological knowledge from the pragmatic thinking of the modern world in which the knowing subject masters its object in order to dominate it, and to reinstate, by contrast, that participatory knowledge in which the subject opens himself to the other in wonder and love, perceives himself in mutual relationship with the other, and so can be changed. Such an emphasis fits easily within Moltmann's later trinitarianism, in which reality is characterized by mutual, non-hierarchical relationships – within the Trinity, between the Trinity and creation, and within creation.

Secondly, Moltmann's theology is characterized by its openness to dialogue. He resists the idea of creating a theological 'system', as a finished achievement of one theologian, and stresses the provisionality of all theological work and the ability of one theologian only to contribute to the continuing discussion within an ecumenical community of theologians, which itself must be in touch with the wider life and thinking of the churches and the sufferings and hopes of the world. His theology is also in principle open to dialogue with and input from other academic disciplines. This openness is a *structural* openness inherent in his theology from the beginning, since it results from the eschatological perspective of his theology of hope. Theology is in the service of the church's mission as, from its starting-point in the cross and resurrection of Jesus, it relates to the world for the sake of the future of the world. The genuine openness of this future ensures that theology does not already know all the answers but can learn from others and from other approaches to reality. At the same time the christological starting-point, in the light of which the future is the future of Jesus Christ, keeps Christian theology faithful to its own truth and so allows it to question other approaches and enter *critical* dialogue with them. Later, from *The Church in the Power of the Spirit* onwards, this structural openness is reinforced by the principle of relationality which becomes increasingly important to Moltmann: to recognize that one's own standpoint is *relative* to others need not lead to relativism but to productive relationship.

CONTENT: ESCHATOLOGY, THEODICY, CHURCH, GOD, CREATION, POLITICS

Eschatology

One of the most important achievements of Moltmann's theology has been to rehabilitate future eschatology. This was in part a response to the demonstration by modern biblical scholarship that future eschatology is of determinative significance for biblical faith. Whereas Schweitzer, Dodd, Bultmann and many others had thought biblical eschatology unacceptable to the modern mind unless stripped of its reference to the real temporal future of the world, Moltmann, along with some other German theologians in the 1960s, saw in future eschatology precisely the way to make Christian faith credible and relevant in the modern world. He wished to show how the modern experience of history as a process of constant and radical change, in hopeful search of a new future, need not be rejected by the church, as though Christianity stood for reactionary traditionalism, nor ignored, as though Christianity represented a withdrawal from history into purely subjective authenticity. Rather, the eschatological orientation of biblical Christian faith towards the future of the world requires the church to engage with the possibilities for change in the modern world, to promote them against all tendencies to stagnation, and to give them eschatological direction towards the future Kingdom of God. The gospel proves relevant and credible today precisely through the eschatological faith that truth lies in the future and proves itself in changing the present in the direction of the future.

Christian hope, for Moltmann, is thoroughly christological since it arises from the resurrection of Jesus. His famous claim that 'from first to last, and not merely in the epilogue, Christianity is eschatology, is hope'[1] was possible only because it was a claim about the meaning of the resurrection of Jesus. It also depends on setting the resurrection of Jesus against its Old Testament and Jewish theological background – a recovery of the Jewish roots of Christian theology which is very characteristic of Moltmann's work. The God of Israel revealed himself to Israel by making promises which opened up the future : against this background God's act of raising the crucified Jesus to new life is to be understood as the culminating and definitive event of divine promise. In it God promises the resurrection of all the dead, the new creation of all reality, and the coming of his kingdom of righteousness and glory, and he guarantees this promise by enacting it in Jesus' person. Jesus' resurrection entails the eschatological future of all reality.

When this concept of the resurrection as promise is related to Moltmann's dialectic of cross and resurrection (see above), important aspects of his eschatology emerge. In the first place, the *contradiction* between the cross and the resurrection creates a *dialectical* eschatology, in which the promise contradicts present reality. The eschatological kingdom is no mere fulfillment of the immanent possibilities of the present, but represents a radically new future: life for the dead, righteousness for the unrighteous, new creation for a creation subject to evil and death. But secondly, the *identity* of Jesus in the total contradiction of cross and resurrection is also important. The resurrection was not the survival of some aspect of Jesus which was not subject to death: Jesus was *wholly* dead and *wholly* raised by God. The continuity was given in God's act of new creation. Similarly God's promise is not for *another* world, but for the new creation of *this* world, in all its material and worldly reality. The whole of creation, subject as it is to sin and suffering and death, will be transformed in God's new creation.

Christian eschatology is therefore the hope that the world will be different. It is aroused by a promise whose fulfillment can come only from God's eschatological action transcending all the possibilities of history, since it involves the end of all evil, suffering, and death in the glory of the divine presence indwelling all things. But it is certainly not therefore without effect in the present. On the contrary, the resurrection set in motion a historical process in which the promise already affects the world and moves it in the direction of its future transformation. This process is the universal mission of the church. This is the point·at which Moltmann's *Theology of Hope* opened the church to the world as well as to the future. Authentic Christian hope is not that purely other-wordly expectation which is resigned to the unalterability of affairs in this world. Rather, because it is hope for the future of this world, its effect is to show present reality to be *not yet* what it can be and will be. The world is seen as transformable in the direction of the promised future. In this way believers are liberated from accommodation to the status quo and set critically against it. They suffer the contradiction between what is and what is promised. But this critical distance also enables them to seek and activate those present possibilities of world history which lead in the direction of the eschatological future. Thus by arousing *active* hope the promise creates anticipations of the future kingdom within history. The transcendence of the kingdom itself beyond all its anticipations keep believers always unreconciled to present conditions, the source of continual new impulses for change.

Theodicy

It was characteristic of Moltmann's theology from the beginning to give prominence to the question of God's righteousness in the face of the suffering and evil of the world. In the first phase of his response to the problem, in *Theology of Hope*, he proposes an eschatological theodicy. Innocent and involuntary suffering must not be justified, as it would be if it were explained as contributing to the divine purpose. The promise given in the resurrection of Jesus gives no explanation of suffering, but it does provide hope for God's final triumph over all evil and suffering, and thereby also an initiative for Christian praxis in overcoming suffering now.

This approach to the theodicy problem in terms of the hope for God's future righteousness is by no means abandoned, but in *The Crucified God* it is deepened by the additional theme of God's loving solidarity with the world in its suffering. When Moltmann turned from his focus on the resurrection to a complementary focus on the cross, he was concerned to extend the traditional soteriological interest in the cross to embrace 'both the question of human guilt and man's liberation from it and also the question of human suffering and man's liberation from it'.[2] He uses the double expression 'the godless and the godforsaken' to refer to the plight both of sinners who suffer their own turning away from God and of those who are the innocent victims of pointless suffering. This is the plight of the world, in the absence of divine righteousness, with which Jesus was identified on the cross.

In *The Crucified God* Moltmann's thinking moved back from the resurrection as the event of divine promise to the cross as the event of divine love. In this movement he was asking the question: how does the divine promise, established in Jesus' resurrection, reach those to whom it is addressed, the godless and the godforsaken? His answer is that it reaches them through Jesus' *identification* with them, in their condition, on the cross. His resurrection represents salvation *for them* only because he dies for them, identified with them in their suffering of God's absence. The central concept of *The Crucified God* is love which suffers in solidarity with those who suffer. This is love which meets the involuntary suffering of the godforsaken with another kind of suffering: voluntary fellow-suffering.

To see the cross as God's act of loving solidarity with all who suffer apparently abandoned by God requires an incarnational and trinitarian theology of the cross. By recognizing God's presence, as the incarnate Son of God, in the abandonment of the cross, Moltmann brings the dialectic of cross and resurrection within God's own experience. The cross and resurrection represent the opposition between a reality which does not correspond to God – the world subject to sin, suffering and death – and the promise of a reality which does correspond to him – the new creation which will reflect his glory. But if God is present in the godlessness and godforsakenness of the cross, then he is present in his own contradiction. His love is such that it embraces the godforsaken reality which does not correspond to him, and so he suffers. His love is not simply active benevolence which acts on humanity. It is dialectical love which in embracing its own contradiction must suffer. Of course it does so in order to overcome the contradiction: to deliver from sin, suffering, and death.

If Jesus the divine Son suffers the abandonment of the godforsaken, as the cry of desolation shows, the cross must be a trinitarian event between the incarnate Son and his Father who leaves him to die. Moltmann interprets it as an event of divine suffering in which Jesus suffers dying in abandonment by his Father and the Father suffers in grief the death of his Son. As such it is the act of divine solidarity with the godforsaken world, in which the Son willingly surrenders himself in love for the world and the Father willingly surrenders his Son in love for the world. Because at the point of their deepest separation, the Father and the Son are united in their love for the world, the event which separates them overcomes the godforsakenness of the world. The love between them now spans the gulf which separates the godless and the godforsaken from God. The trinitarian being of God includes this gulf within it and overcomes it.

In Moltmann's understanding, the cross does not solve the problem of suffering, but meets it with the voluntary fellowsuffering of love. Solidarity in suffering – in the first place, the crucified God's solidarity with all who suffer, and, in consequence, also his followers' identification with the suffering – does not abolish suffering, but it does overcome what Moltmann calls 'the suffering in suffering': the lack of love, the abandonment in suffering. Moreover, such solidarity, so far from promoting fatalistic submission to suffering, necessarily includes love's protest against the infliction of suffering on those it loves. It leads believers through their solidarity with the suffering into liberating praxis on their behalf.

The Church

Moltmann describes his ecclesiology alternatively as 'messianic ecclesiology' or 'relational ecclesiology.' Both terms serve to situate the church within God's trinitarian history with the world, more specifically within the missions of the Son and the Spirit on their way to the eschatological kingdom. In the first place, Moltmann's ecclesiology is rooted in his eschatological christology. The church lives between the past history of Jesus and the universal future in which that history will reach its fulfillment: the former directs it in mission towards the latter. But this also means that Moltmann's ecclesiology is strongly pneumatological. For, in Moltmann's understanding of the trinitarian history, it is the Holy Spirit who now, between the history of Jesus and the coming of the kingdom, mediates the eschatological future to the world. If the church is an anticipation of the messianic kingdom, it is so because it is created by and participates in the mission of the Spirit. Its defining characteristics are not therefore its own, but those of the presence and activity of Christ and the Spirit. At every point ecclesiology must be determined by the church's role as a movement within the trinitarian history of God with the world.

If 'messianic ecclesiology' characterizes the church as orientated by the missions of Christ and the Spirit towards their eschatological goal, 'relational ecclesiology' indicates that, because of its place within the trinitarian history, the church does not exist in, of or for itself, but only in relationship and can only be understood in its relationships. It participates in the messianic history of Jesus, it lives in the presence and powers of the Spirit, and it exists as a provisional reality for the sake of the universal kingdom of the future. Since the mission of the Spirit on the way to the kingdom includes but is not confined to the church, the church cannot absolutize itself, but must fulfill its own messianic role in open and critical relationship with other realities, its partners in history, notably Israel, the other world religions, and the secular order.

Within this context, the church can only adequately fulfill its vocation if it becomes a 'messianic fellowship' of mature and responsible disciples. Here Moltmann, with his eye especially on the German Protestant scene, proposes radical reform and renewal of the church. His criticism is of the extent to which the church is still the civil religion of society, a pastoral church *for* all the people unable to take up a critical stance in relation to society, unable to foster real community and active Christian commitment. The ideal is a church *of* the people, a fellowship of committed disciples called to responsible participation in messianic mission. Membership of the church must therefore be voluntary (from this follows Moltmann's critique of infant baptism) and characterized not only by faith but by discipleship and a distinctive lifestyle. The messianic fellowship will also be a free society of equals, since the Spirit frees and empowers all Christians for messianic service (from this follows Moltmann's critique of traditional doctrines of the ministry). Its life of loving acceptance of the other, however different, Moltmann is fond of characterizing as 'open friendship', since friendship is a relationship of freedom and the church's life of friendly relationships is always essentially open to others (from this follow Moltmann's proposals on the meaning and practice of the eucharist). Finally, the church's open friendship must be modelled on that of Jesus and therefore take the form especially of solidarity with the poor: not simply charitable activity for them, but fellowship with them. Unlike the pastoral church, with its inevitable tendency to accept the status quo in society, the church as a voluntary fellowship of committed disciples is free to be a socially critical church, identified with the most marginalized and the most needy.

Doctrine of God

Moltmann's mature doctrine of God, as it developed from *The Crucified God* onwards, could be said to hinge on a concept of dynamic relationality. It understands the trinitarian God as three divine subjects in mutual loving relationship, and God's relationship to the world as a reciprocal relationship in which God in his love for the world not only affects the world but is also affected by it. He relates to the world as Trinity, experiencing the world within his own trinitarian experience, and so his changing experience of the world is also a changing experience of himself. The trinitarian history of God's relationship with the world is thus a real history for God as well as for the world: it is the history in which God includes the world within his own trinitarian relationships. All this Moltmann takes to be the meaning of the Christian claim that God is love.

Moltmann's distinctive development of the doctrine of God really began, in *The Crucified God*, from the principle that the doctrine of the Trinity is the theological interpretation of the history of Jesus. His interpretation of the cross as the event of God's suffering solidarity with the world required him to take three crucial steps in developing the doctrine of God. In the first place, as an event between the Father and the Son, in which God suffers the godforsakenness that separates the Son from the Father, the cross required trinitarian language of a kind which emphasized inter-subjective relationship between the divine persons. (The Spirit, however, is less clearly personal at this stage.) Secondly, it also necessitated a doctrine of divine passibility, not only in the narrow sense that God can suffer pain, but in the broader sense that he can be affected by his creation. In rejecting the traditional doctrine of divine impassibility, Moltmann is careful to make clear that not every kind of suffering can be attributed, even analogically, to God. But suffering which is freely undertaken in love for those who suffer Moltmann claims to be required by God's nature as love. Divine love is not merely the one-way relationship of active benevolence, but a genuinely two-way relationship in which God is so involved with his creation as to be affected by it. Moreover, because his experience of the world, on the cross, is an experience between the Father and the Son, it is in his own trinitarian relationships that God is affected by the world.

The third consequence follows: that Moltmann abandons the traditional distinction between the immanent and the economic trinities, between what God eternally is in himself and how he acts outside himself in the world. The cross (and, by extension, the rest of God's history with the world) is *internal* to the divine trinitarian experience. Because God is love, what he is for us he is also for himself. The doctrine of the Trinity is thus not an extrapolation from the history of Jesus and the Spirit: it actually *is* the history of Jesus and the Spirit in its theological interpretation. It can really only take narrative form as a history of God's changing trinitarian relation-ships in himself and simultaneously with the world. In his later work Moltmann elaborates his narrative in various forms, eventually including creation.

In all this, Moltmann found himself talking of God's experience. If it is as love that we experience God, then in some sense in experiencing God we also experience his experience of us, and if it is as trinitarian love that we experience God, then in some sense we experience even his threefold experience of himself in our history. On this basis, especially in *The Trinity and the Kingdom of God*, Moltmann develops his fully social doctrine of the Trinity. Signifi-cantly, for this to be possible, Moltmann had to recognize an activity of the Spirit in which he acts as subject in relation to the Father and the Son: his work of glorifying the Father and the Son. This makes it clear that the divine persons are all subjects in relation to each other. It also makes clear that there is no fixed order in the Trinity: the traditional, 'descending' order of Father–Son–Spirit is only one of the changing patterns of trinitarian relationship in God's history with the world. Behind and within these changing relationships is the enduring trinitarian fellowship, in which there is no subordination, only mutual love in freedom.

Moltmann constantly opposes any 'monotheistic' or 'monarchical' doctrine of God which would reduce the real subjectivity of the three persons. Instead he insists that the unity of God is the unity of persons in relationship. Three points can be made about this. First, it is *in* their relationships to each other that the three are persons. They are both three and one in their mutual indwelling (*perichoresis*). Secondly, since the unity of God is thus defined in terms of love, as perichoresis, it is a unity which can open itself to and include the world within itself. The goal of the trinitarian history of God is the uniting of all things with God and in God: a trinitarian and eschatological panentheism. Thirdly, Moltmann sees 'monotheism' as legitimating 'monarchical' relationships of domination and subjection, whereas social trinitarianism grounds relationships of freedom and equality. In himself God is not rule but a fellowship of love; in his relationship with the world it is not so much lordship as loving fellowship which he seeks; and in his kingdom (where 'kingdom' needs to be redefined in relation to the social Trinity) it is relationships of free friendship which most adequately reflect and participate in the trinitarian life.

Creation

The doctrine of creation, relatively neglected in Moltmann's earlier work, receives full attention in *God in Creation*. Its explicit context is the ecological crisis, which, as a crisis in the human relationship to nature, requires, in Moltmann's view, a renewed theological understanding of nature and human beings as God's creation and of God's relationship to the world as his creation.

The kind of human relationship to nature which has created the crisis and must be superseded is that of exploitative domination. In its place, Moltmann advocates a sense of human community with nature, respecting nature's independence and participating in mutual relationships with it. Human beings, as the image of God, have a distinctive place within nature, but they are not the owners or rulers of nature: they belong with nature in a community of creation which, as *creation*, is not anthropocentric but theocentric. But in order to ground theologically this emphasis on mutual relationships in nature, Moltmann appeals to his doctrine of God, whose own trinitarian community provides the model for the life of his creation as an intricate community of reciprocal relationships.

Not only is the trinitarian God a perichoretic community and his creation a perichoretic community, but also God's relationship to his creation is one of mutual indwelling. Because God is transcendent beyond the world it dwells in him, but because, as the Spirit, he is also immanent within the world, he dwells in it. With this dominant notion of the Spirit in creation, Moltmann is able also to take the non-human creation into his general concept of the trinitarian history of God. The whole of creation from the beginning has a messianic orientation towards a future goal: its glorification through divine indwelling. The Spirit in creation co-suffers with creation in its bondage to decay, keeping it open to God and to its future with God. Humanity's eschatological goal does not lift us out of the material creation but confirms our solidarity and relatedness with it. In all of this Moltmann achieves a strong continuity between creation and redemption, and a thorough-going assimilation of the creative and salvific activities of the Spirit.

Political Theology

Moltmann has never reduced the gospel to its political aspect, but he has consistently emphasized it. It was in the years immediately after *Theology of Hope* that he developed his thought into an explicitly political theology in the sense in which that term came into use in Germany at that time, that is, in the sense of a politically critical theology aiming at radical change in society. Moltmann's praxis-orientated dialectical eschatology was not difficult to translate into an imperative for radical political change, but Moltmann's political writings in the late 1960s tend toward a rather generalized rhetoric of revolution. What appealed to him in Marxism at this stage was its vision of a new society of freedom, rather than its economic analysis or its strategy for revolution.

Moltmann's turn to the cross brought with it the requirement of a political praxis of solidarity with the victims, which deepens the praxis of hope. The latter was rescued from the danger of a rather romantic vision of revolution or of confusion with the ideological optimism of the affluent by the requirement that desire for radical change must result from real solidarity with the victims of society and be rooted in their actual interests.

Political concerns continue to feature in, though not to dominate his later theology. His social trinitarianism in *The Trinity and the Kingdom of God*, for example, provides a theological basis for democratic freedom in society. But probably the most important later development in his political theology has been the prominence of the notion of human rights, which he grounds in the created dignity *and* eschatological destiny of humanity as the image of God. It is by means of the concept of human rights that Moltmann's political theology is able to formulate specific political goals. The two earlier themes of revolutionary hope and solidarity with victims gain concreteness especially in this form. Eschatological hope finds its immediate application in striving for the realization of human rights – new dimensions of which can constantly come to light in the movement of history towards the fulfillment of human destiny in the kingdom of God. Solidarity with victims takes political effect in the attempt to secure their rights and dignity as full members of the human community. One could almost claim that human rights come to play the kind of role in Moltmann's political theology that Marxism plays in the liberation theology of Latin America. The concept of human rights is a way of specifying the concrete implications of political theology, and a way of doing so which makes contact with non-Christian political goals and activity, thus enabling Christians to join with others in a common struggle for liberation.

DEBATE

Some of the issues which have been raised in criticism of Moltmann's work are as follows:

1 Critics of Moltmann's early work frequently complained of one-sided emphasis on some theological themes at the expense of others. Especially this was said of the emphasis on the future in *Theology of Hope*, which appeared to deny all present experience of God. However, in retrospect this one-sidedness can be seen to be a result of Moltmann's method, in the early works, of taking up *in turn* a number of complementary perspectives on theology. In the context of the whole trilogy, the one-sidedness of each book is balanced by the others. Present experience of God, polemically played down in *Theology of Hope*, is fully acknowledged in later work, but given an eschatological orientation which preserves the intention of *Theology of Hope*.

2 Much criticism focused on the political implications of *Theology*

of Hope, though not always with due attention to the subsequent essays in which these were fully developed. From the liberation theologians of Latin America, themselves influenced by Moltmann, comes the criticism that the eschatological transcendence of the kingdom beyond all its present anticipations sanctions the typical European theologian's detachment from concrete political movements and objectives. From some more conservative theologians comes the opposite complaint that Moltmann reduces eschatology to human political achievements. Both criticisms miss the careful way in which Moltmann relates the eschatological kingdom to its anticipations in history, though there is something in the liberationists' charge that Moltmann's political theology is *relatively* lacking in specific explicit context and concrete proposals. From a different perspective, Pannenberg blames Moltmann's dialectical eschatology for the commitment to *revolutionary change* which characterizes both European political theology and liberation theology, and it is certainly true that Moltmann's dialectical language was sometimes too simplistically applied to the political sphere.

3 Criticism of Moltmann's doctrine of God has claimed that, in rejecting the traditional doctrines of divine aseity and impassibility, he compromises the freedom of God and falls into the 'Hegelian' mistake of making world history the process by which God realizes himself. To some extent such criticisms provoked Moltmann, after *The Crucified God*, into clarifying his view. He does not dissolve God into world history, but intends a real interaction between God and the world. The problem of divine freedom leads him to deny the reality of the contrast between necessity and freedom of choice in God. Because God's freedom is the freedom of his love, he cannot choose not to love and as love he is intrinsically related to the world. A different kind of criticism finds it hard to distinguish Moltmann's social trinitarianism from tritheism.

4 Many critics, especially in the Anglo-Saxon tradition, find Moltmann's work lacking in philosophical analysis and logical rigor. This is a question of theological style, and Moltmann's way of doing theology has other merits, such as breadth of vision, which more analytical treatments lack. But it is true that it sometimes obscures conceptual problems in his work which could otherwise come to light and be overcome more quickly. Related to this criticism is the charge that Moltmann is insufficiently aware of the necessarily analogical nature of talk about God, so that his discussion of the divine *experience* too often becomes unconsciously mythological.

5 Though not often commented on, two related tendencies in his later work call for criticism. In the first place, elements of undisciplined

speculation seem increasingly common, and secondly, whereas his earlier work was carefully rooted in current biblical scholarship, his use of biblical material seems increasingly to ignore historical-critical interpretation and to leave his hermeneutical principles dangerously unclear. One reason for both tendencies is that, whereas his earlier work at its best moved between the concreteness of the biblical history and the concrete situations of the modern world, he now seems increasingly drawn into the concerns of the theological tradition for their own sake.

ACHIEVEMENT AND AGENDA

Perhaps Moltmann's greatest achievement, especially in the earlier works, was to open up hermeneutical structures for relating biblical faith to the modern world. The strength and appropriateness of these structures lie in their biblical basis, their christological center and their eschatological openness. They give Moltmann's theology a relevance to the modern world which is achieved not only without surrendering the central features of biblical and historic Christian faith, but much more positively by probing the theological meaning of these in relation to contemporary realities and concerns. By recovering a christological center which is both dialectical and eschatological, Moltmann's theology acquired an openness to the world which is not in tension with the christological center but is actually required by the christological centre, and which is not an accommodation to conservative, liberal or radical values, but has a critical edge and a consistent solidarity with the most marginalized members of society.

The most notable feature of the later work is Moltmann's sustained attempt to reconceive the doctrine of God in order to do better justice than the tradition to the Christian perception of God as trinitarian love. This attempt has its problems, but the importance of the issues cannot be doubted, and the open, dialogical intention of Moltmann's theology makes it a challenge to the further thought which is certainly needed in this area.

Moltmann himself has already stated his agenda for future work (see *Survey* above) but within this scheme new developments, such as have occurred in all his major works so far, must certainly be expected. As he works towards the final projected volume on theological method, we may hope that some of the methodological criticisms mentioned above will be considered and met.

NOTES

1 *Theology of Hope*, p. 16.
2 *The Crucified God*, p. 134.

BIBLIOGRAPHY

Primary

Moltmann, J., *Theology of Hope* (London, 1967).
—, *Religion, Revolution, and the Future* (New York, 1969).
—, *Theology and Joy* (London, 1973).
—, *The Crucified God* (London, 1974).
—, *Man* (London, 1974).
—, *The Experiment Hope* (London, 1975).
—, *The Church in the Power of the Spirit* (London, 1977).
—, *The Trinity and the Kingdom of God* (London, 1981).
—, *On Human Dignity* (London, 1984).
—, *God in Creation* (London, 1985).

A bibliography is to be found in D. Isling (ed.), *Bibliographie Jürgen Moltmann* (Munich, 1987).

Secondary

Bauckham, R., *Moltmann: Messianic Theology in the Making* (Basingstoke, 1987).
Meeks, M. D., *Origins of the Theology of Hope* (Philadelphia, 1974).

List of Dates

1884	Rudolf Bultmann b.
1886	Karl Barth b.
	Paul Tillich b.
1904	Yves Congar b.
	Bernard Lonergan b.
	Karl Rahner b.
1905	Hans Urs von Balthasar b.
1906	Dietrich Bonhoeffer b.
1913	Thomas F. Torrance b.
1914–1918	*First World War*
1914	Edward Schillebeeckx b.
1919	*Karl Barth's Epistle to the Romans, First Edition*
1923	Ernst Troeltsch d.
1926	Jürgen Moltmann b.
1928	Hans Küng b.
	Wolfhart Pannenberg b.
1933	*Adolf Hitler Chancellor of Germany*
1934	Eberhard Jüngel b.
1939–1945	*Second World War, The Holocaust*
1945	Dietrich Bonhoeffer d.
1948	*World Council of Churches formed*
1962–1965	*Second Vatican Council*
1965	Paul Tillich d.
1968	Karl Barth d.
1984	Bernard Lonergan d.
	Karl Rahner d.
1988	Hans Urs von Balthasar d.

Glossary

a posteriori
: Latin phrase referring to thought or knowledge based on or arising consequent to experience.

a priori
: Latin phrase referring to thought or knowledge which arises from a concept or principle, or which precedes empirical verification, or occurs independently of experience.

absolutism
: A position which makes one element, text, person, ideology, or reality supreme or absolute in relation to everything; or, an understanding of the absolute (ultimate reality) as existing independently and unconditionally.

aggiornamento
: Italian word for renewal, bringing up to date (especially used with reference to the reforms of the Second Vatican Council).

alienation
: Estrangement, lack of identification or commitment.

anhypostasis
: Greek term in christology after Chalcedon which understands the human nature of Jesus Christ to have no personal locus of its own independent of the divine Word or Logos (compare **enhypostasia**).

anthropocentric
: Referring to a view of life and the universe with humanity at the center, or to an approach whose starting point is humankind.

anthropology
: The study of the nature of human being; or, the scientific study of humankind.

anthropology, theological
: The theological study of being human.

anthropomorphism
: Ascribing human attributes and characteristics to God.

apocalyptic
: Literally, the unveiling of what is covered or hidden; a genre of literature concerning the last things and the end of the world; more widely, revelatory literature concerned with eschatology, often containing dreams, allegories, and elaborate symbolism.

apologetic	Maintaining a given position; explanation from a given position; defence of orthodox doctrine in the face of opposition.
Arian	Relating to the teachings of Arius (*c*.250–*c*.336), who believed that Jesus Christ was not eternally divine and whose views were condemned at the Council of Nicea (AD 325).
aseity	The quality of God as completely self-sufficient and independent of all other beings, having his being from himself alone.
atheism	The belief that God does not exist, that there is no God.
atonement	Literally, at-one-ment; the work of Jesus Christ on the cross reconciling the world to God; the doctrine of the salvific work of Christ.
Augustinian	Of or relating to Augustine of Hippo (354–430), bishop, theologian, and saint.
autonomy	State of being self-directing, independent.
behaviorism	A position regarding human being whereby all explanation is capable of being based on observable behavior, and change is best accomplished by modifying behavior patterns.
biblical theology	Theology conceived from and with constant reference to the Bible, especially applied to a movement producing such theology mainly in 1940s and 1950s.
biblicism	Idolatry of the Bible; absolutizing of the Bible.
Calvinist	Referring to John Calvin (1509–64), Protestant Reformation leader, and his followers and theology.
Cartesian	Referring to the philosophy of René Descartes (1596–1650), often indicating the separation of subject from object, knower from known, and affirming that the individual thinking self is the best starting point for philosophy.
catholic	universal, comprehensive; often used to refer to those churches which affirm continuity of faith with the Christian creeds of the first five centuries.
Chalcedonian	Relating to the Council of Chalcedon (AD 451) and especially to its definition of the person of Jesus Christ which affirmed his full divinity and full humanity.
charismatic	Relating to the gifts of the Holy Spirit, such as prophecy, healing, words of wisdom, discernment of spirits, speaking in tongues, interpretation of tongues; also, relating to a Christian movement (sometimes called Neopentecostalism) beginning in the 1960s, which encourages the exercise of gifts of the Holy Spirit.

christocentrism	Thought or theology which makes Jesus Christ central.
christology	Branch of theology concerned with the doctrine of the person and work of Jesus Christ.
christomonism	A theological system where Jesus Christ is used as the overriding regulative principle.
classical theology	That which is the paradigm for subsequent theology; in Christianity usually referring to patristic theology of the first five centuries.
cognition	The act of knowing; intellectual knowledge.
conciliar	Relating to councils of the church, e.g., Nicea, Trent, Vatican II.
confessionalism	Theological position based on a particular confession of faith (usually one of the Reformation statements); more widely, a stance or position adopted from the inside as distinct from phenomenology or observation from the outside.
consubstantial	With or of the same substance or being; corresponding to the Greek word *homoousios*, which was incorporated into the creed at the Council of Nicea, AD 325, in order to designate the relationship of Jesus Christ to God.
consummation	Fulfilment.
contextualization	Viewing, placing, or considering in a particular setting.
contingency	Fortuitous character or non-necessity of an event or being.
correlation	Literally, a one-to-one correspondence; in theology since Tillich, the relating of questions and issues of modernity with answers or symbols from the tradition.
cosmology	Study or comprehensive understanding of the cosmos or universe.
covenant	Agreement; in the Bible, an agreement initiated by God between God and his people.
deductive	Relating to deduction, a method of reasoning in which the conclusion is the logical and necessary consequence of the premisses.
demythologizing	Process of interpreting traditional texts considered mythological (in the sense that they express their meaning in terms of an outmoded or mythological worldview), with the aim of showing that their continuing existential or practical relevance can be grasped despite their mythological expression.
dialectic (Hegelian)	Rational process of reality uniting the movement of the object (the 'in-itself') and the movement of the subject ('for-itself') in the movement of the whole ('in-and-for-itself'), oriented towards the uniting of all in absolute spirit.

dialectical theology	Theology of the period after the First World War (initiated mainly by Barth's *Epistle to the Romans*) which radically negated (above all by reference to the crucifixion) all human ways of knowing and relating to God, and stressed the corresponding need for God's initiative in revelation; also known as crisis theology because of its stress on God's judgment (Greek *krisis*) on church and world.
diaspora	The dispersal of the Jewish people around the Mediterranean world after 586 BC; more widely, any dispersion of a group from its original location.
dichotomy	Split or division into two, e.g., mind and body, fact and value, sacred and secular.
dogmatics	Coherent presentation of Christian faith through its doctrines.
Dominican	Member of, or relating to, the Roman Catholic religious order of preaching friars founded by St Dominic (1170–1221).
doxology	Address of praise to God, especially 'Glory be to the Father, and to the Son, and to the Holy Spirit, as it was in the beginning, is now and ever shall be, world without end, Amen'; more widely, the study of praise and worship as theology.
dualism	View of the world which holds that there are two ultimately distinct principles or spheres, such as good and evil, or matter and spirit.
ecclesiology	Understanding or doctrine of the church.
eclectic	Coming from diverse and varied sources.
economy, divine	God's plan for salvation incorporating the whole universe.
ecumenism	From a Greek word for the whole inhabited world; in Christianity it is a movement for worldwide unity among Christian churches; sometimes used of reconciliation and cooperation between religions.
efficient causality	That which causes something else to be or to change (one of Aristotle's four types of causality, the others being material, formal, and final).
egocentricity	Understanding which starts from the ego or self; not to be confused with 'egoism' or selfishness (contrast with **exocentricity**, below).
eirenicism	Peacefulness or absence of crisis in a position (from the Greek word for peace).
election	Doctrine that God chooses people for salvation (and, within some traditions, for damnation).
empirical	Approach to knowledge based upon what can be arrived at through sense experience.

enhypostasia/ enhypostasis	Term in the development of christology after Chalcedon which indicates that Christ's human and divine natures can have no existence independently of each other.
epiclesis	Invocation of the Holy Spirit upon the bread and wine within the eucharistic prayer so that they become the body and blood of Christ.
episcopate	The bishops of a particular church, or the state of being a bishop.
epistemology	The study of human knowing, regarding its bases, forms, criteria.
eschatology	Understanding or doctrine of the **eschaton**, or ultimate destiny of the world.
eschaton	The consummation or end time of world history, traditionally known as the Last Day or Day of Judgment.
essentialism	Understanding of objects from their essence.
Eucharist	Sacrament or celebration of the Lord's Supper (from a Greek word for thanksgiving).
evangelical	Relating to the New Testament concern for preaching the Gospel; also a term for the Protestant Church in Germany and Switzerland; also a term for a diverse movement, spanning many Protestant Churches, with special concern for the final authority of Scripture, personal salvation and holiness, and evangelism.
exclusivism	In Christianity, belief that God will not grant salvation to those outside the Christian church, or outside faith in Christ.
exegesis	Detailed and methodical interpretation of a text.
existentialism	Movement of thought, most influential in philosophy, theology, literature, and psychotherapy, which focuses on individual existence and subjectivity, affirms that existence precedes essence (especially in the sense that a person's decisions and responses to contingent events, rather than his or her supposed essential nature, constitute who that person essentially is), upholds the freedom of the will and its irreducibility to anything else, wrestles with the darker aspects of the human predicament such as anxiety, dread, inauthenticity, meaninglessness, alienation, guilt, anticipation of death and despair, and is suspicious of generalization, abstraction, rational overview, systematization, claims to objective knowledge regarding human existence, and fixed ethical principles.
exocentricity	The receiving of one's center from outside oneself; or an understanding which starts from outside the ego or self (contrast with **egocentricity** above).

expiation	Understanding of sacrifice as that which makes amends for past wrongdoings.
extrinsicism	Understanding of values or attributes as attaching externally to an object rather than belonging internally to it.
fatalistic	Assuming that human destiny and development is predetermined and beyond human control.
fiduciary	Relating to a position of trust with regard to an object of faith.
filial	Regarding the relationship of son to father; in theology, usually referring to the Son's relationship with the Father within the doctrine of the Trinity.
filioque	Latin word meaning 'and from the Son', added by the Western Church to the Nicene Creed to indicate that the Holy Spirit proceeds not only from the Father, but also from the Son.
finitude	Inability of an object or person to transcend the boundaries of their existence; limitation, especially to the natural order.
form criticism	Approach to a text which focuses upon its constituent units and their particular functions for the original audience or readers.
foundationalism	Approach to philosophy or theology which affirms certain truths as the bases and criteria for all other truths.
functionalism	Understanding of an object or discipline in the light of its purpose or function.
fundamental theology	Branch of theology which tries to ground as comprehensively as possible the whole enterprise of theology, usually with extensive consideration of the contributions of philosophy and other disciplines.
fundamentalism	In Christianity, a varied movement usually affirming a set of basic beliefs by reference to the authority of a literally interpreted, inerrant Bible.
Gnosticism	Name (derived from the Greek word *gnōsis*, knowledge) given to a varied and diffuse religious movement which saw creation as the work of an inferior god, sharply divided the physical from the spiritual, and offered to initiates exclusive knowledge enabling them to escape from the world and physicality to union with the supreme divine being.
Hegelian	Referring to the philosopher G. W. F. Hegel (1770–1831), his thought and his followers.

Hellenism	Greek culture and ideas influential in non-Greek areas (such as Palestine) during the period after Alexander the Great (356–23 BC).
hermeneutical theology	Approach to theology which concentrates upon issues of interpretation and meaning.
hermeneutics	Study of interpretation and meaning.
heteronomy	State of being governed by, or subject to, outside or alien control (opposite of **autonomy**).
heuristic	Approach intended to open up an issue or argument for further questioning and discoveries.
historical theology	Approach to theology which concentrates upon its development through historical contexts.
historical-critical method	Approach to a text which seeks to determine its meaning in the light of what it would have meant in its earliest form and context, and to understand beliefs, institutions, and practices in terms of how they were produced by historical conditions and events.
historicism	Approach which tries to describe and explain history purely in terms of the historical-critical method.
humanism	Originating in the Renaissance, an attempt to understand human life without recourse to higher (divine) authority; more widely, a worldview cultivating respect for humanity, and confidence in its possibilities.
hypostatic union	Definition of christology agreed at the Council of Chalcedon (A.D. 451) which affirms the dynamic union of two natures, divine and human, in the one person or 'hypostasis' of Christ.
hypothetico-deductive	Approach to knowing which assumes a hypothesis in order then to measure its validity against data arrived at by experiment.
idealism	Philosophical tradition originating in Plato which understands the mind, ideas, or spirit as fundamental to reality. The forms of idealism most influential on modern Christian theology have been Kant's transcendental idealism and the absolute idealism of Fichte, Schelling, and especially Hegel.
ideology	Structure of concepts and beliefs governing the action and understanding of a group of people; often used pejoratively to describe beliefs and ideas which are rationalizations justifying vested interests or an oppressive system or practice.
immanence, divine	Presence of God within the world, including everyday events and situations.
immanent Trinity	Understanding of the Trinity as God's being 'in Himself' rather than in relation to the world and humanity (to be contrasted with the **economic Trinity**)

immutability, divine	The divine attribute or aspect which means that God is not subject to change.
impassibility, divine	The divine attribute or aspect which means that God cannot suffer.
incarnation	Literally, becoming flesh; the event of God becoming a human being.
incognito	Unknown or unrecognized.
individualism	Attitude or position favoring the rights, value, or salvation primarily of persons, understood as autonomous and not essentially social.
infallibility	Inerrancy, being incapable of making a mistake; more specifically, the Roman Catholic dogma that Papal pronouncements made *ex cathedra* are without error.
infinite	Unlimited, inexhaustible, without boundaries.
interiority	A person's subjectivity, especially the capacity for self-consciousness, reflective judgment, and decision.
inter-subjectivity	Mode of relating between persons, understood as human subjects with interiority.
Jesuit	A member of the Roman Catholic Society of Jesus, founded by St Ignatius of Loyola in 1534.
justification	Being pronounced or made righteous; the act of God, through the death and resurrection of Jesus Christ, bringing about reconciliation between himself and human beings.
justification by faith	Justification understood as a free, unconditional gift of God received in faith.
kairos	Significant, pivotal time in history; for Tillich, a crisis or turning-point which demands decision.
Kantian	Relating to the philosophy of Immanuel Kant (1724–1804) and his followers.
kenotic christology	Understanding of the incarnation of Jesus as involving the self-emptying (Greek, *kenosis*), or laying down of certain divine attributes (e.g., glory, omnipotence), in order to become fully human.
kerygma	From the Greek word for a herald's message; a term used for the proclamation of the New Testament church about Jesus.
laity	The members of a church, often distinguished from its clergy.
liberalism	In theology, a movement attempting to open theology to modern experience, worldviews, and criteria, and especially to the contributions of other academic disciplines; more specifically, nineteenth-century liberal theology tended to stress religious experience, historical

consciousness and the need for freedom from traditional dogma and frameworks in recovering Christianity.

liberation theology
: Theology originating in Latin America in the 1960s in contexts of political and economic oppression which seeks to apply the Christian faith from the standpoint of the needs of the poor and exploited.

liturgy
: Official worship of God (from a Greek word meaning action of the people); more specifically, a term for the various aspects of prescribed public worship.

logico-deductive
: Referring to a method which holds that the conclusions of an argument or thesis will logically and necessarily follow from its premisses.

logos
: Greek for 'word'; more widely, the rational or ordering principle in something or in reality as a whole; in christology, used to refer to Jesus Christ as the Word of God, God's self-disclosure.

logos christology
: Christology whose key concept is Jesus understood as the historical expression of the eternal, divine logos through which everything was created.

Lutheran
: Referring to churches, traditions, or theologies stemming from the Reformation tradition begun by Martin Luther.

Manichaean
: Referring to some aspect, or an adherent, of Manichaeism, a religion founded in the third century AD which held an extreme form of dualism, believing in two ultimate powers, one good and the other evil.

Marian
: Referring to Mary, the mother of Jesus.

mariology
: Branch of theology concerning Mary, the mother of Jesus.

materialism
: Philosophical position concerning the constitution of the world, with special emphasis on matter as the only reality and on the denial of the spiritual realm.

mechanistic
: Understanding the world according to the analogy of a machine, with a special concern for tracing effects to causes.

messianism
: Hope for the coming of a messiah or savior who will liberate from oppression.

metaphysics
: Study of reality in general; the science of being, existence, and knowing, aiming to encompass and understand the basic constituents of reality.

metaphysics, christological
: A Christ-centered understanding of reality.

metaphysics, classical
: The metaphysics of Plato, Aristotle, and their followers.

metaphysics, idealist
: Metaphysics of Berkeley, Descartes, Kant, Hegel, and their followers.

meta-theological	Relating to the discussion of theology in general, its nature, bases, methods, and purposes.
methodology	Reflection on the systematic approach to a topic or field.
modernism, Catholic	Position of some late nineteenth- and early twentieth-century Roman Catholic theologians who sought to come to terms with the intellectual climate of modernity. It was officially condemned by the Holy Office in 1907.
monarchia	From a Greek word meaning 'one origin' or 'one rule'; referring in trinitarian theology to the Father as the source of the Son and Spirit.
monarchianist	Referring to the second- and third-century heresy of monarchianism which stressed the unity of the Trinity at the expense of the distinction between its members, and which understood Jesus as divine in a secondary sense.
monergism	Understanding that the Holy Spirit is the sole agent responsible for the regeneration of Christians (contrast with **synergism, synergic**).
monotheism	Belief in only one God as ultimate reality.
mysticism	Strand in many religions stressing the knowledge of God or the transcendent through experience, often in the form of immediate intuition or other direct communication or sense of union, and often denying the possibility of adequate linguistic communication of such experience; often contrasted with knowledge of God through indirect means such as reasoning, scripture, or tradition.
mythology	Study of, or a collection of, myths – which in theology are usually understood as expressions of religious meaning through stories and symbols, often using premodern worldviews.
natural theology	Theology attempting to know God and God's relationship to the world through nature and human reasoning without divine revelation.
naturalistic	Relating to naturalism, a position affirming that the world can be understood (especially through the natural sciences) without reference to any explanatory factor beyond the natural order, which is usually understood in a materialist way.
necessitarian	Relating to necessitarianism, a position which views all events as happening by necessity and denies freewill; often used synonymously with determinism.
neo-Kantianism	Movement of revived interest in the philosophy of Kant after the decline of Hegelian idealism; in theology it especially emphasized Kant's distinction between pure

and practical reason as a means to meet scientific challenges to the validity of religion and theology.

neo-orthodoxy

Term applied to the Protestant theological movement, associated with the work of Barth, Emil Brunner, and Reinhold Niebuhr, referring to their attempt to counter the 'unorthodox' liberal nineteenth-century theology by regrounding theology on the principles of Reformation Protestantism.

neo-Protestantism

Term interchangeable with neo-orthodoxy.

neo-scholastic

Relating to the nineteenth- and twentieth-century Roman Catholic movement of neo-scholasticism which revived the theology of Thomas Aquinas, and made it the norm against which all other theology and philosophy was judged.

Neo-Thomism

Term interchangeable with neo-scholasticism.

noetic

Referring to the mind or intellect, or to understanding gained through human rational processes.

nominalism

Understanding of universal categories as class names which have no reality outside the individual particulars which make them up (contrasted with **realism**).

objectivity

State of being detached from and external to whatever is being perceived or affirmed, often seen as aiding neutrality and therefore accuracy in judgment, but sometimes seen as impossible or inappropriate in matters of religion.

occasionalist

Referring to occasionalism, a position denying all-embracing causal relationships in the natural realm and regarding events as occasions through which God, the sole cause of all, effects change.

omnipotence

Possession of all or infinite power.

omnipresence

Presence everywhere, at all times, to all things.

ontic

Referring to existing reality.

ontology

Branch of philosophy concerned with the study of being, of reality in its most fundamental and comprehensive forms.

original sin

Doctrine of the radical corruption of all humanity through the sin of Adam and Eve, receiving its classical formulation from Augustine.

orthodoxy

Right belief in and adherence to the essential doctrines of a faith as officially defined; or, conventional or traditional belief.

orthopraxis

Right belief combined with right practice, a term specially used in Latin American liberation theology, often in contrast with an orthodoxy seen as insuffi-

	ciently interested in the practical and political content of faith.
panentheism	Understanding of all creation as existing in God yet without negating the transcendence of God; often also holding that the world and God are mutually dependent upon each other for their fulfillment.
pantheism	Understanding which identifies God and the world as one, either without qualification, or with the world as a divine emanation, body, development, appearance, or modality.
paradigm	Model, pattern, ideal type, or basic set of ideas serving to integrate or explain reality.
parousia	Expected appearance of Jesus Christ (the 'second coming') before the consummation of history in the eschaton or last judgment.
paschal	Referring to the suffering and death of Jesus Christ.
passibility	Capability of undergoing suffering or pain, or of being changed by an external power.
patristic	Referring to the fathers of the church and their period, usually covering the first five centuries AD.
penultimate	Next before the last or ultimate; referring to the stage immediately prior to the final or ultimate event; in Bonhoeffer, referring to everything prior to God's act of justification.
perdition	State of damnation or of being lost.
perichoresis	Greek term for the mutual indwelling or coinherence of the three members of the Trinity. (The Latin equivalent is *circumincessio*.)
personalism	Philosophical movement, beginning in the nineteenth century, stressing the human personality as the ultimate value and key notion in understanding reality.
phenomenology	Philosophical movement aiming to ground philosophy in a descriptive and scientific method, which understands religious and other phenomena in non-reductionist terms as they reveal themselves to consciousness, and which seeks the distinctive laws of human consciousness, especially in its intentional character.
philosophical theology	Branch of theology that relates theological and philosophical thought, usually concentrating on areas of mutual concern.
pietism	Originally, a seventeenth- and eighteenth-century Protestant movement reacting against the rationalism and rigidity of traditional Lutheran orthodoxy with an emphasis on the personal, devotional, and practical aspects of Christianity; more widely, a type of faith combining deep feeling, stress on personal salvation

	and holiness, and lack of concern for theological elaboration.
Platonism	The thought of the Greek philosopher Plato (c. 427–347 BC), and of the various philosophical and theological traditions stemming from him.
pleroma	Fullness or plenitude or completeness, usually referring to the nature of God or Christ.
pluralism	Situation or understanding which embraces a diversity of contrasting cultures, values, ideas, religions, or other major elements seen as independently valid.
pneumatology	Branch of theology dealing with the doctrine of the Holy Spirit.
polemic	Confrontational, controversial statement directly challenging an opposing position.
political theology	Theology that works out the political implications of faith; more specifically, that project as carried on in the context of a modern capitalist society.
positivism	In the nineteenth century, a movement associated with Auguste Comte (1798–1857) which saw history in terms of inevitable progress culminating in the 'positive' stage of scientific knowledge, technology and an atheist religion of reason and humanity; in the twentieth century, logical positivism has been a philosophical movement stressing empirical verification, natural scientific method, and the rejection of metaphysics.
postmodernism/ post- modernity	Position regarding the present intellectual and cultural situation, especially in advanced capitalist societies, as in discontinuity with modernity and representing a new stage beyond it.
pragmatic	Practical, aiming at usefulness and effectiveness; in philosophy, relating to pragmatism, a position stressing knowledge derived from experience and experiment and used to solve practical problems, with truth tested by its practical utility and consequences.
praxis	Greek term for action, practical ability or practice, used in Marxism and adopted by Latin American liberation theology to denote a combination of action and reflection aimed at the transformation of an oppressive situation.
predestination	Doctrine of the eternal decision and knowledge of God with respect to the destiny of human beings as regards salvation or damnation (sometimes called the doctrine of election and rejection).
prevenient	Literally, coming before or first; usually referring to God or God's grace as having the initiative in relation to human action, and being its prior cause or condition.
process theology	Theological movement, following the philosophy of A. N. Whitehead, which emphasizes notions of move-

	ment and becoming (process), rather than being and substance, and which affirms divine participation in process.
procession (trinitarian)	Derivation (proceding, procession) of the Son and the Holy Spirit within the trinitarian being of God.
projectionism	Transferral of an attribute or need of a person or group onto another object; in Feuerbach God is explained as a projection of ideal human nature onto an imagined being.
prolegomena	Work of a preliminary, introductory nature, preparing for a fuller treatment.
proleptic	Of an anticipatory nature; used, for example, of the resurrection of Jesus as an anticipation of the final consummation.
propaideutics	Set of introductory ideas or principles required for the study of a subject.
propositionalism	Method of asserting or proposing statements that are capable of being judged true or false.
Protestant	Name for those Christians and churches which separated from the Roman Catholic Church at the Reformation, and for other churches and groups descended from them.
purgatory	Intermediate condition between death and heaven, where those destined for heaven do penance for sins and are purified.
rationality	That which is characterized by conformity with reason, adhering to qualities of thought such as intelligibility, consistency, coherence, order, logical structure, completeness, testability, and simplicity.
realism	Philosophical position (in opposition to **nominalism**) affirming that a universal category (e.g., animal) may have a reality outside its individual manifestations (e.g., lion, cow) and independently of human consciousness; or, a philosophical position (in opposition to **idealism**) affirming that reality exists independently of the human knower, that it requires the human mind to correspond to it, and that what is known about a thing exists in the thing known and would exist without the knower.
realism, theological	In the twentieth century, usually referring to a position (contrasting with theological idealism or liberalism) which stresses the reality and initiative of God in revelation and the need for human knowing to correspond to that; also, a position in ethics and politics which stresses the imperfection of the world and the limits of human attempts to improve it.
reconciliation	Reestablishment of a state of harmony or good relationship between God and humanity or amongst human

	beings; often used interchangeably with redemption or atonement or salvation.
redaction	Editorial ordering of material in a text.
redemption	Literally, buying back: a financial metaphor (relating originally to ransom payments and slave-buying) for atonement, reconciliation, or salvation; the act or process by which liberation from bondage (described variously in Christian theology as sin, death, the law, the devil, the world) takes place.
reductionism	Explanation of complex data in inappropriately simple terms; in theology, often referring to the attempt to explain beliefs referring to, e.g., God, in terms that do not assume the reality of God, e.g., in psychological, sociological, philosophical, or other terms.
relativism	A position holding the impossibility of attaining final, eternal truth or values, and stressing diversity among individuals, groups, cultures, and periods; sometimes also ruling out the comparison of truth claims or values.
ressourcement	French word for return to original sources in order to inform modern understanding.
revelation	Disclosure of what was previously unknown; in theology, usually the disclosure to human beings by God of his nature, salvation, or will.
revisionist	Relating to revisionism, the questioning and reconceiving of the core of a tradition.
sacrament	Action, ceremony, or celebration in which created things become channels and symbols of God's activity and promises (in Roman Catholicism: baptism, eucharist, confirmation, matrimony, holy orders, penance, and extreme unction; in Protestantism: usually baptism and eucharist); more widely used to refer to the ways in which God and salvation are communicated through action and material reality.
salvation history	Those events which the Bible narrates as revealing God's action for the salvation of the world.
sanctification	Process of being brought to a state of holiness.
schism	Divergence of opinion between two groups; in relation to the church, a breach of unity on doctrinal grounds, leading to deliberate separation from an ecclesiastical community.
scholasticism/ scholastic theology	Education, methods, and theology of the thirteenth-century Christian thinkers, often called the Medieval schoolmen, and of their followers in later times, notable especially for their application of logic to theology and their systematic attempts to reconcile faith and reason.

secularism	Position advocating the elimination of religious influence in the state, social institutions and the understanding of reality as a whole.
soteriology	Branch of theology concerned with the doctrine of salvation (or reconciliation, atonement, or redemption).
sovereignty	Relating to God, an attribute of the divine nature referring to its complete independence, freedom, and power to act in relation to creation.
speculative	Referring to speculation, the attempt to project an overall understanding of the truth of a matter using rational thought.
subjectivity	State of being a self-conscious, thinking agent; or, state of being personally involved so that one's perceptions and understanding are relative to one's individual experience or characteristics.
subordinationism	Trinitarian understanding of the nature of the Son which subordinates Him to the Father in a way which is considered to compromise the Son's full divinity.
substitutionary	Relating to the death of Jesus, the understanding which sees it as a voluntary act through which he took the place of sinful humanity.
supernaturalism	Thought dealing with that which is conceived to be beyond the natural order.
synergic	Referring to synergism, an understanding stressing the cooperation of the Holy Spirit, the word of God, and the human being in the act of regeneration.
synoptic	Referring to the Gospels of Matthew, Mark, and Luke.
systematic theology	Type of theology seeking to give a rationally ordered, comprehensive account of the content of a religion, especially its doctrines and their interrelationships.
theism	Belief in, or set of beliefs about, God.
theocentric	God-centred; revolving around the reality of God.
theodicy	Justification or explanation of belief in God in the face of the existence of evil.
theonomous	Referring to God being primary or in control or the constitutive reality for an action, person, or situation in accordance with its own nature and integrity; contrasted with both **autonomous** (referring to independence from God) and **heteronomous** (referring to subjection to an alien control or principle).
theopaschite	Referring to a sixth-century AD Monophysite group which held that the divine nature of Jesus Christ suffered on the cross.
Thomism	Term for the theology of, and the schools of thought stemming from, Thomas Aquinas (1226–74).

traditionalism	Position appealing to past forms of a religion, culture, or other form of belief, understanding, or behavior; more specifically, a reaction to modernity, holding that religious knowledge cannot be derived from human reason or experience, but only through faith in divine revelation communicated through tradition.
transcendent	Existing, going or leading beyond; of God, referring to his being beyond all created reality; of self, going beyond one's present state, often by knowing, willing, or some other mode of consciousness.
transcendental philosophy	Usually referring to the philosophy of Kant and his followers.
transcendental theology	Theology concerned to explore the fundamental conditions of theological knowledge, beyond any particular instances of such knowledge.
transcendental Thomism	Movement in twentieth-century theology (e.g., Maréchal, Rahner, Lonergan) concerned to marry the theology and philosophy of Thomas Aquinas with the philosophy of Kant and post-Kantian philosophers, and especially focusing on the knowing and willing human subject.
transcendentalism, Kant's	Understanding of the fundamental conditions for any human experiencing and knowing, which go beyond empirical experience because they are pre-supposed by all experience.
Trinity	Christian understanding of the Godhead as three in one: the Father, the Son, and the Holy Spirit.
Trinity, economic	Trinity in relation to creation and the revealing of God through history.
Trinity, immanent	Trinity understood in itself through the interrelationship of its three members.
Trinity, social	Trinity conceived in interpersonal terms as a society of three.
tritheism	Belief in three gods, often referring to doctrines of the Trinity in which the unity of God is seen as compromised.
triune	Being three in one.
unitarianism	Understanding and religious movement associated with rejection of the doctrine of the Trinity, denying a differentiated understanding of the Godhead and the divinity of Jesus Christ and of the Holy Spirit.
universal history	The totality of history, with special reference to its unity, purpose, and pattern.
universalism	Understanding of the all-encompassing nature of salvation, including the belief that ultimately all will be saved.

vicarious   Relating to a state of being or an action which is undertaken on behalf of others, usually referring to the humanity or the death of Jesus Christ.

Index

revelation (*cont.*):
  in Tillich 5, 140–3
  in Torrance 22
revisionism 3, 11
Riches, John 217, 237–54
Ricoeur, Paul 104
Ritschl, Albrecht 109–10
ritual, neglected in Jüngel 104
Robinson, J. A. T., *Honest to God* 65–6
Roman Catholic Church
  and history 8
  use of Bible 172
  see also Küng, Hans; Rahner, Karl;
    Schillebeeckx, Edward
Rosenzweig, Franz 294
Rössler, Dietrich 258
Rousselot, Pierre 185

sacraments 38, 56, 127, 153, 158
salvation
  by faith alone, in Bonhoeffer 61, 66
  in Congar 226
  in history 5
  in Moltmann 300–1
  in Rahner 194, 197
  in Schillebeeckx 155–6, 157, 159–60
  in Tillich 143–4, 261
salvation history 117, 127, 225
sanctification
  in Bonhoeffer 61, 64
  in Jüngel 100
  in Tillich 143
Schelling, Friedrich 134, 148, 274
Schillebeeckx, Edward
  on the Church and the world 107,
    154–5, 157–8, 162
  and correlation 3
  and existentialism 107, 153, 154
  on experience and belief 157–60,
    163, 172
  and history 155, 158, 161
  influence 162–3
  on intuition 157–8
  life 152–4
  and personalism 153, 154
  and revelation 156, 157
  and Roman Catholic Church 153–4,
    158, 160–1, 175, 239
  on sacraments 154
  see also christology; creation; ec-
    clesiology; epistemology; escha-

tology; God, doctrines of; grace;
  Holy Spirit; Kingdom of God;
  ministry; praxis; resurrection;
  salvation; soteriology; suffering
Schlatter, Adolf 51
Schleicher, Rüdiger 54
Schleiermacher, Friedrich 54, 110–11,
  119, 124
  Barth on 11, 28–30, 31–2
  on religious consciousness 10–11,
    12, 14, 28, 33, 123
Schlink, Edmund 257, 269
Scholasticism 153, 154, 181, 219, 224;
  see also Aquinas, Thomas; neo-
  Thomism
Schreiter, Robert 107, 152–63
Schwöbel, Christoph 255, 257–91
science, and theology, *see* Torrance,
  Thomas F.
Scotland, theological tradition 22
secularism 67–8
Seeberg, Reinhold 51
Sellin, Ernst 51
sin 5, 27
  in Barth 166, 245
  in Pannenberg 263
  in Tillich 142, 149 ;
  see also evil
Smart, Ninian et al. 9
society, and theology 16–17
Soelle, Dorothée 68
soteriology
  in Barth 37–8
  in Bonhoeffer 59
  in Panneberg 261
  in Paul 121
  in Schillebeeckx 155–6
sovereignty of God 98–9, 159, 244
Strauss, David Friedrich 10, 13
subordinationism 196–7, 199, 281, 305
suffering 5
  of God 95, 96, 98–9, 304; *see also*
    theopaschite group
  in Moltmann 293, 300–1
  in Schillebeeckx 156, 158–9
supernaturalism 109, 122
Sutz, Erwin 51
Sykes, Stephen 13, 16, 22
symbol
  in Congar 227
  in Rahner 198

Index by Meg Davies